The Nations of Wales

WRITING WALES IN ENGLISH

CREW series of Critical and Scholarly Studies
General Editors: Kirsti Bohata and Daniel G. Williams (*CREW*, Swansea University)

This *CREW* series is dedicated to Emyr Humphreys, a major figure in the literary culture of modern Wales, a founding patron of the *Centre for Research into the English Literature and Language of Wales*. Grateful thanks are due to the late Richard Dynevor for making this series possible.

Other titles in the series

Stephen Knight, *A Hundred Years of Fiction* (978-0-7083-1846-1)
Barbara Prys-Williams, *Twentieth-Century Autobiography* (978-0-7083-1891-1)
Kirsti Bohata, *Postcolonialism Revisited* (978-0-7083-1892-8)
Chris Wigginton, *Modernism from the Margins* (978-0-7083-1927-7)
Linden Peach, *Contemporary Irish and Welsh Women's Fiction* (978-0-7083-1998-7)
Sarah Prescott, *Eighteenth-Century Writing from Wales: Bards and Britons* (978-0-7083-2053-2)
Hywel Dix, *After Raymond Williams: Cultural Materialism and the Break-Up of Britain* (978-0-7083-2153-9)
Matthew Jarvis, *Welsh Environments in Contemporary Welsh Poetry* (978-0-7083-2152-2)
Harri Garrod Roberts, *Embodying Identity: Representations of the Body in Welsh Literature* (978-0-7083-2169-0)
Diane Green, *Emyr Humphreys: A Postcolonial Novelist* (978-0-7083-2217-8)
M. Wynn Thomas, *In the Shadow of the Pulpit: Literature and Nonconformist Wales* (978-0-7083-2225-3)
Linden Peach, *The Fiction of Emyr Humphreys: Contemporary Critical Perspectives* (978-0-7083-2216-1)
Daniel Westover, *R. S. Thomas: A Stylistic Biography* (978-0-7083-2413-4)
Jasmine Donahaye, *Whose People? Wales, Israel, Palestine* (978-0-7083-2483-7)
Judy Kendall, *Edward Thomas: The Origins of His Poetry* (978-0-7083-2403-5)
Damian Walford Davies, *Cartographies of Culture: New Geographies of Welsh Writing in English* (978-0-7083-2476-9)
Daniel G. Williams, *Black Skin, Blue Books: African Americans and Wales 1845–1945* (978-0-7083-1987-1)
Andrew Webb, *Edward Thomas and World Literary Studies: Wales, Anglocentrism and English Literature* (978-0-7083-2622-0)
Alyce von Rothkirch, *J. O. Francis, realist drama and ethics: Culture, place and nation* (978-1-7831-6070-9)
Rhian Barfoot, *Liberating Dylan Thomas: Rescuing a Poet from Psycho-Sexual Servitude* (978-1-7831-6184-3)
Daniel G. Williams, *Wales Unchained: Literature, Politics and Identity in the American Century* (978-1-7831-6212-3)

THE NATIONS OF WALES 1890–1914

WRITING WALES IN ENGLISH

M. WYNN THOMAS

UNIVERSITY OF WALES PRESS
2016

www.uwp.co.uk

British Library CIP Data
A catalogue record for this book is available from the British Library

ISBN 978-1-78316-837-8 (hardback)
978-1-78316-838-5 (paperback)
eISBN 978-1-78316-839-2

Typeset in Wales by Eira Fenn Gaunt, Cardiff
Printed by CPI Antony Rowe, Chippenham, Wiltshire

I'r dyfodol —
Joseph ac Elliott —
er cof am ran o'u gorffennol

Contents

Series Editors' Preface

The aim of this series, since its founding in 2004 by Professor M. Wynn Thomas, is to publish scholarly and critical work by established specialists and younger scholars that reflects the richness and variety of the English-language literature of modern Wales. The studies published so far have amply demonstrated that concepts, models and discourses current in the best contemporary studies can illuminate aspects of Welsh culture, and have also foregrounded the potential of the Welsh example to draw attention to themes that are often neglected or marginalised in anglophone cultural studies. The series defines and explores that which distinguishes Wales's anglophone literature, challenges critics to develop methods and approaches adequate to the task of interpreting Welsh culture, and invites its readers to locate the process of writing Wales in English within comparative and transnational contexts.

Kirsti Bohata and Daniel G. Williams
CREW (*Centre for Research into the English Literature and Language of Wales*)
Swansea University

In a press interview at the Savoy Hotel, London, on July 15, Marilyn Monroe, dubbed 'the anatomical bomb,' was asked whether she would visit Wales. She replied, 'Where is Wales?'

The Welsh Nation, July, 1956

[CYMRU]

Byw brwydr bob awr ydyw
brwydr fawr ein bryd ar fyw.

Gerallt Lloyd Owen, 'Cywydd Croeso', *Y Gân Olaf*

PREFACE

History never repeats itself, that we know; but it can seem uncannily fond of rhyme. The resemblances between the Wales of today and that of yesterday with which this volume is concerned can seem striking. The decay of the chapels and attendant fade of Nonconformity (examined in my previous volume *In the Shadow of the Pulpit: Literature and Nonconformist Wales*) left a kind of identity vacuum in late Victorian and Edwardian Wales that intellectuals and artists rushed to fill, and the terminal collapse of the industrial society that for much of the twentieth century had sustained an image of Wales as a proletarian socialist nation has triggered a similar reaction. Despite all public rhetoric and political initiatives, the question of whether Wales can evolve into a really stable, mature, bilingual and bicultural society remains extremely moot, as it was when T. Gwynn Jones reflected on the issue in a great anguished and conflicted 'national' elegy (examined in chapter 6). What Lloyd George at the turn of the century despairingly termed Wales's 'morbid rugby footballism', the product of a first 'golden age' of spectacular victories, paved the way for today's barren 'cenedlaetholdeb y bêl' (rugby ball nationalism). Back in the 1890s, it was the turbulent Irish who were setting the political pace, while the cowed and anxiously respectable Welsh, complacently anti-Catholic and averse not just to violence but to serious political agitation of any kind, tut-tutted from the wings while hoping to benefit from the fall-out. Now, at the beginning of the twenty-first century, the Scots are the troublesome trend-setters, and once more Wales demurely sits out the dispute, deploring such unmannerly behaviour but ready to feed off whatever scraps may fall its way. As J. Arthur Price suggested in

1890, just as Wales was England's very first dependency, it seems set fair to be its very last. Particularly during the rugby season, there even continues to be vague talk in popular discourse of Wales as a Celtic nation, as there was back in the 1890s; and the Welsh have at long last, with whatever seeming reluctance, secured those minimal powers of self-government dreamt of by several leading politicians and thinkers exactly a century earlier than the narrow devolution vote of 1997.

This book is no more than an attempt to explore a few of the images of Welsh identity that were placed in circulation by intellectuals and artists during a fascinating period of roughly a quarter of a century. There is no attempt to be exhaustive – two important features of these years are particularly notable by their absence. The first is the increasing role of women; the second is the gradual emergence, in embryonic form, of the image of the Welsh working class in the figure of the miner. Fortunately, both of these cultural formations characteristic of the period have already been effectively studied elsewhere – by such critics as Jane Aaron in the case of the former, and by such scholars as Stephen Knight and Hywel Teifi Edwards in the case of the latter. As for the dates bracketing this particular study, the year 1890 has been chosen to symbolise, rather than precisely to mark, the emergence of the Cymru Fydd movement for national regeneration (discussed at length in chapter 1) that left a profound mark on Wales's cultural life if not so much on its political destiny. And 1914 obviously stands for the Great War that changed everything in Wales, as in the rest of the world, forever.

And the epigraphs? The first sharply voices a question to which, in more than seventy years of living, I have yet to find an answer. In some moods, Wales seems to me to stand much where it did during the period covered by this study; a 'nation' more mirage than reality. The Welsh seem then destined to be forever a fitfully *wannabe* people. Now you see them, now – as when (ever obliging) they enthusiastically assent to silent incorporation into 'Team GB' – you don't. But at other times my view of 'my people' manifests itself wistfully as dream – not the 'eunuch dream' of that sadly quintessential modern Welshman Dylan Thomas, but the kind of dream in which, as Yeats was fond of insisting, more satisfactory realities can sometimes begin. Hence the second epigraph, from the late Gerallt Lloyd Owen, which roughly translated cautions that to believe in our 'Cymru/Cymry' will involve constant effort – the endless effort of a small, unremarkable, stateless people's will to live. This study is my own small contribution to that struggle.

My debts to friends, colleagues and institutions are none the less sincere for being too many to mention. As for the University of Wales Press, this is the fifteenth book of mine it has published over a thirty-year period during which, in my grateful experience, its performance has consistently rivalled that of the best academic presses worldwide. I am indebted beyond measure to Helgard Krause and Sarah Lewis and, in connection with the present volume, to Eira Fenn Gaunt, Siân Chapman and Dafydd Jones. And while the dedication is, with an eye to the future, to my two enchanting little grandsons, my loving devotion goes equally to Elin, Bob and of course to Karen.

1

EMBLEMATISING THE NATION

Magnificent monument to Welsh commercial wealth and industrial muscle; dropsical symptom of civic elephantiasis; an Edwardian allegory in stone and marble of Imperial Wales; the mausoleum of one vision of modern Welsh nationhood: Cardiff City Hall may be viewed in several different ways, as it encapsulates many different defining features of early twentieth-century Wales.[1] And, in so far as the building was also in its heyday an attempt to harmonise powerful ideological forces that had the potential to conflict as readily as to converge in real life, it could further be read as a Temple of Civic Peace. An elaborate confection it most certainly is, a civic and national folly almost as false and fantastical in its way as the two pseudo-medieval Victorian inventions that are its neighbours – Cardiff Castle and (out at Tongwynlais) Castell Coch. Both were the brainchildren of the third Marquess of Bute, Wales's answer to the 'mad' King Ludwig of Bavaria and the greatest baron of the Welsh industrial aristocracy. It was thanks also to his august family's gracious munificence that City Hall came to be built in a tiny corner of what was known as 'Lord Bute's own town'.[2]

Modelled on English and French Renaissance architecture, the building, grandly fashioned out of soft Portland stone, adorned with a clock tower, and crowned with statutory cupola, was completed in 1904. It stood in one corner of a substantial tract of land to become known as Cathays Park, once the grounds of a Georgian mansion owned by the Butes but sold by the family to the (then) town of Cardiff in 1898 for a knock-down price of £159,000.[3] The clock tower may have been a slyly asymmetrical feature of the ensemble, but in every other respect, down to the smallest detail, the building was consciously designed to convey the stability of equilibrium – a mature balancing of potentially conflicting roles, obligations and interests. Take the mottos engraved on the five bells in the tower (pure copper, of course – after all, 90 per cent of British copper was smelted in west Wales). Three are in Welsh, two in English, and all were carefully chosen to reflect the supposedly different 'temper' of the two linguistic cultures of Wales at the beginning of the twentieth century. The Welsh is nobly principled and piously otherworldly: 'Y gwir yn erbyn y byd' (The truth against the world); 'Duw a phob daioni' (God and every good); 'A gair Duw yn uchaf' (And God's word over all). Tellingly, the modern guidebook to City Hall manages to mistranslate every single one of these proverbs. The English mottos, by contrast, are businesslike and briskly practical in their brusque injunctions: 'I mark time, dost thou?'; 'Time conquers all and we must time obey.' For anglophone Cardiffians, there was no time to lose when there was money to be made.

The figures carved on the west façade also perform their own ballet of balance. Far above messy ground level they execute an exalted high-wire act of fair play between cultural, political and economic interests. The constituent groups represent 'Science and Education', 'Music and Poetry', 'Commerce and Industry', 'Welsh Unity and Patriotism'. As for the 'large groups of monumental statuary' on the external wall, flanking the grand main window of the Council Chamber, these again are elevated public masterpieces of euphemism and elision. Representing 'the sea receiving the City's three rivers, the Taff, the Rhymney and the Ely', they calm the raw competitive and exploitative realities of coal production into bland establishment allegory, obscuring from sight the real, unsightly, volatile sources of the wealth of a city described by the American consul as 'the Chicago of Wales'. Cardiff's affluence came from the great mining valleys of the south Wales coalfield, their sides steeply terraced with workers' housing, their cramped communities nervously and electrically alive to ceaseless change, their deep pits throbbing with life and danger, their ever-growing workforce increasingly restless. Here was to be found 'the distinctive, sardonic, complex, warm, picaresque, soft-hearted and malicious, hard-headed and cock-eyed, ambitious and heroic and daft world of the miners, whose disappearance [from the present-day Welsh landscape] has left south Wales a cubit shorter in spirit'.[4] Nothing of that world was reflected in the decor or architecture of Cardiff City Hall.

Tastefully vague sculptural reference to 'the sea' in the fabric of the building scarcely does justice to the colourful cosmopolitanism, frontier culture and ruthless economic activity of the docks area of Cardiff during the period when 'the metropolis of South Wales' (before its eclipse by its purpose-built neighbour, Barry) was the world's premier coal-exporting port, thanks to its great Bute docks complex. In the very heart of dockland stood City Hall's commercial twin, the Coal Exchange in Mount Stuart Square, built between 1884 and 1886 to the design and deluxe specifications of the architectural firm of James, Seward and Thomas, and replete with such Jacobethan features as fine filigree coving, oak balcony and hardwood panelling. Trade on the floor of the Exchange in its Edwardian heyday could be euphorically buoyant – early in the twentieth century it was reputed to have witnessed the world's first ever £1million business deal (over £100 million in today's money).

Money talked in Cardiff; and money also built – erecting what Yeats would call 'monuments to its own magnificence', but in a tastefully disguised form that provided new wealth with the patina of culture, civility and gentility. In the Coal Exchange, even the most cut-throat of coal trades could be conducted in a 'civilised' ambience redolent of the plush, well-upholstered interior of one of London's superior gentlemen's clubs. Similarly, City Hall repaid the brashly competitive modernity that had financed it by supplying it with a respectably ancient pedigree. In the great Council Chamber directly underlying the dome, the seats are placed in the round, an arrangement reminiscent of Arthur's fabled Round Table; the Chamber's walls are decorated with the Celtically intertwined initials VC – Villa Cardiff, a reminder that the city's origins can be traced all the way back to Roman times; and while the 'four massive pillars of Italian Breccia marble' supporting the dome are capped with bronze models of ships in recognition of modern Cardiff's huge debt to the sea, the armorial bearings displayed in the canopy above the elevated Lord Mayor's chair carry two mottos, in the aboriginal language of Wales, one proudly laying claim to the antiquity of both city and nation, the other emphasising the modern revival of patriotic sentiment. These respectively read 'Y Ddraig Goch ddyry cychwyn' (The Red Dragon will show the way) and 'Deffro, mae'n ddydd' (Awake: it is day).

* * *

'Deffro, mae'n ddydd': the motto may have carried echoes of a sleeping Arthur stirring back to life, but whereas the old legend had prophesied that the hero would reawaken only in his nation's hour of direst need, City Hall was a proud proclamation in stone of an ancient people's modern reawakening to spectacular success. Historians have had the best part of a century to polish their extensive sophisticated narratives, but still the barest summary of some of the most basic facts about the transformation of Wales between the mid-nineteenth century and the First World War from a remote fringe region into one of the powerhouses of British Industrial and Imperial ascendancy can scarcely fail to astonish.[5] In 1898, 70 per cent of UK slate was quarried in north Wales, most of it in the world's biggest quarries at Penrhyn and Dinorwic; 1902 saw the world's largest nickel works ('the Mond', established by the noted chemist and industrialist Ludwig Mond) built in Clydach; in 1914, 75 per cent of UK zinc was produced in the Swansea hinterland. Initially hard-hit by the McKinley tariff of 1890, the tinplate industry concentrated between Llanelli and Port Talbot thereafter recovered its position among the world leaders. The population of the Rhondda grew from 12,000 (1861) to 128,000 (1891), and then mushroomed further after the turn of the century when the rate of migration into the coalfield was exceeded only by the rate of immigration into the US. By 1911, the million and a half population of Glamorgan alone exceeded that of the whole of Wales in 1851; in 1901, the great ports of Cardiff, Swansea, Barry and Newport supplied 46 per cent of Britain's coal exports to Europe; by 1913, south Wales was producing about one third of world coal exports; by the time of the First World War, around a quarter of the Welsh population was working in the mines of the southern industrial belt.

Such economic dynamism generated, and was in turn generated by, galvanic social transformations that were massive, radical and complex in character. A Welsh society, the structure of which had changed relatively little over centuries, was suddenly subject to volcanic upheavals that left it stratified in an entirely new way. The spectrum of wealth of the burgeoning professional and commercial middle classes of the urban areas was largely the product of a huge new industrial working class slowly consolidating into an alienated proletariat. As the centre of social and economic gravity shifted sharply from rural to industrial Wales, the countryside that had seen unrest in the form of the Rebecca Riots and Tithe Wars, that had struggled to break free of the grip of large, anglicised landowners, and that had become the stronghold of the 'Nonconformist Nation', settled into a slow decline concerning enough by the 1890s for rural conditions to be reviewed by a Royal Commission on Land (1893–6). Ostensibly flush with spiritual authority and commanding substantial social influence, the Nonconformist chapels were nevertheless feeling the strain of competing for custom with the glamour of the new attractions of sport and mass public entertainments. A momentous culture-shift was dryly registered in the Census statistics of 1901 which demonstrated that, for the first time since the emergence of Welsh 'peoplehood' a millennium and a half earlier, the majority of the people of Wales no longer spoke the Welsh language.

Wales was, however, undeniably booming and the architects of the new social order were the Liberal politicians, among them populist idols and Westminster grandees such as T. E. Ellis and Lloyd George. The Liberal Party's capture of 33 out of the 34 Welsh Parliamentary seats in 1906 was the seal of the Welsh people's approval on a quarter century of dramatically transformative reforms. The system of primary education introduced following the Aberdare Report of 1881 had been followed in 1889 by the Welsh Intermediate Education Act that established a network of County Schools. A Charter was granted for a University of Wales in 1893, building on the pre-existence of colleges at Aberystwyth (1872), Cardiff (1883) and Bangor (1884) to form a new federal university. The 1888 Local Government Act creating County Councils (followed in 1894 by the establishment of urban and district councils) weakened the traditional grip of the church, gentry and landed classes on society by significantly democratising a vitally important decision-making tier. This radical transfer of social influence and political power had been made possible by the passing in 1884 of the Third Reform Act, not only effectively enfranchising the bulk of the male population in both town and country, but for the first time embracing a substantial section of the working class. The result in Wales had been immediate and dramatic. Of the 34 Westminster seats, 30 were captured by a Liberal Party many of whose candidates represented the interests both of a new commercial elite and of a reformist, broadly middle class, Dissenting culture hitherto largely excluded from political power by the traditionally Tory ruling class of landowners. In 1902, 175 north Wales local councillors out of a total of 260 were Liberals; in south Wales the figure was 215 out of 330. For the quarter of a century after 1884, the whole country was to be a Liberal fiefdom, its political agenda dominated initially by the Tithes debate and subsequently by the issues of 'educational reform, land reform, disestablishment of the Church of England in Wales [granted in 1914] and some measure of devolution' (*W*, 3).

The Liberals in Wales were quick to create new instruments of management to consolidate this new political order, forming the Liberal Federations of North and South Wales in 1886 and 1887. Reflective as they were of two strikingly contrasted socio-cultural regions, the political profiles of these Federations were very different and potentially incompatible. This was eventually made apparent in the fateful 1896 meeting at Newport, when Lloyd George failed to gain the backing of a south Wales federation (whose interests were hard-headedly commercial and many of whose anglophone members were suspicious of the ambitions of the Welsh-speaking north), for his North Wales Federation's campaign for political devolution. That defeat marked the effective end of the political influence over Welsh Liberalism of a broad-front Cymru Fydd/Young Wales movement, whose cultural vision nevertheless continued to be a very potent influence on Welsh Liberal policy and practice, climaxing in the series of nation-building initiatives enabled by the Liberal victory in the 1906 General Election: a Welsh Department of the Board of Education, a National Library, a National Museum, a Welsh Insurance Commission and a National Council for Wales for Agriculture.[6]

* * *

Since a reasonably well-informed familiarity with the Cymru Fydd phenomenon is important for the discussions that follow in this book, some sense of its scope and complexity needs to be established at the very outset.[7] From the mid-nineteenth century onwards, the heavyweight periodicals produced by the Nonconformist denominations evinced an active interest in the nation-building alliance between culture and politics, most strikingly evident in the Young Italy movement that was the driver of Risorgimento movements for national self-determination across Europe from 1848 onwards, involving Italians, Germans, Irish, Romanians, Hungarians and many of the Slavic peoples. Mazzini (the pure idealist to Cavour's canny pragmatist) became, in this context, a figure of particular interest to Welsh intellectuals, at the expense of overlooking his hostility to the aspirations of small, sub-state nations like the Irish (and, by extension, the Welsh).[8] And, indeed, some cautious Welsh attention even began to be paid to Thomas Davis (known to be proud of his Welsh descent) and his

Young Ireland movement, in the wake of the growing interest of talented young Liberal politicians from the mid 1880s onwards in the activities of the Irish Land League under the inspired leadership of the sometime Fenian Michael Davitt. Radicalised in part by his example, this new cohort of spectacularly gifted rising political talent was concerned to add a devolutionist dimension to the traditional Liberal agenda that had hitherto reflected the interests of the four dominant constituent groups of established Welsh politicians. These were the church Disestablishment group (including Thomas Gee and Rendel); the Manchester group (including Henry Richard, Bryn Roberts and Henry Rathbone), devoted to economic liberalism, free trade and temperance; the champions of land reform (instanced by Michael D. Jones and Pan Jones); and the Social Radicals (prominently instanced by Mabon, leader of the South Wales Miners), who were pioneering what became a new Lib-Lab politics.[9]

While the brilliant young T. E. Ellis and his enthusiastic associates were careful to be respectful of veterans such as this, his election in July 1886 as MP for his native Merionethshire, on a platform supportive both of Irish Home Rule and of a like measure for Wales, marked the beginning of a brand new era in Welsh politics. These were heady days, and the ever-wily Gladstone was quick to recognise the rise of this new tide of nationalism in a speech he delivered on the shores of Swansea bay in 1887. Implicit in his remarks was an awareness of the common cause being made between Cymru Fydd and the 'respectable' political wing of the Irish Nationalist Home Rule Movement. When Cymru Fydd published its historic Manifesto in 1889, it envisaged a pan-Celtic alliance with both Ireland and Scotland (whose own Home Rule Association had been founded in 1886, with Keir Hardie and J. Ramsay MacDonald as Vice Presidents) and the same year members of the movement took part in O'Brien's demonstrations in Battersea Park and the Irish Prisoners' demonstration in Hyde Park. A Welsh-Celtic conference was held in the National Liberal Club in London in February 1890, which resulted in a joint committee on Home Rule and an agreed model for a federal Britain – a four-nation model intriguingly endorsed by Friedrich Engels in a letter of 1891 (*CF*, 109). In Wales, some enthusiasts even proclaimed the centenary year of the French Revolution (1789) to be the year of the Welsh Revolution. Viewed in such a glamorising light, the election of Lloyd George as MP for Caernarfon in 1890 could have been regarded as the arrival of the Welsh Napoleon.[10]

In the early days of this new political activism, there was a strong feeling that it was the natural extension of the nineteenth-century struggle of rural Welsh Dissent for social and religious justice. 'In issuing the first number of a Nationalist publication,' wrote T. J. Hughes in his editorial launching the periodical *Cymru Fydd* in 1888,

> We feel that no apology is necessary. Welsh mind and aim have during the past two years been unceasingly and decisively directed towards the remedy of home grievances, social and political. The irresistible constraint of external conditions has made political quietism no longer possible amongst us. State Churchism, educational monopoly and jobbery, a landed system which has degenerated into rude despotism: – these and other baleful evils have oppressed beyond the bounds of further endurance the life of the people of Wales.[11]

'Cymru Fydd,' he concluded, 'is intended to serve in this epoch of transition as an outlet for the national feeling in its protest against wrong.' But as his editorial had unconsciously revealed, the 'wrongs' that his movement were so concerned to correct were more those of a region and religio-cultural faction than those of Wales as a whole 'nation', and the new movement of which Hughes was such an impassioned advocate would continue throughout its lifetime to be hamstrung by this ultimately fatal anomaly.

These significant political initiatives were matched by corresponding developments among a new generation of cultural activists when a group of young intellectuals at Oxford, who had established the Dafydd ap Gwilym Society as a forum for historical, literary and philological discussion, began to turn their attention more directly to the contemporary scene. An expatriate group, they encouraged similar developments among the Welsh diaspora first in London and then in the industrial cities of the Midlands and the North. Meanwhile, Ellis, already the incomparable visionary, was proclaiming that 'Men are longing for – and men are labouring for – an adequate history of the people and literature of Wales, lovers of art and archaeology hope for the establishment of a National Museum and Art Gallery for Wales; educationalists work for a complete system of national education, while the demand is every day growing louder for an instrument for the orderly and progressive self-government of Wales.' (*CF*, 28) Over the next decade, the editors of a portfolio of Welsh periodicals, in both Welsh and English, would work tirelessly to disseminate this vision. And while the movement, on both its cultural and political wings, was to remain overwhelmingly masculine in character, it attracted female support of sufficient prominence to encourage the formation in 1891 of the Liberal Union of Welsh Women. From the very first, though, the uneven distribution of support between north and south for the political as much as the cultural goals of the movement was ominously signified in the time-lag between its initial effective consolidation into an active organisation in north Wales in the later 1880s to the formation of the first south Wales branch in Barry by W. Llewelyn Williams in 1891, with its accompanying paper, the *South Wales Star*. Nor were the problems confined to the north–south divide. When, in 1895, Lloyd George published an article in *Young Wales* floating the idea of prioritising the cause of 'Home Rule all round', and arguing that Disestablishment could best be delivered by a Welsh Parliament, the debate that ensued made it clear that the majority of Cymru Fydd activists still regarded Disestablishment as a much more pressing concern than devolution.[12]

The exact relation of Cymru Fydd to Welsh political Liberalism remains a murky subject, since attempts made during the 1890s, with Lloyd George to the fore, to merge the movement with mainstream politics both in Wales and at Westminster met with repeated opposition, not least from D. A. Thomas (the future Lord Rhondda), an early supporter who was alienated by Lloyd George's attempt to hitch (as Thomas saw it), the South Wales Liberal Association to his own ascendant political star. Nevertheless, Cymru Fydd did help effect a significant reorientation of political consciousness to the new magnetic pole of national awareness, evident as early as November 1888, when for the first time a Welsh Liberal Parliamentary Party was formed. But the compromises with the established order necessary for effective operation at Westminster soon began to take their political toll, with T. E. Ellis's commitment to the cause dimmed, and tarnished in the eyes of some, once he had been appointed Deputy Whip by Gladstone in 1894.[13] The gadfly of the movement, the trenchantly unorthodox intellectual J. Arthur Price, was moved to elegy, pithily noting that 'all hope of Welsh Nationalism doing anything for some time ended when Ellis grasped the Saxon gold.' (*CF*, 129) Two years later, Lloyd George's defeat at Newport ensured a similar defection.

As late as 1895, however, the editor of *Young Wales* (with a nod to the examples set by the kindred movements of Young Italy, Young Switzerland and Young Ireland) could grandly declare in that periodical's very first issue that 'the present decade is witnessing a remarkable revival of national sentiment in Wales. In every direction there are unmistakeable signs of a true *renaissance*. Our prestige as a nation was never so high, and the recognition of our national individuality never so marked and thorough.' Between 1894 and 1896, Lloyd George briefly intensified his efforts to advance some of the key reforms the movement was championing, most particularly that of Disestablishment. His brinkmanship went so far as to lead him, along with a group of like-minded radicals (including D. A. Thomas and Herbert Lewis), to announce that in the interests of the cause of Welsh Disestablishment they would be refusing the Liberal Whip. His transient appetite for a national uprising of Welsh Liberalism even prompted him, in 1896, to refuse support for the Home Secretary Asquith's measure for Disestablishment. The same years also saw the construction of an extensive network of Cymru Fydd organisations across towns in Wales and in England. But the mistrust bred by all these developments among the leaders and rank-and-file members of the Liberal Associations of both north and south Wales served only to prepare the way for the heated 1896 showdown at Newport that effectively marked the end of Cymru Fydd as a political force.

It was at that meeting that 'Mr Bird . . . stated in a phrase, which is now famous, that "thousands of cosmopolitan Englishmen between Swansea and Newport" will not submit to the domination of Welsh ideas.' So wrote W. Llewelyn Williams in *Young Wales* immediately after the event.[14] Mr Brown, secretary of the Liberal Association of Newport, had, Williams added, declared 'it was time to face the fact that English Liberals in Wales were out of sympathy with Welsh national aspirations'. The Revd Fuller Mills from Carmarthen had gone on to assert 'that a Liberal Federation had as little to do with the preservation of the Welsh language as with the preservation of the salmon in the river Towy'. An incensed Llewelyn Williams roundly concluded, in the light of such exchanges, that 'if Liberalism means the suppression of Welsh nationality, the sooner we know it the better'. 'If,' he went on,

> the teachings of Mr Gladstone and Mr John Morley are to be applied only to Ireland and Scotland and the struggling nationalities of the Continent, if in Wales an enlightened and ardent Nationalism is to be construed into disloyalty and treason against the Liberal party, then, I say, the sooner we are rid of Liberalism the better.

As history was, however, very soon to prove, the Newport meeting presaged not the end of the Liberal hegemony in Wales but rather the end of Cymru Fydd's (ever tenuous) political influence over Welsh Liberalism.

The turn towards an all-Wales politics of a socio-cultural movement rooted in the interests and values of an essentially rural, Nonconformist, Welsh-speaking constituency had been an uneasy one from the first. Additionally, that movement had in its frequently rather unfocused political incarnation been far from homogeneous, being instead an unstable alliance of different and potentially conflicting groupings. The political aims of its supporters ranged right across the spectrum, from a radical model of devolution to a view of Wales embedded ever more firmly within the Union and its Empire. There was a divide between secular and religious versions of the desired nation, with the latter's advocates intent on building on what still seemed to be the firm foundations of the nineteenth-century Nonconformist nation. Lloyd George's own brother, William George, even insisted that '[n]o Welsh Nationalist movement which ignored the religious aspirations of the people could be considered a true expression of the National Spirit of Wales'.[15] Secularists, by contrast, trusted to education's powers to build a broad-based civic society, and deplored the adverse effects of inter-denominational rivalries on the movement. Some activists were keen to align Cymru Fydd with existing 'mainstream' political tendencies such as Reform Liberalism, while others argued it should remain resolutely apolitical (in order to ensure the broadest possible alliance of supporters) or that it should provide the basis for an entirely new, independent Welsh political initiative. The issue of language was also a live and frequently contentious one, with the exact status of Welsh being anxiously debated and the steady ever more powerful advance of English noted with great approval by some and even greater apprehension by others. And always, there was the deep regional divide which reflected what might grandiosely be called a clash of cultures. Even in the pages of that optimistic first issue of the periodical *Young Wales* mentioned above, W. Llewelyn Williams couldn't refrain from striking a balefully prophetic note:

> But now the Nationalism that withstood centuries of armed oppression, of silent night, of contemptuous scorn, is withering before the blighting influence of Industrialism . . . The enemy which Young Wales will be called upon to fight in the future is the industrial and commercial

> Philistinism of Englishmen and Welshmen. Let the issue be made clear! Young Wales fights for culture, for true national development.[16]

'Young Wales fights for culture': that was the nub and, indeed, the rub. Whose culture? In which language? What exactly was meant by 'culture' (a word routinely used in Cymru Fydd circles as if it were synonymous with 'nation'), and what exactly did it have to do with politics? In that first issue of *Young Wales* (1895), the editor J. Hugh Edwards pledged to use his new periodical to broker a marriage between culture and politics, recognising 'the insufficiency of mere political organizations' and emphasising 'the absolute necessity of establishing a union between the literary and the political forces of our country'. 'History testifies,' he added, 'that that nation alone becomes truly prosperous in which these two distinct forces act together in warm co-operation.' As he proceeded to make clear, he had in mind the example set by Risorgimento nationalisms across Europe. In Wales, however, the conditions for a union such as he envisaged were far from propitious, and the kind of marriage he was (already rather belatedly) proposing could never be more than a shot-gun wedding. A year later, at Newport, it ended in acrimonious divorce, with the consequences that Edwards had indeed foreseen in an editorial that he had so hopefully entitled 'Salutatory', but that might have been more accurately entitled 'Ave atque Vale'. The danger, he had there described, was that politicians would 'lose sight of ideals in the pursuit of, perhaps, a necessary policy of expedience – to forget the goal in the worry and crush of the thronging pilgrims that line the route' (the religious imagery is significant). As for 'the men of culture', the risk with them was that they would 'withdraw from the arena and become mere negative critics, instead of bringing their wide knowledge of the country's best and of the broader principles of statesmanship to reorganize and to a great extent build upon anew the national life'.[17]

In 1896, the very year of the great Welsh Schism, Edwards returned to his theme in the editorial to the second issue of *Young Wales.* His periodical's primary aim, he announced, was still 'to preach the gospel of the national unity of Wales'. The discussion that succeeded, however, served only to demonstrate that a call to unity on such terms as Edwards was capable of conceiving was bound to fall largely on deaf ears. Recalling the hostile forces with which Llywelyn the Last and Owain Glyndŵr had had to contend, he warned his readers that 'we have to set ourselves in array against far subtler enemies for the overthrow of Welsh Nationality.' He pointed to an article in which Ernest Rhys had accurately identified these enemies when asserting that 'the Cockney is a more dangerous enemy than ever was Saxon or Norman. We have to encounter all kinds of smug cosmopolitanism [the very word made notorious that year by Bird's approving use of it at Newport], and resist all kinds of cheap commercial bribes – all those things in short that seek to destroy the national sentiment, and make Wales into a London suburb, and Snowdon – the sacred mountain of our fathers! – into a railway station!'[18] Such a dismissal, in effect, of the mass culture that was attendant upon industrialisation augured ill for Edwards's wish, as expressed elsewhere in his editorial notes, to reach out beyond the Welsh-speaking 'peasantry' to those 'certain parts in the Principality where the English language has gained a strong footing' (*YW* 1, 50), and to 'serve as the medium of expression to the new activities which are now marking the young life of Wales'.

* * *

The 1903 issue of *Young Wales* carried a poignant elegy by Llewelyn Williams for 'his' Cymru Fydd. Gone with the great defeat of the Liberals in the 1895 General Election, he wrote, was the confident spirit of a progressive and nationalist Welsh Liberal politics. What had replaced it was eight years of 'gloom and depression'. 'Our young men,' he sadly remarked, 'no longer dream dreams, and our elders have no hope. Never, since Wales awakened to a consciousness of her nationhood, has her political affairs appeared so colourless and monotonous.' The great causes of Disestablishment, land reform and self-government had all faded. He obstinately continued, however, to dream of a Welsh Education Department, a Welsh Office with its own Secretary of State, and a National Council for Wales consisting of representatives of all the country's county councils.[19] For developments in these utopian directions he pinned his hopes, somewhat wanly, on Lloyd George whom he judged to be 'fast becoming the political dictator of Wales'.[20]

Even as Llewelyn Williams was writing his article, Cardiff City Hall was rising apace. The product of that industrial anglophone elite with which, as the 1896 meeting in Newport had conclusively demonstrated, Cymru Fydd had failed catastrophically to come to satisfactory terms, it consciously tried in its design and contents to project its own unified vision of a Wales which could reconcile its gloriously dynamic commercial present with its (carefully neutered) ancient past. It also attempted to fuse an unthreatening model of a modest, safely ancient, Welsh cultural nationhood with a fervent and devoted commitment to a majestically modern British Imperial political identity. The ingratiating spirit of this latter version of Welsh contributionism had been captured in all its odious fulsomeness in the poem produced by the ineffable Sir Lewis Morris to mark the installation of the Prince of Wales as first Chancellor of the new University of Wales on 26 June 1896:

> Here on the sounding margin of the sea
> Whence the shy Mountain-Spirit dwells not far
> We of hills and sea the children are
> Unite today in joyous pageantry
> Today rejoice! On this auspicious morn,
> From War to Peace re-born
> Our lost Llywelyn seems again to come,
> For love of learning to his ancient home;
> While with her fair-grown daughters twain
> Our gracious Royal Lady smiles again![21]

That likening of the future Edward VII to Llywelyn, the lost, last native prince of Wales, is a reminder that Cymru Fydd, like Welsh Liberalism at large, could happily accommodate ardent Royalists and Imperialists in its ranks. Even crusading religious Dissenters like William George bent the knee to Queen and Empire far more readily than to Westminster. 'Both our local history and the general policy of the Empire, of which this country forms a part,' George wrote in *Young Wales*, 'points to the urgent necessity of greater insistence in the present day upon the observance in the political world of those moral principles which Wales is practically unanimous in professing.' As for Lewis Morris himself, he declared at a public meeting held by Cymru Fydd in 1895 that, while Wales was indeed a distinct nation, it would be fruitless for her to attempt to recover her lost independence, and yet it would also be irresponsible to disown the duties required of her as a participating nation by the British Empire. The failure of any part of that Empire, Morris added, to develop in keeping with the law of evolutionary progress, would be certain to inhibit the advance of the Empire as a whole, and thus delay the progress of humanity itself.[22] But Morris was insufficient of a 'jingoist' – that is, of a New Imperialist of the Joseph Chamberlain persuasion – to be appointed Poet Laureate on the death of Tennyson (or so Welsh Liberals claimed). In 1896 the incoming reactionary Conservative government under Salisbury appointed Alfred Austin to that post (on the refusal of William Morris), much to the indignation of *Young Wales*.

City Hall's Royalist credentials were prominently evidenced in the official opening of the building by the King and Queen in 1905, an occasion which also saw Cardiff being granted city status. As for its associations with Empire, those were shrewdly incorporated into City Hall's nicely calculated symbolic projections of Welsh nationhood. Of the two grand staircases each side of the main foyer leading to the upper floor, one features 'a memorial to Captain Robert Scott and his courageous companions, who sailed (minus Scott himself) from Cardiff on the *Terra Nova*, on their ill-fated expedition to the South Pole in 1910'. This relic of empire is matched on the pairing staircase by 'another bronze memorial, this time to the poet and writer Sir Edward Reed, who had served Cardiff as a Member of Parliament'. Well before his team's departure, Scott had declared his aim to be 'to reach the South Pole, and to secure for the British Empire the honour of this achievement', and for long after his death his story was regarded in the popular imagination as an iconic tale of tragic derring-do encapsulating the qualities of modest courage, daring and endurance that had created the Empire itself. The major polar historian Beau Riffenburgh has even suggested that 'if one were to select a specific time for the birth of the popular imperial spirit, it could well be a conjunction of events in the first half of 1868, the year in which Scott was born'.[23] And he has also noted that it was a Welshman, Henry Morton Stanley, who had earlier in the century been the influential scribe to the imperial adventurism of Disraeli's government.

The choice of Cardiff by Scott as port of embarkation for his expeditionary force came to be regarded by the city as a signal honour, an acknowledgement of the unparalleled contribution it had made to imperial progress by supplying the navy with the bulk of its steam coal and by establishing coaling stations right across the world. Scott's attention seems first to have been drawn to Cardiff by Lieutenant E. R. G. R. Evans (later Baron Mountevans), who, in 1909, having gained experience from participating in Scott's first expedition, contemplated an expedition of his own. This proposal attracted the attention of the editor of the *Western Mail*, William Davies, who discussed with Evans the idea of leading a Welsh National Antarctic Expedition (modelled on the lines of W. S. Bruce's Scottish National Antarctic Expedition, which had been down south at the same time as Scott's first expedition). Although this idea never came to fruition, Davies retained sufficient interest in a Polar expedition with a strong Welsh connection for him to lobby Cardiff businessmen and industrialists for support when Scott announced his own expedition to the South Pole. Beau Riffenburgh has summarised the response as follows:

> So much support was offered from Cardiff that Scott decided it would be his final departure site. Terra Nova spent five days there finishing preparations. It has been reported that 300 tons of Crown Patent Fuel, 100 tons of steam coal, and 500 gallons of engine and lamp oil were donated at that point by Welsh coal companies, although I don't have evidence as to which ones. The expedition's cooking utensils were donated by the Welsh Tin Plate Company of Llanelli. The Intermediate School in Cardiff presented one of the expedition dogs (officially named Scamp, although the school had named it 'Tua'r Goleuni' [Towards the Light]); this is the way all of the dogs were officially obtained, although they came from Greenland. Cardiff also raised £2500 for the expedition, reportedly more than from any other city.
>
> Two of the expedition's most enthusiastic Cardiff supporters were the leading Cardiff shipowners Daniel Radcliffe and William J. Tatem. Radcliffe at this stage was the chairman of Evan Thomas, Radcliffe and Company, one of the most prosperous and best-known Cardiff-based ship-owning companies, established in 1882 by Evan Thomas and Radcliffe's older brother, Henry. Tatem, later Baron Glanely, was a Cardiff-based shipowner, horse breeder, and philanthropist. The two played a significant role in raising funds and sponsorship throughout South Wales, and helped make sure Terra Nova received dock facilities. Scott was so pleased with the support he received in Wales, that he designated it Terra Nova's home port; she returned there at the end of the expedition. There is correspondence between Radcliffe and Evans quoted in *Scott of the Antarctic and Cardiff*.
>
> In the section on 'Outfit and Preparation' at the end of Scott's Last Expedition, Lieutenant Evans wrote: 'It only remains to acknowledge the unbounded hospitality of the Cardiff citizens, with Mr Dan Radcliffe at their head, who docked and coaled the ship for us, gave freely in money and kind, and made their generosity so felt that Captain Scott promised that Cardiff should be the home port of the Terra Nova.'[24]

Cardiff thus played a vital part in what became one of the most legendary and symbolically charged of all British Imperial adventures.

And then, of course, there was the heroic role played by the Welshman Edgar Evans from Rhossili in the epic story of the ill-fated Antarctic expedition. Reputedly a 'huge, bull-necked, beefy figure', Evans was valued by Scott as a 'giant worker'. Way down the pecking order, a willing pack-horse and devoted underling, the large-hearted and immensely courageous Evans, who almost literally worked himself to death in the service of others, in some ways epitomised the strictly subaltern position of the Welsh working class within the governing hierarchy of the British Empire.

As for the now forgotten Sir Edward Reed, commemorated on the other City Hall grand staircase, he was a Kentish man who had been Chief Constructor of the British Navy from 1863 to 1870, overseeing the building of several boldly experimental ironclads. Lavishly lauded and rewarded, he became Liberal MP for Pembroke in 1874 and for Cardiff in 1880, and was appointed Lord of the Treasury by Gladstone. During his two different periods in Parliament he managed also to amass a fortune as a railroad magnate. A champion of Empire to the core, he was a fervent supporter of the Boer War. The links of Scott and of Reed with Cardiff, let alone with Welshness, were very transient and tenuous, but that in itself was very much to City Hall's purpose. By commemorating them, the city's intention was to dissociate itself from any 'narrow', 'provincial' nationalism and to advertise Cardiff's 'international' status as one of the premier cities of global Empire; a 'cosmopolitan' centre, as Alderman Bird would have it.

Ascend these two grand, imperial staircases, however, and you enter a very different world, a veritable Welsh Valhalla. This is the Marble Hall, home to 'the Heroes of Wales' in the form of a dozen statues, every one male, with the exception of Boadicea, who was an embarrassed afterthought. This grand display of the Pride of Wales was the end product of a half century during which the country had gradually, and at times seemingly reluctantly, reconciled itself to the presence of the fine arts. What with the confirmed prejudice of Welsh Nonconformity against any kind of sensuous aesthetic, and the blinkered preference of commercial and industrial interests for the strictly practical and utilitarian, the fine arts had had to struggle long to win a degree of respect and to gain a firm foothold in Wales. But from 1862 onwards the National Eisteddfod cautiously began to accommodate some work by Welsh artists in its 'Social Science Section', and when the Eisteddfod was held at Aberystwyth in 1863, it boasted the first 'Exhibition of the Art, Industry and Products of Wales'.[25] Much was made over the succeeding years of the 'civilising' influence of the visual arts, prompting Cardiff in 1870 to organise a Fine Art and Industrial Exhibition. Thereafter, two of the senior partners in the architectural firm that was to design the Cardiff Coal Exchange, T. H. Thomas and Edwin Seward, busied themselves with efforts to establish a permanent exhibition space in the town and, having failed to persuade local government worthies to provide a home for the Royal Cambrian Society (founded as a national academy at a Denbigh meeting attended by seven artists in 1881), they switched their efforts to a campaign to establish a National Museum. This goal was finally achieved after many twists and turns, delays and hiccups, with the opening of the building in Cathays Park to the public in 1922. With the national awakening of the 1890s, whose powerful cultural engine was Cymru Fydd, a generation of patriotic artists found a new, pertinent, source of inspiration for their work in the Celticism of the period, while a renewed interest in things ancient prompted the National Eisteddfod to invite the German-born painter Hubert Herkomer to design new regalia for members of the Gorsedd.

As early as 1860, an appeal was being made by the Welsh Mancunian John Francis (Mesuronydd) from the stage of the National Eisteddfod (that year held in Denbigh) for a programme of public monuments to commemorate key figures in Welsh history. 'It was an evidence of decay,' he declared, 'when nations or peoples forget the great men whom God has risen up to be their protectors and deliverers, and it was the best possible proof of the strength and vitality of a people when it could be seen that they revered, and honoured the memory of their noble dead.' (*IN*, 277) Such a dream was to be vigorously revived and forcefully promoted in the context of Cymru Fydd and the new Liberalism by T. E. Ellis in a number of important lectures during the early 1890s. Ellis also pressed for a National Museum (and National Library), and was strongly supported by other prominent cultural leaders such as Brynmor Jones, who believed that the establishment of such seminal national institutions was needed to provide Wales with parity with England and Scotland. By such important initiatives, 'we should thereby advance another step in that forward movement which had for its objective the conversion of Wales from a mere aggregate of counties into a province of the British Empire, having an active and conscious national unity of its own' (*IN*, 304).

* * *

It is, then, in this context that the provision within City Hall of a space for a pantheon of national heroes should be set. Significantly, the sculptures were commissioned eight years after the civic building had opened, a delay sufficiently long to ensure that the very last tiny shock wave of the political impact of Cymru Fydd had died safely away. What remained, being merely innocuous cultural sentiment, could be comfortably displayed in sculptural form in this prestigious 'national' space. Equally significant was the identity of the two towering figures of wartime Welsh Liberalism who were prominently associated with this civic initiative. The group of sculptures had been funded by D. A. Thomas, that early enthusiast for Cymru Fydd, who had helped engineer the defeat of the political wing of the movement at the Newport meeting. By the time the statues were officially unveiled on 27 October 1916, Thomas had been elevated to the peerage as Lord Rhondda, had turned empire-builder in the world of commerce by amassing a fortune in the US and Canada, and was soon to be appointed Food Controller in the wartime government over which his friend and rival Lloyd George presided as Prime Minister. And Thomas embodied an even more striking irony. As the leader of the Cambrian Combine, he had been centrally implicated in the violent showdown between owners and miners at Tonypandy in 1911: in light of this, 'his' sculptures could be viewed as the equivalent of blood-money. As for the official opening of the pantheon of heroes, that honour was naturally reserved for the Prime Minister Lloyd George himself, the grand affair being 'celebrated in a massive group portrait painted by Margaret Lindsay Williams', still on display in the Marble Hall. An illustrated catalogue was published to accompany the exhibition, and its text makes for amusing and illuminating present-day reading.[26]

Ten sculptures were planned, to be chosen by a panel of three (Thomas Powel, Professor of Welsh at University College, Cardiff; Sir Thomas Marchant Williams, a notoriously scathing QC nicknamed 'the Acid Drop'; and W. Llywelyn Williams, a leading Cymru Fydd Welsh Liberal MP).[27] Members of the public were also canvassed for their choice, with the result that the list was headed by Owain Glyndŵr, followed by Hywel Dda; Saint David (Dewi Sant); Bishop William Morgan; Llywelyn the Great; Dafydd ap Gwilym; William Williams, Pantycelyn; Llywelyn the last Prince of Wales; Griffith Jones Llanddowror; and Gerald of Wales, in that order. The contributing artists, all selected by the sole specalist consultant to the project, J. Havard

Thomas, were 'mostly . . . younger English sculptors of conservative inclinations' (*IN,* 338). As for the sculptures that were eventually commissioned, Peter Lord has pointed out that 'all the main strands of early twentieth-century national sentiment were expressed in the pantheon: the early church (Saint David), Nonconformity (William Williams, Pantycelyn), poetry (Dafydd ap Gwilym), and both anglophile British political sentiment (Harry Tudor and Sir Thomas Picton) and the independent Welsh tradition (Hywel Dda, Llywelyn ap Gruffydd and Owain Glyndwr)' (*IN*, 337–8). The late addition of the token female, Boadicea, he has further noted, was a belated nod to the ancient Celtic roots of the Welsh, newly fashionable and also recently scrupulously traced by contemporary Welsh scholarship.

An examination of the case of these marble worthies yields interesting insights into a number of different, and often competing, ideas of Welshness influential in the period. Take the figure of Lieutenant Governor Sir Thomas Picton, for instance (19th in the public vote). A native of Haverfordwest , reputed to be foul-mouthed, irascible and readily given to brutality, the estimable Picton gained fame by leading a crucial bayonet charge that led to his death during the battle of Waterloo and to his being mentioned in despatches by Wellington. He had already served to notable effect in the bloody and murderous Peninsular War, subsequent to serving a term as governor of Trinidad that had culminated in his facing charges of torture and of ruthless suppression of disorder. (The illustrated catalogue of 1916 disingenuously regrets that Picton hadn't taken steps to eradicate the prevailing culture of torture on the island.) T. Mewburn Crook's sculpture has him looking lithe, a coiled spring of threatening energy.

A gaudily decorated hero of Empire, Picton also represented, for an influential section of ruling class opinion in 1906, the long and glorious contribution made by the Welsh to English military history from the battles of Crécy and Agincourt to the desperate affair of Rorke's Drift (1879) – a 'Welsh' affair more in legend than in fact. The great cheer-leader for this gung-ho image of his countrymen was the incorrigible 'Owen Rhoscomyl', a colourful adventurer of multiple identities, some of whose own escapades rivalled in daring even those outrageous antics in the service of Empire celebrated in the *Boys Own* paper. Consciously renouncing that 'feminised' representation of the 'Celtic' character so influentially peddled by Matthew Arnold and made popular in the cartoon figure of Dame Wales, Rhoscomyl set out to advertise Welsh 'manliness'. In the very year that City Hall opened

(1906) Rhoscomyl published his novel *Old Fireproof* (to be studied in chapter 4), a tale closely modelled on his own adventures with Rimington's Guides during the Boer War, and featuring his remarkable romantic feat of winning the heart and hand of an Afrikaaner girl.

Harry Tudor was the darling of all Unionists, and therefore confidently took his place in this pantheon despite coming a lowly 23rd in the popular vote. Adorned with a crown, he is already in effect Henry VII in this marble effigy. The red dragon on the standard he holds slightly to his rear was, undoubtedly, meant to suggest he had the whole of Wales solidly behind him, but the retreating banner might be more cynically viewed as a sign that he had already begun to leave Wales in his triumphal wake. Raised by Henry after landing with his tiny band at Milford Haven, the banner, or so the 1916 illustrated catalogue informed its readers, combined the dragon of Cadwaladar with the white and green colours of another of Henry's ancestors, Katherine, widow of Henry V. This, legend had it, was the origin of the modern Welsh flag.

As for the armed figure kneeling by Henry's side, he is Rhys-ap-Thomas, Henry's chief supporter in Wales who was reputed, by the poet Guto'r Glyn, to have personally slain Richard III. Of Rhys-ap-Thomas, the 1916 illustrated catalogue approvingly reports that he had been singled out on Bosworth Field itself for praise by Henry, who had loudly declared, in religious phraseology, 'This is my well-beloved.' Interestingly, given the aggravated state of the 'Irish Question' at the time, the 1916 catalogue goes on to claim that 'In Henry VII we find many things which may have been due to his nationality.' This king was, the catalogue continues, reputedly 'free from English prejudice', which meant he could more readily 'understand Ireland'. And as it did in the case of so many of the sculptural pieces on which it was commenting, the catalogue bolstered its claims for Henry's achievements by quoting from English literature, in this case the passage from Shakespeare's *King Henry VI* (Part iii, Act iv, scene 6) invoking Henry as 'England's hope'. Implicit in all these quotations was the supposition that, even when celebrating the 'heroes' of the Welsh past, English poetry carried an authority that Welsh poetry entirely lacked.

Both the Unionist camp and the Warrior Tendency in the Wales of the day are again catered for by the inclusion of Boadicea (27th of the public's favourites) in this gallery of the Welsh immortals. A warrior queen, she had long been claimed by the English as a great heroine of their proud 'island' history of resistance to foreign tyranny. She was a particular favourite of Victorian England, and her cult culminated in the sculpture of her in a war chariot, its wheels bristling with scythes, erected on the Victoria Embankment, next to Westminster Bridge and the Houses of Parliament. The accompanying snippet of text from William Cowper's eighteenth-century poem in her honour made it clear that this Boadicea was the Iron (or at least bronze) Lady of the British Empire: 'Regions Caesar never knew,' it read, 'Thy posterity shall sway.'

In choosing to include Boadicea in the sculptural group, the Welsh were coming late to the game. But as a 'Celt', she qualified as an authentic 'British' heroine and moreover, since the English had glorified her martial qualities, the Welsh chose to represent her contrastingly as an ancient Welsh 'mam', protectively clutching, one either side, the daughters whose rape by the Romans had according to Tacitus triggered her rebellion. Such a mild projection of Boadicea's image is particularly interesting when one considers the circumstances and context of the commissioning of the figure. It was a late call, consequent upon the shamefaced realisation that the 'hall of heroes' was, indeed, just that – an all-male space. The omission of any female figure would have been particularly unfortunate at a time when the world of Liberal Wales, as elsewhere, was coming under increasing pressure from the Women's Movement.[28] The figure seems, therefore, to have been a compromise. Its very commissioning ensured at least a token representation for women, while in its finished form it turned what could easily have been a threatening figure of female rebellion into a reassuring image of female domestic tenderness. But the commentary in the 1916 catalogue interestingly balanced the mild impression left by the sculpture with an expression of the dying queen's defiance of her Roman conquerors. Following the example set in the case of the Embankment effigy, it turned to Cowper and his poem predicting the eighteenth-century expansion of England's first English Empire:

> Ruffians, pitiless as proud,
> Heaven awards the vengeance due;
> Empire is on us bestowed,
> Shame and ruin wait for you. (25)

The catalogue thus ensured that its warlike Boadicea was fit to be placed alongside her Embankment twin to form a formidable pair of Imperial matrons.

While the choice of William Williams, Pantycelyn, as the representative of Welsh Nonconformity seemed to have about it something of a Calvinistically predestined air, the selection of Saint David, equally obvious on the surface, was altogether more tricky in its deeper implications. Saint David was claimed as founder by the beleaguered Anglican Church in Wales, who needed every bit of popular 'native' support it could get if it was to make a fair fist of defending itself against the Nonconformists' jeering charge of its being an alien church. But Saint David was claimed with at least equal conviction and fervour by the chapels, who believed they had reinstituted that 'simple' and 'pure' mode of religious life so famously adopted by the saint himself. Represented in marble as delivering the famous sermon at Llanddewibrefi ('Gwnewch y pethau bychain'/ 'Do the little things'), during which the ground turned from molehill into hillock under his very feet, David was a saint who, in his own legendary person, could unite the bitterly opposed factions of Welsh church and chapel. And so, again contrary to appearances, could Gerald of Wales (Giraldus Cambrensis), whose strong ecclesiastical associations (albeit Catholic in character) endeared him to Welsh Anglicans, while his stubborn fight to free the Welsh Church from fealty to Canterbury by establishing a separate Archdiocese for Wales, centred on the ancient Episcopal seat of St Davids, endeared him to the influential Nonconformist wing of Cymru Fydd. And as a bonus, he was the great-grandson, through his mother, of the last relatively independent native ruler of Dyfed.

The note of reconciliation of warring contemporary factions struck in the memorials to both Saint David and Gerald of Wales is sounded again to good period effect elsewhere in this judiciously assembled sculptural group. Bishop William Morgan, child of Union and Reformation, ambassador of the New Learning of the Renaissance, was credited with being the great architect of the magnificent Welsh Bible of 1588. As such, his statue testified to the huge contribution made by the Church of England to Welsh life and culture. But 'Yr Esgob Morgan' was also naturally revered by all Welsh Nonconformists, those 'people of the Book' who had been brought up on Morgan's inspired language. Even Hywel Dda, although there was no concealing his threatening status as an enormously admired 'native' ruler, was a figure sufficiently remote in time and peaceful by reputation (renowned not for fighting but for his legislative code) not to trouble the Edwardian peace. Moreover, although he had retained nominal independence as a Welsh 'prince', Hywel was known to have actually paid homage to the English king and even to have been much influenced by 'the noble life', as the illustrated catalogue obsequiously put it (34), of that great fount of English nationhood, King Alfred the Great.

As for Dafydd ap Gwilym, the sculptural representation of that most sly, mercurial, prodigiously inventive and at times wittily obscene of poets, fashioned at a time when the new Welsh scholarship was busily laying the solid foundations of his cult as Wales's answer to Chaucer and Shakespeare, is a masterpiece of spin. 'In this conception of Dafydd ap Gwilym,' so the modern official guide straight-facedly advises us, 'the romantic Welsh poet is represented as a youthful and gentle bard, with a sensibility to every mood and manifestation of nature. He carries a harp, and is represented as though he is about to burst into song.' The 1916 illustrated catalogue couldn't have put it better. Its Dafydd had owed his medieval success, apparently, to the magnanimity of King Edward III, who had restored to the Welsh bards the freedom and confidence they had lost following the defeat of Llywelyn in 1282, thus making possible the holding of eisteddfodau. And this Dafydd was a sentimental Victorian at heart, given to wandering disconsolately from place to place in search of the 'lovely Morfudd', all the while producing such couplets as 'The dark-eyed maid my love has won, / And hence all food and rest I shun.' He sounds like a comically lovesick swain in a Gilbert and Sullivan operetta.

Then, of course, there are the two fascinating problem cases of Llywelyn ein Llyw Olaf, last native Prince of Wales, and the great rebel nationalist himself, Owain Glyndŵr, who had actually topped the popular poll. Partly prompted by the mid-century publication of Glyndŵr's statesman-like correspondence with the King of France, his reputation, steadily augmented by the cultural nationalists of Cymru Fydd, had grown to cult status between 1880 and 1914. Ernest Rhys's view of him, expressed in an essay on 'The Grave of Glyndwr' in *Young Wales*, was typical of his wing of the movement:

> The untamed mountain-spirit of Glyndwr still quickens for us, whether we are in London or in Rome; the effect, the magic of his name still exists. The Welsh national sentiment is the more alive today because of him.[29]

As Professor E. Wyn James has astutely noted in a valuable study, Glyndŵr's popularity with the Cymru Fydd faithful lay in his confirmed appeal (in his own time as thereafter) to the ordinary people of Wales (the sacred rural *gwerin* of late nineteenth-century Welsh-language culture). One of the social elite of his day he may have been, but (unlike Llywelyn) he could be convincingly represented as 'one of the people'. The remarkable, visionary, political programme outlined in his letters to the French king corresponded quite closely to the aims of the progressive, nationalist wing of Welsh Liberalism – 'the creation of national institutions, including a university; the disestablishment of the church; the formation of a Welsh Parliament'.[30] The consequent extent of Glyndŵr's appeal may be measured, as James points out, 'in the torrent of novels, poems, dramas, passages for recitation and performance as song, and so on'. A generation of parents began enthusiastically to name their sons Glyn (short for Glyndŵr).

The modern visitor information guide to Cardiff City Hall nicely captures the diplomatic image of a potentially Welsh insurrectionary figure produced by the obliging sculptor Alfred Turner: 'The statue represents the great Welsh patriot as the soldier statesman – the enthusiast with lofty ideas and noble aims – not a mere ambitious rebel so wrongfully depicted in English histories . . . Spiritual aspirations rather than desire for material success is depicted in the figure.' In other words, Glyndŵr has been turned into a Great Victorian. The 1916 illustrated catalogue, as ever, turned to English poetry for sanction, taking its cue from Shakespeare's gullible, boastful, superstitious 'Owen Glendower', who rashly claimed 'I am not in the role of common men'. But the catalogue then settled down to the no-nonsense work of re-producing Glyndŵr as a good Welsh reforming Liberal:

> Centuries have passed since that great Welshman died, but his name will be ever honoured by the Cymry although the English called him traitor. He was the champion of the Welsh peasant and his dreams for the education of his countrymen are now being realised (43).

Glyndŵr's convenient 'rehabilitation' had already been effected by Beriah Gwynfe Evans, the newspaperman, vapid historical dramatist, Cymru Fydd stalwart and Lloyd George supporter, who had been commissioned to write a pageant drama about Glyndŵr as part of the 1911 celebrations of the Investiture at Caernarfon of the Prince of Wales. Evans's soap-opera for Royals – not the first treatment of the Glyndŵr story by this impassioned patriot who had for years been turning out what Hywel Teifi Edwards memorably termed 'theatrical éclairs' – was a consummate exercise, so typical of Victorian and

Edwardian Wales, in reconciling cultural nationalism with deep and sincere loyalty to Royalty and Empire. The key to this ideological sleight of hand was the division of history in two. The first period (when England oppressed Wales) ended with Henry IV; the second period (which saw Wales become happily devoted to England) began with Henry V, and led via Agincourt to Bosworth. Since Glyndŵr (and likewise Llywelyn) clearly belonged to the earlier period, then an early twentieth-century Welsh Royalist such as Evans saw no contradiction between celebrating his anti-English uprising and celebrating the Investiture, the latter ceremony being for Evans the gracious 'recognition by Royalty' of Wales as a distinct 'national entity' (*GGG*, 64). Such sentiments (involving Welsh loyalty to Crown and Empire rather than to Westminster) were commonplace in the period. Elfed, a prominent Cymru Fydd stalwart, Nonconformist minister and hymn-writer, hailed the Prince of Wales as a 'True branch of Tudor's root', and 'the Empire's pride' (*GGG*, 65–6). Beriah Gwynfe Evans even resurrected the old vatic traditions of the Medieval Brut for this auspicious Royal occasion, claiming that the Abbot of Strata Florida's prophesy of Arthur's return in the person of Glyndŵr had also included the forecast of the return of Arthur himself in the person of the twentieth-century Prince of Wales (*GGG*, 67).

As for the 1911 Investiture for which Evans composed his pageant drama, it was, as the poor young Edward himself protested, a rum affair that did full justice even to the more bizarre paradoxes of the culturally mixed-up Wales of the day. It owed much, as its primary historian John Ellis has demonstrated, to the romantic nationalism of Owen Rhoscomyl, who had in effect already staged his own dress-rehearsal for precisely such an occasion, in the form of that grand epic, The National Pageant of Wales, produced against the backdrop of Cardiff Castle in 1909 (see chapter 2). The Investiture was planned in considerable secrecy by a tight-knit cabal of the loyalist and royalist great and good, working primarily through a 'National Committee'. As a result, the event expressed, in all its colourful absurdities of pseudo-feudal dress and ritual, 'a view of Welsh national identity formulated by a handful of the Welsh elite, comprising members of the Welsh gentry and Church [the Bishop of St Asaph played an influential role] as well as Liberal politicians [including, of course, Lloyd George] and nonconformists' (*I*, 66).

It can sometimes be difficult to fathom, let alone credit, the depth of Welsh royalist sycophancy in this period, which makes it all the more interesting to come across satirical commentary on it. Conscious, no doubt, that (as the historian John Davies has noted) Victoria had spent only seven nights in Wales during her entire reign, O. M. Edwards adopted the pen name of 'John Jones MA, Oxford' to publish in 1889 a gushing piece on the queen's imagined visit to Bala. 'My respect for her is endless,' John Jones swooned, having complimented the queen on speaking Welsh of such purity that it was unintelligible to her listeners, 'and I believe that the English crown is as perfect a form of government as any on the face of the earth.'[31]

While most of the documentation relating to the planning of the Investiture seems to have been subsequently deliberately disposed of to protect the mystique (and no doubt the political manoeuvrings) surrounding the occasion, ephemera still remain, including the bilingual document officially outlining the programme of ceremonial for the event.[32] There was a fair amount of music by Wagner mixed in with sentimental Welsh airs, rousing military marches and statutory hymn, at what was an event altogether Valhallan in the scale of its ambition. Present in force and with much pomp were representatives of the highest echelons of the English aristocracy, attended by such exotics of the heraldic calling as Garter King of Arms, Caernarvon Pursuivant (Extraordinary), Fitzalan Pursuivant (Extraordinary), Portcullis Pursuivant (Extraordinary) and the presumably more ordinary Rouge Dragon Pursuivant. It was to the likes of these that the newly crowned King George presented 'Our Most Dear Son, Edward, Albert, Christian, George, Andrew, Patrick, David, Prince of the United Kingdom of Great Britain and Ireland, Duke of Cornwall and Rothesay, Earl of Carrick, Baron of Renfrew, Lord of the Isles and Great Steward of Scotland, Duke of Saxon and Prince of Saxe-Coburg and Gotha', commanding them to recognise him hereafter as Prince of Wales and Earl of Chester. In response, young Edward undertook to 'become your liege man of life and limb and of earthly worship and faith and truth'. With this, little Wales was at last allowed its brief, eager moment of glorious basking in the Imperial sun. Appropriately enough, King George was to preside at the Imperial Durbar in India a few months later (*I*, 112), and strong parallels were drawn between the situation of the Welsh and that of the Boers, whose states, newly granted self-government, had just become part of the Union of South Africa under the Crown in 1910 (*I*, 110). 'Through the investiture,' then, 'the state recognized Wales as a full member of the British imperial enterprise.' (*I*, 110)

The various souvenir booklets produced for the occasion clamorously echoed this note of Empire. It sounded loud and clear in the text Owen Rhoscomyl prepared for schoolchildren in the area of Swansea's Local Education Authority.[33] He began by informing his young readers that to mark the coronation of King George in June, 1911, 'one fifth of the whole earth' would be on holiday, 'for that is the size of the wonderful British Empire.'(1) And just when the rest of the Empire would be returning to work, for Wales there would 'still [be] a dearer day to come' (2), the day of the Investiture of the Prince of Wales, following ancient precedent stretching way back into the mists of time when one 'without blemish' would be chosen by the chiefs of the clans across Wales to be 'Head of All the Cymry'. 'A ring of gold was put upon his finger and a rod of gold in his hand. Then a great hirlas horn was brought, containing a drink made from the Elder Tree. The left arm of the King was bared, and from it three drops of blood were caught in the hirlas.' (4) With like liberal imaginative licence, Rhoscomyl then traced the tradition of princely Investiture down to the present, and to 'the ceremony at Caernarvon [that] will be for a mark to all the world that Wales is a special country in the Empire, with a proud past behind her, and a prouder future ahead, if we do but continue to work for her, resolved to bring her to the front in the Empire; to make her a land to which the Empire may look for help and strength in the hour of temptation and in the day of danger' (16).

While the souvenir booklet produced for north Wales by the London and Manchester *Daily News* was a more sober affair, it was equally enthusiastic in puffing Wales's Imperial mission. The forthcoming event, it announced, had been organised to mark 'the distinctive place filled by the Principality in the union of peoples which makes up the Empire of the British Crown', and to demonstrate that, 'though in area one of the smallest countries in the world, Wales ranks in fame among the foremost'.[34] It also couldn't resist having a sly dig at the bitter contest there had been between Caernarfon and Cardiff for the honour of hosting the Investiture. 'Cardiff is, of course,' it archly remarked, 'much the largest and the richest town in Wales, and on the strength of its size and prosperity it is fond of constantly asserting the claims to be regarded as the Welsh metropolis. It also has a castle; only, unfortunately, that castle happens to be the private residence of a nobleman . . .' (2). It was a point repeated elsewhere by the north Wales press. Cardiff's castle was synthetic, just like the mongrel upstart city itself, they sniffed; Caernarfon castle, in contrast, was ancient and authentically Welsh, just like the pure, traditional culture of the surrounding area.

The deep linguistic and cultural divide between the traditional, rural, Welsh-speaking and Nonconformist Wales of the west and north, and the new, increasingly anglophone, cosmopolitan communities of the industrial valleys funnelling down to Cardiff and Newport has been dramatically emphasised by John Ellis in his absorbing study of the Investiture. It was a divide further embittered by the xenophobic tendencies evinced by some in the Caernarfon camp and the colonial, anti-Welsh views expressed by some supporters of Cardiff. As Ellis has shown, the victory of Caernarfon meant the Investiture was designed to showcase the vaunted qualities of the *gwerin*. Gorsedd, Eisteddfod, Cymanfa Ganu, 'traditional' Welsh costume, harp – these were the key stage props of an occasion in which the Welsh language was assigned a prominent part, the 'ich dien' of the Prince of Wales' motto being regularly 'translated' as 'eich dyn' (Welsh for 'your man'). Any acknowledgement in all this orgy of 'traditional Welshness' of the new troublesome proletariat of the cosmopolitan industrial south (or, indeed, of the oppressed and exploited workforce of the Penrhyn quarries in the Caernarfon neighbourhood) was carefully avoided by the vigilant representatives of a Welsh-speaking middle class. As that class had come increasingly under pressure following the shift of power from the *gwerin* to the 'proletariat', it had formed a highly effective, if unholy, alliance with leading figures from the ranks of their erstwhile enemies, the Welsh gentry and aristocracy, who were intent on seeking influential new symbolic roles in the wake of their own similar loss of traditional social and political power.

As John Ellis has graphically demonstrated in his excellent study, beneath its grand charade of national unity the Investiture hid an extensive network of cracks in the structure of social and political Wales that were directly related to competing notions of Welsh identity. One of these featured the ongoing hostility between Church and Chapel – while Nonconformist ministers were placated with minor roles in the celebrations, the prominent roles were all reserved for the bishops and clergy. And whereas nineteenth-century Nonconformist Wales had long demonstrated a sympathy for pacifism, the Investiture showcased the contribution of the Welsh to countless English military adventures from Crécy and the Agincourt of 'Harry of Monmouth' (the future Henry V) to the Imperial present.

Much was made in the Investiture of the 'Celtic connection' of the ever compliant and tractable Welsh (explored in chapter 5), with a particular view to commending their model example of loyalism to the attention of the increasingly dissatisfied and restless Irish. And most striking of all was the way the Investiture was used both inside and outside Wales to distract attention from the violent clash between miners, police and troops during what was being deliberately misrepresented as 'the Tonypandy riots'. In this connection, John Ellis has drawn attention to a striking detail in the Investiture pageant. A prominent part in its ceremony was played by Winston Churchill, the Home Secretary who had ordered in the troops to clear the Tonypandy streets of 'rioters'. 'It was Churchill who read the letters patent as the Prince was invested.' (*I*, 87) Little wonder, then, that the industrial valleys displayed very little interest in, let alone enthusiasm for, the gaudy, ostentatious royal carnival being organised, in the name of all Wales, in distant, tiny, peripheral Caernarfon. 'In the Rhondda,' reported the *Western Mail*, 'the industrial dispute overshadows everything, and no public rejoicings will be held.' (*I*, 88)

* * *

The sculpture gallery of City Hall represented Cardiff's similarly ideologically compromised attempt, some five years after the Investiture, to construct a composite symbol of pan-Welsh identity, complete with a pantheon of 'representative' Welsh heroes, one of whom remains to be examined. If the marble case of Glyndŵr presented some difficulties, then that of Llywelyn ein Llyw Olaf presented even greater problems, as had been underlined by repeated failures over half a century to establish any substantial public memorial to him.[35] From 1856 onwards, Eisteddfod dignitaries had several times attempted to raise funds and launch competitions to commemorate Llywelyn. Their failure to attract significant widespread public support or to raise even modestly sufficient funds contrasted strikingly with the conspicuous success of like initiatives in contemporary Scotland and Ireland. A towering memorial to Wallace was erected on the outskirts of Stirling in 1869, and a statue of O'Connell was erected in Dublin in 1882 in the middle of the street that was then renamed for him in 1884. And England, of course, found no difficulty in erecting memorials to Alfred in Winchester and Cromwell at Westminster, while in Trafalgar Square a skyscraping Nelson, raised triumphantly higher than the mainmast of any of the vessels he had commanded, ruled the roost aloft with the pigeons.

Meanwhile in Wales, even the most insipid and inoffensive proposal to commemorate Llywelyn met only with a mixture of nervousness, indifference and apathy that condemned it from the start. When the gifted young sculptor Edward Griffith exhibited a plaster model of Llywelyn in 1878, he failed to attract money enough to convert it into bronze or marble, but compromised some twenty years later by producing a painted stone effigy atop a pillar for Conway. A serious attempt to establish a memorial fund was made in 1894 by a cross-section of Welsh establishment figures, mostly associated with Cymru Fydd, meeting at a Fleet Street hotel, with the (absent) Marquis of Bute undertaking to contribute a sum of £100. This fund-raising effort – which duly failed – was greeted with predictable nervousness by the *Western Mail*, the paper pledging to support it only if it 'be absolutely free from all political taint' ('political taint' being code for incendiary nationalist sentiment). Despite innumerable committee meetings, appeals and events, all that had been raised by the end of 1895 of the £1000 was a paltry £100. Sporadic attempts were made thereafter to revive public memory of Llywelyn, but all foundered, for reasons that seem obvious and inevitable today. There was nothing about his 'aristocratic' story to interest industrial Wales, its growing working class or prosperous bourgeoisie; and as for the *gwerin* of rural Nonconformist Wales and its middle-class representatives, their infatuation with Empire and its 'local' embodiment, the Prince of Wales, condemned the last native Prince of Wales to the obliging convenience of oblivion. On such rare occasions as he was indeed recalled, it was in a form that made of him a 'Chocolate Soldier', to be remembered not as a warrior but as the sentimental lover of the king of England's daughter.

Ironically enough, it may have been the Investiture of 1911 that brought Llywelyn most vividly back to national memory, this time in a context favourable to public commemoration. The legend of the conqueror Edward I's presentation of his baby son to the 'nobles' of Wales as their very own Prince had been trotted out interminably during the course of the official celebrations, and newspapers had carried reproductions of Sir John Gilbert RA's 1873 painting of the event, depicting the wide-eyed adoration by the Welsh of this new Messiah. The coast was therefore clear for the committee to decide to include a statue of Llywelyn in the City Hall pantheon of Welsh heroes. The commission was entrusted to Henry Pegram (1862–1937), a middle-aged sculptor who had a few years earlier completed a series of monumental statues for the University of Birmingham representing giants in the fields both of Science and the Arts, and embodying the founding vision for the university of Joseph Chamberlain, the arch late-Victorian Imperialist. It may well have been the fact that Pegram was an English outsider with impeccable credentials of such 'Imperial' service that allowed him the liberty to produce – in his sculpture of a defiant warrior Llywelyn for City Hall, clenched fist raised, flanked by a fallen Welsh soldier and harp – the most arresting and stirringly 'nationalist' of all the figures in this group of monumental statuary. There is spirit enough in the figure to satisfy the requirements recorded in a poem by 'Gwaenfab', published in *Cymru* (1895), that Wales should commission a warrior image of Llywelyn:

A rhoddwch lun grymus o Ryddid urddasol
Fel cadarn Hercules mewn dillad swyddogol;
Fel gwron diarswyd, yn herio pob gelyn,
A'i gleddyf yn ysgwyd, ar golofn Llywelyn.

(And place [on Llywelyn's column] a powerful image of noble Freedom, like a staunch Hercules in official garments; a fearless hero, defying every enemy, brandishing his sword.)[36]

Another significant contributory factor to the re-emergence of Llywelyn was the increasing attention being paid, from the early 1890s onwards, to the history of Wales – one of the most important and consequential symptoms, in the wake of the 1848 'year of revolutions', of the growth of a new 'national' consciousness in subordinated peoples across Europe.[37] Initiated by the influential periodicals of the period, particularly those affiliated to the Cymru Fydd movement, these sallies into the past eventually took the more substantial and lasting form of book-length studies, ranging from rollicking efforts such as Owen Rhoscomyl's buccaneering *Flamebearers of Welsh History* (1905), and solidly responsible popular introductions such as O. M. Edwards's *Wales* (1901) and *The Welsh People* by John Rhŷs and David Brynmor-Jones (1900), to J. E. Lloyd's classic two-volume *History of Wales from the Earliest Times to the Edwardian Conquest*, a publication consciously intended to demonstrate the professional sophistication of the new 'scientific' Welsh historiography. A late efflorescence of the Cymru Fydd spirit, Lloyd's study was published in the very year of the Investiture, and included a memorable account of the death of the last native Prince of Wales. To convey the measure of the loss, and the devastation of a whole culture, Lloyd paraphrased several lines from the great contemporary elegy by Gruffudd ab yr Ynad Coch, but was then careful to offset the effects of that anguished threnody with the remark that '[i]t was for a far distant generation to see that the last Prince had not lived in vain, but by his life-work had helped to build solidly the enduring fabric of Welsh nationality' (*JEL*, 113).

* * *

So what, then, do the professional historians of our today make of that Wales of a century and more ago? The doyen of them, K. O. Morgan, has asserted in a recently collected essay on Edwardian Wales that it was a time when 'Wales experienced an unprecedented period of optimism, a golden glow of hope. The present writer, in a literary conceit, once pronounced it to be, in Gibbon-like terms, "Wales's Antonine Age"'.[38] His case, he adds, rests on four propositions. First, that the 'Wales of the years before 1914 was a land of unprecedented prosperity' (147); second, that 'Welsh and more specifically Welsh-language literature was never more thriving' (148); third, that 'Wales was a land of political stability . . . provided by the overwhelming ascendancy of the Liberal Party [which] reached its climax in 1906, when Wales became a Tory-free zone' (149); and fourth, that 'the fact of Welsh nationality was being increasingly recognized at the highest level' (150). In like spirit, Gareth Elwyn Jones opened a discussion of the condition of Wales, 1880–1914, by roundly asserting that '[b]y the criteria conventionally used to measure the stature of nations, Wales [in this period] was a vibrant, proud, successful country' (*W*, 1).

Historians are, however, ever careful to balance such a sanguine outlook with a quick recital of more unsettling facts. In 1894, an explosion at Cilfynydd colliery killed 250, while twenty years later, in 1913, a catastrophic 439 were killed in the Senghennydd colliery disaster. As the nineteenth century closed, 1898 saw a six months stoppage in the coal industry, and 1900 marked the beginning of the Penrhyn Quarry dispute, a landmark event in British industrial history: the strike lasted an epic three years, resulting by 1907 in a mere 800 of the original labour force of 2,700 still in employment. In 1901, a

National Census established that, for the first time, English-speakers outnumbered Welsh-speakers in Wales.[39] In 1900, Keir Hardie was elected as an Independent Labour Party MP for Merthyr, an augury of huge changes to come. Beginning in 1910, the violent disturbances in Tonypandy continued into 1911, a year in which two railwaymen were shot dead by troops in Llanelli. One year after Lloyd George's historic National Health Insurance Act was passed in 1911, the gospel of a radically alternative, syndicalist, social vision was preached in the *Miners' Next Step*, a pamphlet that advocated a wholly different approach to labour relations from that which was represented by Mabon, the lay-preaching miners' leader, who had during the closing decades of the nineteenth century pursued moderate, conciliatory policies. Mabon's days had, in a sense, been numbered ever since 1898, when 'Mabon's day' (the holiday he'd negotiated for miners on the first Monday in every month) had been discontinued. This was an early sign of the growing, tense estrangement of owners from labour that, following the great coal stoppage later the same year, paved the way for the emergence of a new, militant unionism.

Implicated in these developments, as Gwyn A. Williams shrewdly emphasised, was the demise of Nonconformist Wales, the social ideology that 'was the integument which joined together a whole constellation of interests and passions in Wales which were potentially inimical to each other.' (*WWW*, 234) 'The very success of the economy,' Williams added, had 'subjected that synthesis to intolerable strain; by 1900 it was already beginning to come apart.' The archetypal myth of the (rural, Welsh-speaking) *gwerin* was crumbling at the very moment it had gained maximum potency, while the archetypal myth of the 'working class' that was to replace it during the interwar years was already in the fledgling stages of production – assembled in part out of the very materials of the *gwerin* myth it had helped dismantle, just as Welsh farms once had walls built out of stones 'salvaged' from the ruins of the monasteries (*WWW*, 237).

While this present study is interested in precisely such rival images of Wales as those of the *gwerin* and the 'working class', it is written from the viewpoint not of a historian but of a cultural historian with a special, and specialist, interest in literature. In his influential study, K. O. Morgan described the period in Welsh history from 1880 to 1980 as involving the *Rebirth of a Nation*. But for the past three decades or so, cultural historians have fought shy of using any such natural, organic terms for the development of 'conceptions of peoplehood', preferring to emphasise the constructivist aspects of the process by referring instead to 'nation building'. As distinct from common earlier assumptions that 'national character' was a fixed, given, inalterable constellation of cultural traits and psychological syndromes, the present wisdom is that

> [n]ational culture is malleable and mobile. It is the outcome of a constant process of cultural production. A national culture is constantly being moulded as individuals and groups confront their social worlds and try to (re)form them. Out of such confrontations emerge nationalist ideologies from which, in turn, a national culture gets produced.[40]

Moreover, national communities are usually, at any given time, the product of negotiation, competition, and often conflict, between several different national ideologies, each a rival 'consciousness or perception of what the nation is or should be' (*NI*, 4).

> Struggles among nationalist ideologies – contests over ideas as well as conflicts between people – may propel one nationalist ideology into dominance and leave others by the wayside. A national culture is always 'temporary' because, whether antique or recent, its character and puissance are a matter of historical practice; they are plastic constructions, not cultural givens. (*NI*, 4)

In short, 'national culture is not an inevitable output of infrastructural investment. It is a contingent product of history, of struggle.' (*NI,* 10)

This study is a study of precisely such a struggle, the struggle between several competing models of Welshness that were circulating, often merging, but also conflicting, during the momentous years between 1890 and 1914, much in the manner suggested by Gwyn A. Williams. To notice this is to realise that during this period, as during any other, national identity was developed 'not as something "essential" but as a dialogue between a variety of interacting discourses'.[41] Frequently implicated in these ideological struggles were rival versions of what were supposed to be authentic Welsh 'tradition' – although present-day theorists would conversely argue that the idea of any such 'authenticity' was wholly misguided, because 'traditions are not the unitary voice of an organic whole but the dialectical engagement between opposing value systems which define each other precisely by their intertwined opposition' (*MSN*, 32–3).

One thing all these conflicting models had in common was the assumption that Wales was, and should remain, a 'sub-state nation'.[42] Another common feature was the crucial role played by intellectual and creative artists in the production and dissemination of these different formulations of identity. In recognition of this, modern scholars often speak of the emergence of a 'National Symbolic', an aspect of the 'National Imaginary' in the maintenance and development of which the arts, prominently including literature, played a very important part. Much of this first chapter has been concerned with examining arresting instances of the semiotics of contested identity, in the symbolic form of the art and architecture of Cardiff City Hall and the ritual of Investiture, and with demonstrating how rival artistic images of Welshness were the epiphenomenon of different social, political, economic and cultural circumstances.

As for this study as a whole, it pays attention at several points to the construction of the 'National Symbolic' by means of semantically subtle and dense texts that are rich in cultural implication but that, in the hallmark manner of literature, mediate the societal realities of their time only in complex, indirect ways. This study could therefore be said to engage with the textual refractions of a socially, politically and culturally fractured Wales. It claims to be not a magisterial account of the rebirth of a nation, such as that already influentially offered by K. O. Morgan, but merely a tentative investigation of some of the nations of Wales during the quarter of a century or so preceding the First World War, a period when the concept of 'Welshness' was particularly vigorously contested and models of nationhood were energetically multiplied.

2

Performing political identity

One thousand 'fairies' tastefully arranged to form a living map of Wales; the august Marchioness of Bute masquerading as 'Dame Wales'; the hero of the 'Charge of the Light Brigade', Lord Tredegar, proudly strutting his stuff as Owain Glyndŵr; five hundred rugby players, led by stars like Rhys Gabe, 'storming' Cardiff castle. What could all this be, in the summer of 1909, but a 'National Pageant', no less?[1] This was a production to rival in scale the future Hollywood film epics of Cecil B. DeMille, and it was produced on the Elysian fields of Sophia Gardens, with Cardiff Castle – itself an 'historically challenged' mélange of Norman authenticity and nineteenth-century synthetic medievalism – as an appropriate backdrop. Pageant fever had seized towns and cities across the UK following the huge success of the Sherbourne Pageant of 1905, and Cardiff, freshly promoted to city status in that same year, was determined not to be outdone. The event was a fashionable sensation. 'All agog, "bright young things" asked one another, "Are you going to 'padge'?"' (*NPW*, 10) 'We have beaten the world at [rugby] football,' Henry VIII (who slummed it in ordinary life as President of Cardiff Rugby Club) trumpeted at the carnival's end, 'and now we have beaten the world, also, at pageantry. I thank you.' (*NPW*, 9)

Thanks were indeed due. The pageant had been a monumental effort at constructing a 'usable past' – a 'history' of Wales fit for the purpose of a raw, dynamic city ruthlessly intent on securing a prominent yet loyally subordinate place in the imperial sun. The whole affair was an orgy of carefully sanitised, ideologically policed, 'patriotism'. The *South Wales Daily News* understood the matter perfectly:

> The glorious history of the Principality set forth as an object lesson could not fail to instil into the minds of the young the higher patriotism that in their forefathers kept Wales a distinct and national unity and made her a powerful factor in Imperial progress because she was true to herself. (*NPW*, 5)

What Cardiff – and the 'new' Wales it represented – wanted was a 'history-lite' version of the past. While a claim to 'ancient' origins, and to 'national' status, were essential to the city's self-aggrandising image, it also anxiously sought to avoid incurring any substantial obligations to the past of Wales. Ties to that potentially embarrassing past – as to the language and the culture that embodied it – needed to be minimised in the very act of being acknowledged. The National Pageant of Cardiff (the term is an historical and cultural oxymoron in some respects) was an inspired wheeze, a brilliant public relations exercise organised and enacted by the new, proto-international elite of a rapidly ascendant industrial-commercial metropolis.

But in dabbling with the past at all, in an effort to claim a 'national identity' on its own highly selective terms, that elite was playing with fire. For one thing, the pageant operated as a powerful bonding process, binding not only performer to performer but also performers to audience, and, indeed, binding members of the audience to each other. This forged a group or communal identity under the sacred authenticating auspices of nationhood. In this way, however unintentionally, theatrical performance enabled a 'nation-building' process. The *soi-disant* 'national pageant' fostered in Cardiffians – first and foremost 'citizens' of a city situated within a global industrial-commercial network – an undeniable sense, however vague, of being significantly located in Wales; of being Welsh. But they were made partial to a version of the past that was itself decidedly partial in scope and character, 'a picturesque object-lesson to the present generation' (*NPW*, 5).

Much has been written over the last few decades insisting that identities, both personal and social, are to be understood as not so much given as constructed, and constructed largely through 'performance'. 'Fake it till you make it', is Leo McGarry's shrewdly sage advice to his staff at the White House in the up-market soap opera *The West Wing*, and rulers in particular have been immemorially aware of the importance of convincingly regal performances, of the remorseless need to keep up appearances. Judith Butler has been one of the most influential – and controversial – of recent advocates of performance theory in the context of the study of gendered identities, and her emphasis on the opportunities for adopting new social roles when momentous upheavals destabilise established communities is pertinent to our understanding of the National Pageant of 1909.[2]

That the roles there on offer carried a degree, however small, of historical 'depth' is all the more noteworthy given that for centuries the Welsh had been afforded extremely few educational, institutional or cultural opportunities for forming an acquaintance with their own past. As Hywel Teifi Edwards has crisply put it, the Pageant furnished 'a banner-waving historical narrative for an untutored audience long adrift from its own story' (*NPW*, 11). As such, the event needs to be understood in the context of other contemporary efforts, albeit far better informed and more sophisticated, to recover the past in an attempt to reconnect with it. One of the first university-trained generation of historians, partly inspired and sponsored by the Cymru Fydd movement, was very aware of the part played by history in the emergence of new national communities across Europe. Modelled on sophisticated Continental historiography, and completed for the most part in institutions of higher education, their Welsh historical studies laid implicit claim to the authority that could alone come from impartiality. Yet, magisterial though they could be at their best – witness J. E. Lloyd's great *History of Wales from the Earliest Times to the Edwardian Conquest* – these academic histories, too, were inevitably ideologically compromised in their prospectus. Resolutely uninterested, for instance, in tracing the antecedents of the new anglophone, industrial Wales that had created modern Cardiff, they concentrated instead on exhuming the alternative story of an Old Wales. This ran from the deep history of the Celts through the golden age of semi-independence of the princes to the post-Tudor narrative of the gradual making of a pious rural *gwerin*, whose culture exultantly climaxed in nineteenth-century 'Nonconformist Wales' and the apotheosis of a Reforming Liberalism.

* * *

Just as the National Pageant promoted, through its cheerfully vulgarised version of history, the agenda of a new, anglophone Wales, product of the heavily industrialised south-eastern regions, so other almost equally crude historical dramas promoted the agenda of the Welsh-language elite still so powerfully influential in the ranks of the Cymru Fydd movement. Many of these plays were the products of Beriah Gwynfe Evans (1848–1927), a highly versatile and prodigiously industrious editor of *Y Genedl Gymreig*, a weekly published in Caernarfon, then the Mecca of Welsh-language journalism.[3] A rapid glance at his life and career shows Evans to have been constantly operating at the interface between different socio-cultural zones and historical periods.[4] Born in industrial Monmouthshire, he was raised in a thoroughly Welsh-speaking and chapel-going society at a time when the region was about to undergo a radical culture-shift in favour of English.[5] The place of his south-east corner of Wales in the international vanguard of industrial civilisation must have registered early with Evans, since his father, a Congregational minister, followed his own father's example and emigrated to the US when Evans was twenty-one, eventually dying in Arkansas. By then, Evans himself was already settled into a teaching post in Gwynfe, a rural village nestling in the shadow of the Black Mountain that separated it from the rapidly expanding industrial settlements of the Swansea, Amman and Gwendraeth valleys.

He was to regret to his dying day that, as a young teacher, he had been the means of anglicising this thoroughly Welsh-speaking Carmarthenshire community, and his subsequent career may be interpreted as a lifelong attempt at linguistic and cultural reparation. It may also be seen as a consistent attempt to reconcile the different social, cultural and linguistic worlds between which he himself had had to navigate his course. Where others saw and history was duly to decree divergence, Evans dreamt of and worked for convergence. Like many others of his persuasion in the Cymru Fydd movement, he became obsessed with the problem of how to connect Wales's past meaningfully with its potentially self-estranging present, gradually recognising, along with the cynically perceptive Tancredi in Lampedusa's great novel *The Leopard*, that 'for everything to remain the same, everything needs to change' ('Se vogliamo che tutto rimanga com'è bisogna che tutto cambi'). After eighteen years teaching in Gwynfe, he became a journalist in Cardiff before being head-hunted by Lloyd George for a post as editor of the local newspaper that the Welsh wizard had just bought in Caernarfon.

In a sketch of Beriah Gwynfe Evans, another notable journalist of the time, E. Morgan Humphreys, recalled him wielding his pencil like a club and relished his sly professionalism and his sharpness of both eye and tongue.[6] A dogmatism and inflexibility that were, in

Humphreys's opinion, the unfortunate legacy of Evans's early years as schoolmaster, made him a far better journalist than editor – but it was these very same traits that were to make him such a loyal supporter of the Cymru Fydd movement in all its manifestations and a tireless worker on its behalf. This was a period when the new brilliant breed of Liberal politicians in Wales was becoming increasingly aware of the vital part played by the press in reporting political events to a wide reading public.[7] From the MPs' point of view, sympathetic accounts in the local papers of their exploits both in their constituencies and at Westminster were clearly of the first importance. Their achievements had to be grippingly translated into popular story. And after all, there was no shortage of good vivid copy. From the early 1890s onwards, there were ample materials for a good tale – not to say stirring drama, as we shall see – in the heroics of that dazzling duo of young Liberal Turks, T. E. Ellis and Lloyd George. Astute as ever in any matter pertaining to his own advancement, the latter was particularly quick to realise how advantageous it would be for the press in his own constituency to be unfailingly attentive to his achievements. Consequently, he enabled a local company to buy, and therefore to control, *Y Genedl Gymreig* – and it was he, too, who was effectively responsible for the appointment of Beriah Gwynfe Evans as its editor. A by-product of Evans's appointment, as we shall see, was a singular 'theatrical' novel about events at Westminster consciously intended, like the National Pageant, to advertise new roles for the Welsh to play, but this time in a version of the New Wales that reflected a Cymru Fydd perspective on the past rather than the version of it that had been performed in the Cardiff pageant.

Eventually published under the title of *Dafydd Dafis: sef Hunangofiant Ymgeisydd Seneddol* (*David Davies: the Autobiography of a Parliamentary Candidate*), the novel originated as a series of columns in Evans's newspaper, purporting to be authentic up-to-the minute reports from Westminster.[8] An avid reader of such major organs of the Cymru Fydd movement as *Cymru Fydd* and *Young Wales*, Evans had acquired a shrewd understanding of the seminal role played by the press in the formation of a new cultural consciousness. As Benedict Anderson has famously noted, '[it was the new forms of] the novel and the newspaper . . . [that] provided the technical means for re-presenting the *kind* of imagined community that is the nation'.[9] One figure in particular in late-nineteenth-century Wales displayed a genius for understanding this and acting accordingly. That figure was O. M.

Edwards, a phenomenon who placed all his expertise first as an Oxford history don and then as visionary Chief Inspector of Schools for Wales at the service of ordinary Welsh readers, endeavouring to educate them in their own cultural history through a prodigious variety of publications, including the extraordinarily compendious popular journals he edited. Edwards recognised that a long history of national subjection and fragmentation had conditioned the Welsh to identify not with a 'nation' but with their own, particular localities, and he cunningly designed his journals to mirror this. They gave prominence to passionate accounts of local dialects, local histories, local celebrities, local folklore and local geographies, but in so doing they informed those localities about each other, and thus deliberately operated to construct a view of Wales as a community of communities. And alongside such pieces, his journals included important 'overview' articles, informed by the latest scholarship, on Welsh literature, history and culture, thus presenting the country as a single, national totality. Edwards's journals therefore constitute 'classic' examples of Anderson's theory of nation-formation in action.

But for all his brilliance as editor, Edwards had his limitations. Much more of a cultural than a political nationalist, he resolutely omitted from his periodicals any discussion of the momentous political affairs of his day. For him, politics was inevitably bound to be divisive, and so wholly inimical to the work of national unification to which his publications were dedicated. Beriah Gwynfe Evans, by contrast, was an ardent (although not uncritical) supporter of Lloyd George and the new Welsh Liberalism that promised to be both culturally transformative and politically liberating. Naturally enough, he was therefore very concerned to educate the substantial segment of the Welsh population newly enfranchised by the momentous Local Government Act of 1894 in their rights and opportunities. To that end, he prepared a very useful handbook that spelled out with simple clarity the extensive implications of an act that had brought a new system of parish and district councils into being.[10] In so doing, he emphasised that this quietly radical measure had for the first time furnished voters with the ready means of decisively breaking the stranglehold that landowners, squires and Anglican priests had since time immemorial exerted over the systems both of justice and of local government in Wales. 'The Parish Councils Act,' he wrote in an article for *Young Wales*, 'has been rightly called "The People's Charter." What Magna Carta was to the nobles six-and-a-half centuries ago, that – and more

– may the Parish Councils Act prove to the village and rural communities before the end of the present century.' And he went on to foresee such initiatives as the building of cheap housing for workers, and appropriate recreational facilities.[11] But for all its revolutionary potential, Evans emphasised, the Act would be rendered toothless unless voters took full advantage of it. And before they could do so, they needed to understand the full remarkable extent of the opportunities it afforded.

But alongside his impassioned advocacy of local government, Evans also nursed a passion for the much grander political stage at Westminster. Just as he felt that in their innocence of the recent major reforms in the structure of local politics ordinary Welsh voters were in real danger of once more falling victim to the old, rotten governing class, so he believed that ignorance of subtle and sophisticated political affairs in the distant Houses of Parliament could result in those same voters failing to ensure that their own interests were being properly represented there. He wanted them fully to realise that they had now been empowered to be actors, and not merely spectators, in the political and civic arenas. In his eyes, the true champions of the people's interests were T. E. Ellis, Lloyd George and their brilliant new generation of Welsh Liberal politicians.[12] Consequently he set out, in his columns for *Y Genedl Gymreig*, to report the comical adventures of an aspiring Welsh MP, a device that enabled him to provide a weekly commentary, enlivened by fantasy and humour, on the contemporary political adventures of the Welsh at Westminster. The column ran from 1892 to 1894, after which it was reworked and expanded before being published as a novel in 1898.

* * *

Dafydd Dafis: sef Hunangofiant Ymgeisydd Seneddol (David Davies: the Autobiography of a Parliamentary Candidate) purports to be the autobiography of a proudly self-made man.[13] Beginning life as a poor lad from Cardiganshire, its subject and 'author' follows the classic Welsh upwardly mobile path of his kind by migrating to London, where, after a period of sleeping rough, he makes his fortune selling milk. The very idea of a politician's autobiography was shockingly new to a Welsh-speaking Wales used only to biographies (in the hagiographic form of 'cofiannau') to the great, exalted eminences of the Welsh pulpit. But Beriah Gwynfe Evans, himself a minister's son, had grasped that the world of his youth had shifted sharply on its axis. A new Wales demanded new celebrities, and the rising stars were not the mighty preachers of yore but such political striplings as Tom Ellis and his own patron David Lloyd George. Elected to Westminster in 1886 and 1890 respectively, they were both promisingly troublesome Westminster greenhorns in Gladstone's fourth administration (1892 to his resignation, aged 84, in 1894) at the time Evans wrote his fictive columns. The fact that it was a minority government ensured there would be plenty of political theatre, and the Irish Question continued to dominate proceedings, even in the aftermath of Charles Stewart Parnell's tragic downfall, and death in the autumn of 1891, with Gladstone's Second Irish Home Rule Bill passing the Commons but defeated in the Lords in the autumn of 1893.[14] Along with Home Rule for Ireland, Gladstone had pledged himself, during his election campaign of 1892, to disestablish the Anglican Churches in Wales and in Scotland, and much of the energies of Welsh Liberal MPs was, as Beriah Gwynfe Evans's novel reminds us, to be devoted during his final ministry to the fruitless attempt to get the wily old man to be as good as his word. At the outset the outlook seemed promising:

> With the General Election of 1892, and the return of the Liberals to power with a majority of 40 only, a new situation was created. The Welsh Gladstonians, 31 in number, were now more than sufficiently numerous in the House to defeat the Administration had they chosen. Mr Gladstone had realized the danger. Recognizing the influence of Mr T. E. Ellis among the Welsh Members, he offered him a Junior Whipship.[15]

In Evans's novel, Dafydd Dafis tastes the first fruit of his new financial success by marrying the redoubtable Claudia – the pair make a fine comic double act throughout – a flirtatiously scheming young woman from a wealthy English bourgeois family whose political astuteness is matched by her social ambition. Their paths first cross in a scene that seems a deliberate parody of romance fiction: he saves her from disaster when the horses drawing her carriage suddenly bolt. By degrees, and in partly reluctant response to her shrewd promptings, he becomes increasingly privy to the shenanigans of the Welsh Liberal Party, and is thus able to provide a day-by-day, intrigue-by-intrigue account of its affairs, in the process offering vivid pen portraits of all the chief actors in the great Westminster dramas of the day.

The novel is designedly multi-media in character. By including cartoons throughout, many of them by leading young Welsh artists whose work is showcased alongside that of established cartoonists from *Punch* and other mainstream publications, it seeks to accord the image the same prominence and status as the word. The novel thus embodies the expansively inclusive approach to the arts crusadingly championed, as noted elsewhere in this study, by T. E. Ellis and by a Cymru Fydd movement keen to see Wales demonstrate its new maturity by embracing a progressive approach to cultural life.[16] Such a vision is both instanced and emblematised by the title page of *Dafydd Dafis*. It features a stylishly dressed young lady and gentleman gazing upward adoringly at the handiwork of an artisan atop a ladder, who is identified as 'Sion Gymro, Peintiwr Perbarlau Trefedigaethol Mr Balfour' (John Welshman, painter of the civic coat of arms of Mr Balfour). He is putting the finishing touches to a florid coat of arms adorning the fashionable address of 963 Park Lane, the Davies home. Scattered around the foot of the ladder are numerous scrolls blazoned with such Cymry Fydd campaigning slogans as 'National Library [and] Museum', 'Land', 'Education', 'Tithe', 'The Church', 'The Rights of Wales, the Welsh and the Welsh Language'. The image in its entirety thus forms a composite design which is itself roughly heraldic in character, as if it were functioning as a kind of mock coat-of-arms for the whole Cymru Fydd movement. It fuses the politics of social reform and self-government with the arts, while implicitly advertising a catholic view of culture.

The novel treats Westminster as the setting for a prolonged soap opera, and the manoeuvrings both between the different factions within the Welsh Liberal group and between them and the sly Old Man Gladstone are mirrored in the relationship between the relative innocent Dafydd Dafis and his amusingly domineering wife, the feisty Claudia. The central character's innocence is, in fact, a crucial narrative device that allows Beriah Gwynfe Evans to educate his readers in the strange ways, shifting alliances, political feints and labyrinthine intrigues of Westminster; also, by showing how Dafis is at once teased but also respected by the Welsh Liberal MPs, it is implied that the latter, although become sophisticated and metropolitan in their ways (and thus well able to hold their own in the rough and tumble of Parliamentary affairs) have not lost their common, homely, Welsh, touch.

The novel deals, on its own amusing terms, with many of the key issues of Welsh Liberalism in the last decade of the nineteenth century – with Disestablishment, of course, dominating all others. As K. O. Morgan has pointed out, 'The evidence that the Welsh Church was showing some signs of awakening from its slumbers and that the rate of growth of nonconformity was slowing down made Welsh Liberals all the more passionate. A series of motions between 1886 and 1892 effectively drew the attention of the House of Commons to the central arguments . . . Further, the growing importance of the Celtic nations within the Liberal Party materially helped their cause.' (*RN*, 41) *Dafydd Dafis* tracks the several (unsuccessful) attempts made at different times by different groupings to force the resourcefully slippery Gladstone – a former opponent of Disestablishment – to turn his ambiguous high-minded statements on the subject into decisive action by threatening otherwise to remove their support from the minority Liberal government. Particular attention is paid to the brief rejection of the Liberal Whip by Lloyd George, D. A. Thomas and two other Liberals from April to May, 1894, the decidedly anticlimactic high water mark of Welsh national 'rebellion'. The following year, Gladstone's successor in the premiership, Lord Rosebery, set in train the developments that eventually led to Welsh Disestablishment some twenty years later.

In *Dafydd Dafis*, Evans hints at the difference not only in character but in political strategy between the two rising stars of the new Welsh Liberalism: T. E. Ellis and Lloyd George. As J. Hugh Edwards shrewdly noted in 1896, Lloyd George was strongly inclined to follow the example of the Irish, believing that 'Wales will not receive her due share of the attention and support of the English Parliament, and certainly not the realisation of her most cherished hope of a Parliament of her own . . . unless she . . . welds her Parliamentary representation into one solid homogeneous whole, characterised by such absolute distinctiveness as to make it the effective medium for the expression of the national will and the symbol of the national individuality of her people.' Ellis, by contrast, modelled his own strategy on that of the Scots, who had steadily packed the front benches of Westminster until they had 'captur[ed] the whole range of Parliamentary vantages', and were thus in a position to dictate terms.[17]

Even when its humour is most low-key and domestic, therefore – as when dealing with the relationship between Dafydd and Claudia – *Dafydd Dafis* seems to be registering significant pressure points in the world of Cymru Fydd. And when the text tries to deal with the most serious and most uncomfortable of such areas of tension, the humour tends to become outrageous to the point of burlesque. So, growing dissatisfaction with the endless prevarications of the Liberal leaders over the issue of Disestablishment of the Church in Wales is underlined by a fantastic scene in which Lord Salisbury, no less, the aristocratic leader of the Tories, comes calling in his august person on Dafydd Dafis with a tempting invitation to throw in his lot with the Conservatives. As for that bitter episode of 1894, when Lloyd George, with three followers, attempted to force the Government's hand on the Disestablishment issue by acting the rebels and withholding their Parliamentary support for Liberal measures, it is conveniently disposed of through the extravagant expedient of having Dafydd Dafis kidnapped, and thus sidelined, for the entire duration, by an Irish faction incensed by his supposed success in advancing Welsh above Irish interests

* * *

In writing his columns, and subsequently when constructing his novel, Beriah Gwynfe Evans relied heavily on his wide experience as a dramatist, stout believer as he was in the key role the theatre could play in promoting a consciousness of nationhood informed by an educated, mature historical awareness.[18] Naturally sensitive therefore to the theatrical aspects of life at Westminster, he was also shrewdly aware of how new forms of Welsh social identity were in process of being formed by being 'performed' there. After all, never before in the long history of Wales had MPs actually arisen from among the ordinary people themselves. A recurrent theme of his fiction is the remarkable transformation of the 'local lads', 'Cynlas' (T. E. Ellis) and Lloyd George, into cunningly effective political operators on the parliamentary stage, and that at a time when much of the whole wide world seemed to be ruled from Westminster. In thus assiduously registering the evolution of a new kind of Welshness, the adventures of Dafydd Dafis may be said to confirm Judith Butler's shrewd comments about the 'performative' nature of identity, whether that be gendered or social in character. 'That identity is performative,' she writes, 'suggests that it has no ontological status apart from the various acts that constitute its reality. This also suggests that if the reality is fabricated as an interior essence, that very interiority is an effect and function of a decidedly public and social discourse.' (*GT*, 173) As we shall see, one prominent feature of the novel is the way in which it registers the strange, new kind of 'discourse' that the novice Welsh MPs had had to master.

As noted above, in commissioning cartoons from leading Welsh artists of the day Evans was implementing a policy of advertising the high quality of the contemporary visual arts in a Wales that seemed singularly reluctant to value them. 'The author takes pride,' noted Evans in his introduction, 'in thinking that he has succeeded in demonstrating to the world that Wales is capable of producing talent of the first rank, that that talent is comfortably able to take its place in the homely literature of the nation, and that Welsh publishers are able to do justice to the visual culture of Wales.' (*DD*, vi) But those exaggerated, stylised illustrations also perform another function. In turning the figures they illustrate into larger-than-life characters, they underline the fact that the novel's focus is on 'actors' and on the political parts they are taking in the grandest drama of all: the drama of Westminster politics.

This thespian aspect is signalled from the very beginning of the novel. As has already been mentioned, the frontispiece consists of an elaborate visual design centred on a sign-painter at work putting the finishing touches to the coat of arms of a newly ennobled Dafydd Dafis above the door of an obviously substantial urban residence. The tradesman's handiwork is being admired by a fashionably dressed pair, but where alongside the painter's ladder the door of 963 Park Lane should appear we have instead a portrait bust of the author, Beriah Gwynfe Evans, dapper in bow tie. And the frontispiece is framed by the hint of curtains of a theatre, drawn back left and right to reveal Evans, like some old-style Victorian actor-producer, ready to take his bow. Readers are thus from the outset treated as spectators at a theatrical event. Like the fashionably dressed pair gazing in rapt admiration at the blazon, they furnish Dafydd Dafis with an audience appreciative of his melodramatic transformation (with Claudia's help, of course) from Welsh country bumpkin into an aficionado of Westminster and (comically) sophisticated man-about-town. Evans draws further attention to these theatrical aspects of his novel in his author's introduction, where he congratulates himself on having succeeded in 'affording a glimpse of [political] life behind the curtains so accurate that the very actors themselves had supposed it must have been one of their own company who had been responsible for such treachery' (*DD*, vi). The reference is to the baffled speculation among Welsh MPs with regard to the author's identity at the time when the anonymous newspaper columns first appeared.

Dafydd Dafis is undoubtedly at its best when Evans deploys the skills at dialogue he had learnt from writing so much for the popular stage. The exchanges between Dafydd and Claudia are particularly entertaining:

> 'Ies, David, diar,' ebe'r wraig eilwaith, 'Ei wont tw get iw intw ddi hows!'
> 'Be, andros,' ebe fi wrthyf fy hun, 'sy ar Claudia 'rwan?'. . .
> 'Hwot dw iw mîn 'y nghalon i?' meddwn. 'Ei am in ddi hows now, mei diar!'
> 'Ei *dw* wish iw wd toc sensibli David,' ebe hithau, gan guro blaen ei throed ar y ffwtstwl sidan – arwydd sicr nad oedd hi yn meddwl cymeryd dim lol. 'Now dw pwt ddat horid paper owt of iwar hand ffor a minit, and listen.'
>
> ['Ies, David, diar,' said the wife a second time, 'Ei wont tw get iw intw ddi hows!'
> 'What the devil,' said I to myself, 'is up with Claudia now?'. . .
> 'Hwot dw iw mîn, my heart?', said I. 'Ei am in ddi hows now, mei diar!'
> 'Ei *dw* wish iw wd toc sensibli David,' said she, tapping the tip of her foot on the silken footstool – a certain sign that she would take no nonsense. 'Now dw pwt ddat horid paper owt of iwar hand ffor a minit, and listen.'] (*DD*, 2)

It is the first of innumerable instances where 'David' (the change of name, of course, indicates a change of social role, and of status) proves to be inept at mastering foreign languages – not only the arcane discourse of Westminster, but also the modish slang of stylish London society. He has a long way to go before his transformation into one of the English bourgeoisie is complete. Evans makes effective comic capital out of his terminological blunders:

> 'Ddi ffact of the ddi mater is, David, iw myst get a teigar!'
> 'Tad anwl!' llefis, gan lamu ar fy nhraed, a rhodio'n wyllt rhyd y stafell. 'Be da chi'n feddwl w i, deydwch?' [. . .]
> Chwarddodd Claudia wrth weld fy anesmwythder.
> 'Mi ryda chi, David, yn un digri,' ebra hi. 'Mae'n faich arno chi i gadw fyny ag arferion yr oes, ond mae'n rhaid gwneud neu mynd yn gyff gwawd i rei llawer is na chi. Mae pawb sy'n rhywun y dyddia yma yn cadw teigar, a gyn eich bod chi wedi mynnu'r dogcar newydd uchel yna, mae'n rhaid i chitha gael teigar i fyn hef fo.'

> ['Ddi ffact of ddi mater is, David, iw myst get a teigar!'
> 'Dear Lord!' I wailed, leaping to my feet and wildly pacing the room. 'What on earth do you mean?' [. . .]
> Claudia laughed at my agitation.
> 'You are a funny one, David,' said she.' It's such a strain on you to keep up with the fashion of the time, but you have to do it, or you'll be a laughing stock for those beneath you. Every one who is someone these days keeps a tiger, and since you've insisted on a new high dog-car, you'll have to get a tiger to go with it, like everybody else.'] (*DD*, 173)

And despite Dafydd's strenuous protestations, get a tiger indeed he must, as Claudia's word is always his law. Having succeeded in securing a suitable animal, he brings it home and shuts it in the kitchen one morning when Claudia is out, only to be shortly startled by blood-curdling screams emanating from that direction. On investigation, he finds the young servant girl, Sarah, perched precariously on a stool, hysterical with fear. At her feet lies poor Fido, Claudia's pet dog, dead in the jaws of a contentedly munching tiger. It is all an unfortunate misunderstanding, of course. 'Tiger', so Dafydd is all-too-belatedly informed by Claudia, is the fashionable term for a combination of livery servant and ostler.

And once Dafydd, urged on by the irrepressible and irresistible Claudia, ventures to explore life on the floor of the Houses of Parliament, his bewilderment at the language spoken there is a useful device for Evans to educate his readers in the machinations that underlie the grand issues of the day. Welsh Liberals focus obsessively on the Disestablishment of the Anglican Church in Wales, while in contrast the Irish campaign for Home Rule with an impressive political guile, reinforced by an extra-political turn to violence that the anxiously respectable, law-abiding Welsh loudly deplore.

Such, however, is Dafydd's innocence of the foreign ways of Westminster that he fails even to understand where it is that Tom Ellis MP has in mind that they meet. As he explains to a mildly exasperated Claudia,

> 'Wel, deyd mae o am i mi weitied iddo fo yn y lobi, fel taswn i ryw ffwtman iddo fo! Aed Ellis a'i Hows of Comons i'w grogi cyn rhosa i iddo fo yn y lobi! Fasa fawr gyn i iddo gael lle imi yn y wêtingrwm gan nad sut. Lobi'n wir! Mi ro i lobi iddo fo!' a theflais ei lythyr ar y bwrdd.

> ['Well, what he's saying is for me to wait for him in the lobby, as if I were his footman! Ellis and his House of Commons can go to hell before I stop for him in any lobby! I'm sure it wouldn't have been hard for him to find a place for me in the waiting room, if he'd wanted. Lobby indeed! I'll give him lobby!,' and I flung his letter on the table.] (*DD*, 7)

Things then proceed from bad to worse for him. Having gained admission to the House's holy of holies, he completely fails to understand the meaning of a reference to a 'Difishon Bell', and then goes on to mention a 'Mr Majority Banks', when he means to refer to Mr Marjoribanks, whom insiders know well to call 'Mr Marshbanks'. 'Oh, Dafydd! Dafydd', exclaims Tom Ellis on hearing his gaffe, upon which both the MP and Marjoribanks fall about

> a'r ddau yn chwerthin am y gora fel dau ffŵl gwirion, a'm gadal ina'n ffŵl gwirionach fyth i sbio arnyn nhw heb wybod beth oedd yn bod. A dyna lle 'roedd y bobol erill yn y lobi o gwmpas, byddigions i gyd, yn spio'n syn ar y ddau wirion rheiny'n chwerthin fel tasa nhw mewn pantomeim.
>
> [laughing like two idiots, leaving me feeling even more of a fool than they for failing to see what on earth the joke was. And all around us in the lobby there were the crusty aristocrats gazing in astonishment at the silly pair as if they were pantomime performers.] (*DD*, 51)

The analogy is apt, because pantomime is indeed what plays out on the political stage in Westminster from time to time, as the novel repeatedly shows. Politicians cannot afford not to be highly versatile players.

Learning the language of Westminster is at times rather like cracking a secret code. Accordingly, Dafydd Dafis has slowly to realise that references to 'Room Fifteen' are shorthand for mentioning the caballing of the Irish MPs who always congregate in that room, and that 'the Cave' refers to the group of disaffected Liberal MPs who are busily plotting to rebel against the government. Dafydd is particularly tickled by the English meaning of the word 'clos' ('clause') with which he is familiar only in its homespun Welsh meaning:

> Mi wyddwn i'n iawn be oedd clos cyn imi 'rioed ddod i Llundain; clos penglin fasa nhad yn i wisgo bob amser. Mae'n wir wedi imi ddod i gyffyrddiad â rhai o bobl y South, Towyn Jones 'rŵan, a rhei felly, mi

> gefis allan mai nid peth i wisgo ydy clos yno, ond buarth. Ond 'toedd dim buarth yn yr Hows of Comons, a'r unig clos welis i yno oedd y clos penglin a wisgid gan rai o'r swyddogion. Ond wrth wrando a sylwi a pheidio deyd llawar, mi ddois i i wybod mai 'Adran' feddylid wrth 'Clos' yn iaith y Senedd.
>
> [I knew very well what 'clos' meant to me before coming to London: 'clos penglin' were the knee breeches my father always used to wear. It's true, though, that once I'd come across Welshmen from the South, Towyn Jones and his like, I came to realise that 'clos' to them meant not an article of clothing but the yard of a farm. But there was no farmyard in the House of Commons, and the only breeches I ever saw there were the knee breeches worn by some of the liverymen. But by listening, noticing, and saying very little, it dawned on me that 'Section' was what was there meant by 'Clos', in Parliamentary language.] (*DD*, 79)

'Parliamentary language': the script to which every MP has to adhere if he wishes to play his appropriate part in the drama of the Commons.

While most of the novel is devoted to chronicling the story of the struggle of Welsh MPs to secure the Disestablishment of the Anglican Church in Wales, it does nevertheless find a little room for other prominent issues of the day, including, most interestingly, the campaign to secure political rights for women. For women to begin to take themselves seriously as potential actors on the political scene meant little less than a revolution in their conception of themselves as women. It meant transformation of habits of speech, dress and conduct. In short, it meant performing a radically different role. The late Ursula Masson has traced very thoroughly the history of the movement for women's suffrage within the heavily patriarchal ranks of nineteenth-century Welsh Liberalism.[19] It began, she notes, with the efforts of a small group to reform the established political order. As it grew, it spread to include the determination of a more radical wing of the movement to broker a working alliance with the WLA (the Women's Liberal Association) and in particular with the WUWLA (the Welsh Union of Women's Liberal Associations). The inaugural president of this last Association was Norah Philipps, one of the most prominent of the leaders of the women's rights movement in Wales,[20] and she attracted to her cause others of such calibre as the novelist Gwyneth Vaughan and Sybil Thomas.[21] As Masson has noted, 'it is clear that Philipps saw the future of the women's organization in being joined to the nationalist movement' (*UM*, 53).

Between 1895 and 1897 Philipps edited, and contributed to, a series of reports on the women's wing of Welsh Liberalism in *Young Wales*, beginning by recalling the important meeting held by forty women in Aberystwyth in March 1892, that resulted in the formation of the WUWLA. She concluded her first bulletin by deploring contemporary society's waste of the talents both of the working classes and of women:

> We curb their energies, we restrain their individuality, we limit their opportunity, we neglect their education; all this we do, not so much with a conscious desire to degrade and injure them, but because we have not yet learnt that to liberty and to knowledge we owe all the progress, the civilization, the happiness, and morality of humanity, and that out of an extension of these, good must come and that from their limitation evil and sorrow and wrong inevitably spring.[22]

Later in the same year she argued that women had their part to play in the developing of Welsh nationhood – Wales having long been one of the many 'subdued nations' of Europe – while emphasising that Welsh aspirations could best be fulfilled by the cultivation in its people of 'a passionate patriotism for this great empire – great, not only in extent, but far more, in the intent of her civilization', while they strove 'with joy and pride and devotion' for their own small country, 'that part of the great whole to which we, by special love and human linking of family, language and religion, belong'. It was a sign of the progressiveness of Welsh politics, she added, that support for female suffrage was so well advanced there – as had been evidenced in the actions of the fifteen Welsh Liberal MPs who had 'voted on the Local Government Act of 1894 in favour of qualified married as well as single women having votes for Parish and District Councillors.'[23]

In her pioneering study of the women's movement of this period in Wales, Ursula Masson emphasised it was important to do more than simply trace the course of 'events, and cause and effect'. It was necessary to be

> concerned with women's political language. It is my contention that, in the 1890s, women placed themselves at the 'spoken centre' of the Welsh nation. The phrase is Patrick Joyce's: he suggests that Gladstonian discourse brought women to the 'spoken centre' of British Liberalism in the 1880s. The religious and moral appeal of Gladstone's 1879

> Midlothian campaign, and his direct call on women to involve themselves in Liberal politics as a peculiarly womanly and moral duty, had been remembered as a watershed moment by Liberal activists, and the terms and tenor of his address were often to be echoed in the speech of Nonconformist Liberal women of Wales. Joyce has represented this as a development in which women exercised no agency, and from which they derived no power; they were included in a discourse of nation and 'the people', but had no role in shaping meanings. (*UM*, 3)

There is evidence aplenty in Evans's novel of his unease at the new vocalism of women who 'interfered' with a political order long the exclusive domain of the men. Anxious though he was to champion the cause of the 'New Welshman' represented by Tom Ellis, Lloyd George – and of course Dafydd Dafis! – Evans was far from being as supportive of the 'New Welshwoman' whom he saw appearing like a nightmare before his very eyes. There was no room in his Cymru Fydd/ Young Wales for such a monstrosity as that, and in order to set his fears to rest he defused what was for him a threatening development by ridiculing it in his novel as a subject for comic melodrama.

Evans's anxieties were also played out through the uneasy sparring between Dafydd and Claudia, which leaves no room for doubt as to which of the loving pair is the boss: 'no man chooses his path – particularly if he's married, his wife living, and she somewhat similar to Claudia' (*DD*, 5). While by no means a campaigning feminist, Claudia exemplifies the new assertiveness that typified the crusading women of the period across the UK. Indeed, it is she, rather than her limply ineffectual and chronically bewildered husband, who is a politically astute operator and she repeatedly demonstrates how keen are her political instincts, witness her handling of one of the prominent Welsh Liberal MPs of the day, Bryn Roberts.[24] The relevant chapter is ominously entitled, 'Claudia charms Bryn – and roasts him' (136). 'I knew,' muses Dafydd,

> fod Claudia am sugno'i waed o; ac eto ddyliach chi byth mo hyny wrth ei gwelad a'i chlywad hi hefo fo ar y ffordd i'r deining-rwm. Mi roedd ei chwerthiniad hi mor ysgafn a pherorus a chlychau arian, a'i llygid hi'n dawnsio yn ei phen hi, ac mi roedd yn debycach lawar i hogan deunaw oed yn scwrsio hefo'i chariad nag oedd hi i ddynes wedi cynllwyno i ddal Aelod Seneddol diniwad i'w rostio fo'n fyw.

> [that Claudia wanted to suck his blood; and yet you'd never say as much if you saw her and heard her with him on the way to the dining room. Her laugh was as light and as tuneful as silver bells, and her eyes danced in her head, and she was much more like an eighteen-year-old flirting with her lover than a woman who'd conspired to catch an innocent Member of Parliament and roast him alive.] (*DD*, 139)

And that's exactly what Claudia proceeds to do, by squeezing Bryn into a corner and forcing him to confess to his indiscretion in sending a letter to the *Times* criticising the conduct of the hotheads who were campaigning for a degree of devolution of parliamentary powers to Wales. Confused by her sudden change of tack to poking fun at him, Bryn blusters: 'I do not think, Mrs Davies, that women were intended by the Almighty to interfere in matters such as this.' (*DD*, 141) It is a crucial mistake because, on cue, all the other ladies whom Claudia has invited to lunch proceed to pile in with gustatory gusto:

> 'Rhag cwilydd i chi, Mr Roberts!' ebra hitha, gan ddropio'i ffishfforc ar y plat. 'Did iw hiar ddat Mrs Philipps?'
> 'No. Hwot was it?' ebra'r westyes.
> 'Ranc heresy,' ebra Claudia.
> 'Byt dw sei hwot it was,' ebra un arall o'r ledis.
> 'Wel,' ebra Claudia, wedi llwyddo i dynu llygid pawb atyn nhw'ch dau. 'Mr Bryn Roberts ses ddat Profidens nefer intended wman two tec part in pyblic affers.'
> 'Oh, Mr Roberts, how cwd iw!' Ebra Mrs Wingate yn f'ymyl.
> 'Eim shoct!' ebra Mrs Philipps. 'And iw ar two tec ddi tsher at mei miting at Carnarvon necst Thyrsde.'
> 'Ei nefer cwd haf thot iw capabl of sytsh a sentiment, Mr Roberts!' ebra Mrs Brynmor Jones, gan chwyddo'r corws.
> 'Men wer disifers efer,' ocheneidiai rhyw hogan ifanc y pen arall i'r bwrdd.
>
> ['Forshame, Mr Roberts!' exclaims Claudia, dropping her fish-fork on the plate. 'Did iw hiar ddat Mrs Philipps?'
> 'No. Hwot was it?', says the guest.
> 'Ranc heresy,' says Claudia.
> 'Byt dw sei hwot it was,' says another of the ladies.
> 'Wel,' says Claudia, having succeeded in fixing every one's eyes on Bryn and herself, 'Mr Bryn Roberts ses ddat Profidens nefer intended wman tw tec part in pyblic affers.'

> 'Oh, Mr Roberts, how cwd iw!' cries Mrs Phillipps, 'And iw ar two tec ddi tsher at mei miting at Carnarvon necst Thyrsde!'
> 'Ei never cwd haf thot iw cepabl of sytsh a sentiment, Mr Roberts!' adds Mrs Brynmor Jones, swelling the chorus.
> 'Men wer disifers efer,' sighs some young girl the far end of the table.] (*DD*, 142)

Disguised though it is as humour, Beriah Gwynfe Evans's unease at such a baying chorus of Harpies is evident enough. For him, the sooner that the women intent on a place at the 'spoken centre' of Welsh political life are silenced and relegated once more to the margins, the better.

The fear aroused in men by newly assertive womanhood is made visually manifest in the nervously grotesque cartoon by Dyer-Davies entitled 'Roasting the Members'. The setting is a Victorian kitchen, in which three matrons are seen boldly confronting the reader and shamelessly flaunting their skills as savage cooks. On the left, Claudia is basting the heads of two Welsh MPs (D. A. Thomas and Bryn Roberts) on a slowly revolving spit in front of a roaring fire; centre-stage, Mrs Wynford Philipps (Norah Philipps) proudly displays the severed head of another Welsh MP she's holding by his long, feathery hair, while seemingly groping behind her back for a kitchen knife placed chillingly close to hand on a table; and on the right of the picture, Mrs Brynmor Jones kneels next to a post crowned by the head of Sir T. D. Llewellyn MP, while the head of Humphrey Owen MP dangles limply from her hand. Other MPs, heads still thus far attached to their chicken bodies, scratch around on the floor. Backdrop to the scene is a sturdy Welsh sideboard on which are displayed the pickled heads of Alfred Thomas and Tom Ellis.

The cartoon in its entirety is a visual digest of late Victorian male disquiet at contemporary women's campaigns for social and political equality. The violence of the fears stirred up in men's breasts is obviously projected onto the women, whose activities are, with queasy jocularity, openly associated with head-hunting and cannibalism. The 'unnaturalness' of the new roles in public life being claimed by women is underlined by a cartoon featuring the supposedly perverse uses to which the Victorian kitchen, that peaceful domestic domain in which women had long been supposed to reign supreme, was now being put, while the traditional image of the mother as nutritionally nurturing is likewise given a new, sinister twist. And from the post-Freudian perspective, of course, the whole scene is strongly suggestive of male fears of castration, loss of one's 'manhood' being equated with loss of virility. Women, the cartoon makes clear, have abandoned the traditional role assigned to them by nature itself, and have opted to 'act' in disturbingly new, unnatural ways. Male opposition to the women's movements often focused particularly fiercely on the intrusion of women onto the political 'stage,' as is shown in a *Young Wales* article by 'K. Lentzner PhD', in which the author condescendingly assents to greater educational opportunities for women but draws the line at the 'retrograde' step of a female suffrage based on the assumption of gender equality.[25]

In *Dafydd Dafis*, the female of the species proves far more dangerous to Welsh politicians than the male. Claudia is pitiless once roused. Several of the giants of Welsh Liberalism are savaged by her, one by one, including Lloyd George himself. Through guile, she actually succeeds in extorting a scribbled note from that notoriously reluctant and dilatory correspondent. And she gives the Chancellor of the Exchequer, the formidably aloof Liberal Grandee Sir William Harcourt, such a tongue-whipping that he confesses to Dafydd Dafis:

> 'Iwar weiff is a remarcabli ffein wman, Mr Davies, in meni respects ei meit se a gloryis wman, won in fact of hwm eni man wel ffil prowd. Ei congratiwlet iw mei diar ffelo on hafing sytsh a weiff – byt ei thanc hevn shi is *not* Ledi Harcort!' (*DD*, 245)[26]

In his house, clearly, the woman is still an appendage to her husband. Signficantly, the Welsh word for 'woman' – 'gwraig' – is also the word for 'wife', and this lends (spurious) authority to the conflation of the one with the other. As for Claudia, who could never remotely be considered an appendage of Dafydd Dafis, she is bold enough even to mount a frontal assault on the Grand Old Man himself, William Gladstone. She persuades Dafydd to track him down all the way to his secret retreat in Biarritz, so that Dafydd can be the very first to discover, and subsequently to reveal, the Grand Old Man's bombshell of an intention to relinquish the premiership and to resign at long last as leader of the Liberal Party.

One chapter of *Dafydd Dafis* in particular encapsulates the tense relationship between the women's movement and the mainstream Liberal Party in Wales. Dafydd has tried to retreat to bed, claiming he's a little worse for wear after an evening's heavy drinking. In reality, he's attempting to avoid having to admit to Claudia that he's disobeyed her orders. But she, as usual, is too shrewd to be deceived. Next day, she enthuses to him about her new friendship with a 'Mrs Wynford Philipps', '*Sytsh* a neis litl wman. And oh! *sytsh* a tôcer! Iw nefer herd won leic her.' (*DD*, 33) 'Mrs Philipps' (she exists, it seems, only as a function of her marital status) implicitly does not speak in the fashion that the likes of Dafydd would expect from a married woman. What Claudia deliberately *doesn't* disclose is what the topic of conversation had been with Norah Philipps. Although 'Mrs Philipps', Claudia proceeds to inform her husband, can't speak Welsh, she has nevertheless agreed to fashion a slogan for the women's movement: 'Y gwŷr yn erbyn y byd.' It is, alas, a verbal solecism. Norah Philipps has coined a slogan for the female suffragist movement that has 'men' (*gwŷr*) not 'truth' (*gwir*) – in Welsh they are pronounced identically – boldly outfacing the world. It is a Freudian slip, *avant la lettre*, and Dafydd naturally greets it with relieved hilarity. In proudly brandishing the slogan, Claudia has in fact for once accomplished the very opposite of her designs. But she is too sly to be so easily out-done. 'Oh, ddat's ol reit,' comes her tart reply, 'That's exactly what I wanted to say anyhow. I want to make sure my husband has the courage to face the world.' Which not only puts poor Dafydd back in his place but places him once more firmly under her thumb.

In the remainder of the chapter, Claudia and her female chums, sisters all in 'the cause', stubbornly hold their ground in the face of hostile challenges from the leading Liberal politicians of the day, including the two greatest luminaries, Tom Ellis and Lloyd George. The whole struggle unnerves Dafydd, and in the last paragraph he confesses to more than a frisson of fear:

> Dyna'r tro y deuthym i ddeall gynta fod merched eraill 'blaw Claudia'n teimlo dyddordeb mewn gwleidyddiaeth; ac wrth wrando ar Mrs Wynford Philipps a Mrs Williams Idris, ac erill o honyn nhw, yn siarad a Claudia, mi ddechreuais feddwl fod anhawsderau a pheryglon Aelodau Seneddol yn debyg o gynyddu yn hytrach na lleihau yn y dyfodol. Mae plesio dynion yn orchwyl calad yn y byd yma, ond mi fasa plesio'r merched i gyd yn amhosibl. Po fwya oeddwn i'n feddwl am y peth lleia i gyd oeddwn i'n leicio'r rhagolwg o fynd yn AS ar gais Claudia na neb arall.

> [That was the time when I came to realise that women other than Claudia took an interest in politics; and as I listened to Mrs Wynford Philipps and Mrs Williams Idris and the rest of them talking to Claudia, I started

> to think that the difficulties and dangers MPs faced were likely to increase rather than to decrease in the future. Pleasing men is a difficult task in this world, but pleasing women as a whole sex would be impossible. The more I thought of the situation, the less I liked the prospect of becoming an MP to satisfy Claudia or anyone else.] (*DD*, 37)

The point is underscored by a detailed cartoon by 'Ab Caledfryn', the artist William Williams (1837–1915) who had been trained in his youth by Hugh Hughes and who went on to establish a reputation primarily as a portraitist. Entitled 'The Emancipation of Women', the cartoon features a man carrying a whip and displaying the legend 'The Oppression of Law'on his back. In front of him are grouped nine women, protectively surrounding another who is reclining on the ground, her wrists manacled together. Her chain bears the two inflammatory little words 'Vote' and 'Justice'. Seven of the nine ladies in the surrounding group are seated respectably enough, although words like 'Women's Institute' and 'Freedom' are scattered ominously over their dresses. But the bearing of the other two is quite different. One carries a basket with a cornucopia of grain and flowers, labelled 'University Degrees'. The other, sporting traditional Welsh costume, brandishes a broom threateningly over her head, inscribed with the words 'Woman Suffrage'.

Beneath the cartoon is the artist's interpretation of it, couched in a language clearly parodying that of the *Book of Revelation*:

> And behold, in my vision, I saw the Woman pressed to earth by the weight of her burdens, and bound hand and foot by the fetters of traditional inferiority. Over against her stood Man, the Oppressor, armed with his Whip of Power, and wearing the badge of Oppressive Statutes; while, with the broom of Woman suffrage uplifted in brawny arms, Gwyneth Vaughan aimed a vengeful blow at the Oppressor's head. Gertrude Stewart, by means of the 'Vote' File, was releasing the Woman from her fetters, Lady Henry Somerset at the same time relieving her of her burdens; Mrs Wynford Philipps brought the Women's Institute Medicated Bowl to wash her wounds and bruises; Mrs Howell Idris hurried forward with the Tea Tray of Freedom to revive her; and Mrs Brynmor Jones brought a tempting bucket of the luscious fruit of University Degrees to slake the poor creature's thirst for knowledge; while ready as ministering angels to render further assistance, were a host of others led by Miss Gee,[27] Edith Oldham, and Eluned Morgan. (*DD*, 32–3)

The emphasis, once again, is on the disturbingly 'unnatural' character of the female actors in the tableaux. They prominently display all those sentimental qualities and virtues the Victorian Age loved to assign to women – those of supporting and protecting their husbands, tending their families, ministering to the sick and the weak. But this group of women actually perverts these qualities by dedicating them to the cause of women's suffrage and turning them into weapons in a deadly struggle against men. As for the two female figures set apart, they present an even more troubling aspect, fierce and Amazonian no less. The depiction of Gwyneth Vaughan, 'with the Broom of Woman Suffrage uplifted in brawny arms', is clearly a sinister variant of the reassuringly cosy and familiar customary image of Dame Wales, used ubiquitously in press cartoons of the day to represent a country sycophantically obsessed with appearing unthreateningly obedient to established British interests.[28] What is more, the entire, disruptive, scene is played out in the setting of a parlour – that domestic shrine dedicated to the Victorian ideal of respectable family life centred on the wife and mother. And it is no accident that the artist models his explanation of the cartoon on the Apocalyptic discourse of the *Book of Revelation*. Millenarian anxiety was beginning to run high in 1898, the year the autobiography of Dafydd Dafis was published in satirical novel form. Ominous, malignant signs of the End of the World were detected everywhere.

What the picture makes graphically evident is that femininity is now beginning to be 'performed' in new ways that most men found threatening. A cartoon achieves its effects by exaggeration and distortion. Ab Caledfryn's image thus inescapably highlights the theatrical aspects of the politics of women's suffrage, implicitly acknowledging the social provenance of gendered identity. As Judith Butler has noted,

> In the place of an original identification which serves as a determining cause [i.e. the supposition that any given gendered identity is preordained by Nature itself], gender identity might be reconceived as a personal/cultural history of received meanings subject to a set of imitative practices [i.e. performances] which refer laterally to other imitations and which, jointly, construct the illusion of a primary and interior gendered self. (*GT*, 176)

Those social and performative aspects of female identity are further underlined by the tableaux composition of Ab Caledfryn's image as a whole. It even so happens that the artist's very pseudonym betrays the patriarchal character of the dominant ideology of the Victorian Age that his cartoon embodies, because 'Ab Caledfryn' is a patronymic ('Caledfryn's Son'). William Williams (another patronymic) is a man who, true to the custom of his day, traces his descent only through the male line, totally obliterating his matrilineal inheritance.

* * *

Even as *Hunangofiant Dafydd Dafis* conspicuously devotes itself to the proleptic envisioning of Cymru Fydd – emergent Wales with its glorious future – and purports to endorse, through enthusiastic illustration, the performative aspects of this transformative process, it is also beset with the anxieties attendant upon such a vision that were constantly voiced by enthusiasts for the Young Wales movement. Would the committed vigorous promotion of a Wales for, and of, the future inevitably entail the severance of hitherto cherished connection with the Wales of the past? Would that Wales, *Cymru Fu*, simply be eclipsed by its near-homonym, *Cymru Fydd*? Beriah Gwynfe Evans tries to counter this anxiety in his novel by repeatedly insisting that in undergoing social transformation into a prosperous London Welsh dairyman, Dafydd Dafis has not lost contact with his early life as an impoverished Cardiganshire milkman. Dafydd's ascent to the dizzy heights of that highly desirable address at 393 Park Place does, he must admit, mean submitting to Claudia's continuing efforts to improve his English, bowing to her insistence that 'I mix with learned doctors so that now I use the occasional big, heavy, clumsy word' (*DD*, 255). Nevertheless, he maintains, he remains true to his early background and stubbornly refuses to forget his roots: 'I've retained this much of the country: I dislike having *sheets* on the bed.' (*DD*, 305) His unpretentious preference is to be cosily wrapped in the familiar, homely comfort of warm blankets made of Welsh wool.

While the 'Cynlas' of old is by now respectfully referred to as 'Mistar Ellis, MP', and Howell Williams has chosen to 'improve' his name to Mr Williams Idris, Dafydd himself stubbornly sticks to his baptismal name, resisting his wife's every persistent attempt to rename him 'David'. In the grand dinner held to celebrate the formal inauguration of the University of Wales, Dafydd takes advantage of the occasion to voice his concern about the sweeping social transformations he sees everywhere around him:

> 'Wel dyma ni, 'rwan,' ebra un o honyn nhw, 'ar ben y ffordd i godi'r Hen Wlad yn ei hôl miawn gwirionedd.'
>
> 'Ia,' ebra un arall, 'wedi cael yr Iwnifersiti mi ddaw rhyw lun ar Gymru bellach.'
>
> 'Reit iw ar, mei boi,' ebra y trydydd, 'Ddi lyrned proffeshyns wil now stand sym tshans in Wêls'
>
> 'Cambria redifeifys!' llefai un arall gan daro'r bwrdd nes 'roedd y gwydra'n clecian.
>
> 'Iyng Wêls tw ddi ffrynt!' ebra gŵr y pen arall i'r bwrdd, a dyma hi'n hwre fawr.
>
> 'Rhoswch chi hogia,' ebra fina. 'Mi rydw i gymint o Iyng Wêls a'r un o hono chi, ond mi rydw i'n tybied ei bod yn bosib ini anghofio'r graig o'r hon ein naddwyd, a dibrisio gwaith y rhai aeth o'n blaen ni.'
>
> ['Well, here we are now,' said one of them, 'well on the way to set the Old Country once more proudly on her feet.'
> 'Yes, indeed,' replies another, 'now that we've got a University there'll be some shape on Wales at last.'
> 'Reit iw ar, mei boi,' adds a third, 'Ddi lyrned proffeshyns wil now stand sym tshans in Wêls.'
> 'Cambria redifeifys!' cries another striking the table until all the glasses shake.
> 'Iyng Wêls tw ddi frynt!' enthuses another man at the far end of the table, and with this a loud hurrah goes up.
> 'Stow it, boys,' say I. 'I'm as much Iyng Wêls as any one of you, but I fear it may be possible for us to forget the rock from which we are hewn, and to devalue the work of those who went before us.'] (*DD*, 248)

Upon the word, Dafydd launches into a paean of praise for the 'degree-less' worthies of the past, those pillars of the chapels from the golden years of the eighteenth-century Methodist Revival to the leading lights of the last decade of the nineteenth century. Who can be seen sitting at Dafydd's side, enthusiastically nodding agreement and loudly chorusing their approval, but the stars of contemporary education and politics, the two fields of 'national progress' upon which Cymru Fydd stalwarts so congratulated themselves; Isambard Owen, medical man, scholar and architect of the new university system in Wales, and T. E. Ellis, Chief Liberal Whip. And when he finally falls silent, Dafydd Dafis realises he's been the lead actor in a scene emblematic of the achievements and aspirations of Young Wales:

> Mi rydw i'n hoffi aros, mewn dychymyg 'rwan, ar yr olygfa hono, gwrogaeth ddigamsyniol yr hogia bywiog pan ddeallasant pwy oeddwn i, a chyfeillgarwch cynes Isambard a Tom Ellis a'r gwŷr mawr y treuliais i awr bellach yn eu cwmni difyr cyn cychwyn adre.
>
> [I like to dwell, if only in imagination now, on this scene, on the unmistakeable homage of the lively lads, once they'd realised who I was, and on the warm friendship of Isambard and Tom Ellis and the other great men whose genial company I stayed to enjoy before turning for home.] (*DD*, 252)

His concerns about the possible disconnect between past and future in Wales are far, however, from being completely allayed. As the novel draws to its close, so his fears concerning the prospective decline of 'y werin' – that legendary rural community of ordinary, pious, self-educated 'folk' regarded by Cymru Fydd faithful as the very soul of the Welsh nation – noticeably increase.

As it speeds towards its conclusion, *Hunangofiant Dafydd Dafis* grows ever more hectic and fantastical. The hero spends a whole year imprisoned by Irish extremists who have kidnapped him to ensure that it is they, rather than the Welsh Liberals, who have the whip hand in Parliament. So, poor Dafydd ends up on the verge of a nervous breakdown. In his mental turmoil, he is haunted by nightmares in which the comic is mixed with the absurd. These are the *Gweledigaethau Dafydd Dafis*, visions consciously modelled by Beriah Gwynfe Evans on *Gweledigaetheu'r Bardd Cwsc*, the great eighteenth-century classic of Welsh religious prose by Ellis Wynne. Whereas the latter's visions were concerned with the grand contemporary parade of sin and corruption denoting the parlous state of the human soul, those of the mentally distressed Dafydd Dafis pertain to the bewildering succession of events in the political drama of Wales at Westminster. These include that traumatic episode captured in Ab Caledfryn's cartoon when the established order was so rudely and violently 'threatened' by the tribe of the aggressive New Woman. And as we read of these, we realise that the pace of political change at Westminster has now so manically quickened that Dafydd is totally unable to cope with the dizzying drama of it any more. No longer can he follow his script: no longer is he comfortable with his part.

But at the very height of his crisis, release comes from the customary direction of the formidable Claudia, and once more it's signified through the use of the language of the theatre. So eye-catching have been her ingenious efforts to free him from imprisonment that he has become a national celebrity. On his release, he is honoured with the grand title of Earl Dafydd in a dramatic ceremony conducted by none less than Queen Victoria herself. It is during this ceremony that he learns his wife's true name, in a twist of plot parodying popular Victorian melodrama: she is 'Baroness Gwladys of Dafydd in Carnarfonshyr and of Ypland Cort in Iorcshyr' (*DD*, 334). By now, the novel has turned into pure comic farce, and the events that follow Dafydd's ennoblement by Victoria in her own 'droing rwm' ('drawing room', when he seizes the opportunity to invite her to tea) provide Beriah Gwynfe Evans with the means of voicing his considerable misgivings about the 'New Welsh' who tread the boards of the Commons.

Since the novel approximates more and more to drama as it nears its end, it's appropriate that, in the final pages, we discover that 'it was in the thiatr, or rather the thiatr lobi' (*DD*, 315) that Dafydd and Claudia unexpectedly met for a second occasion, some time after the original 'heroic' episode involving the runaway horse and carriage. This second encounter proves to be even more melodramatic in character than the first. This time, Dafydd saves his future wife from the clutches of two rogues intent on kidnapping her and holding her to ransom, and in the process he floors the attackers one after another as only a Superman of the Victorian stage could do. Appropriately enough, therefore, *Hunangofiant Dafydd Dafis* concludes with the author-actor-producer's farewell, on behalf both of himself and of his characters, to readers who had also throughout been treated as spectators at a contemporary political drama:

> ANERCH FFARWEL CYNYRCHWYR 'DAFYDD DAFIS'
> (Yr Awdur, yr Arlunwyr, a'r Cyhoeddwr, yn ymddangos ar y llwyfan yn ffrynt y llen – gwel y darlun gyferbyn)
>
> 'Pa le mae Dafydd? Ble mae Claudia wen?'
> Ha Gyfaill! Wele hwynt tu draw i'r llen!
> Ond erys gwersi eu bywydau mad
> Yn wersi i bob Cymro ym mhob gwlad.
> Mae'n hysgrifbin, a'n pwyntil yn ddigoll
> A thlyswaith yr argraffydd, un ac oll
> Yn dweyd yn groew, yn iaith Dafydd bur,
> Ac a llais Claudia yn adseinio'n glir: –

'Os cynt drwy lawer dyrnod frad
Cadd Cymru anwyl aml glwy,
Rhowch chwithau help i wneud ein gwlad
Yn Gymru Well — yn Gymru Fwy!'

[FAREWELL ADDRESS OF THE PRODUCERS OF 'DAFYDD DAFIS'
(The Author, Artists, and the Publishers all appear on the stage in front of the final curtain – see picture opposite)

'Where's Dafydd? Where is Claudia fair?'
Ah, Friend! Behold beyond the curtain there.
Their life's lessons recently at hand
Remain for Welsh in every land.
Our pen, our pencil, the printer's splendid art
And this work's off'rings in every part
In Dafydd's fair tongue clearly declare,
With Claudia's own voice ringing clear: –

'If past by many a treacherous hand
Foul blows have hurt our dear land,
For you to help is not too late
To make Wales better — to make Wales great!'] (*DD*, 336)

It is the drama, therefore, that is allowed the last word in this novel. It underlines the similarity between the text and the eighteenth-century *Interludes*, those travelling folk entertainments, rhyming commentaries on contemporary personalities and affairs, made famous by the remarkable talents of Twm o'r Nant. Just as they were intended to offer a mirror to the life of their times, so too was *Hunangofiant Dafydd Dafis*. It was the product of years of tumultuous change in the economic, social, political and cultural life of Wales and, as Judith Butler has emphasised, the fluid, amorphous character of such periods tends to encourage radical personal transformations and related experiments with social identity. Like the National Pageant, Evans's novel thus conforms to the classic definition of productions 'in which as a culture or society we reflect upon and define ourselves, dramatize our collective myths and history, present ourselves with alternatives, and eventually change in some ways while remaining the same in others'.[29] Cultural performance does not only enact change, it actually contributes to enable it – hence what theorists recognise as its 'efficacy' – and Dafydd Dafis's autobiography was clearly intended to help realise its author's dream of the transformation of the old Welsh-speaking Wales into a new, sophisticated, politically aware Wales; a proud, dynamic *Cymru Fydd*, still loyal, nevertheless, to the cultural values of *Cymru Fu*, the Wales of yesteryear.

* * *

As has been suggested above, however, Beriah Gwynfe Evans's faith in performing a new identity, one appropriate to the growing political maturity of a new Wales, was by no means simple and unquestioning. Very much a product of Welsh Nonconformity, he couldn't be entirely indifferent to old, deep-seated chapel suspicions about acting and the stage. He was accordingly always alive to the possibility that performance was, at worst, the artful, cunning, practice of deception, and, at best, hollow pretence. One of the recurrent themes of *Hunangofiant Dafydd Dafis*, as the scholar Teddy Millward has shrewdly emphasised, was the possibility that, when it came to the political crunch, the Welsh Liberal MPs were all act and no real action:

> When Claudia and Dafydd seek an interview with Sir William Harcourt, the chancellor of the exchequer, he laughs off the idea that there are 'rifolters' [revolters] among the Welsh members. They will kick up a row, says Sir Williams, but do nothing . . . Dafydd is determined that the Irish Home Rule question should not be allowed to push disestablishment and Home Rule for Wales into the parliamentary sidelines. This, it is revealed, is why he was kidnapped [by the Irish] and kept prisoner for a year.[30]

Evans, Millward concludes, 'clearly thought that too many of the *Cymru Fydd* generation were indulging in political play-acting' (*DD*, 172).

Evans's fascination with the ambivalent character of performance may partly account for his long-standing fascination with that most virtuosic of actors on the political stage of the day, David Lloyd George. Following his failure at the infamous Newport meeting to mobilise the whole of Wales behind his Home Rule agenda, Lloyd George came to be viewed by some as a defector who had thrown in his lot with mainstream unionist and imperialist Westminster politics.

Not so by all, however. Such were his gifts, and his magnetism, that others were very reluctant to believe he had been entirely lost to the cause. One such was Evans, his long-time friend and associate, whose 'campaign biography' *The Life Romance of Lloyd George*, written in July 1915 at a time when its subject was proving to be a highly successful Minister of Munitions, reads in part like an attempt, enthralling but futile, to produce a credible Cymru Fydd 'script' for his political matinee idol who had now stepped out boldly onto the world stage. Evans's underlying misgivings about the authenticity of Lloyd George's performance are, however, indirectly registered at the very outset, in the form of a cartoon from *Punch*. Sub-titled 'The Arch-druid of Drowning Street', it shows Lloyd George, crowned with laurel and garbed in the bardic robes of the Eisteddfod Gorsedd, seated at a harp and, mouth agape, heartily roaring the words of the Welsh national anthem, *Hen Wlad fy Nhadau*. Beneath the sub-title appears an acid quotation from a 'musical correspondent at the Eisteddfod', who reports: 'The Chancellor of the Exchequer, in his rendition of the famous . . . song, gave its full site value to every note.'

Evans was exceptionally conscious of the element of performance in Lloyd George's success because he had witnessed at first hand the precocious talent the Grand Young Man had shown at the very outset of his career in controlling the image of him being circulated by the media. As the journalist who had been hand-picked by Lloyd George in 1892 to edit the influential local Caernarvonshire paper he'd recently shrewdly purchased, Evans could be said, as he very well knew, to have been the wizard's very first spin doctor. When, therefore, he discusses Lloyd George's innovative strategies of media manipulation in his biography, he does so very much with the astuteness of an intimate insider.

Notoriously reluctant to commit himself to paper, even in the form of a scribbled note (partly, perhaps, because he instinctively understood that any such informal communication could be difficult to control), Lloyd George was almost obsessively concerned to manage every published report of his speeches and activities. The more inspirationally improvised his silver-tongued public comments appeared to become, the more meticulously did he seek to control printed copies. As Evans dryly remarks

> No man living has made more effective use of the press – from *The Times* upwards and downwards. This is neither the time nor place to reveal

> professional secrets, but it is permissible to say and to demonstrate that working journalists all over the kingdom owe him a debt of gratitude for lightening their task of recording his speeches. That he, too, owes them more than he perhaps recognizes, is certainly no less true. (*LRLG*, 8)

Lloyd George, Evans notes, had long been in the habit of briefing a small 'ring' of journalists ahead of a speech, dictating to them 'what he proposed saying' (*LRLG*, 9). But, by 1915, his practice was to have his private secretary 'meet the pressmen and dictate from a typewritten copy what Mr Lloyd George will say'. When he spoke in Welsh, he avoided the 'risk of having his peroration mauled and his views possibly distorted in translation' by supplying 'his own "authorized English translation"' (*LRLG*, 10). It was Lloyd George, or so Evans claims, who had perfected the art of the political pamphlet in modern times, and had created 'a specialized literature to launch the administration of the Insurance Act'. Indeed, 'never was there in the whole history of British legislation such a campaign as that of Mr Lloyd George to explain the provisions and effect of the Insurance Act. In Erse and in Gaelic, in Welsh and in English, the whole kingdom was, by means of the printing press, instructed' in its unparalleled complexities (*LRLG*, 10–11).

Message and image: Lloyd George could sometimes seem preternaturally gifted at managing both to his own advantage. Evans's biography is, in its turn, an experiment to determine how far his own preferred image of a Lloyd George who, through all the various roles he'd performed, had remained true to his Cymru Fydd origins, could be made to conform to the reality of one who was evidently on the verge of becoming a world figure. But even as Evans tries hard to fit his elusive, mercurially shape-shifting hero into a passably traditional Cymru Fydd narrative, he seems at times to realise it would have been easier to measure Merlin for a Sunday school suit. As it proceeds, his text, affirmative without being uncritical, seems quietly to accumulate a sub-text of deep, quiet reservations and regrets. What slowly becomes apparent is that this most spectacularly successful of all attempts to form a new kind of Welsh identity through performance on the grandest of political stages has resulted – as perhaps may even have been inevitable – in a form of Welshness that can seem compromised and questionable if viewed in the light of the original Cymru Fydd intentions of Lloyd George and Beriah Gwynfe Evans alike.

Evans highlights the Great Social Reformer's several measures to redistribute wealth and to alter radically the existing structure of power within society. The roots for these historic initiatives, so Evans persuasively argues, lay in Lloyd George's early experiences, as a Welsh Nonconformist, of the extortionate power of a largely 'alien' established class of gentry and clergy. He can even convincingly propose that those experiences were, at the time of writing in 1915, helping to make Lloyd George a highly effective wartime Minister for Munitions. 'The cry of the oppressed,' we are confidently informed of Evans's Lloyd George, 'ever appealed to him.'

> That sight and that cry greeted him in childhood; they greet him still today. The Welsh evictions of 1868 made him a land agitator; the German Rape of Belgium twelve months ago has manifestly transformed him into one of the strongest advocates of the World War of today, as did the Invasion of the Transvaal make him an equally ardent Apostle of Peace fifteen years ago. And it is the cry of the British soldier in the trenches which has now further developed him into the Minister of Munitions, creating great guns and high explosives almost literally by word of his mouth. (*LRLG*, 4)

In that final remark lies thinly disguised the fantasy of supreme power craved by a tiny, impotent Wales, 'oppressed' as Cymru Fydd imagined the nation to be. And how typical a product of a Nonconformist Wales fixated on preaching is that other fantasy made evident here, the fantasy of the irresistible power of word not simply made flesh but turned instantly into deadly steel and gunpowder. As Evans proudly proceeds to boast, no doubt fully aware of his subject's notorious dilatoriness as correspondent, Lloyd George's 'power is emphatically that of the tongue rather than of the pen' (*LRLG*, 7).

Then, from Cymru Fydd's point of view, there was the ideological gift of Lloyd George's origins in a humble rural cottage. All his prominent gifts as a politician, Evans firmly informs us, are owed to this 'parentage': 'all that is best in village life, exercised the influence of heredity upon the village boy, and upon his development into the Imperial Statesman' (*LRLG*, 12–13). This *gwerin* myth is, of course, the Welsh equivalent of the fabled US journey 'from log cabin to White House'. And in further compliance with this myth, Lloyd George is invested with prophetic power by being represented as a figure out of famous Biblical narrative: 'as the child Samuel grew up in the house of Eli, so did the little David grow in the house of his uncle, Richard Lloyd' (*LRLG*, 16). Like T. E. Ellis, Evans tells us, Lloyd George had been a child of the heady 1859 religious revival in Wales and still readily confessed, now that his political power had reached its zenith, to having been in thrall, throughout his early formative years, to the great preachers of the day. Hence, Evans adds, the fervent eloquence with which he preached his political evangel. At one point, or so Lloyd George liked to claim, he had even entertained a wish of entering the ministry – an intriguing possibility, given what we now know about his hearty pagan appetites of the flesh. Mention of this chapel background allows Beriah Gwynfe Evans to argue that Lloyd George's crusadingly reformist brand of politics is a secularised expression of the religious culture in which he was raised, and that as a politician he had based his performance on the legendary actors of the Welsh pulpit:

> when Lloyd George was but a child of five, he witnessed the great Miracle of a Renaissance, whereby Welsh Nonconformity and Welsh Nationalism first became synonymous, inspired by a common motive, and dedicated to a common mission. The dry bones of political Nonconformity which had laid quiescent in the valley of humiliation almost from the days of Walter Cradoc and Vavasour Powell two hundred years earlier, were being shaken in Lloyd George's childhood. The trumpet voice of many an angel of the Welsh pulpit was calling the bones together; there grew upon them sinews and flesh, and the miracle was accomplished when the Spirit of Nationalism breathed upon them, 'and they lived and stood upon their feet, an exceeding great army' which has practically held the political representation of Wales ever since. (*LRLG*, 36)

The young Lloyd George is therefore explicitly represented by Evans as a latter-day peripatetic preacher, a social radical in the proto-Nonconformist tradition of those turbulent seventeenth-century Puritans Cradoc and Powell, and therefore one of those young politicians of his generation fervently dedicated to the 'public preaching now of that Nationalist Gospel'. In transferring his political act from the local Welsh to the 'national' Westminster stage, then, Lloyd George had remained true to the Cymru Fydd principles and values that had originally inspired his performance.

Next, as if wishing to mirror in his own text that metamorphosis of the religious into the secular about which he has just been writing,

Evans proceeds to substitute Owain Glyndŵr, a hero from Welsh secular history, for the Biblical Samuel as Lloyd George's role model. If, like Samuel, he had 'as definite a mission as any prophet of old', then he 'had politically only a single aim – the enfranchisement of the Welsh people. "A Free Church, for a Free People, in a Free Land" – Owen Glyndwr's great motto – in a sense possessed his soul.' (*LRLG*, 105) Through the deployment of such devout phraseology, Evans strives to replace the common contemporary image of Lloyd George as a crafty, unscrupulous political opportunist with that of a selfless, dedicated patriot: 'Personal ambition had little, or no, place in his thoughts – the fulfilment of his people's aspirations much, practically all.'

Thus does biography reveal itself to be hagiography, and hagiography brazenly reveal itself to be a fictional genre. In some of its aspects, Beriah Gwynfe Evans's work can perhaps be regarded as a fascinating example of popular political romance – as its author himself highlights when entitling it *The Life Romance of Lloyd George.* Included in the text are romantic domestic interludes and pastoral idylls of the kind so beloved of Victorian fiction:

> By heredity the son of a village schoolmaster; by adoption and tuition the son of a village shoe-maker; politically the son of a village nationalist; in religion the product of the humblest of village meeting-houses – all his environments, influences and instructors, have been essentially of the village. But the village has ever been the backbone of Britain's power on sea and land, in court and schools – as it is today the heart that pounds the life-blood pulsing through the veins of Welsh Nonconformity. (*LRLG*, 12–13)

This 'fiction' also features the dilute version of Romantic nature-mysticism favoured by the Victorians. 'It were as easy to demolish the everlasting rocks which constitute the foundations of the Snowdonian mountains that encompass his childhood's home, as to uproot the sense, the love of Nationalism implanted in [Lloyd George's] nature.' (*LRLG*, 212) It is a hopelessly belated attempt to put the genie back in the bottle. Lloyd George had long since joyously escaped the confines of Snowdonia, as indeed of Wales. And far from finding in Nature monitory images of stability and continuity, he found only vindication everywhere in its untroubled amorality for his own restless, furious, heedless, headstrong energies.

'The love of Nationalism [had been] implanted in [Lloyd George's] nature': that is the claim Beriah Gwynfe Evans wanted his text so desperately to confirm, only to find that his subject's passionately expressed original ambition for Welsh Home Rule was the one aspect of the Cymru Fydd programme that the politician's spectacularly successful subsequent career rather clearly demonstrated he had long since abandoned. It was in this crucial regard that the performance of a new Welsh identity had, in Beriah Gwynfe Evans's carefully muffled opinion, so tragically miscarried. The first half of his study is studded with eloquent affirmations lifted verbatim from Lloyd George's early speeches, of blazing commitment to this particular cause. But then, as the book approaches its half-way point and Lloyd George's career leads him inexorably towards a Cabinet post, a silence suddenly falls on this seminal issue during which, at one point, Evans uncharacteristically allows his text to betray his own misgivings about whether 'Lloyd George, the Cabinet Minister . . . was essentially still the Lloyd George the Rebel of 1894, and Lloyd George the Guerilla Chief of 1900, pursuing as unfalteringly as then the same objects' (*LRLG*, 118).

Evans had earlier tentatively anticipated such a conclusion when he had admitted that, of the three objectives Lloyd George had set himself as a young politician, 'so far as the recognition of the separate national entity of Wales is concerned, the only part of his dream of a quarter of a century ago which has been realized, and which is directly due to his initiative, is that in the "mighty Armageddon" to which "the people of Europe are thronging today" . . . Welsh soldiers are fighting under the Red Dragon of Wales.' (*LRLG*, 51) What, then, had become of the dream of Home Rule? Nothing but a 'Battalion of Welsh Life Guards' and a *soi-disant* 'Welsh Army, under Welsh-speaking officers' (*LRLG*, 51). As much, Evans concedes, could have been said of the Welsh mercenaries in the English armies 'on the Fields of Cressy and Poictiers' (*LRLG*, 52). It is almost certainly a coincidence, but at the point where Evans's misgivings about Lloyd George the Welsh nationalist are most clearly voiced, a photograph is inserted in his text that could be said to emblematise his reservations. In it, Lloyd George is seen pointing proprietorially to a Welsh dresser. His family's initials, we are duly informed, are carved into the wood, thus implying he's a chip off that sturdy old block. But is he? The image is so carefully staged that it seems actually to invite mistrust of its evidently contrived message. That dresser looks suspiciously like a stage prop.

Evans's biography is a piece of special pleading primarily memorable, perhaps, for the evidence it reluctantly offers of its author's failure entirely to convince even himself. To the very end, he strives to find consoling evidence of the British Minister for Munitions' continuing fidelity to his nationalist origins, concluding by relaying his loudly professed concern to advance the Cymru Fydd agenda of self-rule for Wales within the 'community' of a post-war Empire reconstructed along federal lines.

Two years after the appearance of *The Life Romance of Lloyd George*, Woodrow Wilson was to announce in a famous speech the 'Fourteen Points' upon which the Treaty of Versailles – negotiated on behalf of Britain, of course, by Lloyd George – was to be based. The fifth of these points influentially advocated 'a free, open-minded, and absolutely impartial adjustment of all colonial claims, based upon a strict observance of the principle that in determining all such questions of sovereignty the interests of the populations concerned must have equal weight with the equitable claims of the government whose title is to be determined'. This opened the door for the drastic redrawing of the map of Europe after 1918, to allow the emergence of a plethora of small nations from the wreck of the once-mighty Austro-Hungarian and Ottoman Empires.

Anticipating some such development, Evans's biography of Lloyd George ended by advancing – in keeping with Cymru Fydd thinking – an alternative future for the British Empire that would allow it to survive in modified form while also allowing for a significant degree of 'self-determination' by nations such as Wales, Scotland and Ireland – all of whom, as the proposed arrangement implicitly recognised, had been agents of Empire as well as dependent subjects of it. Such a move was also a reminder to Lloyd George of the logical post-war implications of that affecting parallel he had so potently drawn between the situation of Wales and that of 'poor little Belgium', when he was the ultimate Recruiting Sergeant for the British Army. With Belgium being hopefully on the brink of complete 'liberation', it was time for Wales to benefit in like terms from an Allied victory.

That link between Wales and Belgium was implicitly reinforced in the introduction to Evans's volume supplied by Charles Sarolea, a Belgian academic, who was at that time Professor of French at Edinburgh University and used by the Belgian government to try to persuade the US to enter the war. Fearful that British Imperial interests might trump the interests of Continental nations at any forthcoming peace conference, Sarolea placed his trust in Lloyd George to speak up for the rights of nations. He, said Sarolea, was one to whom the French could warm and rally, since his 'was the inspired voice of another great Celtic country' (*LRLG*, xii). The new post-war diplomacy would 'have to be a diplomacy of the nations', and as a Welshman Lloyd George was the British politician best qualified to acknowledge this: 'the profound understanding of the value of nationality which has been such a marked characteristic of the Welshman will be of infinite value in the conduct of negotiations' (*LRLG*, xv). In historical retrospect, Sarolea's comments are liable to resonate with irony. At Versailles, it was to be another case of 'for Wales, see England' – or 'for Wales, see Britain' – even as Lloyd George did indeed settle the fate of Europe's various nations, the small along with the large.

Evans's evident aim in his biography was to attribute to Lloyd George a loyalty to principle and a consistency of purpose his opponents cynically but correctly doubted the great opportunist and consummate actor possessed. But the biographer was not solely, or even principally, concerned to advance his subject's reputation or to advance his political interests. Evans's study was primarily an anxious attempt to reassure himself, as much as his readers, that Lloyd George was not after all a defector from the ranks of Cymru Fydd; that he was still true to his original nationalist agenda; that his scintillating 'performance' as Chancellor and as Minister for Munitions was still consistent with the original Welsh 'script'. Parallels can therefore be drawn between Evans's biography of Lloyd George and his comic novel about Dafydd Dafis. Both these 'political fictions' are designed to fashion their respective subjects into figures representative of the new, politicised Wales, and are thereby intended to function as proleptic texts endowed with obstetric powers. They are powerful discursive agents for turning the dreams of Cymru Fydd into political actualities. Mastery of performance is recognised in both texts as the prerequisite for playing the new, sophisticated roles that alone can enable the Welsh to influence the turbulent political life of the day. But *Hunangofiant Dafydd Dafis* and *The Life Romance of Lloyd George* also betray their author's deep misgivings about the heady allure of the political stage and its power to turn the heads and warp the characters of those who venture to tread its treacherous boards.

3

O. M. EDWARDS: KEEPING TRACK OF THE *GWERIN*

A neat old lady in a recognisably Welsh dress, spectacles on her nose, bends over a book as she sits in a primly upright high-backed chair beside a roaring open fire. Steaming away by her side is a small cauldron, suspended by a hook from an old-fashioned high mantle, on which stand sundry simple ornaments – candlesticks, a jug, a pot. Below the mantelpiece hangs a hunting gun. A bellows is conveniently placed to keep the fire merrily burning, and next to it stands a plain, if imposing, Welsh dresser adorned with a teapot and other pieces of unpretentious earthenware. In front of the left-hand wall, pierced by a small, low, multi-paned window, there stands a sturdy kitchen table of bare wood. The floor is uncarpeted so that the heavy 'flags' (large paving stones) stand clear, and the thick wooden beams supporting the low ceiling are likewise prominent. The whole room is spick and span in its domestic frugality.

An overnight traveller on the train from Paddington to west Wales dreams, as the border is crossed, of Newport entirely submerged by the sea, a golden ridge of islets alone left peeping above the cold, white-crested waves. All that remains of Cardiff is its ancient fortifications, now smothered in a forest of clinging ivy and brambles, the ocean having long retreated to an immense distance. Neath and Swansea remain obscured in ominous, desolate darkness, save that a rim of light over the bay gives faint notice of the coming dawn. For this traveller, then, the train journey through south Wales has been a journey 'o wlad y nos i wlad y bore', from the land of night to the land of morning.

These are two scenes from the beginning and end respectively of perhaps the most influential of books about Wales to be published in the last decade of the nineteenth century. *Cartrefi Cymru* (*The Homes of Wales*, 1896), by the indefatigable and indispensable O. M. Edwards, became a classic virtually overnight.[1] It literally grounded the seminal, self-aggrandising Nonconformist concept of *y werin* (the naturally cultured and devout rural 'volk') in a lovingly traversed national landscape that was a patchwork quilt of different localities, whose nodal cultural points were the modest old farmhouses that had been home to Wales's greatest religious and cultural figures.[2] The book is an engaging collection of travel essays, recounting the learned author's leisurely visits to several of these scattered sites. In them he is able to preach, like some latter-day peripatetic Dissenting minister, a series of inspiring sermons on the modern secular faith of patriotism. In the first of the scenes described above, then, the spirit of his whole enterprise to advertise *y werin* is distilled into the pencil sketch that was published as frontispiece to *Cartrefi Cymru*.

As for the second scene, it occurs towards the conclusion of that book, at a point where Edwards the inveterate traveller is bound for St Davids, on the distant romantic coast of west Wales. It is a vision of a landscape lost to huge, obliterating, invasive forces. The importance of the episode is that in it, Edwards allows carefully coded expression to a great fear he is otherwise reluctant to acknowledge but that underlies the whole of his book, secretly determining its very character. His fear is that the immensely powerful anglicised society of the industrial south-east that has already devoured a large portion of Wales during the closing years of the nineteenth century will soon spell the doom of the old, aboriginal, Welsh-speaking rural areas, several of whose key cultural strongholds are identified and celebrated in *Cartrefi Cymru*.

The volume was consciously conceived by its author as belonging to the vanguard of the great contemporary attempt of progressive Welsh political Liberalism to build a new Wales on the values of the late nineteenth-century 'Nonconformist nation'.[3] But, viewed from the unkind perspective of this darkly prophetic train journey, the work appears instead, as Edwards's unconscious reluctantly recognises, to be the rearguard action of a largely marginalised and increasingly beleaguered cultural elite. In *Cartrefi Cymru*, the concept of *y werin* displays, not for the first time, some of the tell-tale features of a back-formation. Dafydd Johnston has usefully defined this key concept of the later nineteenth century in Wales as centred on a belief in 'the high-minded spirituality of the Welsh people . . . [and] the supposed reverence for education in Wales'.[4] 'The whole idea of the *gwerin* must,' he has shrewdly added, 'be regarded as a myth,'

> [n]ot only in the negative sense that it was a distortion of reality, but also in the positive sense of that term as representing the aspiration of a people, their chosen self-image, and an ideal which was of central importance in the literature of the early twentieth century.[5]

That 'myth' had originated in Welsh Nonconformity's outraged response to the grotesque misrepresentations of the rural Welsh-speaking poor placed on damning official record in the Government's 1847 report on education in Wales, which came to be known as *Brad y Llyfrau Gleision* (The Treason of the Blue Books) in reference to the report's blue covers.[6] Now, half a century later in 1896, the defensive features and stress fractures of this powerful ideological structure reappear as it is threatened anew by the latest powerful manifestations of anglicisation. But what is also noteworthy is the ingeniousness of the strategy Edwards is adopting. Following the 1847 report, a Victorian Welsh Wales that had meekly learnt all too well the lesson that the modern, progressive world belonged exclusively to the English people and their language, obediently accepted the commissioners' recommendation that the use of Welsh be confined entirely to the hearth and to the family circle. On the surface, therefore, Edwards's hymning of hearth and home as the traditional custodians of the Welsh language and its culture seems to be entirely consistent with established conservative Victorian philosophy. But in also demonstrating the potently national and indeed incipiently nationalist dynamic of this ostensibly homely cultural base, Edwards actually succeeds in converting an ideology of cultural passivity into one of politico-cultural assertiveness. It is an ingenious act of reversal, akin to that contemporaneously accomplished by Yeats when he turned the feminised Celticism of Matthew Arnold into the aggressively masculine Celticism of his nationalist hero, Cuchulainn.[7]

Nevertheless, Edwards is ever-aware of the increasing pressure of an ever-encroaching Englishness on his *gwerin* community. And, indeed, before *Cartrefi Cymru* is concluded, those subconscious fears allowed expression by Edwards only in a nightmare train journey begin ominously to disturb his waking hours. Leaving the train at Haverfordwest, he is immediately reminded that he has reached Little England beyond Wales, that substantial part of Pembrokeshire whose anglicisation dates back to the original plantation of Flemings there in the Middle Ages. The driver of the light carriage he hires turns out to be resolutely English, and his crass uncultured ignorance quietly appals his passenger. The man knows nothing of Arthur; cares as little as he knows about chapels, Sunday schools, ministers and the like; is full of casual profanities; and will talk of nothing except dogs, hunting, otters and fishing. The encounter with him serves to highlight in quite crude terms the contrast, as Edwards sees it, between the anglicised working class of the largely industrialised south of Wales and the supposedly cultured and classless society of *y werin*, whose company he has up to this point enjoyed wherever in rural Welsh-Wales he has travelled.

There is, therefore, an allegorical dimension to Edwards's journey from Haverfordwest to St Davids. Passing through anglicised Pembrokeshire, he eventually crosses the linguistic frontier at Newgale into the magical ancient land of remote Dyfed, redolent of 'pagan' legend as well as instinct with Christian spiritual significance ever since the age of the Celtic saints. As Edwards explicitly recognises, he is following the old path of spiritual pilgrimage and, beset by modern threats and anxieties, is instinctively heading back to a primitive, primal, revivifying source.[8] An Oxford don and renowned professional historian, he is fully aware both of the circumstances of the original Saint David, and of the political implications of the cult of the saint carefully fostered by Gerald of Wales for his own (self-serving) purposes in the Middle Ages. And both of these aspects speak directly to his immediate contemporary concerns.[9]

In keeping with members of all the Welsh Dissenting denominations, Edwards believed that Nonconformity could legitimately trace its roots back to St David and the very early Christian centuries, since the professed aim of the chapels was to recover the pristine form of 'primitive' Christianity that the Celtic church represented.[10] But as a progressive Welsh Liberal of the late nineteenth century, dreaming of more political as well as cultural autonomy for his country, Edwards also strongly sympathised with Gerald of Wales. For many years, Gerald – Giraldus Cambrensis – had persisted in arguing that Saint David had been recognised during his lifetime, long before Augustine was to convert the pagan Saxons to Christianity, as Archbishop of the whole of Wales. Therefore, the medieval Welsh church should not be held accountable to the remote and 'foreign' Archbishop of Canterbury. And, enthused by his visit to Saint David's seat, Edwards brings to mind Owain Glyndŵr's dream, when first he raised the banner of national rebellion, of making St Davids the ecclesiastical centre of the archbishopric of an independent Wales. Like Gerald of Wales, Edwards was alive to every opportunity to enhance the prestige of St Davids at the expense of the English. In a note in his periodical *Cymru*, the very year in which *Cartrefi Cymru* was published, Edwards emphasised that one of the key texts of early English history, the Life of Alfred (*Vita Ælfredi regis Angul Saxonum*), was written at the king's court by Asser, a ninth-century monk from St Davids.[11]

* * *

That Edwards's text, at least to modern eyes, should so clearly betray the flaws and limits of its governing ideology should not, however, prevent us from recognising the significance of its achievements, fully appreciated only when one becomes aware of the adverse socio-cultural conditions prevailing at the time of composition. The relevant facts are as damning as they are simple. The indigenous population of Wales, subject for centuries to rule from England, had long been socially, politically, and economically subordinated. The native culture's confirmed subaltern status had immeasurably damaged its capacity to produce its own extensive and sophisticated structure of social meanings, as it had also affected its ability to reproduce itself save in the limited, narrow terms afforded, from the mid-eighteenth century onwards, by chapel piety. In *Cartrefi Cymru*, as we shall see, Edwards set out to repair just a little of this accumulated damage.

But while such remedial work was concerned to engage with this situation only on an ideological and discursive level, it was informed by a practical awareness, hard-wired into Edwards from his earliest years, of the adverse socio-economic factors that governed ideological production. As the son of a poor tenant-farmer who had rented his few acres from the vast Williams Wynn estate, Edwards well knew that very little of the Welsh land he so lovingly celebrated as a precious national asset in *Cartrefi Cymru* actually remained in the possession of the ordinary country people to whose cultural welfare his book was dedicated. And as a monoglot Welsh pupil who had been force-fed English at his village school, he nursed a legitimate lifelong grievance, not against the English language per se but at the abuse of it in Wales as a tool of cultural colonialism: 'I knew a language, and that language was not used to help me to learn . . . to English education I was indebted for nothing until I had a Welsh-speaking teacher to instruct me in Welsh.' (*OME*, 9)

For the most part, these bedrock social realities – a native population dispossessed of land and, in being denied education in its own language, effectively deprived of both living acquaintance with its own past and a say in its own future – constitute only the subtext of *Cartrefi Cymru*. From time to time, this awareness of the connection between economic depression and cultural suppression does trouble even the carefully controlled, equable surface of Edwards's narrative. A visit to the home of the noted minister Ap Fychan (1809–80), north of Bala, prompts the casual aside that his father had needed the express permission of the manager of the Williams Wynn estate to convert even a derelict cottage into the most primitive of homes. Edwards, with quiet outrage, notes the shocking state of Welsh cottagers' lives during the lean years of what well-heeled nineteenth-century English historians liked complacently to describe as the triumphant aftermath of the Napoleonic Wars. For weeks at a time during his childhood, so Ap Fychan had reported in his memoirs, there would be nothing to eat save boiled turnips; on one grim occasion, the overseers of parish relief had invaded the home to remove the family's feather bed; many a time, Ap Fychan himself, a ragged urchin, had been reduced to wandering the surrounding countryside for fifty miles and more, scraping moss off stones and selling it for a penny. And in one of those many cunningly artless scenes in *Cartrefi Cymru* that are actually contrived to function as suggestive cultural emblems, Edwards mentions how one of Ap Fychan's contemporaries remembered seeing the little boy tramping the countryside in a coat many times too large, one of whose capacious pockets held the precious harvest of collected moss, while the other contained a Bible. Little wonder that so many youngsters from such a deprived area had headed straight for America.

The Welsh countryside through which Edwards was himself travelling, three quarters of a century later than the period of Ap Fychan's childhood, displayed no such livid scars of poverty. But it did bear the signs of the dramatic depopulation occasioned both by prolonged economic slump and the migration of the young in large numbers to the lucrative new region of the industrial south-east. On a visit to Llandovery, in search of the seventeenth-century home of Vicar Prichard (1579–1644), author of *Canwyll y Cymry* (1658–81), a collection of homiletic verses hugely loved by Nonconformists, Edwards is dismayed at the dilapidated state of a country town that had once been the Mecca of Welsh drovers. Signs of its sleepy stagnation are everywhere, from the empty shops and idle carts to the grass serenely growing through the cobbles of the marketplace. And other places he visits likewise display the unmistakeable signs of abandonment, of life having moved elsewhere. En route to the Llŷn home of 'Dafydd y Garreg Wen' (David Edwards, the supposed eighteenth-century author of one of Victorian Wales's favourite sentimental ballads, 'David of the White Rock'), Edwards at one point comes across a neglected driveway which he glumly supposes leads to 'the palace of desolation'. He likewise notices that the many ruins in the countryside are those of cottages abandoned for the 'mud houses' that form a growing settlement on the fringes of Criccieth.

The psychological depression, then, that Edwards briefly confesses to feeling at the state of Llandovery is revealing. It's a symptom of the stresses and strains arising from the constant effort of preventing the subtext of *Cartrefi Cymru*, with its narrative of rural decline, from disrupting the surface text, intent as is the latter on promoting rural Wales as the heartland, past and future, of the nation. A greater threat by far, however, than that of socio-economic decline faced Welsh-language society in Edwards's opinion. This took the form of ignorance – the alarming ignorance of the country people of their own history and culture. It was this deficit that *Cartrefi Cymru* was primarily intended both to expose and to address. The book is studded with examples. The young maid laying the table of the inn in the tiny village of Llangair, not far from Harlech, is wholly unaware that Ellis Wynne of Y Lasynys (1671–1734), author of the religious classic *Gweledigaetheu y Bardd Cwsc* (The Visions of the Sleeping Poet, 1703), was laid to rest in the church graveyard. 'Maybe so,' is her comment, 'but I didn't know him.' (*CC*. 109) A farm servant at Llanfhangel yng Ngwynfa has, indeed, heard of the hymn-writer Ann Griffiths from neighbouring Dolwar Fach – but has no idea that a colourful local character, Sian Hughes, Pontrobert, is the daughter of Ruth, the maid who had preserved those hymns by committing them to writing. In their unabashed ignorance, such characters display none of the much-vaunted attributes of the *gwerin*, a reminder that the term tended to comprehend not the rural population at large, but that more limited segment of it roughly corresponding to the yeoman and artisanal classes in England.

Core members of the *gwerin* constituted what Frantz Fanon would term a 'native intelligentsia', a cohort of intellectuals self-educated independently of the socially acknowledged institutions of learning that acted as the unofficial custodians of the religio-cultural values of their subaltern society.[12] It had, in some ways, been easier for such an indigenous social grouping, formed largely under the auspices of the chapels, to exert influence on the *gwerin* during the period when, as was constructively highlighted in the otherwise devastatingly damaging officially-titled 'Government Enquiry into the State of Education in Wales' of 1847, no efficient let alone comprehensive state system of school instruction had existed in the country. This was the period when 'Welsh society was characterized by a range of social, cultural and educative influences, particularly Sunday schools and eisteddfodau.'[13] A network of such unofficial initiatives was reinforced by a range of intellectually heavyweight denominational journals 'with an estimated circulation of 120,000' (*HEW*, 71). And for decades after the 1847 report, the status and influence of native intellectuals educated by these means had been immeasurably enhanced by their key role in defending the rural Welsh against the outrageous charges of egregious immorality levelled against them (most particularly women) in the Government Report.

* * *

In 1870, however, the situation changed with the passing of the pioneering Elementary Education Act. This provided for a system of state-supported Board Schools to supplement the existing network of National and British schools, sponsored by the Anglicans and Nonconformists respectively. Instruction in these new state schools, as in the pre-existing schools, was to be entirely in English, so as to prepare Welsh children (most of whom in rural areas spoke only Welsh) to operate efficiently in the modern world whose language was English. There was never any question, of course, of instructing the children in the basic history of their own distinctive society and culture (*HEW*, 84–5).

We read how the consequences of this alien and alienating educational dispensation worry Edwards constantly in *Cartrefi Cymru*. Searching for the grave of Ann Griffiths he encounters an old man whose son has departed for England, and learns that 'there is little mention of Ann Griffiths here on the borders of Montgomeryshire these days, and as little singing of her hymns, compared to the old days.' (*CC*, 9) As he approaches the grave, he finds himself surrounded by a genial, noisy crowd of inquisitive youngsters from the neighbouring school who, it is implied, have little comprehension of where he's headed (*CC*, 10). The same is his experience when he encounters lively, curious schoolchildren in the neighbourhood of Ellis Wynne's grave in Llanfair, near Harlech (*CC*, 108). As for his visit to Ann's home at Dolwar Fach, that uncovers further ominous signs of cultural erosion. While the present owners of the house are familiar enough with her story, their lodger is the local English schoolmaster who speaks feelingly of the difficulties he faces in trying to teach intelligent local children whose only language is Welsh. As for Ann Griffiths, 'he had heard not a single word about her, and he looked at me suspiciously as if I were a confirmed liar when I informed him he was living in the home of the world's greatest female hymn-writer.' (*CC*, 18)

These instances of the cultural identity-crisis rapidly developing in rural Wales are ruefully recorded in the early chapters of the book, but by the penultimate chapter Edwards's patience has worn thin. One encounter with a young girl provokes him to angry, forthright comment. The exchange with the child occurs when he's looking for the rock traditionally associated in popular memory with the song 'Codiad yr Ehedydd'.

> 'Fedri di ganu?'
> 'Medra.'
> 'Fedri di ganu "Dafydd y Garreg Wen" i mi? Neu "Godiad yr Ehedydd"?'
> Edrychodd y plentyn yn syn arnaf.
> 'Wyt ti ddim yn dysgu canu yn yr ysgol?'
> 'Ydw.'
> 'Wyt ti'n dysgu canu Cymraeg?'
> 'O nag ydw!'
> 'A ddysgodd neb erioed i ti ganu alawon Dafydd y Garreg Wen, a thithau'n byw yn yr un wlad â fo?'
> 'Naddo.'
> 'Be fedri di ganu?'
> '"Little Ship" a "Gentle Spring."'
>
> ['Can you sing?'
> 'Yes, I can.'
> 'Can you sing "Dafydd y Garreg Wen" for me? Or "Codiad yr Ehedydd"?'
> The child gazed at me in astonishment.
> 'Don't you learn singing in school?'

> 'Yes, I do.'
> 'Do you learn singing in Welsh?'
> 'Oh, no, I don't!'
> 'Didn't anyone ever teach you to sing airs like Dafydd y Garreg Wen, since you live in the very landscape that produced it?'
> 'No, no-one ever did.'
> 'What can you sing?'
> '"Little Ship" and "Gentle Spring."'] (*CC*, 127)

He has, Edwards reflects, been confronted with the same sad testimony wherever in Wales he has travelled. In some cases the failure to familiarise children with the best of their own local culture has resulted from the teachers' complete ignorance of the Welsh language. In other cases, the teachers may be Welsh-speaking but lack acquaintance with their own inheritance. Very much to blame in every case have been the paid servants of the state who regard Welsh simply as an irritating inconvenience: school inspectors with an extremely shaky grasp of the language at best; teachers who have unlearnt their naturally good Welsh in order to acquire a smattering of poor English; and ignorant supervisors who believe all the blessings of heaven and earth will be showered on their children if only they can acquire even such poor, basic English as is heard spoken by Welsh drovers at Chester markets (*CC*, 128). Outrage at this state of affairs prompted Edwards to edit *Cymru'r Plant* from 1892, the year in which he established this important pioneering magazine for the children of Wales, until his death in 1920. And it was also what motivated him to leave his comfortable, prestigious post as Fellow and Tutor in Modern History at Lincoln College, Oxford, in 1907, for the challenging role of Chief Inspector of Schools at the newly established Welsh Department of the Board of Education in London. As modern historians have concluded, 'Edwards must be regarded as the educationist with the highest profile in twentieth-century Wales. His philosophy of education was embraced so firmly that he was determined to use his official position, one without any parameters of precedent, to practical effect.' (*HEW*, 113)

School teachers were not the only signs encountered by Edwards of the sinister encroachments of an alien, invading English on Welsh-speaking Wales. Arrived in Llangammarch, he hears the sound of a heavy tread, 'like the marching of a line of soldiers', and a policeman heaves into view. Heartened, Edwards asks him in Welsh for directions to Cefn Brith, only to receive the brusque reply, 'I don't know what you say, you should speak English.' (*CC*, 89) This he takes as a reminder that 'on the borders of South Wales many of the ideas of the old Lords Marchers continue to prevail as the authorities suppose it their role to govern the Welsh not to serve them.' In this disgruntled state of mind he proceeds to Cefn Brith, where John Penry (1563–93) was born, and there pays deeply felt tribute to this martyr of early Welsh Dissent fittingly revered in Nonconformist tradition. Penry's crime, in the eyes of Elizabethan bishops, was to have campaigned not only to have the Bible read to his people in the only language they could understand, but to have Gospel truths explained to them by competent preachers. This was a period, Edwards notes, 'when the rulers of Wales were afraid of the Welsh tongue' (*CC*, 95) – the analogy with his own late Victorian times is, of course clear, as is the relevance of that recent encounter with the hostile English policeman.

Of all the figures eulogised in *Cartrefi Cymru*, John Penry is the one with whom Edwards seems most closely to identify, as is apparent when he emphasises how the natural environment left an intimate, formative imprint on his character. Wandering from the farmhouse of Cefn Brith out across the adjacent fields, Edwards lifts his gaze from the hedgerows to the mountain range beyond where 'there were no rocks or rough crags only smooth majesty and silence. Viewing the lovely swellings of the Eppynt brought ease of mind, not the ease that leads to laziness but the ease that leads to labour. Here is restfulness like that of heaven, that awakens the intelligence and strengthens it for work.' (*CC*, 97) That is nicely said, but the sentiments are those of a Victorian devotee of Ruskin, rather than those of the Elizabethan Penry, as is confirmed by a moving passage quoted from one of Penry's last letters to Lord Burleigh, where he describes himself as a 'poor young man, born and raised in the mountains of Wales. I am the first, since the recent blossoming of the Gospel in these present days, to have sown the blessed seed on these bare, desolate hills.' (*CC*, 100) The affinity that Edwards clearly feels for Penry has blinded him to what the latter has actually written, and led him to attribute his own sentiments of a much later day to the Elizabethan. This difference between their two ways of viewing the mountains – what was a green desert for the one is now a green paradise for the other – alerts us to a seminal feature of *Cartrefi Cymru*: the many ideological uses to which, in this book, Edwards puts the landscape of Wales.

Cultural geographers have, for several decades, been fascinated by the way topography is invariably also tropography. Local, ephemeral belief systems are universalised and eternalised by assuming natural form, merging deceptively with the very lie of the land (a phrase that has in turn been repeatedly mined for its punning implications).[14] Nature thus serves as an important site of cultural struggle – of contesting perceptions, values and beliefs – and so changes its appearance constantly depending on who is viewing or representing it. Geographers routinely speak of 'the social production of landscape', of resulting 'power geometrics'. Landscape, they note, is the product of 'social work' but it also 'does work' by helping to produce, and sustain, a given social order. The natural world has always been a rich source of 'metaphors to live by', they add, so that every landscape becomes 'a cultural image, a pictorial way of representing, structuring or symbolising surroundings'. Particular attention has been paid to the contribution made by these 'maps of meaning' to the construction of national identities. 'Every mature nation', it has been argued, 'has its symbolic landscapes. They are part of the iconography of nationhood, part of the shared ideas and memories and feelings which bind a people together.' In such connections as these, landscape becomes a kind of 'text, part of the cultural signifying systems through which we make sense of our worlds'.

Armed with such concepts as this, it becomes quickly apparent both how central the act of representing landscape is to O. M. Edwards's purpose in *Cartrefi Cymru*, and how much it there contributes to the fashioning, through the geo-graphing (i.e. land-writing), of the icons of his own particular version of Welsh nationhood. Indeed, the very act of travelling all over rural Wales, minutely recording the distinctive physical features of the several localities he visited, was, for the author, the physical enactment of his dream of developing an inclusive, holistic vision of the country in an historically fissiparous native population whose horizons had long been confined, both physically and mentally, to their native patch, their local *bro*. In *Cartrefi Cymru*, a new enlightened parochialism is demonstrated to be perfectly compatible with a devolved model of nationalism that aims not to supersede localities valued historically for their hallmark features, but to connect them into a single summative national entity that, in its multifaceted wholeness, is greater than the sum of its parts. Wales's *broydd* (its beloved localities) should be treated, he urged, as examples of *pars pro toto*; each acting as synecdoche, that is, for the country as a whole. In his seminal study, *Imagined Communities*, Benedict Anderson rightly proposed that the widespread consciousness of belonging to an extended community termed a 'nation' grew as the technologies for circulating information and for easy travel – the newspapers and the railways – began to develop from the eighteenth century onwards.[15] Edwards's travels around Wales complemented the work done by his compendious periodicals. Those Victorian omnibuses encouraged contributors from all over the country to place on central record and to bring to national attention the historical figures and events, legends, geographical features and dialects that constituted the unique glory of their own particular neighbourhoods.

* * *

For Edwards, landscape seemed not solely to exist in the present, but to be the repository of deep time. It seemed to possess its own memory; to bear still the impress of its past inhabitants; to be ghosted by its particular history. Entering the locality so intimately associated in his imagination with the writings of Elis Wynne, the 'Bardd Cwsg' (the so-called 'sleeping poet' because his early eighteenth-century masterpiece was a dream-work), he supposes it natural to term this region 'the Land of Sleep'. 'I supposed there was something strange about the light there,' he writes, 'and that stillness surged in waves through its air still . . . It was as if I were dreaming even as I walked through that land.' (*CC*, 101) And as consistently happens in *Cartrefi Cymru*, he proceeds to imagine that it is the site of some intimate transaction, a mystic wedding contracted between landscape and author. The terrain has not only been permanently marked by Elis Wynne's writing, it has, in its turn, entered deeply into his work, metamorphosing into the mental landscape of the celebrated book in which he traverses the regions of heaven and hell. In Edwards's opinion, Elis Wynne's chiarascuro, worthy of a Rembrandt painting, is a textual reflection of the dramatic interplay of light and dark over Harlech bay. This fusion of text and landscape means that Edwards repeatedly feels that as he treads the land so is he also stepping back in time. In *Cartrefi Cymru*, Edwards the traveller turns into Edwards the time-traveller: 'see, there, a shaft of light brightening from behind that yellow-white cloud, the very [sight] the Sleeping Poet saw when, praying in the grip of the Fairies, he declared he saw "some light from afar breaking out, O so beautiful!"' (*CC*, 102)

Repeatedly in *Cartrefi Cymru*, landscape is translated into text, as texts by the writers with whom Edwards is concerned are shown to retain the contours of the landscapes in which they were written. And texts correspondingly possess a geomorphic power to reshape landscape. It is this process of interpenetration and interanimation that makes the land numinous, for him, with the culture that for centuries it has sustained. His essay on Ann Griffiths (1776–1805) constantly interweaves passages from her hymns with descriptions of the countryside around her home at Dolwar Fach. She drew repeatedly on the latter, it is implied, when imagining heaven and its delights, and even when mystically straining to capture the ineffable beauty of Christ's divinity. That indefatigable traveller for Christ, the Methodist evangelist William Williams, Pantycelyn (1717–91), wrote hymns which, as Edwards demonstrates, were in part marching songs for pilgrim souls, full of references to the actual physical obstacles that the rough, mountainous terrain of Wales had, in Williams's experience, so abundantly to offer.

Equally suggestively, when visiting the Llŷn peninsula, Edwards avidly records the verses inscribed on tombstones – these are calcified texts, so to speak, simple graffitied poems by anonymous versifiers intent on leaving their mark on the very stones of their localities. Tombstone verses are also markers in other senses of the word. They invite travellers to pause and mark this particular spot. And for Edwards, they are markers of cultural identity, evidence of who has so long 'owned' this particular land by living and dying there. They are also invitations to mark not only the grave and its occupant(s) but to mark the surrounding scene. In this connection, Edwards resurrects the genre of graveyard poetry beloved of English eighteenth-century poets so as to give it new and different life in a Welsh context by completely changing its register. Instead of inclining him to melancholy, the graveyard of Treflys affords a sublime prospect, embracing not only the uplands of Llŷn but the majestic Snowdonia range in Arfon and the more distant mountains of Merioneth. And it is the verse engraved on the tombstone of a local poet, 'Bardd Treflys', that has, Edwards implies, opened his eyes to the grandeur of the scenery before him, text teaching him where and how to look and thus turning into landscape before his very eyes (*CC*, 125).

The hymns of Pantycelyn and of Ann Griffiths contributed substantially to the concept, so popular in nineteenth-century Welsh chapel culture, of Wales as a second Holy Land, a country blessed by divine presence immanent to the land itself.[16] But while Edwards allows a faint shadow of this belief to fall occasionally across his text, in general his vision of the Welsh landscape owes much less to religion than to the nineteenth-century secular religion of Romantic nationalism, one of whose most common and most crucial formative tropes was the interpenetration of people and land over many centuries to constitute a grounded national community hallowed by history. On such a view, landscape assumed the aspect of the solidification into perdurable matter of a long past, an aspect that enabled the land to serve 'its' nation as a cultural mnemonic. This concept is repeatedly mobilised by Edwards in *Cartrefi Cymru* to counter the hard truth – so evident 'on the ground' as he travelled – that the country of Wales was, in fact, largely in the possession of landowners who, even when not actually English, were invariably anglicised. But if much of the landscape of rural Wales was the property of foreigners, it was truly owned – in an altogether different and deeper sense – by the ordinary farmers who had for centuries not only sanctified it with their labours but had made it part of their very selves by incorporating it into their culture. That was the insistent – and defiant – 'postcolonial' message of *Cartrefi Cymru*.

At no time is this more clear than when Edwards chooses to summon the landscape into being by ritually reciting the Welsh names for its salient features, as he does when searching for Bryn Tynoriaid, home to that incisive champion of Welsh Nonconformity and scourge of the 1847 enquiry commissioners, Ieuan Gwynedd (1820–52):

> Ar ein cyfer dacw'r Hengwrt Ucha: a thraw ar fin y mynydd, uwch ei ben, dacw'r Blaenau, cartref Rhys Jones, cynhullydd *Gorchestion Beirdd Cymru*. Ymhellach fyth y mae'r Rhobell gawraidd yn edrych i lawr ar y llethrau a'r dyffryn.
>
> Cefais ymgom ddifyr â llawer amaethwr y diwrnod hwnnw. Dywedent fel y byddai pawb ar ei dir ei hun unwaith – Pant y Panel, Coed Mwsoglog, Coed y Rhos Lwyd, Maes y Cambren, Brith Fryniau, a llu ereill – oll erbyn heddiw wedi eu gwerthu i dir-feddiannwr mawr. Sylwais gymaint yn dlysach oedd yr hen dai na'r tai sydd newydd eu codi; ond nid oedd amser i holi beth oedd y rheswm.

> [Opposite us there's Hengwrt Ucha; and yonder on the mountain edge above it is Blaenau, home to Rhys Jones, compiler of *Gorchestion Beirdd Cymru*. Further off again there is giant Rhobell, gazing down on the slopes and the vale.
>
> Many an enjoyable chat with a farmer I had that day. Everyone, they told me, had farmed his own land once upon a time – Pant y Panel, Coed Mwsoglog, Coed y Rhos Lwyd, Maes y Cambren, Brith Fryniau,

> and many another – all now sold to great landowners. I noticed how much more attractive were the old houses than those newly built; but there was no time to enquire why that should be.] (*CC*, 71)

The rosary of loss is here also a roster of indomitable survival, bearing witness to the long memory of a land that remains inalienably faithful to its familiar old inhabitants. It is as if the landscape answers only to Welsh – as if, indeed, that is the native language of the fields and mountains as well as of the indigenous human inhabitants.

And in the concluding sentence of that passage is buried another crucial 'truth', left unspoken here but consistently stated elsewhere in *Cartrefi Cymru*. The old houses are incomparably more attractive than the new because theirs is a 'vernacular' architecture. Not only do they blend with their surroundings, but several of them seem actually to be virtual outcrops – or rather outgrowths, since Edwards wants to stress their organic character – of the landscape itself. This is how Edwards arrives at the home of Ellis Wynne, in the uplands of the Harlech hinterland:

> Cerddais dros y bryn bychan gan ddod i lawr at gefn Glasynys y bardd – amaethdy a'i wyneb tua'r mynyddoedd. Gwelais ar unwaith ei fod wedi ei adeiladu fel y dylid adeiladu ty ar lethr craig; gyda drws i fynd oddiallan i'w ystafelloedd uchaf, a mor naturiol ei safiad a phe buasai wedi codi, fel blodeuyn, yng nghwrs natur ar ochr y bryn.
>
> [I crossed the hillock and came down to the rear of the poet's home at Glasynys – a farmhouse with its face to the mountains. I immediately saw it had been built in a manner fitting for a house built on a craggy slope; with an upstairs door that opened directly onto the landscape, so that it seemed as natural as if it had grown, like a flower, in the course of time, on the side of its hill.] (*CC*,104)

And just as the building seems the product of its surroundings, so does its name. Glasynys, Edwards suddenly realises now that he's at last arrived at the location, must in this context mean 'Green Island'. The hill on which the farmhouse stands rises from the plain, providing an incomparable view of the distant sea: 'this spot, undoubtedly, was once an island', Edwards concludes, 'and the plain was once ocean' (*CC*, 103). Here knowledge of the name is a *sine qua non* for 'reading' and 'comprehending' the lie of a land whose present form was shaped long ago, in deep time.

* * *

'From the top of the hill' on which Glasynys stands, 'there is a splendid view of sea and mountain', writes Edwards (*CC*, 103). It is one of those moments in *Cartrefi Cymru* when he emphasises that his 'point of view' on the landscape is that of an inhabitant and not of a 'picturesque traveller', of an 'indweller' rather than a visitor. Much has rightly been made of Edwards's (readily avowed) debts to the English Romantic tradition of nature writing, both in poetry and in prose, deriving, of course, from the eighteenth-century revaluation of landscape in the light of the then emergent theories of the picturesque and the sublime. Most particularly, he has repeatedly been described as a Welsh disciple of Ruskin, and indeed traces of the great Victorian's thinking can be discerned everywhere in *Cartrefi Cymru* – hatred of industrial capitalism, love of traditional 'craft' occupations and skills, preference for 'vernacular' architecture, an implicit sympathy with what would nowadays be termed 'environmentalism', and a concern to break down class barriers by feeding and fostering the intelligence of ordinary working people. But in listing indebtednesses there is the danger of overlooking the interrogating, even dissenting, aspects of Edwards's relationship with English Romantic tradition, particularly evident in his treatment of landscape. What he was reacting against was the 'aestheticisation' of landscape that had occurred with the advent of the picturesque; the 'highland clearances' by the eye, so to speak, of an inconvenient native population from the land it occupied so that all that was left to be framed in the picture was 'natural vista' and 'prospect'. And as has repeatedly been demonstrated, this perspective on nature was a ready ally of the colonial outlook that treated others' land as up for grabs.

O. M. Edwards's particular variant of 'geopiety' found expression in a form of landscape writing heavily inflected to serve his own passionate agenda of the reawakening of national consciousness. In so far as it might be termed a 'land reclamation scheme' for the whole of rural Wales, *Cartrefi Cymru* is also – to employ another anachronistic term – an example of 'postcolonial' writing. In its way, it is the discursive parallel to such great, nineteenth-century popular movements of rural protest and revolt in Wales as the Rebecca Riots and the anti-Tithe campaign. But Edwards's uprising is not economic or religious, but cultural in nature and textual in character; an ideological attempt to address and redress the condition of an invisible nation – a nation that had almost ceased to be visible even to itself. At a time when, as we have seen, the education system in Wales did not see fit to take any notice of the very country it was intended to serve, Edwards found in *Cartrefi Cymru* the materials for an alternative education writ large in the landscape of his nation. And since social geographers are nowadays fond of sometimes speaking of the land as a vast 'cultural spoor', it would seem as appropriate as it is suggestive to conceive of O.M. as acting, in *Cartrefi Cymru*, the part of a great 'native tracker' of his Wales.

A striking example of his tracker's eye for the 'cultural spoor' detectable by the initiate in landscape is furnished when he visits Gerddi Bluog, at that time supposed to have been the seventeenth-century home of Edmwnd Prys (1543–1623), the celebrated versifier of the psalms, in the vicinity of Trawsfynydd. His first instinct upon arriving there is to pause on the threshold, not in anticipation of what lies within but so as to take his geo-cultural bearings by reviewing those features of the landscape visible from this particular spot. 'We stopped by the door of the house to see what view could be seen from there. Black pines stood nearby, and the light breeze caused them to shake slowly, like the old women of the Seiat [religious meeting] moved by the breezes of Zion, as if they still heard the music of the psalms.' (*CC*, 43) It is a remarkable instance of the fusion of landscape and religious culture. When eventually he crosses the threshold and enters the old house, Edwards's attention is immediately arrested by the sight of Edmwnd Prys's famous old grandfather clock, and upstairs he is shown Prys's old bed, in whose wood his initials are reputed to have been carved. And there, indeed, faintly inscribed in the timber Edwards is able to make out what seem to be the initials 'E.P.' followed by the year '1592'. Yet, despite showing a dutiful interest in these old intimate relics, Edwards has frankly to admit that '[f]or my part, best of all is to be able to gaze on the scenery that those famous in our country's history once gazed upon' (*CC*, 45). The syntax is contrived to emphasise the mutuality of the relationship between the present and a past made available, visible and tangible in the landscape. Such is the generalised transactional force of the grammatical construction that it is hard to tell which of the elements in the sentence are active and which passive. The result is to persuasively imply that it is the landscape, and not the human dwelling, that is the best guarantor of national permanence, the guardian of cultural continuity, as it possesses the power to spatialise time.

Edwards's project of using his books to help build a national community depended centrally on his being able to establish a similarly transactional relationship with the 'common reader', a sense of solidarity which could have proved a challenge, given his elite academic background. The greatest potential difficulty lay with the social register of the kind of sophisticated language his intellectual training might well have encouraged him to adopt, the temptation being all the greater given the lexically and syntactically tortuous character of what passed for 'educated Welsh' in his day. As commentators have repeatedly emphasised, Edwards's single greatest achievement was therefore to forge an easy, colloquial style of Welsh, free alike from the pomposities of academia and the pulpit and from the limiting features of regional dialect. In effect, he invented a friendly lingua franca for his new Wales, a new, accessible style of writing whose imagined readership was the Welsh *gwerin*. Indeed, so convincingly imagined in textual terms was this readership that Edwards's prose seemed almost to possess a power to call into actual existence the idealised *gwerin* presupposed by its stylistic register.

In keeping with this style, Edwards chose to present himself in *Cartrefi Cymru* not as an Oxford don but as an ordinary man very much at ease when at large among his people. That such a self-image was the result of conscious choice is made apparent in an early passage in the book:

> Peth digon hawdd i bobl ddieithr fel ni, a ninnau wedi darllen papurau newyddion ac yn medru siarad Saesneg, ydyw ei lordio hi dipyn, fel y dywed pobl y fro hon, yng ngwydd pobl wledig.
>
> [It's an easy matter for outsiders such as ourselves, who have read the daily newspapers and are able to speak English, to lord it, as locals here would say, in the presence of country folk.] (*CC*, 26)

Edwards here registers the opportunity afforded by his superior education and social class only to reject it out of hand. Members of the Welsh-speaking *gwerin*, according to his idealised construction of them, constitute a naturally classless society. Anxious to be of their number, he chooses to travel socially incognito, careful always to betray no signs of his privileged status. Accordingly, those of the *gwerin* he comes across on his journeys around Wales are described as expressing an interest not in his social background but in his regional origins and his denominational affiliation. The only exception is the Englishman who picks him up at Haverfordwest station. From the first, his forelock-tugging speech is thick with class consciousness – '"Cloudy mornin', fine day, sir."' (*CC*, 132) Outside the magic circle of the *gwerin*, the English class system rules supreme.

Yet, commoner though Edwards insists on styling himself, he regularly avails himself of his privileged position, as we have seen, to educate his compatriots in their cultural history. And in like manner he attempts to broaden their horizons by setting their land and their lives in a context as wide as that of the continental Europe with which he has become acquainted through extensive travel. Visiting Trefecca College, in the vicinity of Brecon, for instance, a training institution famously established by Howell Harris (1714–73), one of the great figures of the eighteenth-century Methodist Revival in Wales, Edwards is moved to recall his visits to the graves of Dante and of Chateaubriand. The intention, in making such a connection, is not to parade his sophistication; rather, it is to demonstrate how natural a comparison can be drawn, in the absence of snobbish inhibition, between the significant points of origin of three European nations. 'I felt,' writes Edwards of the stone commemorating Harris in Talgarth, 'that there was more than a grave in this church; I felt I was standing on the very spot that had given birth to a new Wales.' (*CC*, 78) Dante, Chateaubriand, Howell Harris: three figures widely separated by time, by country and by circumstance, yet persuasively viewed by Edwards as a single trio of Risorgimento heroes, each responsible for a national awakening.

As this episode suggests, for Edwards the reawakening of Welsh-speaking Wales to its own history necessarily involved recovering an awareness of itself as an ancient European nation. Viewed from the uplands beyond Criccieth, the ocean appears to O. M. Edwards to be of a blue more intense than anywhere save on Mediterranean shores in the shelter of the Ligurian mountains (*CC*, 119). This European connection was a truth set, so to speak, in stone – a truth inscribed, for anyone who had eyes to see in the imperishable rock of Welsh landscape. Striking inland from Harlech, he hits upon the steep stone steps carved by the Romans out of the hillside to form a direct route across the mountains. More than a millennium and a half after its construction, this route is still as easy to follow as an ordinary garden path. As it dips down into dales and passes through dells, he recalls strolling the slopes of the Appenines, turning his journey into a reminder that Wales was once part of a Roman Empire that bound most of Europe into a single entity.[17]

* * *

This awareness of a European dimension to the Welsh case is integral to O. M. Edwards's envisaging of a future for his Nonconformist nation. Improvements in education and increasing ease of travel helped nurture a more international outlook in the intelligentsia of middle-class Wales by the closing decades of the nineteenth century. This, in turn, meant a greater readiness on the part of some intellectuals to imagine for Wales a place in the world beyond England and her Empire. One of the most trenchant advocates of this outlook was Emrys ap Iwan (1848–1906), a passionate Europhile and scathing diagnostician of the deadly 'English fever' from which so many of his compatriots suffered. Having spent periods in his youth teaching and studying in Lausanne, Heidelberg, Bonn and Glessen, he made a point of holiday-ing on the continent most years thereafter. As a writer, he took the social pamphleteers of France as his model (especially the work of Paul-Louis Courier) and set out to act the Socratic gadfly of Non-conformist Wales, launching scathing attacks for two decades in the columns of several leading Welsh periodicals.[18]

Their true religion, Emrys ap Iwan informed the servile chapels whose social climbing he satirised and whose fierce feuding he despised, was not Christianity but Englisholatry. He caricatured relations between England, Wales and Ireland in the form of invented exchanges between John Bully, Paddy and Taffi – this north-Wales Welsh word for sweets being used by Emrys ap Iwan to imply his compatriots were ruinously besotted with the big sugar-daddy beyond Offa's Dyke (*EI1*, 1–13). As for his frequently starry-eyed Europhilia, it was evidently the obverse of an attitude towards the neighbouring English that was bigoted and piercingly perceptive by turns. He proudly styled himself, with considerable justification, a defender of the rights of defenceless nations (*EI3*, xiii) and liked, on occasion, to identify specifically with one or other of the smaller peoples of Europe – adopting, for instance, a Flemish persona to write a commentary on the contemporary state of the British Isles (*EI1*, 92–122). Yet he was also a devotee of the great powers that could challenge English superiority, most particularly of France, a country to which he felt closely connected through his French grandmother. Napoleon was a particular hero of his, not-withstanding the Emperor's notorious indifference to the plight of the many peoples, large and small, his victorious armies trampled underfoot (*EI1*, 123–65).

As D. Myrddin Lloyd perceptively pointed out some seventy years ago, within the Welsh culture of his day, Emrys ap Iwan's Francophilia acted as counterweight to the Germanophilia of that notable scholar Sir John Rhŷs (1840–1915), whose renowned philological scholarship was modelled on the most advanced contemporary German academic practice.[19] 'In France, they study men; in Germany, books,' was Emrys ap Iwan's pithy way of differentiating between the two cultures (*EI2*, 159). And, whereas Rhŷs was Germanically preoccupied with establishing a sound 'scientific' basis in etymology and linguistic history for contemporary Welsh usage, Emrys ap Iwan (ever respectful of the common people's authority, in the best French Revolutionary tradition) consciously modelled his own fluid writing on the best in colloquial speech, particularly as recorded in some of the classic prose works of the Welsh past. John Rhŷs's approach to language matters he dismissed as that of a purist and pedant, believing it resulted only in leaden expression. Very much a linguistic nationalist, he was anxious to demonstrate that Welsh could best renew itself in the French fashion, modernising by drawing on its own inner resources rather than by borrowing from other languages – particularly invasive English. And he was very much in favour of enriching native culture through the importation into Welsh of the work of leading continental authors – late in his short life, he published brief sample extracts he had himself translated from the works of Hans Christian Andersen, F. A. Krummacher, Lessing and Tolstoy.

O. M. Edwards's orientation on Europe, different from that of both Emrys ap Iwan and John Rhŷs, is clearly signalled in the title of his book *O'r Bala i Geneva*. From Bala to Geneva: these two locations, as different as they are distant, were for him the two poles of a single world; his own world; the world of Welsh Calvinistic Methodism.[20] Geneva, of course, was the famed home of John Calvin himself, the titan of sixteenth-century Reformed Protestantism whose radical theological system, recorded in magisterial volumes designed as the handbooks of a new spiritual order, was to provide Europe with a revolutionary new political blueprint. As for the little town of Bala, nestled alongside Llyn Tegid amid the mountains of mid-Wales, from the middle of the nineteenth century onwards it developed into the intellectual powerhouse of Welsh Presbyterianism (as the denomination was also known), following the establishment there in 1839 of a college for training Welsh Calvinistic ministers. Lewis Edwards (1809–87), co-founder and subsequent principal of the college, was one of a galaxy of talents associated with this seminal institution. The neighbouring college established at Bala by the Welsh Independents likewise produced its own luminaries. One such was Michael D. Jones (1822–98), the nationalist (Llanuwchllyn-born, like his disciple O. M. Edwards) whose vision of resettling the Welsh Nonconformist nation overseas, at a safe distance from England and its intrusive language, led first to his tentative explorations in Cincinnati and then to the Patagonian emigration experiment of 1865.

Indeed, *Cartrefi Cymru* can be read as Edwards's answer to Jones's version of the Welsh future. Emigration, the latter had concluded, was the lifebelt of a people otherwise destined to drown in the sea of ever encroaching Englishness. He dreamt of a new start overseas, where 'there will be chapels, schools and a Parliament and the old language will be the medium of worship, of trade, of science, of education and of government. A strong and self-reliant nation will grow in a Welsh homeland.'[21] Refusing to give up on the original historic homeland of Wales itself, Edwards, by contrast, mounted a heroic, if ultimately futile, rearguard action to reserve it primarily for the Welsh language and the culture it had for so long supported. And his travels overseas were not to seek out a new land for a new beginning, but a search for political examples, spiritual sources and cultural resources that would both broaden the horizons of his people and bolster their self-confidence, weakened by centuries of politico-cultural subordination.

In journeying from Bala to Geneva, then, the Welsh Presbyterian O. M. Edwards was following the axis of his personal world in an attempt to place his Wales firmly on the map of Europe. His aim is to help create Welsh Europeans. Accordingly, his route is to run, so his preface informs the reader, between 'hen gartref meddwl Cymru a hen gartref meddwl Ewrob' – from the old home of the Welsh mind to the old home of the mind of Europe. A grandiose formulation, but its faint absurdity is neatly offset by the tone of what follows, as, quoting repeatedly from the letters he wrote on his travels, Edwards charms and disarms his reader by constantly altering the expressive register of this, the first continental travel book ever to be written in Welsh.[22] Thus the sight (recorded in an atmospheric pencil drawing) of seagulls soaring into vision off the Thames between him and St Paul's immediately gives way to an attractively peevish description of the squirming, squealing, grubby child who disturbed his slumbers on the train journey from Liverpool Street Station to Harwich (*OBG*, 10). Later in his journeys, the train is to represent for him both an indispensable modern convenience and a barrier to his stepping fully back into the past by approaching the key towns of Protestant Germany along the very same roads as his heroes of old (*OBG*, 50).

Having crossed the channel, he and his fellow-passengers 'walk from the ship, one long line, like spirits coming from the graveyard' (*OBG*, 13). At its best, Edwards's prose is light of touch, engaging in both senses of that word, and he is particularly adept at alternating the roles of knowledgeable guide, innocent visitor, and genial tourist. The chapter on Antwerp begins with a brief history of its commitment to social freedom and religious liberty, and ends with a comic episode. A Fleming alarms Edwards by producing a knife and running his finger menacingly along its edge. Grappling with him in self-defence, Edwards tumbles his 'assailant' into the river only to discover he'd been miming a request for a light for his cigarette. The episode is clearly a parable for this Welshman's encounters with a continent whose social landscape is as difficult to decipher as the geo-cultural landscape of Wales for those who lack the 'language', including of course the 'correct' historical knowledge, to read it.

Two early chapters lay out the key coordinates of Edwards's own ideological map of Europe. One outlines a history of divinely ordained social, political and religious progress almost entirely confined to the north, in which freedom radiated outwards from the free mercantile towns of the Low Countries whose names he devoutly recites as if telling a Protestant rosary: Antwerp, Utrecht, Ghent, Brussels, Louvain, Liège. These were the sacred sites of late Medieval struggle between town and castle, freedom and slavery, free trade and monopoly by lord and priest, industrious craftsmen and the dead hand of the feudal system; and it was this struggle that eventually came to a head in the form of the challenge of a northern Protestantism to an entrenched, superstitious and oppressive Catholic system whose power-base lay primarily in the south (*OBG*, 22ff). And as in Wales, this history is for O. M. Edwards to be seen still laid out in landscape. Travelling the Rhine, he sees the pinnacles of towns rising wherever the land is flat, while a castle seems invariably to crown every peak (*OBG*, 24).

This militantly anti-Catholic vision is, however, somewhat tempered by the relatively conciliatory chapter he devotes to describing his attendance at a service in Notre Dame cathedral in Antwerp. Here he comes as close as ever he will to manifesting an eirenic spirit. Edwards is far from insensible to the spiritual force of the beauty by which he is surrounded in a cathedral that can boast several glorious paintings by Rubens. The priest, he admits, cannot be faulted for passion, so mesmerically intense is his sermon. And he finds himself surprisingly reconciled even to the rowdy chaos of his fellow-worshippers, who have evidently come directly from their work yet are suddenly stilled to quiet, sincere devotion. 'Could it perhaps be,' he ruefully reflects, 'that even their worldly workaday tasks are sanctified by this kind of worship?' (*OBG*, 19)

* * *

It is the ugly side of Welsh Nonconformist ideology that finds expression in Edwards's scandalous response to the Jews he encounters when visiting what is for him the sacred town of Worms, where Luther famously defied both the secular and the religious authorities of his day:

> A pheth arall, y mae yma nifer anferth o Iddewon. Y maent hwy yn cynyddu tra y mae'r bobl eraill yn lleihau, fel y mae blodau gwenwynig yn blaguro mewn gardd ddiffeithiwyd. Gweli Iddew yn sefyll wrth ddrws ei siop fel pryf copyn, neu a'i hanner allan o'i ffenestr yn rhythu ar dy ôl, – y mae lliw ei lygaid a maint ei drwyn yn ei fradychu. Er cased ydynt gan bawb, yr oedd eu henwau cynefin – Abraham a Jacob, a Levi, a Joseph – yn gwneyd i mi deimlo yn rhyw gynnes atynt.
>
> [And another thing, there are here a huge number of Jews. They increase as other peoples decrease, just as poisonous flowers blossom in a garden abandoned to wilderness. You'll see a Jew standing at his door like a spider, or with half of him hanging out of a window as he stares after you, – the colour of his eyes and size of his nose betray him. Yet hated though they are by all, their familiar names – Abraham and Jacob, and Levi, and Joseph – caused me to feel a certain warmth for them.] (*OBG*, 53)

This response is all the more shocking and disturbing given the geniality of character otherwise everywhere apparent in *O'r Bala i Genefa*. And the obnoxious effect is compounded rather than moderated by that final confession of a sneaking regard for Jews, not as individuals or as a distinct people or as a religious group, but because they so often bear Old Testament names familiar to Nonconformist Wales. The ambivalence of motive behind such a comment may, however, be worth briefly considering. On the one hand it clearly smacks of the common nineteenth-century Nonconformist belief that the Welsh have displaced the Jews as the chosen people of God. On the other hand, it may also be an instance of a perverted kind of sympathetic identification in the form of an inverted self-projection; of the victimised turning victimiser. A Welsh Nonconformist, used to being viewed by some sections of English society with contempt, finds release for his anger and frustration by visiting a similar contempt on the Jews. Either way, the result is a sorry case of rank racism.[23]

The 'Jewish question' receives extended treatment in *O'r Bala i Geneva*. His landlady, Edwards reports, openly regards all Jews as rapacious blood-suckers. A visit to a synagogue in Heidelburg prompts memories of several occasions back home in Wales when the subject of the Jews arose (*OBG*, 56ff). He remembers hearing a farmer in the west curse them for the sorry state of some of his crops. He brings to mind researching, along with a friend, the influence of the Jews on English history, and recalls resisting a plea to sympathise with their repeated sufferings because they had, he felt, largely brought those sufferings upon themselves. His conclusions are all the more unnerving because they are arrived at with the air of a trained historian's dispassionate judiciousness. The expulsion of the Jews down the centuries by various states is, in Edwards's opinion, understandable. On the other hand the pogroms of the past, he emphasises, were clearly barbarous and indefensible, and to blame the Jews for usury is hypocritical, given that their money-lending facilitated the development of the modern world of trade, industry and commerce. Wondering, therefore, whether the hatred of them evident across Europe can be justified, Edwards concludes that yes, indeed, it can. He particularly commends a book written by Jacob Brafman (1825–79), a Russian Jew who condemns his fellow Jews for effectively operating a state within a state in order the more effectively to prey financially on innocent Christians, whom they thereby drive to ruin and destruction. Nothing in the Ten Commandments prevents Jews from so acting, Edwards calmly adds, because gentiles are regarded as fair game, along with all their possessions. Omitting to mention that Brafman was in fact an apostate who had converted to the Greek Orthodox Church, Edwards concludes by carefully conceding that Brafman's book testifies only to the practices of Eastern European Jews: 'I have as yet had no opportunity,' he adds with all the appearance of the utmost scrupulousness, 'of ascertaining with certainty how far the same is true of the Jews of Germany.' (*OBG*, 79) History has, of course, rendered this comment all the more chilling.

Nor is O. M. Edwards yet finished with the Jewish question. That they live under the damnation of God is evident, he insists, if one reads the first six chapters of Ezekiel. And justly so, since they had been destined by the Almighty to bear witness to the truths of the spiritual world, but had opted instead to worship the golden calf. Their present fate has therefore been preordained, as of course has the triumphant march of Protestantism across Europe likewise been predestined, reaching a glorious apotheosis in the spectacular growth of Welsh Calvinistic Methodism. But Jews may yet be granted forgiveness, Edwards magnanimously concludes, provided at long last that they recognise Christ as their Redeemer (*OBG*, 81). This is the standard discourse of nineteenth-century 'conversionism'. The whole discussion is a farrago of the sinister anti-Semitic prejudices dismayingly bred at the dark heart of nineteenth-century Welsh Nonconformist ideology.

* * *

After a very leisurely journey, seemingly lasting several weeks, Edwards duly arrives in Geneva, planning to spend the winter there. He is roughly half way through his book, and no sooner has he arrived at his destination than he attempts to help his reader back home to imagine its layout by superimposing its town plan on that of Bala. No better image than this double exposure could have been devised to capture the very essence of Edwards's vision of the twin centres of Bala and Geneva fused to form a supercharged nuclear core for Calvinistic Wales. And no sooner has Edwards elaborately constructed his doubled image than he redoubles it, but this time in reverse, as he now imagines Wales come to Geneva, courtesy of visits to beautiful Catholic churches in the surrounding countryside that serve only to reinforce his own nostalgic attachment to the simple, unadorned chapels of his native country. These plain buildings, he convinces himself, are the outward signs of the intense inward devotion and purity of spirit that are the defining features of Nonconformist Wales. The fine arts, he argues, flourish only where and when piety begins to slacken. The history of nations follows a parabola divinely ordained by God. First, as in the case of a nineteenth-century Wales renewed by Calvinistic Methodism, the fierce energy of youth produces hymn-writers and evangelists; next, there is the coming of age, marked by the production of historians and statesmen; and finally comes mellow autumnal fruition, attended by artists, sculptors, musicians and novelists (*OBG*, 114).

Geneva is also experienced by Edwards the Oxonian as a refuge from the rigours of a culturally threatening Germany whose university students belong to duelling clubs, whose famed scholarship seems to him overbearingly intellectual, whose new theology undermines traditional faith, and in whose literature he nervously believes it is dangerous to dabble (*OBG*, 125). But Geneva's greatest gift to Edwards is that it allows him, by virtue of both its theological history and its geographic location, to bring the split between Protestant and Catholic Europe into focus and to account, to his own satisfaction, for this great, historically fateful, religious, social, political and cultural divide. In so doing, he lays bare the infrastructure of Welsh Nonconformist ideology.

Edwards was particularly puzzled as to how to account for the considerable Catholic presence in the northern heartland of Protestantism in Europe. He proposed several explanations: the allure of the great cathedrals in all their majestic beauty; the fact that a Protestant faith, driven by conscience, was active, volitional, intensely demanding and judgemental, whereas a Catholic faith was passive, indulgent and comfortable. Edwards clearly thought of the two in stereotypically gendered terms – the virility and vigour of strenuous Protestantism contrasted with the soft, feminine, yielding theology of a Catholic Church that interposed the intercessionary Virgin Mary and a host of petitioning saints between the sinner and 'Duw llidiog' (a wrathful God) (*OBG*, 129). In particular, Edwards assured his reader, Catholicism exploited the vanity of women, who were easily enticed by promises of finer dresses and social status. When addressing this matter, Edwards openly, if unconsciously, displays a fear of his own susceptibility to the sensuous attraction of women. Viewing a Catholic procession in Heidelburg he exclaims uneasily at the sight of so much beauty seductively decked out in white and gaily bedecked with festive flowers, while the 'virginal white' in which young female mourners are dressed at a funeral seems to him to bear sexual connotations, and thus to be not only inappropriate but improper.[24]

In context, it is clear enough that Edwards's reactions to 'the female principle' derived in part from a suppressed awareness of what he felt to be the 'feminine', 'sensuous' side of his own nature. This comes out most strongly in his confession of a strong attraction to painting and sculpture – an attraction that makes him distinctly uneasy, because he finds it easier to recall visual impressions than to register more 'substantial' matters such as ideas. It's as if he fears he may have the instincts of a flâneur and dilettante, delighting in the ever fascinating, ever variegated, ever mobile surface of life but never probing its depths:

> Daw masnachwr croenllyfn, mewn dillad spon, yn prysuro trwy'r eirlaw i'w gartref, ty ardderchog lle chwery goleuni y lampau crogedig ar lestri aur ac arian, ar wydrau tryloewon, ar ddarluniau prydferth, ar y carped esmwyth . . . Daw y gweithiwr wedyn, yn taflu ei goesau allan wrth gerdded, a'i gefn a'i war yn syth fel polyn, ond eto yn rhoi rhyw dro nes y mae lapedi ei got yn chware'n ôl ac ym mlaen gyda'i gamrau.
>
> [A smooth-skinned merchant comes, in brand-new clothes, hastening home through the sleet, a splendid house where the light from hanging lamps shines on gold and silver dishes, on transparent glasses, on beautiful paintings, and on a comfortable carpet . . . Then a workman comes, throwing out his legs as he walks, and his back and shoulders straight as a pole, and yet somehow giving a hitch to his movements so that the lapels of his coat play backwards and forwards in time with his steps.] (*OBG*, 133)

Just for a moment, in such passages as this, the egalitarianism bred of his radical Nonconformist respect for the soul of every individual, high or low, is allowed expression as a fascination with the distinctive physical form and movement – the signature body language – of each and every person he encounters. Of course, such vivid sketches as these owe much to the writings of the nineteenth-century English novelists, essayists and journalists Edwards had read. But they also bespeak a frustration at the prohibition placed by a Welsh Nonconformity obsessed with high seriousness on any sustained exercise of the 'frivolous' talent, such as Edwards knew he naturally possessed, for shrewd observation of the ordinary, passing, everyday world.

Whereas the very title of his book, *O'r Bala i Geneva*, was intended, as we have seen, to suggest the tracing of a closed circle – the closed circuit of the mental world of Calvinistic Methodism – Edwards did take pains to ensure, from time to time, that his journey was also alternatively registered as one into difference, into strangeness – a journey 'abroad'; an excursion, in the root sense of a venturing out into the unknown. Nowhere is this more evident than when, via his exposure to the 'feminine' cast of Catholicism, he tentatively opens himself up to the sensuous side both of the world and of his own nature. And it is in the interests of thus widening his mental horizons that he turns to painting, beginning conservatively by building a reassuring bridge between the foreign painters that attract him and the spiritual and social values of the Welsh Nonconformity he represents. Rembrandt is a particular favourite, because of his devotion to the poor, the sinful, the downtrodden, the dispossessed. Teniers is cherished for his love of fun, his gift for conveying the comical accidents of the everyday. And so truly does Girardet capture the spirit of a children's snowball fight that Edwards, viewing the painting in the company of a boisterous group of schoolchildren, is left uncertain where the frame ends and life begins.

O. M. Edwards found such paintings as these easy to reconcile with his strong Puritan beliefs. 'Were I a believer in metempsychosis,' he writes, 'I should believe also that it was the soul of Calvin that painted Rembrandt's pictures, and that dreamt Hawthorne's *Scarlet Letter*.' (*OBG*, 147) It was likewise easy for the Romantic pantheist in him to approve the work of Salvator Rosa and Claude. More challenging were the sumptuously sensual paintings of Veronese and Titian, whose images were 'earth of the earth, the flesh as if still warm on the canvas' (*OBG*, 148). While his response to these is registered in carefully guarded terms, it nevertheless betrays a genuine fascination: 'Darlunio dynion yn ddynol a wna y rhai hyn, a gwn am lawer hen flaenor fuasai'n galw eu syniadau yn gnawdol odiaeth.' (*OBG*, 148) [These painters concentrate on the humanity of the human condition, and I know of many an old deacon who would consider their ideas obnoxiously fleshly.] It becomes apparent that Edwards is much more inclined to respect the frontal honesty of painters such as this than to commend the coy ruses adopted by such 'Puritans' as Cranach:

> Y mae dosbarth arall yn gwneyd dynion yn angylaidd; y mae'r cnawd yn diflannu, a'r enaid yn dod i'r golwg; y mae *drapery* prydferth o wyn a glas yn nofio oddiamagylch ac yn cuddio'r bronnau noethion a'r aelodau o esmwyth gnawd, ac nid oes yn y golwg ond gwyneb meddylgar, erys yn y cof wedi unwaith ei weled. (*OBG*, 148)
>
> [There is another class of painters who turn humans into angels; the flesh disappears, and the soul comes into view; lovely white and blue drapery floats around, concealing naked breasts and smooth fleshly members, and there is nothing to be seen but a pensive face that, once seen, stays in the mind.]

This, he adds, is a style of painting that leaves him cold.

His adventure among paintings is one of the seminal moments in Edwards's narrative, because it marks the very uttermost of his attempt to use his European journey in order to expand the boundaries of tolerance of his Nonconformist nation. The strain of his effort is accordingly registered not only in terms of the acknowledged break from accepted chapel opinion, but as an ongoing argument with himself arising from the complex sensitivities of his own nature. But in the end, Edwards has no wish to break out of the Calvinistic world confined, symbolically, for him between Bala and Geneva; and so, in the last paragraph of his work, he emphasises the circularity of the journey he has travelled one final time by recycling that key phrase with which his narrative had opened. 'Y peth fu'r Bala i Gymru,' he declares, now with the proven authority of textually demonstrated experience to back him up, 'hynny fu Geneva i Brotestantiaeth Ewrob.' (*OBG*, 182) 'What Bala has been to Wales, is what Geneva, in its turn, has been to Protestant Europe.'

* * *

Cartrefi Cymru and *O'r Bala i Genefa* may, then, be regarded as important complementary contributions to Edwards's lifelong work of constructing an evolved version of the original nineteenth-century 'Nonconformist nation', a version that would be suitable for a new age. That his concept of 'nation' was very heavily influenced by the Liberal Romantic model of nationhood[25] that had violently reshaped the map of Europe during the second half of the nineteenth century is apparent from the first of the notes he appended to *Cartrefi Cymru*. Central to that model was the assumption that nations were not, as the later twentieth century was to insist, provisional social structures wholly contingent on specific historic circumstances, but rather eternal social verities, ordained by the Almighty himself. For Edwards, therefore, Nonconformity and the Welsh nation were not accidentally related but necessarily co-dependent, since a national community was per se a religious community. Moreover, every nation had been ordained by God as an instrument of human improvement, social harmony and international cooperation. It made sense therefore for Edwards to speak of the Welsh landscape as 'sacred' to the nation; of it having been explicitly and exclusively gifted to the Welsh people by the Almighty. And the history of Wales took on a like spiritual complexion, with important historic sites assuming the character of sacred shrines.

The devout faith Edwards accordingly placed in what he termed 'patriotism' is likely only to sadden and disturb us today, in all its culpably innocent utopianism:

> Gallu grymus fu gwladgwarch erioed, ac er daioni pob amser. Y mae hunan-aberth ynddo, collir hunan mewn gwlad; y mae ymsancteiddio ynddo, – llosga hunanoldeb fel sofl sych a difa'r hen lid teuluol sy'n chwerwder bywyd barbaraidd, a dug ddyn yn nes at Dduw. Yng ngrym ei wladgarwch y mae nerth pethau goreu cymeriad dyn; yn erbyn gwladgarwch y mae'r pethau gwaelaf yn ei gymeriad – awydd am elw, cas at ei gyd-ddyn, rhagfarn.
>
> [Patriotism has ever been a strong force, and always for good. It involves self-sacrifice, since preoccupation with self is lost in commitment to country; it sanctifies self, since it burns up selfishness like dry stubble and destroys the old tribal resentments that are the bitterness of barbarian life, thus bringing man closer to God. It is in patriotism that the best of man appears in all its strength; and the worst elements in his nature become manifest when patriotism is slighted – the desire for profit, hatred of one's fellows, prejudice.] (*CC*, 139–40)

O. M. Edwards was, then, a passionate advocate for the God-given right of the 'Nonconformist nation' to exist. Also, like many of the most thoughtful cultural advocates of Cymru Fydd, he was deeply concerned that the emergent Wales whose 'enlightened', 'progressive' qualities and characteristics that a triumphalist Welsh Liberalism was so busily trumpeting, was in danger of losing all meaningful contact with the 'deep history' of the Welsh people. He attempted to address the rapidly accumulating 'cultural deficit' evident in the steadily anglicising industrial regions through a series of publications designed to introduce the cosmopolitan people of this 'new Wales' to the basics of historic Welsh-language culture. But, aware that a long-term lack of systematic education followed by the installation of an alien education system had left Welsh speakers, too, largely ignorant of their own history, he set out in *Cartrefi Cymru*, as in a whole library of other publications, to remedy this serious shortcoming. In a brief note he published in *Cymru*, he succinctly summarised his core aims in publishing his little book. The purpose of it, he plainly stated, was to consecrate the land of Wales in the eyes of her children, so that boys and girls might be moved to spend part of their holidays on a pilgrimage to the ordinary homes that were the nation's most sacred sites. This, he emphasised in a telling coda, would be infinitely preferable to them flocking to those many other places where they could learn only the lessons of vice and sin.[26]

Hidden in that final remark is, of course, the unspoken contrast around which the entire text of *Cartrefi Cymru* pivots, the contrast between the 'pure' world of the Welsh-speaking countryside and the corrupt and corrupting world of the new, anglophone Wales of the densely populated southern industrial belt. *Gwerin* and 'proletariat' were, ultimately, rival myths, incompatible yet in a sense inseparable since the one concept was implicated in the other, and between them they sustained a dialectic crucially constitutive of a modern Welsh identity. But while Edwards was deeply mistrustful of a new anglophone Wales, the threateningly colonial aspects of which he had shrewdly registered, as we have seen, in *Cartrefi Cymru*, he was never to be simply hostile to it. As early as 1895, he had founded and edited a short-lived English-language periodical, *Wales*, with the aim of reaching an accommodation with a growing anglophone society which he recognised, however anxiously and regretfully, as adding a challenging new dimension to the case of contemporary Welsh nationhood. His experiment proved misguided, being based on the naïve and perhaps patronising assumption that these 'new Welsh' could be readily persuaded to embrace the values and vision of the old Welsh-language Wales of Nonconformity. But this in no way impugns his good intentions, apparent again when in 1907 he was appointed Chief Inspector for Education in Wales. In that important role, he made it his business not merely dutifully to serve, but enthusiastically to promote the concept of Wales as a *bilingual* nation. Addressing delegates from across the globe at an Imperial Education Conference held at Whitehall on 2 May 1911, he emphasised that 'we [in Wales] do not regard the bilingualism of our country as a disadvantage in any way. We look upon it as an advantage.'[27] Accordingly, he explained, he had, since assuming office, ensured that a policy of bilingualism was implemented in every part of the country, a step that had involved devising three different teaching protocols, tailored to three different regional profiles. These profiles reflected the fact that Wales could now be divided linguistically into three distinct categories: a predominantly monoglot Welsh Wales; a predominantly bilingual Wales; and a predominantly monoglot English Wales. In its attempt to embrace bilingualism, he added, Wales enjoyed several advantages. 'In the first place, the language problem is not connected, and never has been connected, with either political or religious party questions. In the second place, the two languages of our country have each a literature well adapted for the teacher's purposes.' (*M*, 85)

By the end of O. M. Edwards's relatively short life he could, then, be said to have awoken from the prostrating nightmare he'd reported experiencing, in *Cartrefi Cymru*, during his night-time journey through the heavily anglicised and industrialised landscape of south Wales. He was now enthusiastically committed to the challenge of forming some kind of constructive nation-building relationship between the Welsh-speaking Nonconformist Wales that had produced him and the booming new industrial areas of the country where 'people of all nationalities . . . flocked' (*M*, 88). But sadly, it was an endeavour doomed to failure, for reasons that this chapter has already made apparent. The Romantic Liberal model of a historic Welsh nationhood centred on an 'indigenous' rural *gwerin*; the assumption that the Welsh language and its culture were a *sine qua non* of a national identity; the supposition that there was an indissoluble tie between nation and religion; these and other salient features of his 'patriotism' rendered it unfit for purpose in the new industrial Wales. But they were nevertheless essential for the work he had originally intended – the work of rehabilitating and reinstating a Welsh-language culture that had been subordinated, suppressed and marginalised for many centuries. In this latter context, the 'strategic essentialism' of his patriotic vision – the conceiving, in the interests of effective politico-cultural action, of Wales as a given, fixed entity – proved a great asset. But such a rigid model of inherited nationhood proved a liability once he attempted to extend that patriotic vision to include the new anglophone Wales of the south-eastern valleys and seaports.

There were also other important reasons for the 'failure' of Edwards's larger encompassing vision of a bicultural Wales. Given his background (first rural Bala, then privileged Balliol and Lincoln College, Oxford) he could have no real inward understanding of the radically new kind of social consciousness industrial experience had created in the strange new cosmopolitan world of the industrial proletariat. In particular, as one revealing sentence from his Imperial Conference address makes clear, he had no real conception of the huge pressures, both practical and ideological, at work in coalfield society that overwhelmingly favoured the spread of the English language and disadvantaged Welsh. In that address, he mentioned 'an attempt made [in one of our populous and newest towns] to drop all subjects regarded as ornamental, including the second language [i.e. Welsh].' (*M*, 88) The attempt, Edwards added, had been unsuccessful because the educational advantages of a bilingual education had been persuasively demonstrated. Maybe so, but the population in those new industrial towns was to prove obdurately impervious, in the longer run, to Edwards's enlightened sophisticated reasoning, and the dream of creating a modern bilingual Wales died with his death in 1920. And so the desolating vision of social annihilation, which the author of *Cartrefi Cymru* had experienced decades earlier as nightmare during his night-time train journey through south Wales, proved to have been darkly prophetic of the fate of his Wales after all.

4

Literature and the Political Nation

In 'Salutatory', the editorial that welcomed readers to the very first issue of *Young Wales*, the periodical pledged itself to emphasise 'the absolute necessity of establishing a union between the literary and the political forces of our country'.[1] True to the nineteenth-century belief in the centrality of culture to national identity, the Cymru Fydd movement attempted indefatigably to present an image of the 'Celt' (see chapter 5) as naturally sensitive to the finer products of the human spirit embodied, as influential Victorian sages from Thomas Carlyle to Matthew Arnold had powerfully argued, in great works of literature. And in showcasing the antiquity of Welsh literature, advocates constantly contrasted the refined taste of a nation of chapel-loving poets with that of its politically powerful neighbour. In England, a debased, commercialised popular culture supposedly pandered to the appetites of a population brutalised by industrialisation, addicted to gambling and horse racing, and living a low life punctuated by divorce and murder. Welsh connoisseurs of culture were also liable to view a literature primly free of any hint of sensational or licentious subject matter as a welcome barrier against the new, worryingly unruly working class nurtured in the raw, raucous coalfield society of the south of the country.

And just as politics sought validation from literary culture, so literature found itself attracted from time to time by political events and political personalities. A number of texts therefore appeared – including *Hunangofiant Dafydd Dafis*, as we have seen – that attempted to record important aspects of the dynamic, and frequently highly dramatic, political life of the day. These may be regarded as literature's distinctive contribution to the work of educating the public in an awareness of the emergence of Wales as a newly politicised nation. But these publications were as much narratives as chronicles, and as such may also be considered as textual attempts to weave 'the story of Wales' out of the coarse but robust and vividly colourful cloth of contemporary politics.

One such text appeared in 1904. Two years after T. Gwynn Jones's success with 'Ymadawiad Arthur' in the Chair competition at Bangor National Eisteddfod (to be considered at length in chapter 6), another long poem on the subject of Cymru Fydd very narrowly failed to win the Crown when the Eisteddfod was held in Rhyl. 'Tom Ellis', J. Dyfnallt Owen's elegy for the brilliant young hope of the national movement who had died five years earlier, numbered almost as many pages (thirty-nine) as years lived by its hero.[2] But the poem has weathered considerably less well than has the reputation of its subject. Its high Romantic rhetoric, heavily reinforced by Biblical cadences, decorated with elaborate tropes and peppered with poetical archaisms, makes for decidedly heavy reading. Nevertheless, it remains a compelling cultural document because it skilfully combines most of the seminal myths of Cymru Fydd to create a verbal icon equivalent in political resonance to the monument to T. E. Ellis fashioned by Goscombe John and unveiled in the centre of Bala by John Morley MP before a huge crowd that, along with Lloyd George, boasted no fewer than sixteen serving MPs.[3]

Since the ceremony took place on 7 October 1903, and was widely covered in the Welsh press – a photograph of the occasion forming the frontispiece of *Cymru* – it is not surprising that Dyfnallt (as he was popularly known) should have had the monument very much in mind when composing his *pryddest*. He would also have been aware of the 'medal struck in memory of Ellis, whose untimely death at the age of forty was perceived as a martyrdom in the national cause'.[4] And in a detailed analysis of the allegorical meaning of Goscombe John's monument, one contemporary commentator was moved to emphasise that it formed part of a trilogy of national remembrance, since Bala also boasted heroic sculptures of Thomas Charles (the famous architect of Welsh Methodism) and Lewis Edwards (founder of the great Welsh Presbyterian college for the training of ministers in the town). While Ellis himself was depicted wearing the robes of the Warden of the Guild of Graduates[5] of the University of Wales which he had helped found, the positioning of his monument made the religious antecedents of his nationalism very clear. As for the plinth, it featured his humble rural birth-cottage at Cynlas, the university colleges at Aberystwyth and Oxford (Balliol), and the Houses of Parliament, thus triumphantly allegorising the pilgrim's progress of this cultivated Welsh 'peasant' to power.

And there is one other powerful dimension to this public memorialising and national emblematising of Ellis in stone. A deeply cultivated man, Ellis had thirstily imbibed, while at Oxford, the exalted views of art promulgated by Arnold and Ruskin. Consequently, he was as committed to an ambitious programme to celebrate, enlarge and enrich the national culture of Wales as he was to achieving specific social, religious and political goals. His dreams included the establishing of Arts and Crafts schools across Wales and the founding of a Welsh school of architecture. A natural and totally unsnobbish aesthete, Ellis regretted that the nation had never embraced the visual arts as it evidently had music and literature. Sad evidence of this, he concluded in a lecture on 'The Memory of the Kymric Dead', was the relative paucity in Wales of sculptures and paintings commemorating the heroes of the nation's past.[6]

Such a cultural deficit was, he argued, all the more surprising given the natural affinity of the 'Celt' for the mysteries of the afterlife. To remedy this lack, he suggested a concerted effort should be made, 'with the development of national art' (*SA*, 7), to memorialise publicly those historical figures who had made an heroic contribution to four aspects of public life. These he identified as 'Cymru'n Un' (the unification of Wales), 'Cymru Lân' (the Moral Elevation of Wales), 'Celf Cymru' (the Culture of Wales) and 'Neges Cymru' (Wales's example to the world). His choices for commemoration under each of these headings were predictable enough, given his cultural background and political outlook. To the first category belonged Hywel Dda, Llywelyn Fawr (Llywelyn the Great), Llywelyn ein Llyw Olaf (Llywelyn the Last) and Owain Glyndŵr; the second included Thomas Charles, Daniel Rowland, Bishop William Morgan, John Penry and Griffith Jones Llanddowror; the third included Henry Vaughan, Dafydd ap Gwilym, Richard Wilson and John Gibson; his only nomination for the fourth category was Robert Owen, the father of the cooperative movement and harbinger of Socialism – an interesting choice given Ellis's impeccable Liberal credentials. True to his passionate belief in the untapped potential of the ordinary person (represented at its best for him, of course, in the 'gwerin', the naturally cultured rural 'yeomanry' of Wales), he alluded to Ruskin's core philosophy 'that we cannot have a noble nation or a perfect man, any more than a pyramid or a church, but by sacrifice of much contributed life' (*SA*, 8). Ellis's was therefore a consciously 'democratic' reading of public monuments. The individuals commemorated were to be regarded not so much as isolated geniuses but as representative of the 'life' of a whole community that had 'contributed' to the making of their greatness.

Goscombe John's sculpture may be understood as having been conceived and executed very much in this spirit. It constitutes a memorial not only to Ellis and the 'gwerin' that had produced him, but also to Ellis's dream of a free Wales as proudly aware of its cultural achievements as of its progress in religion, education, politics and science. If it is regarded as a public avowal of the central importance of art to national life, the sculpture is as much about itself as it is about its subject, and as such a fitting tribute to Ellis's vision. A similar claim can be made for Dyfnallt's poem, since T. E. Ellis had been no less deeply appreciative of the national importance of poetry than of the importance of the many other art forms he championed. This throws new light on one of the aspects of the *pryddest* modern readers are likely to find most indigestible: its ostentatious display of its author's familiarity with culture, ranging from the Mabinogion to Botticelli's *Birth of Venus* and Da Vinci's *Mona Lisa*. Implicated in this practice can now be detected Dyfnallt's homage to his hero's exemplary cosmopolitan tastes (a death in Cannes seemed modest for one who had travelled as far afield as Egypt and South Africa). The *pryddest* implicitly acknowledges Ellis's catholic, multifaceted conception of Welsh culture, firmly underpinned by his respect for learning as the *sine qua non* of a mature, modern, national life.

This passion found its most complete and lasting expression in the part Ellis played in the development, during the last decades of the nineteenth century, of a sophisticated system of education for Wales, stretching from primary schools through the intermediate sector to colleges and national university. But even more intimately personal in character was Ellis's devotion to the scholarly work of salvaging, conserving and publishing what had miraculously survived of the historical, legal and literary records of the Welsh past.

In a notable address (17 October 1896) to the Guild of Graduates of the University of Wales, Ellis emphasised that it was the sacred responsibility of the university and its scholars 'to bring something like order into the public presentation, so to speak, of the literature and records of Wales' (*SA*, 147). Recalling the pitiful history of Wales in respect of preserving such invaluable 'remains', he regrets that even such as have not been lost 'are still, in a sense, buried,' hidden from public view and therefore not circulating in the bloodstream of the national life. He then reflects, at intelligent length, on the precarious fate of Welsh books, concluding that their survival could be guaranteed only by some national library of the future. In the meantime, he advocates the establishing of 'a committee of literature and a committee of records' (*SA*, 153). The latter might oversee work in fields ranging from social history to law, while yet another initiative might concern itself with recording 'fauna and flora, Welsh geology and palaeontology' (*SA*, 161). He next charges the putative literature committee with the immediate and express responsibility of managing an ambitious programme of publishing 'in various forms some of the finer parts of the literature of Wales' (*SA*, 153). In particular, the 'national poetry' of Wales demands urgent attention as, for Ellis, it constitutes the chief glory of a literary heritage to the study of which he was particularly devoted.

Indeed, his comments in this latter connection, made just three years before his untimely death, are as retrospectively poignant as they are fervent. In addition to the Herculean political labours of his last and declining years, Ellis struggled against increasing ill health to complete the first volume of a pioneering scholarly edition of the works of Morgan Llwyd, the seventeenth-century Puritan mystic whom Ellis undoubtedly regarded as one of the most important precursors of 'the Nonconformist nation' of which he himself was a proud product and representative. Llwyd was piously Puritan, but studiously eclectic and non-sectarian. He came from staunch 'yeoman' background in rural Gwynedd, but was much-travelled and had intimate experience of affairs at Westminster. A man of action, unafraid to participate in the violent, turbulent political life of Cromwell's New Model Army and subsequent Commonwealth, he was nevertheless naturally inclined to a quietist life of contemplation. Although a radical spiritual individualist, he was desperately concerned for the soul of his entire nation. In all these respects, he offered Ellis a mirror to the dualities of his own complex and in some ways conflicted nature. In addition to being a prominent act of cultural pietas, his editing of Morgan Llwyd's devotional masterpieces, at the Guild's express instigation, was also a public claim to belong to the great spinal tradition of Welsh spiritual, social and political radicalism which, for Ellis, ran directly from Morgan Llwyd through the two towering nineteenth-century figures with strong Bala connections to whom his scholarly edition was dedicated: Lewis Edwards, a theologian, social polemicist, essayist and magisterial educator of Presbyterian clergy at the college he founded in Bala, had been one of the first modern Nonconformists to recognise Llwyd's significance; Michael D. Jones was a Congregationalist divine (and Ellis's earliest mentor) whose renowned patriotism had, as noted in chapter 3, found most famous expression in attempts to establish Welsh settlements first in the USA and then in Patagonia, which would enable him to realise his dream of autonomy for the Welsh people. These were the tutelary spirits of an authoritative edition that, like Dyfnallt's *pryddest*, stands as a memorial to Ellis's commitment to the fusion of culture and politics in the national cause. His edition of *Gweithiau Morgan Llwyd* was, therefore, not only the fruit of a great labour of both scholarly and patriotic love, but also a symbolic act of profound cultural and political resonance.

Among the many tributes to Ellis on the occasion of his death,[7] there were several poems, implicitly recognising him as a man of culture who had also always staunchly been a champion of culture. In 'A Tribute of the Muse to T. E. Ellis', W. W. Williams drew on the revered, classical tradition of the pastoral elegy to commemorate the politician, in the process deliberately foregrounding the early rural origins to whose values, so all his memorialists emphasised, he had remained faithful to the end:

> His were melodic strains as of the nightingale
> That poured its song at night, unseen in shaded vale,
> As if too deeply it had drunk of love.[8]

Sir Lewis Morris, Wales's own unofficial Poet Laureate, likewise created a reverential verse effigy of Ellis as a 'Child of the People', who had been familiar alike with 'the bardic measures' and 'the Tiller's lot'. And he, too, entombed Ellis textually in the landscape of his native locality:

> Here as the silent mountains stand around
> Salem, the blest,
> Comes no rude whisper of contentious sound
> To break his rest.[9]

Ellis is thus solicitously repatriated in death.

His passing continued to be commemorated in Welsh literature for many years after the event. Commenting on the funeral more than five years later, Iolo Caernarvon perpetuated the pastoralising tradition by quoting from an elegy singling out for praise Ellis's fidelity to his rural Nonconformist roots: 'Cedwaist dy grefydd, a symledd y mynydd' ('You retained your religion and the simplicity of the mountain').[10] But he was also moved to recall a passage from an ancient chronicle: 'Y dydd hwn y syrthiodd pen a tharian ein gwlad: y dydd hwn y diflannodd gobaith ac addfwynder holl genedl y Britaniaid.' ('This day fell the head and shield of our country; this day disappeared the hope and mildness of all the nation of the British.') Indeed, several of the Welsh obituarists instinctively sought to set Ellis's death in an ancient, legendary context, as was the case with the editor of *Young Wales*, who envisaged him as a latter-day Arthur, the lost leader who would one day return to liberate his people. 'May we have that same deep presentiment and that keen expectancy,' he wrote, 'which the old Welsh had that the nation's leader is not lost to us, but will come again to take his destined place at the head of the forces that strive for the true emancipation and freedom of Wales.'[11]

In 1902, W. Pari Huws published 'Dygwyl wylo am Tom Ellis' ('A Day of weeping for Tom Ellis'), a poem ingeniously fusing the politician's convalescent visits to Egypt (although he actually died in Cannes) with the Old Testament story of the Israelites' Egyptian bondage:

Yn yr Aifft mae bedd pob arwr;
Bedd yr Aifft yw cred gwladgarwr;
Marw yno'm mrwydr rhyddid
Yw ei eni ef i fywyd
Rhai fu'n gaethion, a'i orseddu
Yn eu calon i deyrnasu.

[In Egypt is the tomb of every hero;/ An Egyptian tomb is the patriot's craving;/ To die there in freedom's struggle/ Is to be reborn/ In the enslaved, to be enthroned/ There in their hearts.]

Huws thus deftly relocates Ellis in the religious and biblical culture from which he had originated, and his paralleling of modern and biblical Egypt allows him to turn Ellis into a latter-day Moses/Joseph, whose death has paved the way for his nation's entry into the Promised Land of freedom:

Cludo'i Joseph idd ei Chanaan
Mae pob cenedl wrth fynd allan
O gaethiwed; cludo'i bywyd
Ydyw hynny, mynd â'r ysbryd
A'i gwrolodd yn ei dagrau,
A'i gwaredodd o'i chadwynau;
Gwobr marw'r Aifft yw Canaan –
Byw yng nghalon cenedl gyfan.

[Carrying its Joseph to its Canaan/ Is the act of every nation as it escapes/ Enslavement; it is to carry with it its own life,/ To take with it the spirit/ That heartened it in its tears,/ And that freed it from its chains;/ The reward for death in Egypt is entry into Canaan –/ Life eternal in the heart of a whole nation.][12]

The reference is to the Israelites' act of carrying Joseph's bones with them, in the Exodus under Moses' leadership, for eventual 'repatriation' in Canaan. For years before his death, Ellis had been likened by Cymru Fydd supporters to a Welsh Joseph or Moses. In J. Hugh Edwards's 1896 portrait of him, he had been compared to 'that Hebrew patriot – that first pioneer of nationalism – who, learned in the wisdom of the Egyptians and with all the avenues to Egyptian statesmanship opening up before him, decided to leave the splendours of Memphin [*sic*], choosing rather to dedicate himself to the task of realising his early dream of the emancipation of his race.'[13]

Dyfnallt's poem was, then, a contribution to an already well established ritual of Biblical troping and literary commemoration. It begins by imagining the dawn of a new age for Wales, characterised by the coming of a bride redolent of the sensuous allure of 'y rhamant a'r mabinogion' (ancient romance and the Mabinogion) (*TE*, 10). Aware that Ellis's native Bala had itself once been a noted region of romance ('[B]ro y traddodiadau hen a chartref hud yr oesau gynt': 'the haunt of old traditions and the home of the magic of past ages' [*TE*, 12]), Dyfnallt is able to suggest that although an innocent child of Nature (raised among the simple shepherds of the hills), his hero had also been tutored early in traditional lore: 'Nid yw Plentyn Rhamant sydd yn Blentyn Natur yn cael cam' (no Child of Romance who is a Child of Nature is ever wronged) (*TE*, 11). His poem thus tries to reconcile at the outset two potentially irreconcilable components of the Cymru Fydd ideology – its valorisation of the simple, ordinary rural 'gwerinwr' (peasant or yeoman) and its privileging of the representatives of the 'new learning' (the cosmopolitan college-educated scholars, poets and intellectuals who were reconnecting Wales with its ancient past). In this poem's version of a miraculous birth (and Dyfnallt consciously mythologises his narrative from the start by employing classical allusions), Ellis is born a 'natural scholar', and thus assumes from the cradle the emblematic role of the cultivated 'gwerinwr', a seemingly oxymoronic figure of pivotal importance, as we have already seen in the case of O. M. Edwards, to the cultural politics of Cymru Fydd.

And by what is made to seem like another divinely ordained coincidence, T. E. Ellis was born in 1859, the year of the Great Revival in Wales. Dyfnallt is thus able to adapt the theology of 'the elect' to suggest his subject is the chosen heir of the great Nonconformist spiritual tradition of Wales, as of course Cymru Fydd also claimed to be. It is a natural step from there for the poem to connect Ellis with a key fourth component of the movement's ideology, its image of itself as the champion of justice for the tenant farmers of Wales and freedom from their oppressive landlords.[14]

Having early mobilised some of the conventions both of Classical and of pastoral elegy, Dyfnallt continues to 'build' his monumental *pryddest* by adding further politically emblematic devices to its textual plinth. He provides each of the scenes of which his *pryddest* is composed with both a summary and a title: 'The Dawn of Romance', 'With the Shepherds', 'Son of the Gwerin', 'The dream of the Revivalists', 'The Bridegroom of Merioneth', 'The Beloved of the Nation', 'The Apostle of Welsh Nationalism', and 'The Mourning of Wales'. This resembles a list of visual tableaux epitomising the images of itself that Cymru Fydd preferred to project. It all tends to the conclusion that the people of Wales are heard 'arguing its right to be hereafter / A *nation* among the British family' ('yn dadleu iddi ei hawl / Yn *genedl* mwy fel eraill o deulu Prydain') (*TE*, 17). As for Ellis himself, the poem depicts him as a learned poet-politician, the dreams of nineteenth-century Nonconformity now having found secular fulfilment in a religion of national culture:

> Breuddwyd yr athraw chwery'n niwl ei obeithion,
> Asbri y llenor ymnydda'n ei galon weithion;
> Gweddia ar dduwies Llên am awen ac yni
> I bortreadu ei wlad o flaen ei oes,

A chymhell ei genedl hoff wrth gario'i chroes,
I gofio'i Duw a'i neges wrth ado'i chyni. (*TE*, 19)

[The dreams of the teacher/professor play in the mist of his dreams,/ The enthusiasm of the writer entwines in his heart now;/ He prays to the goddess of Literature for inspiration and energy/ to portray his country to his age,/ And he urges his dear nation as he carries her cross,/ To remember God and His message as she leaves her travails behind her.]

This use of the prophetic poet-figure to represent a visionary kind of political as well as cultural nationalism is testimony to the strong religio-cultural provenance of the Cymru Fydd movement and it recurs in the memorial lyric to T. E. Ellis published by Eifion Wyn immediately following his death. 'Doesn't his spirit continue to dwell with us in this country,' the poem enquires rhetorically, 'continuing to write his great poetry [?]' (Onid yw ei ysbryd trwyddol/ Gyda ni yn awr,/ yn y wlad yn ysgrifennu/ ei farddoniaeth fawr [?]).[15] The 'poetry' mentioned here is figurative rather than actual, of course, referring as it does to Ellis's eloquent speeches and addresses outlining his vision for Wales and to the central place consistently afforded to literature in that vision.

Dyfnallt depicts Ellis as a reluctant politician, a writer manqué who found it difficult to resist the temptation to retire to a scholar's cell. He had recognised that a campaign for national freedom could succeed only with the support of writers ('rhaid i Dadeni a Llenyddiaeth,/ Asbri rhyddid a'i barabl persain, clir,/ i gerdded law yn llaw tua'r hyfryd dir') (*TE*, 20). But, following the example set by Young Ireland and other national liberation movements across Europe, he had believed in prioritizing political over artistic activity. Even Ellis's marriage is interpreted as prelude to the national duty of producing future activists, and thus as a contribution towards national salvation: 'Geilw Meirion ei chwiorydd i briodi plant y tir' (Merioneth calls on her sisters to wed the children of the soil) (*TE*, 23). But Dyfnallt particularly emphasises the high value Ellis had put on the cultivating of the visual arts in Wales and the importance he had attached to the creation of national memorials: '"Gyda'r Dadeni grymus,"' declares his Ellis, '"y daw argoelion/ Am Gymru yn deffro i swyn y Celfau Cain."' (With the powerful national reawakening/ Come signs of Wales awakening to the charm of the Fine Arts) (*TE*, 27). The dream is of descendants worthy of Richard Wilson, John Gibson, Milo Gruffydd, Burne-Jones (*sic*) and William Morris (*sic*), artists able to image the 'new' nation to itself and to the world. One important feature of Dyfnallt's yearning for such 'uplifting' products is his fear, voiced in the poem, that the new industrial Wales will suck people away from the country and into the ugly towns, where their spirits will be depressed, their minds stunted like their bodies, and the glorious potential of Wales lost for ever from their sight. As was pointed out in the previous chapter, a crucial aspect of Cymru Fydd that it would be easy, but fatal, to overlook is its reactionary character – it was as much an anxious response to the new, industrialised and rapidly anglicising Wales of the south as it was a confident revival, renewal and active politicisation of national life by a professionalised Welsh middle class.

As Dyfnallt's poem proceeds, its discourse associates Ellis ever more closely and intensely with religious and, indeed, Messianic events. As its hero's death approaches, the implications of martyrdom grow stronger. The text first climaxes with a tribute to Goscombe John's monument, erected on the shores of Llyn Tegid, seen as a kind of resurrection of its subject willed by a grieving people. It is also imaged as an altar raised in spontaneous thanksgiving for Ellis's life (*TE*, 32). This first apotheosis of him is immediately followed by a second, crediting Ellis with having awakened the Arthur of his nation from its slumbers. Modern Wales has thus been restored to its ancient rightful place among the nations of Europe, a place first secured when the Arthurian Romances conquered the continent and a Welsh knight was sent travelling to the furthest ends of the earth in search of the Holy Grail (*TE*, 33). Ellis the cosmopolitan Europhile is treated as representative of a new Wales determined once again to break out of the confines of its hills and language in order to reconnect itself with the European mainstream by proudly embracing its Celtic identity. At this point, Dyfnallt openly embraces that intensely pan-Celtic philosophy (see chapter 5) by which he was to continue to be animated for the rest of his life, as he envisages Wales making common cause in the name of freedom with Ireland, Scotland, the Isle of Man and Cornwall (*TE*, 35).

The poem ends with Dyfnallt pledging his eternal fealty to the memory of T. E. Ellis. Reverting to the modes of pastoral elegy with which he opened his deliberately 'internationalised' *pryddest*, he performs the classical commemorative ritual of laying flowers on the grave of the departed, in the process deliberately fusing the Christian with the pagan. And, following the arc traditional to elegy, he concludes by extracting hope from grief and loss and by treating the departed as progenitor of a better future:

> Daw yntau'n ôl yn llanw cry'r amseroedd
> Fel daw y nawfed ton i fin y tir,
> A llais ei ysbryd egyr lwybr clir
> O flaen ei wlad yn anwel y pellderoedd,
> Tra cerdda'i genedl law yn llaw â'r gwir. (*TE*, 39)

[He will return on the strong tide of time/ like the ninth wave crashing ashore,/ and the voice of his spirit will open a clear pathway/ for his nation through the obscurity of distances,/ while his people walk hand and hand with truth.]

As can therefore be seen, Dyfnallt's *pryddest*, whatever its literary credentials, is an elaborate work of cultural and political artifice. Like every such commemorative exercise it presupposes a consensus of values, a 'shared language', and a collective vision. But in so strenuously striving to endorse, reinforce and augment such an ideology, it tacitly admits its questionable solidity and durability – because the assumed consensus was, of course, much more apparent than real. Cymru Fydd's obsessive rallying cry, 'Cymru'n Un' (Wales as One: echoed in Dyfnallt's poem), may have been reasonably credibly grounded in such acts of collective will as the anti-landlord and anti-tithe movements of the later part of the nineteenth century, but it flew directly in the face of the reality of a Wales starkly and seemingly irreconcilably divided between the heavily industrialised, rapidly anglicising regions of the politically progressive south, apparently devoid of 'culture', and the much more conservative, overwhelmingly Welsh-speaking and largely rural communities of the north and west where, in the face of multiplying social pressures, a traditional culture was, as Dyfnallt's elegy to T. E. Ellis clearly demonstrates, anxiously fetishised.

On closer inspection, any claim to Welsh unity such as that made in Dyfnallt's poem proves to have been inconsistent even with the realities of the rural, Welsh-speaking Wales of the time, because, as becomes abundantly clear from the columns and editorials of the various periodicals sponsored by Cymru Fydd, that Wales was deeply divided by religious sectarianism and by the parochialism that was the legacy of the many centuries during which, in the absence of any unifying institutions of Law, Politics, Education and the like, any concept of Wales had in the minds of its ordinary people dwindled to little more than an attachment to their immediate localities, their beloved 'bro'. The challenge consciously faced by Cymru Fydd was therefore very similar to that faced by Mazzini when, following re-unification, he famously commented that having created Italy he now had to create Italians.[16] Leaders of the movement therefore dedicated themselves to the fundamentally educative task of training their countrymen to take a unified view of Welsh history and geography. And in its very format, the omnibus Victorian periodical favoured by Cymru Fydd not only deliberately promoted such national catholicity of outlook but, thanks to its juxtaposition of widely assorted topics from an extensive range of sources, assumed the textual image of a unifying web of interconnections.

* * *

'I godi'r hen wlad yn ei hôl': the motto O. M. Edwards chose for his groundbreaking periodical *Cymru* entered popular discourse. It also divided opinion. The problem lay with its interpretation. Some understood it to express a wish to raise the old country back onto her feet, and loudly protested that princely modern Wales could walk no taller among all the territories of the Empire. Irritated, Edwards replied that its intended meaning was that all that was rich and valuable in the old Wales needed to be restored to the memory of the new Wales. The Welsh past should be revivified so that it could both enable admiring measurement of the progress that had been made and also help fashion the Welsh present and future.[17]

The possible disconnect between past and present was a chronic cause for concern for all those many supporters of Cymru Fydd whose progressive politics was paradoxically rooted in a cultural conservatism. An interesting long poem, 'Ifor Wyn o'r Hafod Elwy', for instance, published in the 1895 issue of *Cymru*, concluded its exploration of the matter with an anxious injunction to its readers: 'A chofiwch hyn bob dydd,/ Fod hanes annwyl Cymru fu,/ Yn rhan o Gymru sydd.' ('And remember this every day; / that the beloved history of the Wales of the past/ is part of the Wales of the present.')[18] The same perceived crisis was given effective fictional expression in the work of Gwyneth Vaughan (Annie Harriet Hughes). As noted in chapter 2, Vaughan was an influential figure in the Welsh Union of Women's Liberal

Associations (WUWLA), vigorously campaigning alongside leaders such as Norah Philipps to advance the cause of female suffrage and social opportunity. In these respects, she was a thoroughly modern reformer; yet, as her talented creative work indicates, her socio-cultural vision inclined towards the nostalgically conservative in character, and manifested mistrust of the new social structures evolving in the industrial south.[19] Her outlook remained significantly shaped by her upbringing in a rural, Welsh-language society that had fallen victim to colonising English power. She rooted her Cymru Fydd politics in the hope that the gentry class that had once provided Wales with its cultural and political leadership, but had become progressively anglicised and alienated since the Act of Union, might be persuaded (or educated) into recognising once more its duty of national leadership. This, conservative, aspect of her otherwise progressive political ideology is inscribed in the very structure of her two interesting Welsh-language novels, *O Gorlannau y Defaid* (From the Pens of the Sheep, 1905) and *Plant y Gorthrwm* (The Children of Oppression, 1908).[20]

Both are historical novels, the first an imaginative revisiting of the Great Religious Revival of 1859. As such, it is a conscious tribute to the spectacular 1904–5 Revival that was under way at the time of writing, and also interesting confirmatory evidence that (as will be further explored in chapter 7) one element in the complex nexus of social, cultural and religious causes of that latter Revival was deep anxiety at the current state of national life, in the wake of the sweeping and radical character of recent social change. In the Preface to *O Gorlannau y Defaid*, Vaughan stresses the 'purity' of the life represented in her fiction and her intention to preserve some of the 'vanishing landmarks' of a morally noble rural chapel society. For all its idealisations and its sentimentality, the novel has its enduring nostalgic charms, its power residing principally in the wonderfully rich, idiomatic Welsh used to convey the impression of an idyllically 'innocent' world, at the centre of which is a religious belief that is in many ways warm, fulfilling and human as well as morally demanding.

It centres on the family life of the Fychans (Vaughans) in their prosperous farmhouse 'Y Foty', invoked in terms that make of it a visual emblem of the 'traditional' values Vaughan was so concerned to elegise. The master is Robert Fychan, a much-loved, forgiving, and highly respected elder in the Calvinistic Methodist Church; and the mistress is Luned Fychan, beautiful, stately, poised, motherly, gently pious, who comes from the stock of an ancient family of 'uchelwyr'

(Welsh gentry). The conservative aspect of Gwyneth Vaughan's social philosophy thus embodied in Luned is placed in tension with the progressive aspects of that philosophy, partly represented by Luned's daughter Angharad, whose character and story allow the author to air her campaigning reformist views on a number of contemporary issues – most notably the education of women. Angharad is allowed eventually to strike out for France and Germany, to acquire an intellectual education suited to her exceptionally lively questioning mind, before she returns to become a loving, dutiful wife. As for Vaughan's yearnings for the return of the genuinely indigenous *uchelwyr* class (gentry), they find expression through a central structural contrast between the anglicised landowner Sir William (who speaks a comical Welsh-English hybrid) and the young Welsh gentleman Dewi, who is conveniently bequeathed a fine old 'uchelwyr' house that used to belong to his father before his close English friend tricked him out of it. This house, implicitly contrasted with that of the upstart Sir William (whose aristocratic pedigree in Wales extends back a mere two centuries), is the visual embodiment of the traditional, 'Celtic' values Vaughan so admired.

Her second novel, *Plant y Gorthrwm*, is, in terms of character, setting, structure and ideological agenda, strikingly similar to her first. This time, the action is set in 1868, the famous revolutionary year when many Welsh tenants, recently enfranchised, cast their votes not for their Tory landlords but for Liberal candidates promising radical land reform, and were then evicted from their farms for their impudent temerity. As Vaughan explained in her preface, her work was intended to draw the attention of young readers to an important episode in Welsh history that was in great danger of disappearing from popular memory. The novel centres on the Vaughan family, tenant-farmers at Hafod Olau, who are fortunate in having as champion Sir Tudur Llwyd, a warm-hearted, open-souled representative of the ancient 'uchelwyr' class, who steps in with assistance when they are 'turned out' by their English absentee landowner. Llwyd is an affectionately comic character, whose bastardised English-Welsh signifies the way even the best of the *uchelwyr* have come to be significantly anglicised. His support takes the practical form of marriage to Rhianon Vaughan, who is forty years his junior. In context, this union symbolises the peaceful take-over of power by the 'gwerin' class (of ordinary people) that was the mainstay of Welsh Liberal ideology. It also suggests that the inherent gentility of the character of the 'gwerin' made that class the natural, legitimate heir of the old Welsh *uchelwyr*. The marriage also signifies the emergence of woman as a new social and political power, since Rhianon (now Lady Llwyd) is much the stronger partner, adored by her awe-struck husband.

Yet, as in *O Gorlannau y Defaid*, Vaughan is careful in *Plant y Gorthrwm* to imply that the emergence of this new woman (also explored in the novel through the case of the intellectually gifted young girl Dyddgu, who rebelliously crops her hair like a boy [169ff] and devours books on the rights of women) is perfectly compatible with (and is indeed essential to) the maintenance of home, family and nation much in the style contemporaneously advocated by Vaughan's associate, Mallt Williams. Sir Tudur's death leaves Rhianon financially independent and entirely her own mistress, but she exercises her new-found liberty only to marry her long-time love Francis Glyn. Their case contrasts with that of their friend Nisien Wyn. He is the son of the kindly local estate manager who is dismissed when Plas Dolau is acquired by an absentee family of landowners who appoint a tight-fisted steward in his place to squeeze their tenants financially. This 'grasping screw' of an agent is the black villain of the novel responsible for the extensive 'turning out' of tenants after he fails to ensure electoral victory for his boss in 1868.

* * *

In this period, Welsh Liberalism had a grip on literature every bit as firm as it had on Welsh politics. Yet dissenting authorial voices were occasionally to be heard, particularly in connection with the bitterly divisive issue of Welsh disestablishment. 'I will fight them with their own weapons,' proclaims Jack Anwyl, a fierce young opponent of Welsh Radical politics in Daisy Hugh Pryce's *The Ethics of Evan Wynne*.[21] Pryce's novel provides an example of that strategy being deployed in the area of fiction. As for her political allegiances, they are made immediately clear in the dedication of the book 'to the memory of Hugh Lewis Pryce, a well-known and well-beloved Anglesey rector'. In his foreword, written as from the Episcopal palace at Abergwili, the Bishop of St Davids commends the novel for highlighting 'the injury that would be inflicted upon social life in Wales were the Government to be allowed to pass into law, behind the backs of the people, its mean little Bill for secularising the ancient religious endowments of Wales'.

Pryce's work could usefully be regarded as a wrenching adaptation of a favourite Victorian genre – that of the ecclesiastical novel pioneered and popularised, of course, by Trollope – to the greatly aggravated social situation faced by the Anglican Church in Wales at the beginning of the twentieth century. The serious threat presented to the prestige, power and status of the Church by the Welsh Dissenters' political campaign for Disestablishment and disendowment meant that no longer could Anglicanism be addressed in the temperate tones of Trollope's genial fiction, with its tolerant ironies and indulgent satire. The anxieties of the established Church's protectors in Wales had, by the end of the nineteenth century, increased to the verge of hysteria, and this is faithfully reflected in the shrillness of Pryce's novel.

The work is likely to be of interest today only as a social document representative of its time, intriguing for the way it mobilises some of the stereotypical *topoi* of fiction for conservative social and political purposes. One instance would be the use to which the convention of the rural idyll is put. The 'out-of-the world parish of Hendremynach', (*EW*, 57) sunk somnolently deep in the countryside not far from the coast, is the home of the benign 'white-haired Archdeacon' (*EW*, 22) Richard Anwyl, who 'preached a good sermon, told a good story, and kept a hospitable table; and to him, as to a father and protector, his people came to have their wills made, their quarrels, their griefs told, their wants supplied.' (*EW*, 22) Into this tranquil scene intrudes the ambitious and scheming young Radical Dissenting politician Evan Wynne, who wins the affections of Enid, Archdeacon Anwyl's beloved daughter. A vehement champion of Disestablishment, the social wrecker Wynne is condemned from the outset by his lack of humble empathy with the beautiful scenery, which to him 'was but an appropriate setting to his own success. He gloried in the wonderful world which was the theatre of his life's drama' (*EW*, 51). He is repeatedly represented as impatient with the settled character of rural existence, fretful even when summer is at its seductive, languorous zenith: 'Day after day the sun shone gloriously from a sky of cloudless blue, and the flowery moorlands along the rocky coast glowed like a landscape painted in colours of gold and opal.' (*EW*, 131) The logic of this kind of conventional symbolism dictates, of course, that 'the weather, which had been fine for so long' must break for the wedding between Evan and Enid, so that they are married 'on a day of driving wind and rain.' (*EW*, 151)

As might be expected of a novel designed to celebrate traditional social hierarchy centred on the Established Church, there is a village chorus of assorted grateful dependants loud in their praise of the traditional order. Particularly vocal are Will Parry, 'the Rectory gardener and odd-job man' (*EW*, 57), and William Jones, the coachman (*EW*, 58). Both are staunch supporters of the familiar authority of the Church and utterly dismissive of an upstart from their own ranks such as Evan Wynne, familiar to them since he was a local urchin. As the novel draws to its conclusion, it is Parry and Jones who become the mouthpiece of the author's warnings to the lower classes of the dangers of supporting disestablishment and disendowment. Together, they muse on the catastrophe that would befall the likes of them were the Church to be robbed of its accumulated wealth. '"There will be no one to pay you and me better wages than other men get in the parish,"' remarks William Jones: '"there will be no one to bring wine and jellies to us when we are ill, and pray with us when we are dying. No one to take singing-meetings, and concerts, and Sunday-school treats – what shall we do then?"' (*EW*, 274) And his partner, Will Parry, is not slow to voice his own similar misgivings:

> 'They say that *perhaps* they will put some of the money to help in the Old Age Pensions . . . but they will use up a good deal to pay the ones that have the job of dividing it, so I do not believe there would be enough left to make any worth of difference to the age when it is to be got now. I do not put much faith in *that*.' (*EW*, 275)

Between them, these two old fogeys, faithful retainers intent on upholding a feudal order, give voice to the central political argument of the novel: the ordinary working people of Wales are loyal adherents not of Radical Nonconformity but of the established Church, and are resentful of the political machinations of malcontents who, having newly acquired middle class status, are ambitiously intent on overthrowing the natural order of things.

This unlikely assessment of the temper of the times, a figment of the anxious imagination of social conservatives such as Pryce, is given central structural expression in her novel by means of the plot. The Oxford-educated Jack Anwyl, the saintly Archdeacon's son and brother to Enid, is intent from the outset on undermining the credentials of the Nonconformists' radical politics by infiltrating their power base – the important slate-quarrying districts of north Wales where a new, 'proletarian' spirit had been created under industrial conditions. So he sets out to improve his rudimentary Welsh, and to disguise himself as an ordinary working man, so that he can work alongside them and thus acquaint himself intimately with their political outlook. Nothing could better illustrate the insuperable cultural distance in this period between the established Church and the Welsh people – the very distance that the novel is at such pains to deny – than Pryce's earnest supposition that such a ruse could possibly work. Her ideological fantasy is further compounded when Jack, in character as 'Jack Morgan', a common working man whose 'hands are hardened with splitting slate in a Welsh quarry' (*EW*, 219), confounds a public meeting called by radicals in London by eloquently exposing, in great detail, the many falsehoods in the Disestablishment case.

One sure index of the nature of the relationship between the Church and mainstream Welsh society at this time was the Anglican attitude towards the Welsh language. Indeed, one of the many grievances of the reformers was that the alien character of the Church was manifest in its reluctance to adopt, either in its services or in its parochial and pastoral duties, the very language of the people whom it purported to serve. The fundamental lack of comprehension by Anglicans of what was at issue is unconsciously revealed by Jack even as, ironically, he attempts to defend his Church against the charge of its being an anglicised colonial institution:

> 'There are more Welsh services in Wales per head for the Welsh people than there are English services for the English people who live there, and, in the cathedrals of Bangor and St Davids, parochial Welsh services are held every Sunday. The reason why they are not given in the others is that they are not wanted. In many parts of Wales – especially in South Wales – there is a population that speaks chiefly English. English is understood everywhere except in a few very remote parts, and it is not at all the same thing as French in England.' (*EW*, 221)

Throughout Pryce's novel, Welsh is condescendingly treated as a declining local patois, so complicated in its primitive structure that learning it as an adult is deemed a near impossibility (*EW*, 75). The prodigiousness of young Jack is accordingly attested to by his remarkable ability to master the language. Welsh is supposed to be in use only among the uneducated and unsophisticated peasantry in 'remote parts', and the faint traces of the aboriginal tongue left on spoken English, in the form of the Welsh accent, are treated throughout the book as a sad badge of social inferiority, and a reliable index of lack of breeding. Attitudes such as these serve only to confirm rather than refute the accusation of Welsh Nonconformity and its politicians that the established Church had long since alienated the affections of the Welsh by aligning itself with a foreign class and a foreign order. But, in her blind allegiance to Anglicanism, Pryce persists in portraying its downfall as due not to its addiction to power and privilege and its snobbish anglocentricity, but entirely to the machinations of unscrupulous Nonconformist politicians as opportunistic and scheming as those she describes spending an evening caballing over dinner at the London home of Evan Wynne and his scandalised young wife, Enid. They are motivated not by principle but by greed, avidly aware that 'The Disestablishment and Disendowment of the Welsh Church is a programme with money in it' (*EW*, 166–7). Nor are they content with such a programme, as they eye further, even more threateningly extreme, goals: 'There's the land; that'll come next – and then the millionaires.' (*EW*, 167) Pryce nervously had in mind, of course, Lloyd George's unbridled appetite for radical social reform, and his is the ghost that restlessly haunts her entire novel.

One of the classic advantages of the flexible romance genre, to which *The Ethics of Evan Wynne* belongs, is that the narrative of courtship and of marriage around which such a work is organised can be used to negotiate and symbolically resolve any social conflicts and tensions that the novelist may care to address. Pryce's novel takes full advantage of this. Beginning by exploring, through the courtship of Evan and Enid, the opposed milieux and philosophies of pro- and anti-Disestablishment advocates, it continues by showing how the fierce antagonisms between their rival beliefs result in marital catastrophe, and concludes by resolving both domestic and social crisis through effecting a reconciliation between a repentant and reformed Evan, broken by his wife's temporary desertion, and a triumphant Enid who rejoices that her husband has at last seen the light. In the novel's final sentence, Evan genially reflects on how

> The whirligig of time brings round queer revenges sometimes, and I suppose that with you [Enid] as his mother, it is not at all impossible that a son of mine may turn out to a bigoted Tory and a pillar of the Church! (*EW*, 317)

It is made clear that his wife's victory, as protector of the Established church, has been in significant part due to her successfully finding her voice as a highly forceful, eloquent and irresistible public advocate of the righteous cause to which she is entirely devoted. Thus Pryce conclusively resolves the running argument throughout her novel (see *EW*, 133) over whether or not women should be allowed to participate actively and visibly in politics. Her self-belief greatly strengthened by her conspicuous success as an activist, Enid is transformed by the end of *The Ethics of Evan Wynne* – from a dutiful wife primarily devoted to promoting her husband's well-being, into the psychologically stronger figure in their partnership:

> Enid loved him once more – not quite as she had done before, perhaps, but none the less deeply and truly. In her feeling for him now, there was something of a maternal element – a pitying and protecting love strangely intermingled with appreciation and pride. Evan trusted to it as to an enduring and unfailing safeguard, and he knew it would be to him a sheet-anchor through life. (*EW*, 316–17)

There is, however, no suggestion that Enid will continue to play a prominent part in the political life of the day. Rather, in keeping with the author's conservative social philosophy, she is clearly destined to resume domestic life and to dedicate all her new-found strength to maintaining her husband, mothering her child, and protecting her marriage.

* * *

'Dr Livingstone, I presume?': as laconic as it became iconic, the (probably invented) clipped greeting that came to epitomise the indomitable spirit of the British Empire was spoken by 'H. M. Stanley', a Welshman (John Rowlands of St Asaph) every bit as prone to fertile fantasy as Iolo Morganwg, who had astonishingly managed to locate a legendary lost Scot (David Livingstone) in the very heart of remotest Africa.[22] An English Imperialist to the core, Stanley bluntly informed the Eisteddfod that he had no intention of 'exciting interest in the Welsh nationality and literature'. The sooner the Welsh spoke English the better. 'How can I talk about Cambria?', he added. 'What *is* Cambria *alone*?' (*E*, 168) As he told his North Lambeth electorate, 'my one over mastering desire is for the maintenance, the spread, the dignity, the usefulness of the British Empire. I believe that we Englishmen [*sic*] are working out the greatest destiny which any race has ever fulfilled.' (*E*, 168) And when it came to Empire building, the Welsh could not remotely claim to rival the Scots, as Stanley was in due course contemptuously to remind his fellow countrymen and women.[23] It was surely no coincidence that when, on the occasion of her Jubilee celebrations in 1897, Queen Victoria ceremonially transmitted by telegraph her august message to her Imperial subjects worldwide, she wore a dress decorated with the emblems of England, Scotland and Ireland – but not of Wales.[24] Turn but a page of any narrative study of British Imperial history and you are very likely to encounter the Scots, or the Scots-Irish, or the Anglo-Irish, in all the pomp and power of their authority as mighty plenipotentiaries of Empire. The Welsh, on the other hand, keep a very low profile, for all the carefully burnished legends of their heroism in the Zulu wars and the proud monuments erected in due course in sundry corners to such 'Anglo-Welsh' Imperial notables as General Nott, General Picton, and Lord Tredegar.

Enthusiasm for Empire in late Victorian and Edwardian Wales was, however, every bit as passionate and vociferous as it was in every other corner of Britain.[25] The periodicals of the time are full both of reflective discussions of Wales's supposedly important contributions to the Imperial order and of spontaneous effusions of pride in it. Even O. M. Edwards could chide a correspondent in *Cymru* by deploring his ignorance of prominent Welsh military participation in notable English Imperial successes down the centuries: 'You will not find a war of importance that the Welsh did not distinguish themselves in, and army and navy currently are full of Welshmen.'[26] Yet, there was no disguising the relative lack of really outstanding Welsh contribution to the military and administrative development of Empire, as even Sir Lewis Morris was forced to acknowledge, while defensively pointing to the historical reasons for it. 'It is notorious that the Scotch, by dint of harder brains and of a Higher Education widely diffused, have reaped more than their numerical share of success in every part of the Empire and in every department of life.'[27] The remedy for him, as for many other leaders of opinion in educational matters, was to establish in Wales a university that could come to rival even the universities of Scotland as a production line for turning out sound loyal servants of Empire. The university, wrote Professor J. Young Evans, responding in part to H. M. Stanley's recent attack in a Swansea speech on his native country's parochial preoccupation with itself, should labour to overcome such obstacles as 'misdirected patriotism which have as yet hindered Welshmen from attaining to such positions in the Empire at large as they are by nature equally qualified to fulfil, with Englishmen, Scotchmen and Irishmen'. Only by being 'brought into closer sympathy with the general thought of the Empire . . . can Wales fulfil that intellectual, moral, and religious work which we are all agreed it is destined to perform'. Evans was obviously shrewdly appealing to his countrymen's Calvinistic belief in predestination and fusing it with the social Darwinism so influential at the time. 'Let leaders of political thought,' he unctuously added, 'do all that in them lies to kindle in Welshmen a pride that they are, after all, members of the greatest empire on earth.'[28]

Nonconformist Wales, though, was often inclined to argue a contrary case for Welsh involvement in Empire. O. M. Edwards himself concluded his forementioned discussion of the prowess displayed by the Welsh in Imperial service by conceding that 'ym muddugoliaethau heddwch, y mae'n wir, y ceir ein prif arwyr ni' ('It is in the victories of peace, it's true, that our heroes can primarily be found'). It was the piety and unparalleled moral probity of the Welsh nation that would provide the whole world of Empire with a model of enlightened conduct. 'Both our local history,' wrote Lloyd George's brother William George, 'and the general policy of the Empire, of which this country forms part, point to the urgent necessity of greater insistence in the present day upon the observance in the political world of those moral principles which Wales is practically unanimous in professing.'[29]

Such sentiments as these were sometimes fused with a Hegelian belief that social collectives evolved according to a preordained world-historical model of moral progress and social refinement. Late Victorian Wales, argued the Revd Richard Hughes in *Young Wales*, had at last reached that crucial, advanced stage in the process characterised by dawning consciousness, in a given society, of its destined place in evolutionary history. Wales had come to realise that 'the evolution which is slowly proceeding in human society is not primarily intellectual but religious in character'. This remarkable progress had been effected not through any radical change in human nature since the time of 'savages', but through steady development of social institutions, pre-eminently including nations, that enabled the collective, cooperative maximisation of individual potentialities.[30]

The most subtle and distinguished Welsh proponent of this philosophy was Sir Henry Jones (the renowned British Hegelian who had famously risen from the humblest of origins to become Professor of Moral Philosophy at Glasgow University), and on it he based what has been described as his 'Imperialism of Moral Ideals'. Believing in nations as indispensable instruments for individual development, Jones further conceived of them as organisms each with its distinctive 'habits of mind . . . moral disposition(s) and political convictions'.[31] Wales was one such nation, albeit advantageously nested within the larger, more socially developed, nation of a Britain which in its turn operated within the even larger collective of its Empire; and so Wales needed significant control over its own affairs, within this wider context, in order to enable future developments suited to its inherent nature. Wales, he wrote in the *Westminster Review*, 'is proud of the inheritance into which it has entered by its long and peaceful union with England in the British Empire; and in asking for some measures of self-government, it only asks for room *to live within that Empire its own life* . . . No nation, however small, was ever expunged without leaving the world poorer for its loss.'[32]

A modest degree of self-government within Empire: that was another model of a modern Welsh national polity canvassed in this period, albeit in the vaguest of optimistic terms. In an essay on 'Nationalism' published in *Cymru Fydd* 2 (1889), Edward Jones argued for a federal structure that would significantly loosen the hold of England over its colonies, allowing them a degree of influence over their own affairs. 'The strength, the stability, the permanence, the peace and the prospects of a great empire depend,' argued Jones, 'in an especial manner, upon the spirit in which the central government deals with the peculiarities of race and nationality subjected to its rule.'[33] Such thinking was broadly in line with Joseph Chamberlain's proposal in 1886 to 'bring all the colonies "into one supreme and Imperial Parliament, so . . . that all should be equally responsible . . . have a share in the welfare, and sympathise with the welfare of every part"'.[34] A federal model had, or so it has been argued, once more come to seem attractive in the wake of successful consolidation, following the victory of the North in the American Civil War, of the federal structure of the United States. Accordingly, an Imperial Federation League was founded in 1884. But the League was riven, from the beginning, by disagreements over the exact kind of federal structure that should be favoured, so that by 1892 'the idea of an imperial council' similar to that advocated by Edward Jones 'was probably the lowest common denominator of agreement'.[35] Moreover, far from being prompted by the decentralising impulse commended by Jones, the kind of federal model promoted by the League, as later by Chamberlain during his period as Foreign

Secretary and staunch champion of 'New Imperialism', was unionist in intention and prompted by the fear that the Empire might disintegrate if no cogent form of central, coordinating control were established. The model attracted very little support either from English politicians, who regarded 'colonials' with condescension and shrank from alienating the US by favouring a different foreign alliance, or from the colonies, some of whom (most particularly Canada) were already successfully trialling domestic federal structures of their own.

Some Cymru Fydd supporters nevertheless remained attracted to the idea of a federated Empire. 'If the British Empire . . . can unite the different portions of its various dominions in an Imperial Senate,' wrote J. Arthur Price in 1890 with some prescience, 'the Imperial statism of the future will have neither the time nor the desire to thwart the free expansion of a subordinate nationalism [such as that of Wales] in any one of the Imperial States. But should that dark and gloomy day ever arrive when the flag of an independent Australian republic wave from the walls of Melbourne and Sydney, when Canada is absorbed in the American Union . . . England will be driven once again, almost in self-defence, to consolidate what remains of her possessions, and that work of consolidation must of necessity prove fatal to the new life of Wales.'[36] It seems to have been some such federal model of Empire, too, that T. E. Ellis discussed with Cecil Rhodes during a period of convalescence in Africa in 1890, 'Rhodes himself being an enthusiast for Irish home rule on imperial grounds. On his return, Ellis delivered a famous speech at Bala in September 1890, in which he appealed openly for a Welsh parliament.'[37]

Some Welsh supporters of Empire based their advocacy on a socio-political Darwinism. 'Imperialism,' wrote the Revd W. G. Edwards-Rees in an essay resoundingly entitled 'The Welsh: A Neglected Imperial Asset', 'connotes the voluntary federation in a close unity of political wholes which at an earlier time would have chosen to remain independent.' While patriotically insisting that the roots of such an idea could be traced all the way back to the polity of Llywelyn Fawr (Llywelyn the Great, 1173–1240), Edwards-Rees claimed that an enlightened British imperialism was also consistent with that very modern discovery, evolutionary law: 'A mixing together of inter-dependent parts, and a fuller and intenser and more specialized life for each part – this is what evolution brings and this is what a sane Imperialism promises.'[38]

'As Welsh Liberals,' Lloyd George thundered in 1891, 'we are Imperialists because we are nationalists.'[39] The dream of a place for

Wales in a grand British Imperial parliament of self-governing states world-wide found intriguing expression in *Lady Gwen, or the Days that are to Be*, an anonymous fictional work that appeared in serialised form in *Cymru Fydd* (1890–1).[40] 'A federated British Empire,' so the preface asserted, 'would at once possess the overwhelming strength of an enormous empire, and . . .would at the same time give to each separate portion of the Empire – whether great or small – the free right to live in its own way.'[41] Opposition to such an idea, the author conceded, was likely to come both from anglicised Welsh supporters of the Wales-domiciled Conservative MP Cecil Raikes and from the Radical wing of Nonconformity, led by Thomas Gee, entirely intent on pitting class against class in the struggle to gain justice for the tenant-farmers of Wales. Set in the utopian Welsh society of 2000, the novel envisages both a leading political role for women (the blonde, harp-playing bombshell Lady Gwen Tudor ends up premier of her country) and the emergence of a society in which the tensions bedevilling late Victorian Wales (centred on the issues of Education, the State Church and the Land Question) have all been resolved so that old-fashioned political radicalism has given way to a moderate social conservatism infused with the values of a more sophisticated Calvinist theology. The work actually instances the kind of pan-imperial co-operation that its author advocated, since it was avowedly modelled (as its preface made clear) on *AD 2000, or a Woman's Destiny*, a novel published by the ex-Prime Minister of New Zealand Sir Julius Vogel.

* * *

No more ardent Welsh servant of Empire could be imagined than that incorrigible adventurer and militant nationalist Owen Rhoscomyl.[42] A more unlikely disciple of O. M. Edwards (which he claimed to be) would be impossible to find. On the very threshold of a new century, Rhoscomyl took the opportunity to dismantle established stereotypes of 'the Celt' in a sprightly article in *Young Wales*.[43] Anticipating post-colonial criticism by the best part of a century, he roundly criticised Matthew Arnold for following Renan in characterising 'the male Celt' as 'no more than half a man smothered in the spirit of a whole nice old lady' (50), and counterattacked by pointing to Welsh renown in war and in business. Both the Scots and the Irish, he perceptively argued, had managed to escape pallid stereotyping as fey 'Celts' because they enjoyed a much higher and sharper public profile that was entirely of their own creation and recognised beyond their own borders. This was thanks largely to the brilliant image-making of two fiction writers: Walter Scott and Charles Lever. By contrast, the Welsh came across as no more than a downtrodden peasantry at best, and a dourly puritan people at worst, cowed by their chapels and preachers. The chapel, however, had never managed fully to 'emasculate' the'careless, witty, drinking, love-making, fighting Welshmen' that the Tudors had recognised, and now, at century's end, it was clear the reign of the ministers was at long last drawing to its conclusion. 'During the century now rising to be gone, it is the chapel which has been the main upholder of Welsh nationality,' but now a new notion of nationhood was needed, and 'one looks round and sees only nationalism within imperialism as at all adequate to lift the burden and swing it up, wave borne, another beach higher on the progress.' (57) 'For our young men then, all those who wish to see Wales not a mere lichen covered buttress of England, but a firm and polished pillar of the Empire . . . let them gird themselves in their own strength and not in that of others.'

As this essay implies, Rhoscomyl was acutely conscious of the role played by fiction in fashioning influential images of national identity, and accordingly set out to be the Walter Scott of Wales, the author of romances calculated to stir the spirits of young Welsh men (Rhoscomyl is indisputably a male chauvinist) to rousing adventure in the service of an empire he hopefully envisaged as British, as distinct from English, in its essential character.[44] In *Old Fireproof*, a very creditable attempt at the kind of tale of military and romantic adventure (such as Rider Haggard's *King Solomon's Mines*) that was so popular in its day, he fashioned a perfect allegory of his stirringly aggressive fantasy of Welsh nationhood.[45] The novel (largely autobiographical) ticks all the boxes. Centre stage is the outrageously brave and morally upright Welsh Captain, the owner of the grand old unpretentious house of Llys Rono. A scion of the ancient Welsh 'nobility' Rhoscomyl so desperately idealised, the Captain has been fated by greatly reduced circumstances to serve as a lowly officer in Roston's Horse, an irregular company of Scouts in the Boer War. Ostensibly a collection of 'riff-raff', a motley group composed of despised colonials and 'even Jews', these apparent drifters in fact operate impressively as a battle-heartened unit whose repeated resourcefulness and courage in action consistently puts the efforts of the regular army to shame. In a phrase dripping with the homoeroticism that occasionally surfaces in the novel, the 'tanned skin' of these men's faces are said to shine 'with a film like the gleam of the bayonets some of them fixed.' (*OF*, 20) Rhoscomyl thus reverses the social perceptions of his day by making the outcasts and marginals of society (including the Welsh) the true heroes and aristocrats of Empire, a strategy further underlined when the English chaplain who narrates the story comes to idolise the Captain and, having proved his courage, is admitted as an honorary member of the dashing Welshman's ragged company according to some supposedly immemorial custom enshrined in the old Welsh laws.

For Rhoscomyl, the only true test of the 'virility' of any people was whether or not it had mastered 'the craft whereon God forges the fate of nations . . . all must in the culmination abide the test of battle.' (*OF*, 17) Men had to undergo a rite of passage, coming to full manhood only by becoming consummate 'players of the red game' (*OF*, 18), and the Captain, who excels at fighting, speaks of entry into battle as a journey into the vale of soul making. Rhoscomyl is anxious, however, to temper his hero's ferocity with a strong dose of morality and even a religious sensibility to Welsh Nonconformist taste: 'at home, yonder in Wales, I used to have a secret of my own – that this quiet breeze was the soul of Christ from Calvary, wandering in sad sorrow, aching in hope if men would still not turn to the love of holiness' (*OF*, 28). One of his most prominent attributes is the paternal regard he shows both for his own men and for all who are weak or oppressed – a quality particularly attractive, no doubt, to Rhoscomyl since he himself had never known his father. His Captain is actually killed saving the life of a despised 'Kaffir', one of several moments in the novel when the Welsh are implicitly aligned not with the powerful but with the disadvantaged. Another example of this is when the sympathy both of Rhoscomyl and of his Captain is paradoxically extended even to the enemy, the Boer farmers being seen as another small people whose dogged courage, strong family values and religious beliefs have come under attack from a much more powerful people in a war cynically described at one point as 'The Great South African Land Trouble and Eviction Campaign' (*OF*, 254). 'Surely,' the narrator muses, 'our demands must have gone beyond the extremes when unprepared men would face even war with the greatest empire in the world rather than yield.' (*OF*, 36)

'The one dominant note of him,' says the narrator of the Captain in another homoerotic passage, 'was mental strength, a mentality that was all one will to prevail, like the molten steel which, splashing from the furnace cauldron, burns its way relentlessly along its course, be that course straight or winding.' (*OF*, 25) The mistake made by the young English society beauty whose hand he had rejected back home in Wales was to attempt to break that supreme masculine will. Widowed very early after marrying an old earl merely for his money, she had set her widow's cap at the lowly Captain, winning him with an invented story of enforced marriage only to lose him when the lie was detected and the hard, 'low', 'gutter-snipe' side of her mercenary character lay exposed. What she had not realised until it was too late was that the inveterate and unconquerable will which made him such a formidable servant of Empire was rooted in pride in his ancient descent from the Welsh warrior class. Their relationship thus becomes an allegory of English attempts to break the spirit of Wales and to force it at last into humble submission after centuries of resistance.

The captain contracts a blissfully happy marriage instead to a stunningly beautiful Boer girl whom he first encounters in an enemy house he has stealthily entered and who consequently becomes a rebel leader whose dash and courage equal his own. Having been captured by the British she quickly succumbs to the charms of a man who marries her at breakneck speed, very much at risk to his own military career, in order to save her from imprisonment in a concentration camp. This politically suggestive Welsh-Boer love match is sealed with the birth of a son who, when the Captain is eventually killed, is destined to fulfil his father's vision. Recalling that, in his own eyes, he (no doubt like Rhoscomyl) had always fought for the freedom of small oppressed peoples like the Cubans and the Greeks, the Captain has dreamt of the day when his own people will win their own freedom within the framework of the Empire. His baby son, he predicts, will long for the sword as did his ancestors stretching all the way back over forty-five generations to the time of Vortigern:

> He will! Don't mistake – he shall be trained to fight for his country if need be. The old Welsh laws were true there. When the boy grew to be fourteen he was handed over to the chief to be trained in all that made a fit and full tribesman . . . No wonder that the nation never could be rooted out, in spite of all the armies that came in endless clouds to do it. And that's my ideal still: and my son shall be taught and trained to war, that he may the better follow this greater vision, for he will know that, when it comes to the steel for it, he can take the steel with the best and the worst of his enemies. (*OF*, 364–5)

Deeply embedded in *Old Fireproof*, then, is a reading of Welsh history that secretly governs the entire action of the novel and that was outlined in detail in *Flame Bearers of Welsh History*, the work Rhoscomyl wrote for use in Welsh schools.[46] The primary aims of a book that, in all its 254 pages, chose to bring the history of Wales no further than the Act of Union, were well summarised by the distinguished scholar Sir John Rhŷs who, along with another distinguished Celticist, Kuno Meyer, supplied a preface to the volume. They were to 'show broadly and clearly that the Cymry are not descended from a race of hares ready to run away at the first approach of an enemy, that on the contrary they were always ready to fight and to fight obstinately even when the numbers arrayed against them were overwhelming' (*FBWH*, vi); and to develop Welsh nationality to the full by avoiding 'slavish imitation of the Saxon and the least progressive element in the composition of the great English people'.

> That development could not help making [the Welshman] both a better man and a better citizen of the mighty Anglo-Celtic Empire, in which the accidents of place and history have made him a piece of the mosaic, and with which his own setting and loyalty have insolubly identified him for ages past. (*FBWH*, vii)

As Rhoscomyl himself put it in the body of the book, 'the self-respect of any nation must come from two sources; the consciousness of what it is capable of accomplishing in the present, and the remembrance of what it has accomplished in the past' (*FBWH*, xxiii). It was the misfortune of Wales, he added, to be largely deprived of the former source of self-respect because it had for so long been entirely deprived of the latter. The Welsh had no reliable source of information about the heroic beginnings of their own society, and no realisation that 'princes of Romance, sheer romance, were the Princes of old Cymru.'[47] (*FBWH*, 137) His own 'scientific' researches, he emphasised, had established that the early post-Roman 'Cymry' had evolved a distinctive polity – as, too, had the invading Saxons, whom Rhoscomyl treats with like respect. Such findings are very much to his purpose, since his book is intended 'to make of Welsh people not only better Welshmen but better Britons' (*FBWH*, xxvii).

'Cymru is part of the Isle of Britain, and true progress and true development doom all the peoples of this isle to union,' Rhoscomyl insisted, consciously adverting to the old belief that the Welsh once possessed the whole island. 'There is no question of that. The only question is, on what terms should that union take place.' (*FBWH*, 187) In his own day, Rhoscomyl believed, those terms had become demeaning ones. As he proceeded to narrate the romantic story of his people, the battling Cymry, from leader (or Flame Bearer) to leader, he kept admonishing his young readers that 'they were of your ancestors, remember' (*FBWH*, 62). But his intention was always to make them all the prouder of belonging to Britain and her Empire. Hence his history naturally not only concluded but climaxed with the accession of the Tudors. Henry Tudor, we learn, 'was striking, not to free Cymru from England, but to seize for a Son of Cunedda, once more, that Crown of Britain which the Norman stranger had wrested from the English at Hastings' (*FBWH*, 238). For Rhoscomyl, British and Imperialist to the core, the history of Wales thus reached its apotheosis with the Act of Union and, he could assure his young readers one last time, 'It is a proud thing still to be a Cymro.' (*FBWH*, 253)

* * *

The publication of Marie Trevelyan's novel *Britain's Greatness Foretold*[48] coincided, as its author proudly pointed out in her preface, with two notable events in the contemporary imperial record: the first was the beginning of the Boer War and the second the preparations afoot to place Thomas Thornycroft's bronze sculpture of the warlike Boadicea in a position of eminence on the Thames embankment (see chapter 1). The novel itself is a monumental advertisement for the virtues of an Empire of 12 million square miles and of 390 million people, trumpeted in 70 pages of self-congratulatory prose by Edwin Collins in his introduction. Whatever its origins in financial self-interest and competition between aggressively powerful European nation states, argues Collins, the Empire has blossomed, during the sixty years of Victoria's reign, into a model of civilised and civilising good order. Its progressively enfranchised 'free' citizenry has evolved into a body of 'Colonials' ever faithfully ready, as demonstrated in the Boer war, to defend 'the British Empire and . . . British prestige throughout the world' (*BGF*, xxxvii). Collins's Empire is, of course, an Empire exclusively of and for the whites – no mention is ever made of Africa at large and very little of India. It is imagined as consisting of colonials who remain British in essence, whatever their native countries, because such is the irresistible power of British civilisation that no culture experiencing its advanced values could ever possibly resist them. Even the United States, that set of colonies which unfortunately got away, remain British in all but name insists Collins, in an attempt no doubt to bridge the divide at the beginning of the twentieth century between those who saw the future of Britain as best tied to the development of its colonies, and those who believed it should look far more to America for direction and collaboration. 'It needs no prophet to tell us,' Collins confidently asserts, 'that our Empire will, ere long, be the most beneficent, the most prosperous, and the most peaceful because the strongest as well as the widest, that the world has ever known' (*BGF*, xx). As for the Boer War itself, it is represented as provoked by Boer mistreatment of African natives and of the *utlanders* (outsiders, mostly from Britain) drawn to Transvaal by the lucrative Witwatersrand gold mines – never mentioned by Collins although these, along with the Kimberley diamond mines, were a major factor in British intervention.

Trevelyan's novel tries to provide Wales with an important place in this triumphalist narrative by following the eighteenth-century poet William Cowper in arguing that the rise of Britain to Imperial power had been 'foretold' and indeed foreshadowed in Boadicea's patriotic defiance of tyrannical Rome. Hers had been a heroic (and tragic) stand for those very values of social justice and personal freedom that a liberated Britain would in due course export to all the countries of its ever-growing Empire. The native Brythonic name for Boadicea, 'the British Warrior-Queen', Trevelyan explained, was Buddug (loosely translatable as Victory or Victoria), and Trevelyan herself, when a girl in Llantwit Major, had been 'accustomed to hear constantly around me the language of which the great queen spoke' (*BGF*, ix).[49]

By smoothly equating modern British identity with Ancient British (Brythonic, or Welsh) identity, Trevelyan is able to argue that all the important characteristics of the 'British race' were already evident in Boadicea. 'In those struggles for national liberty and justice,' she claims, 'we trace the foundations of our present freedom.' But then her very next sentence unintentionally reveals the anxiety of which her confident assertion has in fact been bred:

> In the elements of [Boadicea's] unswerving devotion we behold the origin of the great and unparalleled patriotic revival of 1899–1900 [the period of the Boer War], which has in a measure effaced the names of

> England and the English, and restored to us – ours by birth-right – the broader name of Britain and Britons! (*BGF*, xi)

What Trevelyan there admits, of course, is that in general discourse, both within Britain and across the world, the term 'British' had for long been regarded as interchangeable with 'English'. In its confused way, her novel is her own (ineffectual) Boadicean revolt against such casual absorption of Wales into England; a timidly 'post-colonial' attempt to reclaim a heroine long lost by the Welsh to the English; a pathetic bid to be seen not as a disempowered subject of the 'British' Empire but as an originating partner that had been influential in its construction. Tellingly, though, when Edwin Collins touches on this issue in the briefest of ways in his lengthy introduction, it is not the Welsh but those troublesome neighbours the Irish whom he approvingly singles out as the true 'descendants of the ancient Britons' among the British troops serving in the Boer campaign (*BGF*, xlviii). It seems appropriate that, even as Trevelyan is exulting that the 'statue of Boadicea will be unveiled near the scene of her triumph in old Caerlud, known to us as London, the mother-city of the vast British Empire', we also learn that the name of the person who, as Chairman of the Bridges Committee, has chosen the north-east corner of Westminster Bridge as the exact site, is none other than a Mr Bull (*BGF*, xiv).

Britain's Greatness Foretold is a very feeble fiction, even judged by the forgiving standards of popular romance. But it does display three telling cultural features. First, Trevelyan makes some attempt – as she points out in her preface – to offset the prevailing English view that the Ancient British were only a primitive, barbaric people. Secondly, her whole narrative is centered on the courageous exploits of strong women – not only Boadicea herself but Eurgain (infelicitously translated as 'Golden Beauty'), spirited grand-daughter of Caractacus, and also such marginal characters as Rhonilla (leader of a northern tribe of pre-Celtic warriors) and Senana, who is 'tall, broad-shouldered, and imposing looking, with the strength, activity, and endurance of a man' (*BGF*, 255). These two latter characters embody something of the Amazonian character that a Trevelyan nervous of depicting 'masculine women' is anxious to disown in her preface, but that is allowed a kind of sly life in the sub-text of her narrative. Her attraction to strong women may owe something to her own circumstances. Having discovered that she had contracted a bigamous marriage to a Frenchman, Trevelyan had been forced to rely on her own resources (as a popular author) to earn a living for herself and for her son.

The third signifying feature of the text is the use Trevelyan makes of the established romance device of a convenient marriage, most memorably employed in Scott's first great historical novel *Waverley*, as a symbolic solvent of violent conflict between two very different societies. The love match between Eurgain and Victor the Centurion stands for the eventual fusion between native British and invading Roman values that, in Trevelyan's version of history, made possible the development of the modern British race. The Roman invasion, we learn, 'was to prove the greatest factor in promoting civilization in "the utmost bounds of the west." . . . Britain was to pass through may ordeals, ending at last in perfect regeneration of a race whose valour in ages to come would be a world-word.' (*BGF*, 180) And it is, of course, in this 'contributionist' perspective that she views the modern history of her own people, the Welsh, with Eurgain's marriage to Victor prefiguring Wales's felicitous union with England to form the modern basis of the British and their Empire.

* * *

All of the works considered in this chapter were attempts of their time to put literature to political use. Creative writing was, in each case, regarded as capable not only of reflecting political issues but of decisive, seriously consequential, intervention in social and political affairs. Texts could, so the authors supposed, prove to be valuable agents of change. And in order to actualise their full potential, writers endeavoured to utilise the resources of form as much as of content, implicitly recognising that it is through the complex totality of its signifying structures that even the most unremarkable creative text communicates, and not through its overt message alone.

That texts divergent in genre and in social conviction could, nevertheless, converge on a common set of assumptions is testimony to the latter's centrality to the age. Contemporary Wales, they all agree, is distinguished by its new-found political consciousness. The arts, they further concur, must find and deploy appropriate means of mediating this reality. Moreover, as they all discover in their different ways, narrative proves to be a seminal means of translating political issues into effective agents for contemporary socio-political transformations. These disparate texts, however, engage with contemporary political life each according to the protocol appropriate to its particular 'genre'. In writing his elegy, for instance, Dyfnallt Owen had the advantage of practising a culturally prestigious form (poetry) that, for well over a millennium, had acted as a prime vehicle for Welsh 'nationhood'. In late-nineteenth-century Wales, as in contemporary Ireland, 'it was to poetry and drama rather than prose that cultural nationalists looked to articulate the nation, cultural forms in which *how* you wrote had to answer the serious nature of *what* you were writing about'.[50]

Again as in Ireland, there had been in Wales the long-standing dream of discovering a national epic and, in the absence of any such text, a concern 'with the identification of epic effects [of embodying cultural and political unity] in other, less deserving but more amenable forms' (27). In Dyfnallt's case, this proved to be the elegy. His poem was, in part, an exercise in creating what has recently been termed a 'mnemonic community', centred on an agreed version of the 'national past' intended to promote an agreed version of the national future.[51] Elegy is, after all, a form essentially predicated on a reverence for memory, and so, in cultivating a cherished past narrative of a 'representative' individual life, it simultaneously enables the construction, through a highly selective process of recall, of a 'national history' all the more powerful for being so intimately associated with the death of a popular hero. The novels, on the other hand, necessarily proceeded by very different means. They mostly drew on the romance genre to couch the political issues related to national identity in terms of personal relations and domestic affairs, constructing their respective allegories of nationhood in terms of these established conventions. And for all their differences, all of these texts bear in the very body of their form signs of the strain of their authors having to respond to the political reality of a new Wales requiring appropriate forms of cultural representation.

5

THE CELTIC OPTION

'Allons, enfants de la patrie,/ Le jour de gloire est arrivé': thus opens 'La Marseillaise', the insurrectionary song of the French Revolution duly adopted by a fiercely unitary 'Gallic' nation as its national anthem. But the words were first sung by a motley crew of expatriate Genoese, Corsicans and Piedmontese, 'immigrants' all, advancing on Paris from Marseilles in July 1792.[1] Born in paradox, 'La Marseillaise' therefore encapsulates the disturbingly mixed nineteenth-century history of the construction of modern nations by means of the creation, from a highly selective 'history', of a foundation myth, of an originating moment for 'the nation'. This process necessitated the silent suppression of discordant facts and communities and often fostered a messianic sense of national mission which ironically tended to find expression in imperialist 'liberating' and 'civilising' initiatives. The forging of a national collective was thus a process both intensely constructive and intensely destructive and central to it was the work of producing 'narrative discourses that signified a sense of "nationness"', and the mobilisation of the artist in the development of such generative and regenerative discourses.[2]

As the heterogeneity of Welsh society grew ever more pronounced during the later nineteenth century, owing to both the internal and inward migration so dramatically promoted by the rapidly accelerating industrialising process and the resultant culture-shift, some emergent nationalists naturally (if dangerously) favoured a reassuringly single image of nationhood that unified by the drastic process of exclusive simplification. One such image would seem to be that of a Celtic Wales, which had the advantage of investing modern Wales with an antiquity that satisfied its craving for a validating 'historicity'. But appearances in this case prove deceptive. As the following discussion will demonstrate, the category of the 'Celtic' proved to be susceptible to a range of interpretations, each involving a very different model of modern Welsh identity. Celticism was, for example, capable of being viewed from two diametrically opposed positions, one stressing the primacy of the Welsh language as the sole meaningful connective with the Celtic past, the other understanding the 'Celtic spirit' as being non-language-specific and therefore free to migrate from Welsh to English in a manner that not only conveniently reintegrated the linguistically fractured modern nation and satisfied the needs of expatriate Welsh writers and intellectuals, but also conferred an undemanding Welsh ('Celtic') identity even on individuals of distant, and even dubious, Welsh descent. But despite its claims to a kind of spontaneous self-generation – to be the natural offspring of the ancient Welsh past – modern Welsh Celticism was in truth essentially modern and relational in origin and character, being the binary opposite of nineteenth-century English Saxonism to be further considered in chapter 6.

While this binary had found its most perfect form and influential expression in Matthew Arnold's seminal 'On the Study of Celtic Literature',[3] its constitutive elements had already been firmly established by the 'first wave' of Celticists in the eighteenth century,[4] when Celtic fever gripped Europe in the wake of Macpherson's publication of Ossian,[5] and it was further developed by Carnhuanawc (Thomas Price) and the circle surrounding Lady Llanover (Augusta Hall) in the 1830s.[6] But by the end of the nineteenth century, this antiquarian and frequently highly fanciful Celticism was beginning to be radically revised in the light of the new university scholarship produced by Sir John Rhŷs and Edward Anwyl.[7]

Baffling to present-day imagination, the politico-cultural reach and penetration of the cult of 'The Celt', throughout those decades when the nineteenth century was slowly turning into the twentieth, was largely owing to the hospitable amorphousness of the pseudo-racial concept that underpinned the phenomenon. Since modern-day scholarship has served only to complicate, not to say undercut, the very idea of a 'Celtic' identity past or present, the whole concept may in the present connection best be treated as a multipurpose fiction that operated in both enabling and disabling ways in *fin de siècle* Wales.[8] Several of its uses, as pertaining to the construction of national identities in this period, will be the subject of the following discussion. And what should be clear is that the usefulness of 'Celticism' was directly proportionate to the serviceable vagueness of what was meant by the appellation at this time and, therefore, to the several different forms – linguistic, cultural, racial – that the Celtic could take.

But in all its most popular and influential forms, it continued to owe much to Matthew Arnold's celebrated (although subsequently notorious) back-construction from his England's favourite image of itself as 'Saxon', a brilliant device for highlighting those aspects of his 'philistine' society Arnold so feared, deplored, despised and castigated. The Welsh had fallen hook, line and sinker for Arnold's propaganda, rarely noticing how they were disadvantaged by it. As late as 1898, Kenneth Venmor Morris, writing under his 'Celtic' name of Ceinydd Morus, devoted an essay on 'Progress' to *Young Wales* in which he lauded Welsh indifference to materialistic advancement and devotion to 'dreaming'. 'We may teach the Saxon to put wings to their thoughts,' he wrote with splendidly self-satisfied condescension.[9] In like spirit, reviews of the work of 'Fiona Macleod' (the fey 'Celtic' persona of the four-square Scottish Lowlander William Sharp [1855–1905]) gushed in full Arnoldean mode over 'the spirit of the Celt, with its gloom and superstition, its fixity of purpose and its harshness and nobility'.[10] A latter-day Ossian, 'Macleod' (seen at the time as the Scottish counterpart of the young Yeats in a pan-Celtic revival) thrilled readers with her rendering of a doomed people, impractical because temperamental and poetic.

But the enduring power of 'the Celt' lay in the term's adaptability, in its capacity to serve a myriad different purposes and to answer a multitude of psycho-cultural needs. Arnold's coinage could even be turned inside out and upside down. Contrast his impractical Celt (the antithesis of the practical social creature let alone the political animal) with the version that appears in Beriah Gwynfe Evans's 'campaign biography' of Lloyd George, already examined in chapter 2. In the course of a speech delivered when he was fighting the House of Lords, Lloyd George brought off a typically audacious rhetorical stroke. Having opened by proudly announcing 'I have got Celtic blood in my veins', he proceeded to proclaim that so had the English and that, moreover, it accounted for the very best in them. And what was that best? Turning the image of the Celts as an oppressed 'race' on its head, he argued that their persecution had been due to 'their irrepressible love of freedom', first evidenced in their fierce struggle against Caesar.

At one stroke, Lloyd George had replaced the centuries-old myth, so powerful in English politics, of 'the Norman yoke' (in which it was the 'oppressed' Saxon that had stood for freedom) with that of 'the Saxon yoke' (in which the Celt now stood in the Saxon's place). And he had reascribed that 'liberty' which the English had long claimed as the unique prerogative of their 'Saxon race' to the Celts who, moreover, or so he daringly claimed, represented the 'better self' of the English people. 'The Englishman, without his Celtic blood,' he rousingly asserted, 'would not be strong enough to resist the Lords.'[11] It was fighting talk, as the 'feminised' Celts were suddenly liberatingly endowed with virile 'masculine' qualities. This was, of course, an image of the Celts as a warrior people that assumed sinister new significance with the outbreak of the First World War, and it could result in such singular productions as *Notennon Diwar-Benn ar Gelted-Koz / Nodiadau am yr Hen Geltiaid* (Notes on the Ancient Celts).[12] This was a bilingual Breton-Welsh pamphlet distributed among Welsh and Breton troops in France in 1918, and it promoted the notion that the Celts had always been a peculiarly warlike race. Indeed, it claimed, the German name for the Celts derived from the Old German words for warrior and battle.

Lloyd George's 'masculinisation' of the Celt was broadly in line with a reaction among some 'Celticists' from the late 1890s onwards against Arnold's representation of the Celt as a passive creature of sensibility unsuited to the demands of the modern, practical world. In Yeats's case, for example, such a reaction was, by 1904, beginning to take the form of the repudiation of his earlier 'Celtic Twilight' self: 'I cannot probably be quite just to any poetry that speaks to me with the sweet insinuating feminine voice of the dwellers in that country of shadows and hollow images. I have dwelt there too long not to dread all that comes out of it.'[13] And implicit in such a reaction was the realisation that a 'Celticism' predicated on the feminisation of its subject readily became 'unintentionally complicit with the very imperialism it was adopted to *challenge* and subvert'.[14] Ironically, Lloyd George's deployment of an alternative, 'masculine' model of the Celt in his speech could be said to serve precisely the same colonising purpose.

Lloyd George's virile model of Celticism meets its intriguing alter ego in the thinking of an extraordinary, colourful and at times outrageous figure, Owen Rhoscomyl. Enthusiastic military servant of the British Empire, as noted in chapters 1 and 4, sometime 'Rough Rider' in the Cuban war, a member of 'Rimington's Guides' in the Boer War and reputedly a US frontier scout, Rhoscomyl was to act during the First World War as Lloyd George's recruiting sergeant for Welsh troops to serve on the murderous Western Front. In a vivid article for *Young Wales*, already mentioned in chapter 4, this fiery but distinctly idiosyncratic 'Welsh Nationalist' noted:

> in these last few years, [there has been] an increasing tendency amongst our young men to sit down under the theory that the Celt has certain inherent limits beyond which he may not go. But to compensate, as these young casual thinkers imagine, for this, the Celt is invited to consider himself as exclusively possessed of certain beautiful qualities, which, examined, are mostly mawkish, weak, or merely ornamental . . .[15]

Rhoscomyl demolished this emasculating image by listing evidence of the Welsh Celts' prowess in battle, their role in developing the commerce of England's major cities, and their part in the winning and servicing of the British Empire. Anticipating many of the 'post-colonial' arguments of our own period, he bluntly highlighted the contribution not only of the Welsh but also of the Scots and Irish to the imperial mission.

To cap it all, Rhoscomyl seized on the most recent disclosure of scholarship that the whole talk of significant racial difference between the peoples of the British Isles was, in any case, arrant nonsense. The key factors accounting for the differences between the various constituent peoples, he insisted, were not racial but social and environmental. And it was here the Welsh had been disadvantaged, compared to the Scots and the Irish, when it came to defending themselves against all the forces of anglicisation. The ones who denied this stark reality were, Rhoscomyl shrewdly concluded, 'idealists', romancers who felt 'kin in spirit to all the generations that went before, back to that dim dawn when all glories were possible in the days when earth herself glowed with the flush of her first springtime' (*ASC*, 53). Moreover, many of the Welsh 'idealists' who were accordingly enamoured of the racial cult of the ancient Celtic were in fact simply under the influence of English stereotypes of the Welsh. As a Welsh counter-type much more congenial to himself, Rhoscomyl proffered the roistering image of his people presented, for example, in some Elizabethan and Tudor texts. 'So,' he impatiently concluded, 'let us hear no more of "limitations", of "types"; or of that "Celtic temperament", which in the imagination of certain critics is supposed to make us faithless and unstable.' (*ASC*, 57)

Rhoscomyl thus proclaimed his passionate advocacy for an anti-Celtic and pro-Empire model of modern Welsh nationhood, as illustrated in the previous chapter. And in outlining his own vision of Welsh identity performed on a global stage, he also implicitly recognised that one consideration influencing some Welsh Celticists was their wish to embrace internationalism in a form (pan-Celticism) alternative to that on offer within the smothering embrace of the British Empire.

Others wholeheartedly echoed Rhoscomyl's anti-Celtic sentiments. In advocating 'scientific and technical education in Wales', R. E. Hughes ridiculed the fashion for racial stereotyping – 'this twaddle about temperament and national types' – in insisting 'that the nation that has done what Wales has done during the last ten years is a virile, energetic, business-like, pushing, and ambitious nation, one that is looking to the future, not declaiming on the past, one not much concerned with lyrics, but intensely interested in the development of its own natural resources'.[16] But like so many cultural critics of the present day, Hughes and Rhoscomyl failed to understand that a Celticism so easy to expose as intellectually untenable and no more than a servile fiction nevertheless survived because of the serviceability of the endlessly malleable concept of 'the Celt' in so many arenas of contemporary life – even in that most un-Arnoldean of settings, the world of international politics.

As passingly noted in chapter 2, this was strikingly evidenced in the introduction furnished by Charles Sarolea (1860–1953) for the Beriah Gwynfe Evans biography of Lloyd George. Claiming to recognise in Lloyd George 'the spokesman of an oppressed nationality', ironically raised to supreme power by 'the race which for centuries suppressed the aspirations of his native country', Sarolea trusted the Welshman to protect, in the Versailles negotiations, 'the rights of the small and the weak against the ambitions and encroachments of the strong', to honour 'the principle of nationalities in foreign policy, and of self-government in domestic policy'. Of crucial advantage to Lloyd George in his negotiations with the French, Sarolea further argues, would be the fact that both France and Wales were Celtic countries. There should, therefore, be a natural affinity of temperament on both sides which would 'make sympathy and understanding singularly more easy'.

Sarolea cited the Breton Ernest Renan's (1823–92) seminal 'Essay on the Poetry of the Celtic Race' (1859) – a significant influence both on Arnold and on the brand of Celticism espoused by Yeats in his 'The

Celtic Element in Literature '(1897) – as his reliable 'scientific' authority for confidently predicting this natural, and politically productive, rapport between Welsh and French. In so doing, he thoroughly distorted Renan's account, in which 'racial' affinity exists not between France and Wales but specifically between the marginal, culturally peripheral, regions of Brittany and Wales, and in which furthermore all of Arnold's stereotypes are prefigured in Renan's insistence on the passive, 'feminine', 'childish' character of a 'poetic' race, incapable of progress, seduced by fantasy and doomed to extinction (although in his concluding paragraph he interestingly prevaricates on this final point).[17] He even goes so far as to assert that only a woman (Lady Charlotte Guest) could have proved equal to appreciating and translating the delicate feminine qualities of the *Mabinogion*, a compilation he enormously admired. A juxtaposition of Renan's Celt with Sarolea's therefore encapsulates the extremes of difference capaciously contained within the cult of the Celtic.

So flexible indeed could the concept be that it could readily be adjusted to serve the needs of different social and political ideologies. When an article advocating Socialism appeared in the columns of the periodical *Cymru Fydd* in 1888, it provoked an attack by Ivor Bowen in which any form of state interference with the instruments for the production and distribution of wealth was pronounced to be false to the ancient indigenous spirit of the Welsh people. 'It is one of the most remarkable features of Celtic life,' Bowen confidently claimed, 'that self-reliance and individual enterprise are two qualities always admired and revered.'[18] And complementing this enthusiasm for identifying modern Wales with its 'Celtic' past was a new resentment at the way in which even the most supposedly authoritative of contemporary British historians in England and the United States persisted in perpetuating the myth that 'everything is Anglo-Saxon in the making of Britain', as R. Foulkes-Griffiths trenchantly put it. He objected to 'the complete ignoring of Welsh, or ancient British proceedings in dealing with the origin and making of the British nation'. Concentrating on the Romanised Celts of the early Christian centuries, he argued that such civic spirit and institutions as modern society prided itself on had derived not, as purportedly 'learned' scholars continued to suppose, from Saxon precedents but rather from Roman Britain and were a great Celtic contribution to the development of modern civilisation.[19]

In the pages of *Young Wales*, positive and negative versions of Celticism could sometimes be found on succeeding pages. In the

January issue for 1901, for instance, F. E. Hamer concluded his interview with the reactionary Bishop of St Asaph (Charles Edwards) by quoting his subject's lofty comment that

> The Celtic temperament is constitutionally liable to hypertrophy of self-consciousness, and it will be well for the youth of Wales to study that Platonic self-control or temperance, the essence of which is obedience to authority, and the opposite of which is that spirit of what Plato calls insolence or 'beyondness' – the general spirit, in a word, of setting oneself up against what is higher than oneself.[20]

The good Bishop clearly felt threatened by an 'upstart' Nonconformity whose Liberal politicians were at that time vigorously prosecuting a case for the Disestablishment of the Church of England in Wales. But the very next page featured an enthusiastic commendation by Robert Bryan of a new pan-Celtic periodical (*Celtia*, see below) that lauded the Celt's '"intense spirituality, combined with a keen sense of justice, generated by centuries of suffering"'.[21] While elsewhere a T. R. Dawes, Headmaster of the County School at Pembroke Dock, concluded his interesting comparison of the attitudes of the Belgian and Welsh school systems towards bilingualism with the confident assertion that 'our Celtic volubility, not confined to English or Welsh but extended even to French and German will be a valuable commercial asset', not least in the context of 'our Anglo-Celtic Empire'.[22] His quiet reinscription of Arnold's foundational version of the dreamy, otherworldly, impractical Celt (specifically designed to contrast the philistine commercialism of the Saxon English) as a potent commercial force was, if anything, even bolder than Lloyd George's trumpeted ascription to him of a fearless warlike character.

In addition to the cult's accommodation of many different models of 'Celticness' such as these, any one of them was itself also liable to function differently under different social circumstances. In 1890, for instance, the rising young Welsh star of Welsh Liberalism, T. E. Ellis, published an essay entitled 'Britain's Debt to the Celt'. No more than a rehash of Arnold's celebrated contrast between Teutonic, Celtic and Norman races, it was as undistinguished as it was unoriginal. But when David Lloyd George's wife, Margaret, compiled her volume *Gwlad fy Nhadau: Rhodd Cymru i'w Byddin* (*Land of my Fathers: Wales's Gift to her Army*) as a fund-raising initiative in 1915, she found Ellis's essay to be very much to her purpose because of the new timeliness of passages such as the following that retrospectively assumed a jingoistic character:

> Is it not this Celtic strain that supplies Britain with the specific ability and genius, the special gift that differentiates Britain from Germany, and makes her the superior? Is it not this that makes Britain's religious life more intense, more god-centred and enthusiastic than German religion, that makes British oratory more passionate, stirring and effective than German oratory, and that makes Britain's language [i.e. English] more vigorous, flexible, brilliant and swift than the language of Germany, and that contributes to the making of Britain's contribution to the imperishable wealth of the world of greater import than that of Germany?[23]

Varied and extensive though were the diverse forms that Celticism could take, the cult proved most intensely useful perhaps to those of the period who experienced deep inner divisions and tensions, psycho-cultural in character. Its appeal to expatriates like W. B. Yeats (Ireland), William Sharp (Scotland) and Ernest Rhys (Wales), for instance, rested partly on the powerful means it offered them not only of publicly advertising but of confidently characterising, explaining, and thereby solidifying and stabilising, their sense of cultural displacement and unease.[24] It lent shape and coherent meaning to their inchoate sense of 'difference'. They found in it a means of validating their perceived marginality to central metropolitan culture, and in this they found sympathetic allies in some English northerners made 'outcast' by their industrial, working-class backgrounds, accents, tastes and values. Indeed, Ernest Rhys spent some of his formative years working as a mining engineer in the Durham coalfield, participating enthusiastically in proto-socialist and workers' education movements, supporting the work of the so-called 'Pitman Poet', Joseph Skipsey (1832–1903), and contributing to the 'Canterbury Poets' series established by the publisher Walter Scott to make important creative work available to ordinary working people.[25] Another partner in that enterprise was William Sharp, who subsequently joined the Rhys circle in London. Rhys's egregious instinct to 'place' his 'Celtic' Welshness in this northern context is manifest in his *The Fiddler of Carne* (1896), significantly published not in London but by Patrick Geddes in Edinburgh, thus underlining a further association with the *soi-disant* 'Celtic' nation of Scotland. Set a century earlier in what appears to be a Northumberland seaport, the novel nevertheless includes a Welsh landlord and former sea captain, Mr Ffoulkes by name, whose daughter, Marged, is noted for her plangent singing of a variety of Welsh folk tunes and hymns – 'Ar Hyd y Nos', 'Mentra Gwen', 'Caersalem', 'Bydd Myrdd o Ryfeddodau'.

* * *

The psychic complexities of the investment by some artists of the period in 'the Celtic' are no more dramatically apparent than in the case of William Sharp, whose persona as 'Fiona Macleod' began to crystallise from 1894 onwards. His most recent biographer, Flavia Alaya, has identified some of the component elements of this fictional self.[26] Beginning by showing how the ground may have been prepared by Sharp's early recoil from the 'Southern' Italian temperament to which he had originally been so attracted, Alaya proceeds to show how Sharp's 'Northern turn' gradually assumed a form that allowed him not only to separate his sensitive, creative self from his work-a-day practical self but also to isolate, and to access, a 'feminine' side to his sensibility. This was during a period when a fascination amounting almost to an obsession with the bisexual, or hermaphrodite, aspects of the psyche (that had been influentially explored by Shelley) was a feature of the work both of progressive intellectuals such as Havelock Ellis and Edward Carpenter, and of prominent creative writers such as Meredith and Hardy.

Of particular importance to the Welsh case, however, was Sharp's decision, as a monoglot English Lowlander, to adopt the persona of a Gaelic-speaking native of the Islands and Highlands, 'Fiona Macleod'. A native of Paisley, a town prospering on its textile, engineering and ship-building industries and strongly marked by its Calvinist Scottish Presbyterian culture, Sharp eventually sought escape into his version of Celtic faery. In such cases, influential prevailing models of 'Celticity' proved indispensable. As an anglophone Lowlander, he had already become interested in the Walloon-dominated Belgian Renascence (one of whose prominent organs was *La Jeune Belgique*), because it seemed to provide a compelling example of a 'national spirit' finding expression not in the 'native language' of Flemish, but rather in the 'adopted' language of French. And by masquerading as 'Fiona Macleod' – a Gaelic speaker writing in English – Sharp aimed similarly to demonstrate conclusively how, being inborn and ineradicable, a 'racial and cultural nature' (*FM*, 149) (in his case, that of 'the Celt') could survive linguistic 'translation' wholly intact. Moreover, such a concept could be used to sponsor a version of 'cosmopolitanism' that placed great emphasis on the kind of intercultural trafficking of 'progressive' ideas made possible only by the adoption of a lingua franca (such as French in the Belgian case and English in the Scottish), an ideal enthusiastically championed by Patrick Geddes and his Edinburgh reformers, and supposed to be consistent with 'scientific' belief in an inevitable cosmic progress towards universalism.[27] Such an ideal was based on the confident assumption that the 'Celtic spirit' could blithely survive the total extinction of the (accordingly readily expendable, because merely contingent and redundant) language and culture that had traditionally nurtured it but had been condemned by 'Progress'.

On the island of Iona, Sharp found a landscape emblematic of his psychic fantasies. In the person of Fiona Macleod, he opened *The Sin Eater and Other Tales* (1895) with a letter 'From Iona' addressed to George Meredith, dubbed 'Prince of Celtdom' not least because the manner in which the 'Cymric blood' that supposedly flowed through his thoroughly English veins made him, for Sharp, the very model of the fanciful synthetic Celticness he himself favoured. 'An elemental, among the elemental forces,'[28] Sharp's Ossianesque Celt 'brooded' his remote and lonely way on magnificent, rugged, storm-tossed Iona to inevitable obliteration: 'The Celt falls, but his spirit rises in the heart and brain of the Anglo-Celtic peoples, with whom are the destinies of the generation to come.' (*SE*, 9)

During a period of dramatic linguistic change and culture shift, such as had been experienced in Ireland and was being experienced in Wales, this trans-racial and trans-national model of the 'Celtic', construed only as a marker of *racial* identity and not of linguistic and cultural difference, was particularly useful not least to culturally liminal figures like W. B. Yeats, who would otherwise have found himself wholly excluded from that ancient Gaelic tradition which for him constituted part of the very essence of Irishness. But it was also a version of 'the Celtic' that could not fail to be anathema to many of the stalwarts of the Gaelic League and its associated language movements.

* * *

'It must not be forgotten,' Sharp had perceptively written, 'that "the Celtic Fringe" is of divers colours.' (*SE*, 7) Summarising in passing the respective plights of Brittany, Cornwall and the Isle of Man, he proceeded to emphasise that 'In Wales, a great tradition survives; in Ireland, a supreme tradition fades through sunset-hued horizons to the edge o' dark; in Celtic Scotland, a passionate regret, a despairing love and longing, narrows yearly before a bastard utilitarianism which is almost as great a curse to our despoiled land as Calvinistic theology has been and is.' (*SE*, 13) While the denominator common to all cases was the urgent challenge to language and tradition presented by the incursions of an incomparably more powerful language and culture, it followed from Sharp's intelligent analysis that widely differing coping strategies, each tailored to the locally distinctive crisis, might be adopted across the spectrum of 'Celtic' nations. One of the central recurrent concerns of the Cymru Fydd movement was how to accommodate an evidently unstoppable anglicising process partly originating from amongst those 'within', who regarded English as the language of modern social and intellectual progress, and partly from without in the form of massive anglophone immigration into the booming south Wales coalfield. Had a 'Celtic' model of national identity anything to offer under such circumstances, and if so, which of the several models available (including Sharp's) should it be?

If the situation in Wales differed sharply from that of Scotland, so did it from the case of Ireland, where census figures charted the terminal decline of Gaelic speakers from 23 per cent in 1851 to a residual 14.5 per cent in 1891. But even the champions of the Gaelic League, established in 1893 to initiate a revival in the language, were wisely chary of the cult of the Celtic already flourishing among many of their anglophone compatriots.[29] 'We spend much time,' complained D. P. Moran in an essay on 'The Gaelic Revival' for *New English Review* (1899), 'endeavouring to unravel such mysteries as: – Who are the Celts? As if it mattered to anyone, beyond a few specialised scholars, who they were.' The really 'interesting mystery,' he insisted was 'Who and what are *we*?'[30]

Such misgivings about a Celtic label that could easily conceal a process either of fossilisation or assimilation of a living, lively language were much augmented in the context of Welsh-language culture. There, a 'Celtic' language, still spoken by more than 50 per cent of the population, vigorously supported a thoroughly modern literature increasingly buttressed by a pioneering new scholarship that constantly threw new light on the creative contemporary potential of an ancient poetic tradition. Yeats recognised the distinctiveness of the Welsh situation at the time when he wrote of his own country, in 'The Literary Movement in Ireland', that 'We are preparing, as we hope, for a day when Ireland will speak Gaelic, as much as Wales speaks in Welsh, within her borders, but speak, it may be, in English to other nations of those truths which were committed to her.'[31] For many serious scholars, intellectuals and writers alike, a concern with the Celtic could seem valid only when it took the form of dispassionate research into the deep origins of national history or of search in ancient cultural traditions for creative potentialities that contemporary writers could activate. So Brynmor Jones and John Rhŷs soberly concluded in *The Welsh People* (1900), that 'the Welsh people of today have the satisfaction of knowing they are not the decayed and disconsolate remnant of a once great nation, but that in the main they are the descendants of Celtic races which . . . have succeeded in retaining their language and some of the best characteristics of their ancestors'.[32]

Recent scholarship has remarked on how '[t]he renewed confidence in Celtic origins', following the discrediting of eighteenth-century antiquarian Celticism, 'and their relevance to modern aspirations owed much to the work of John Rhys', whose groundbreaking *Celtic Britain* appeared in 1882.[33] But even as early as 1856, Owen Jones's *The Grammar of Ornament* pioneered the comparative study of Celtic, Indian, Persian and Greek art (*IN*, 319). Artists as well as writers began to quarry the 'Ancient British' past and its later legendary deposits, with Goscombe John's exquisite small bronze of Merlin and Arthur (1902) being completed in the year that saw the Eisteddfod success of T. Gwynn Jones's great *awdl* 'Ymadawiad Arthur' in the Chair competition, while the Crown won on the same occasion by R. Silyn Roberts for 'Trystan ac Esyllt' (Tristram and Iseult) was itself of 'interlacing Celtic design' (*IN*, 321).

A colourful and innocently apolitical group also interested itself – in the spirit of the rather naïve early nineteenth-century patriotism of Lady Llanover and Thomas Price, whose bardic name 'Carnhuanawc' announced his passion for all things Breton – in a linguistically based pan-Celticism that concentrated, through organisations such as the Celtic Association and events like the (frequently pantomimic) Celtic Congresses, not only on language kinship but also on associated cultural products such as folk costume, dance, song and music. Such events attracted both writers like 'Mallt Williams' and 'Gwyneth

Vaughan', and artists like the Celtomaniac J(ohn) 'Kelt' Edwards. The year in which a particularly theatrical and fanciful 'Celtic Congress' was held in Caernarfon (1904), the young Christopher Williams breathlessly informed his wife that 'I have been with two really great men [Hwfa Môn and John Morris-Jones], Celts among Celts, and I have been steeped in Celtic ideals, flooded with early Welsh history and pre-Arthurian tales and mythology.'[34] Over the next few years Williams painted a series of 'Celtic' portraits of Ceridwen, Branwen and Blodeuwedd.

In Wales, though, the strength of the indigenous 'Celtic' language meant that any version of the Celtic that did not acknowledge Welsh to be the primary 'carrier', if not the unique surviving legatee, of the culture was bound to be viewed by most Welsh-language writers with considerable suspicion. Moreover, the Welsh could be jealous guardians of their cultural ascendancy over the other Celtic nations. Noting that the Cardiff National Eisteddfod of 1899 had been invaded by pan-Celts from Ireland, Scotland, Brittany and the Isle of Man (photographs proved his point), turning it into a virtual pan-Celtic Festival, Gwilym Hughes complained that in their naïve enthusiasm the visitors threatened to upstage and indeed overwhelm their hosts.[35] A guarded attitude towards fellow Celts can also be sensed in O. M. Edwards's puzzled comment in the pages of his journal *Cymru:* 'Y mae'r elfen Geltaidd yn gref iawn yn yr Alban, er fod ei hiaith yn aml yn Saesneg.'[36] ('The Celtic element is strong in Scotland, although its language is frequently English.') The tone of his remarks captures Edwards's own ambiguous cultural position, as outlined in chapter 3. An intellectually sophisticated, Oxford-educated product of the rich, heartland Welsh-language culture of Bala and its environs, Edwards was naturally inclined, both by background and by his rigorous historical training, to be sceptical of the synthetic, vaporous Celticism of 'Fiona Macleod' and her kind. But, profoundly aware of the irresistible rise of an increasingly anglophone and industrial Wales, he was also dedicating his formidable energies to the fostering of a new, bilingual and bilateral nationhood, and so had some interest in Macleod's 'Celtic' writings as experiments in what might be termed 'cultural transfusion' of the kind he himself was attempting in his tireless efforts to 'educate' his new anglophone compatriots in their Welsh-language inheritance.

* * *

O. M. Edwards's sympathetic attention to Macleod was a minor instance of the 'pan-Celtic' sentiments that peaked around the turn of the century.[37] These feelings of 'international' solidarity were based on the vague supposition that the surviving 'Celtic peoples' of Europe – the Bretons, Irish, Scots, Welsh, Manx (less certainly) and Cornish (most controversially)[38] – shared common origins, were essentially similar in 'racial character', and might benefit from collaboration.

The most prominent champion of such beliefs at century's end was undoubtedly W. B. Yeats, although his own version of pan-Celticism – powered primarily by his infatuation with Maud Gonne – was distinctly idiosyncratic and overwhelmingly centred on his view of Irish interests. He had been fascinated by the Celtic since his early twenties, a fascination nurtured both in the Dublin artistic circle of his youth and through his connections with the Welshman Ernest Rhys and others in a London milieu that promoted pan-Celtic aspirations. His first volume, *The Wanderings of Oisin* (1889), was consciously conceived of as a Celtic collection; and the formation in 1890 of the London Rhymers' Club, many of whose members boasted real or imaginary Celtic antecedents, provided him with another congenial setting for his interests. These fed into his passion for the occult, since in *The Celtic Twilight* (1893) he characterised his age as that of 'the hour before dawn, when this world and the next were closest'.[39]

Believing the Celts to be uniquely suited to these conditions, Yeats committed himself for a feverish period, with the fervent encouragement of Gonne, to the pursuit of 'Celtic mysteries'. This involved a 'spiritual and mystic discipline devoted to finding the secret of the Grail through a consecrated order of visionaries and the evolution of patterns of ritual' (*WBY*, 233). Further enthused by the heady millenarian convictions of his mystical friend 'AE' (George Russell) that a new Age of the Celtic peoples was about to dawn, Yeats for a time thought of his work as belonging to 'the Celtic twilight' before the glorious new dispensation. And while broadly accepting Arnold's celebrated characterisation of the Celt as sensitively attuned to spiritual rather than brute material realities, he interpreted these qualities as markers not of the Celt's 'passive', 'feminine', delicate character, but of his active, vigorous and heroic nature.

Apart from Ernest Rhys, Yeats's other primary pan-Celtic connection was with William Sharp, whom for some years he believed to be the intermediary between himself and the authentically Gaelic 'Fiona

Macleod'. In June, 1896, for instance, he excitedly wrote to Sharp about 'the need to further "the mutual understanding and sympathy of the Scotch, Welsh and Irish Celts . . . In a vague way I realise that something of tremendous moment is being matured, just now. We are on the verge of virtually important developments. And all the heart, all the brain of the Celtic races shall be stirred."' (*WBY*, 166) A month later, a visit he paid to Aran rekindled his enthusiasm for Fiona Macleod's moody, atmospheric writing. And six months later, with prospective contributions from Macleod in mind, he announced the imminent creation of the 'Celtic theatre' that would soon become the Irish Literary Theatre (and eventually the Abbey Theatre). Within a further year, he would have reason to doubt both the authenticity of Fiona Macleod and the validity of his cherished category of 'the Celt', but even at the end of 1897 he was still declaring Macleod to be the 'real voice of the Celt' (*WBY*, 196) and, as late as the Pan-Celtic Congress held in Dublin in August 1901, he gave an impassioned address in which he declared that the pan-Celtic movement '"had created a revolution, the whole thought of the nation had been changed by the movement; and if it went on as it had been doing it would be shaking governments."' (*WBY*, 246) On this colourful occasion, 'Yeats enjoyed himself greatly amid Druidic ceremonial, "traditional chanting", and arguments about the Celtic credentials of Cornwall. He enthusiastically entered into the debate on a "national costume", advocating an authentically Irish evening-dress as well as day-wear.' (*WBY*, 246)

Present at that Dublin Congress were the two Welsh sisters 'Mallt' and Gwenffreda Williams, who published fiction under the pseudonym 'Y Ddau Wynne' (The Two Wynnes). Their report, along with that of William George, was published in *Young Wales*.[40] They ranged over the extensive debates, addresses, entertainments and resolutions without a single mention of Yeats's contribution, and were generally approving of the impact made by the Welsh National Eisteddfod through its ceremonies and officials, although the Gorsedd's '"fripperies and furbelows"', along with the protracted conduct of its proceedings, proved altogether too much, or so George recorded, for the patience of the *Irish Times*. This 'family reunion after a separation extending over many centuries' was defiantly celebrated by George, despite English scoffing 'at the expense of enthusiasts who can discuss with such gravity the advisability of adopting the heather as "the symbolic flower of the Celtic race"'. 'Let our prosaic predominant partner beware also lest he should, in one of his incendiary moods, set that heather on fire,' George ominously retorted, 'otherwise he may find his "game" very much upset, and his sport sadly spoilt.' (233) Wherever and whenever Celts proudly gathered, it seems, they were doomed sooner or later to view their activities through the jaundiced eyes of the sceptical English. 'The love of colour and the love of the picturesque are strong in the Celt,' the *United Irishman* defensively concluded, after conceding that to any 'Whitechapel wit' the Gorsedd's peacock struttings at the Congress would have seemed no more than an amusing 'circus', 'and we felt for a moment lifted out of the drab dreariness of so-called Anglo-Saxon civilization.'

A full report of the first Pan-Celtic Congress was carried by *Celtia*, the pan-Celtic monthly magazine that had been launched in Dublin seven months earlier on 1 January 1901, primarily dedicated to the regeneration of the 'national languages' of surviving Celtic societies.[41] Flying the Gorsedd Motto, 'Y gwir yn erbyn y byd' (The truth against the world), from its masthead, the periodical announced its devotion to 'the [purely cultural] preservation of those characteristics which distinguish the Celtic nationalities from their powerful neighbours'. *Celtia* recognised that political divisions, assiduously promoted by the powerful nation states of which they constituted a subordinate part, had long divided the Celtic peoples, but it was confident that a solid pan-Celtic 'intellectual alliance' could be formed. The magazine proposed to serve as a multilingual platform for the international exchange of views and information, while making clear its commitment to an exclusively linguistic definition of Celticism, consistent with its guiding maxim 'no language, no nation'.[42] It was this desire for international exchange of cultural experience that made some Celticists of the day, reluctant to accept English as their lingua franca, ardent advocates of Esperanto. Setting the pan-Celtic development to which it was committed firmly in the context of the nineteenth-century 'awakening of peoples' across Europe, *Celtia* emphasised that all the small nations that had consequently emerged were 'national units' established on 'the basis of language'. It recognised that the Celtic languages varied greatly in strength from case to 'national' case, with the flourishing condition of the Welsh language in Wales clearly functioning in this regard as the model to which the others should aspire. 'The forcible extinction of the language of a conquered people by the conqueror,' it asserted, was the equivalent 'in the world of nations to "murder" in the world of individuals', while the abandonment by a people of its language to its fate, as had happened in Ireland, was the equivalent of 'suicide'.

In the course of welcoming the first issue of *Celtia* very warmly in *Young Wales*, Robert Bryan incidentally demonstrated how ideologically flexible pan-Celticism was. He highlighted *Celtia*'s sentiments that the Celts' 'centuries of suffering' made them the natural 'advocate of the oppressed, and the representative of moral force in the affairs of mankind'.[43] Therefore, 'The Celt will have to prepare himself, not merely for a leading position in his own country, but also for a great mission in the world at large.' This was the 'export', socially and politically 'progressive', version of Celtic identity that Lloyd George was to embrace and publicise so flamboyantly in due course, and it was in these terms that his hagiographic followers and biographers were to couch the narrative of his most famous achievements. Such rebranding, which was an effective means of combating Arnold's image of the fading, ineffectual Celt, was designed to align the modern Celtic people with the 'evolutionary', socially progressive and politically radical movements of the era, placing them in the very vanguard of human advancement.

The pan-Celtic cause had, in fact, been championed in *Young Wales* by E. E. Fournier d'Albe, Honorary Secretary of the Irish Committee of the Pan-Celtic Congress before *Celtia* (which he was to edit) had been brought into being. Fournier was an astonishing polymathic figure, who went on to publish many books on chemistry, physics, astronomy and parapsychology, and was also the author of an account of crossing the Sahara by car. His scientific background undoubtedly predisposed Fournier to conceive of Celticism in the (pseudo-) scientific terms of race, and to conclude his advocacy of the pan-Celtic alliance with a biological analogy: 'Deep down in the soul of the Celt there is the intuitive perception of a great Truth, that nature makes for diversity and not for uniformity, and that no organism is healthy which is forced to live any but its own natural life.'[44] But in a companion article published in *Young Wales* a few months later, his plea for pan-Celtic solidarity took the form of a parable about two brothers, Bryth and Goidel, and their respective sons: David, Yves and Ian being those of Bryth and Patrick, Colin and Michael being those of Goidel. The vicissitudes of their separate histories are sketched in crudely simplistic terms to underline the need for belated trans-Celtic rapprochement.[45]

As for the first issue of *Celtia*, it featured a preface by Lord Castletown, who also delivered the presidential address at the first

Pan-Celtic Congress. One of the grandest of Anglo-Irish grandees, this eminent soldier of Empire could endorse the pan-Celtic movement very enthusiastically, secure in the knowledge that it was purely linguistic and cultural in its aims, and had no intention of upsetting the political applecart. Indeed, some of the advocates of pan-Celticism were not only apolitical, but specifically anti-political. In one number of the 1899 issue of *Young Wales*, a Dr J. Llewelyn Treharne from Cardiff waxed lyrical about his recent visit, as one of a Welsh delegation, to the Breton Eisteddfod at Vannes. The link between Welsh and Bretons, he felt, was closer 'than that between us and the other peoples of Celtica . . . Their subdued melancholy, their deep religious feeling, their love of song, their clinging to old traditions, their cleanliness, their white-washed cottages in the country districts – all remind one of Home.'[46] Treharne was, however, very anxious to emphasise that this should in no way imperil the majestic national unity of France and Britain respectively: 'The highest aim' of both Celtic peoples should be to become 'true and loyal citizens' of 'the great nations they were geographically attached to' (215). Scotland alone, Treharne felt, had hitherto triumphantly discharged this duty without losing its independence of spirit, and while retaining the respect of the English. For those in Wales of his persuasion, the value of the pan-Celtic movement was not, as it was for some others, that it could pave the way for a political campaign in favour of a devolution of political power, but that it actually helped safeguard the status quo by cultivating a safe and purely cultural form of national identity. All that he really asked was that England be more prepared to recognise the multicultural character of Britain. But an alternative and very different political lesson could, of course, be drawn even from a broadly 'contributionist' Celticism that respected the status quo. 'In the evolution of the modern State,' a *Celtia* editorial announced, 'the doctrine of the Divine Right of Kings has been replaced by that of the Liberty of the Subject. In the evolution of the modern Empire it remains to replace the doctrine of the Superior Race by that of the Liberty of the Subject Nation.'[47]

Treharne was not unaware, however, of the potentially negative consequences of espousing Celticism. He shrewdly admitted the danger that the cult of the antique Celt might render Welsh-language Wales 'a mere specimen (although an interesting one) in a world's museum', by making its vibrant living culture seem anachronistic and moribund (214). And he also realised how potentially divisive a linguistically-based form of Celtic identity might be. An advocate of a future bilingual nation, in which Welsh would continue to play a vital part, he nevertheless implicitly recognised that in contemporary Wales, any undue emphasis on the language was bound to be factional and sectional in character. He therefore oscillated between associating Celtic identity with the Welsh language on the one hand, and concentrating instead on its historical roots on the other. By promoting an awareness of a common 'deep' past in the entire population from Holyhead to Cardiff, Treharne argued, the Celtic movement could help forge a single nation out of a currently divided modern Wales. He no doubt had in mind not only the division between anglophone industrial Wales and its rural Welsh-language counterpart, but also the bitter inter-denominational rivalries that had been the bane of nineteenth-century life in his native country. Just as Celticism offered national misfits like Yeats an Irishness that was not Catholic, so it offered a rapidly secularising modern Welsh intelligentsia an escape from 'Nonconformist Wales'.

* * *

For all its staunch concern to emphasise the exclusively linguistic base of modern Celtic identity, under duress *Celtia* could waver even on this cardinal principle, confirming that it was the ideological flexibility of Celticity, however philosophically deplorable that might be, that made it such a resilient and serviceable term in the maelstrom of the time's debates about national identities and destinies. The magazine was provoked into a temporary modification of its customary stance on the Celtic by a lead article in the *Times*, brought to its attention by *Young Wales*. The Thunderer (as the *Times* was popularly known) opened its editorial with a breathtakingly ignorant and arrogant attack on the Eisteddfod. At best, Wales's national festival only 'amuses some persons' and 'gives a short season of importance to bards and other functionaries', while serving 'as a convenient occasion for airing grievances which, if not very acute, lend themselves to expressions of patriotic sentiments'. Its 'attempt to represent to the world a true Celtic literature is likely to continue to prove disappointing' because eisteddfodic works 'fail to express the thoughts of the best minds about the things urgent and interesting today'.[48]

Having disposed of the Eisteddfod, the *Times* bluntly insisted that a Celtic Revival, 'if it is ever to be more than a passing whim, a fugitive hankering after a past that has gone with generations which slumber in unknown tombs, can be realised only in English verse and prose'. It accordingly next turned its attention to the Neo-Celts – those writers who claimed to be Celtic in character while writing in English – beginning by dismantling the claims of Arnold and Renan that the spiritual sensitivities evident in Celtic literature were an elusive 'essence and . . . aroma' unique to it: 'that swift, serial, super-sensuous way of looking at the world is the prerogative of no race'. Having thus disposed of the very quality that lent anglophone Celtic writing its supposed distinctness, the *Times* listed the writers whose Celticism it had thus effectively disposed of – Fiona Macleod, William Sharp, Neil Munro, W. B. Yeats, George Russell, Nora Hopper, Thomas Moore, Thomas Davis, Clarence Mangan and others. These, it insisted, had contributed not to Celtic but to English literature, a claim that, while arguably not inconsistent with the logic of the core philosophy of *Celtia* itself, the magazine could not allow to pass uncontested. Sensing a cultural imperialism in the *Times*'s lofty arguments, it sarcastically noted how anxious the Thunderer seemed to be to demonstrate that anglophone Celtic writers involuntarily paid 'homage to the soul and spirit of England – the English language'. Such logic, it added, would lead to the conclusion that there was, and could be, no American literature, that Emerson, Thoreau, Melville and Whitman were all doomed to be English writers. And having so supposedly disposed of the *Times*'s somewhat uncomfortable arguments, *Celtia* concluded that 'the Anglo-Celtic writers are our representatives at a foreign court', pending the achievement by the Celtic nations of the British Isles of their cultural independence through triumphant eventual recovery of their original 'national' tongues.

* * *

Of course, Wales was not without its own cultural ambassadors at the court of 'English' literature. One such was Mallt Williams, whose enthusiastic commendation of *Celtia* had been published in the magazine's second issue. As noted previously, Williams usually masqueraded under the plural identity 'Y Ddau Wynne', thus coupling herself with her sister Gwenffreda. But modern scholarship suspects that Mallt was much the more active partner. Hers was a reactionary, patrician model of Celticism consistent with her perceived social position as the scion of an ancient gentry family reduced to bourgeois status, and there were some similarities between her compensatory Celtic dream and that of Yeats. Their resort to 'the Celtic' was, in important part, a response of deracinés to a social world of violent, radical, disorientating change. The later Yeats was to make a virtue out of the resulting inner divisions in his nature by developing a theory of deliberately cultivated multiple personality (his 'Masks') and a ceaseless psychic dialectic haunted by the unattainable ideal of unified sensibility. But the early Yeats dreamt (if somewhat uncertainly and fitfully even then) of resolving all by embracing a quintessential 'Celticness' of being. Even at that relatively early juncture in his development, however, he refused to accept that the price of assuming a single Celtic identity might be to learn Irish, as his friend Douglas Hyde had done, so that he might gain direct access to the original, authentic Celtic sources. Culturally displaced daughter of a would-be patrician anglophone Wales, as Yeats was the culturally displaced son of a bourgeois Anglo-Ireland, Mallt Williams took the step refused by Yeats of 'reconnecting' with native aboriginal sources by learning the indigenous Celtic language. But both she and Yeats alike found their way to a 'racial' Celtic identity that was in many respects a defensive psychic formation fashioned in the image of their respective experiences of socio-cultural deracination.

The regressive, politically reactionary and indeed frankly racist character of Mallt Williams's Celticism is crudely evident in her novel *A Maid of Cymru*, originally serialized in *Young Wales* (1900–1). One set scene, emblematic of Williams's Celtic enthusiasms, is centred on the Gorsedd ceremony at an eisteddfod held on a hillside in the neighbourhood of the 'black country' of the south Wales industrial valleys. It is attended not only by the 'iron and steel workers of Dowlais and Rhymney and Cyfarthfa', along with 'miners and surface workers' (*YW*, 1901, 38), but by 'quarrymen', thus making the audience a composite of the whole 'proletariat' of Wales, north as well as south. The setting, 'Carnedd y Milwyr/ Cairn of the Warriors', has been chosen for its 'associations with the past', and the Gorsedd stones themselves are likewise 'the stone memorials of the great Past'. The Celticness of that past is evident from the Gorsedd robes of Tangwystl Hywel, the tale's heroine, regally garbed as she is in a red robe adorned, at her throat, with 'a striped ribbon of the three bardic colours – blue, white, and green' (*YW*, 1901, 38). Those attending bow the knee to this 'Princess' – the stability that Williams, like Yeats, craved required reversion to an imaginary Celtic society not only antique but rigidly hierarchical, formal and ceremonial. So conceived, it was the opposite of the raucously egalitarian emergent society of the south Wales coalfield. Williams's workers are reassuringly deferential and that in the very year which saw the election in Merthyr of Keir Hardie (1901), the first Socialist MP, presaging the coming age of violent class struggle, labour disputes and radical politics. Incredulous witness to these elaborately choreographed bardic ceremonies is Tangwystl's would-be suitor, Garry Thoyts, quarry manager and a 'descendant of hard-headed, dour North Englishmen' (*YW*, 1901, 40). Between the pair lay 'a great gulf . . . the old barrier of racial division, which is as strong today between a Sais and a pure Cymro, as it ever was' (*YW*, 1901, 40).

> The two must ever remain apart. The Sais is materialistic to his very heart's core – a leader in the utilitarian conquest of the world. The Cymro is at heart a dreamer – a living link with the mighty past, and it is no effort for him to throw himself, heart and mind, back through the Ages – to carry out a role that, from the standpoint of the practical prosaic Sais, appears objectless, puerile, and ridiculous. (*YW*, 1901, 40)

His passion is not eisteddfodau but cricket – but Tangwystl returns scorn for scorn, scoffing at the vulgar English love of low music-hall entertainments and contrasting it with Welsh devotion to the higher things of the spirit.

As the tale unfolds, an impending workers' strike is avoided through a venerable bard's appeal both to their pride in their ancient racial past (although at this point they are invested with an even deeper antiquity, addressed as descendants of the autochthonous dark little people who antedated even the 'yellow-haired, tall-statured Celts' [*YW*, 1901, 112]) and to their religious natures. Williams trusts to these two 'control mechanisms' to manage the volatile proletariat of the new anglophone coalfield. As for Tangwystl, the ardent advances of the passionate Garry temporarily transport her to the Enchanted Isles, before she recovers her senses and returns 'once more [to] the work-a-day world, far removed from that dream-world, which is the natural home of the Celt' (*YW*, 1901, 131). At this point, Arnold's feminised image of the Celt thus finds its apotheosis in an actual woman dangerously prone to fall victim to her own passionate nature. But then, having effectively banished Garry from her life (an interesting parallel is drawn with orthodox Jewish aversion to 'marrying out'),

Tangwystl finds consolation in such projects as a school for Welsh harpists. Taking initiatives in 'our sister nation, Alban' (*YW*, 1901, 205) as her model, she further underlines her proudly professed pan-Celticism by singing Breton songs, having learnt 'the tongue of my brother Celt of Brittany – the tongue most nearly allied to my beloved Cymraeg' (*YW*, 1901, 206).

Since Mallt Williams was raised near Brecon, the daughter of a medical officer who served with the First Brecknockshire Rifle Volunteers,[49] then there may be a note of autobiography in the scene in which General Mortimer and Major Byng Orris sneer at 'the wild natives of the hills', deplore Welsh as a primitive, barbarous, 'guttural tongue', and announce that 'the Welsh classes [i.e. the upper classes] are as English as we are. It is only the *people* who are different.' (*YW*, 1901, 208) The scene, deliberately resembling an Indian, colonial setting (Orris complains 'the Indian cameo' he wore has been stolen by the thieving Welsh), seems to disclose the provenance for Williams's particular upper-class brand of fervent Celtophilia. Tangwystl's eventual betrothal to the cosmopolitan Cadwgan is consequent upon the conversion of that worldly upper-class Welshman to the nationalist cause.[50]

Central to Williams's Celticism was the cult of the Leader. Taking as her model the role of Lord Castletown in Ireland and Lord Archibald Campbell in Scotland, she dreamt of 'a man of ancient Cymric lineage, of high position and influence, an enthusiast for his country, and devoted to the advancement of the Celtic race'.[51] This male fantasy was complemented by a female one. A firm believer in marriage only to a fellow-Celt, Williams encouraged Welsh women firmly to suppress any passion for a cultural 'outsider', advocating the secular equivalent of that 'religion of sacrifice' that, she was convinced, Christianity had been in Wales in days gone by.[52] She herself seems to have lived by her precepts, remaining unmarried until her death, and a recurrent preoccupation of her fiction was with the life of the single woman. In 'The Passing of Mamgu Pali', an old woman recalls her distant wedding day with gratitude for having saved her 'from the reproach of her world (which holds the unmated woman up to contempt)'.[53] Williams's way of dealing with this kind of prejudice is made clear by Tangwystl in *A Maid of Cymru*, when she announces that 'independently of love, and marriage, I have so many interests, in life, that I cannot image myself, ever a lonely and desolate woman. If one likes, one can always keep a young heart, and there will always be Mam Gymru to work for.' (*YW*, 1900, 284) But the end of the tale sees

Tangwystl safely married to her perfect Welsh suitor, Hoel Cadwgan, thus confirming the cultural message already conveyed by the previous tale about Mamgu Pali. That story turned on the miraculous appearance in the sheltered life of Mamgu's beautiful young grand-daughter, Gwenni, of the grandson of the young local fisherman who had been her granny's original beau. The moral of the tale was meant to be that a suitable partner can always be found within one's own immediate cultural circle, as is evident from *A Maid of Cymru* where reference is actually made by Tangwystl to the earlier story: 'Nay, take comfort in Gwenni's creed – that the maid destined to wear the wedding ring may sit at home in the "congl", and ne'er trouble to leave it, for "her man" will appear true to his time, never fear.' (*YW*, 1900, 128)

Williams's politico-cultural philosophy was outlined succinctly in the essay 'Patriotism and the Women of Cymru', contributed by her to *Young Wales*.[54] It announced the launch of a new patriotic female society 'to support and extend the Home Industries of the Principality'. Taking as its model Irish and Scottish initiatives, it pledged itself to revive such traditional occupations as 'spinning and weaving, the most picturesque and graceful of all occupations, for women', as well as 'knitting, carving, pottery, and any other home work'. The instigator of this society was the Irish aristocrat Lady Eva Wyndham-Quin ('a representative of one of the few really old Celtic families of Erin'), while its objectives were identified as being 'to find employment for poor families in the cultivation of their national talents, in their own home and country, thus providing a check to emigration'. This all reflected Williams's determination to 'teach the A. B. C. of patriotism' to Welsh women who 'have not cultivated – hardly recognize' such a virtue. On the contrary, Williams indignantly declares: 'they have banished an ancient Celtic tongue – their *mother* tongue – the tongue of saints and heroes and princes, from the drawing-room, the schoolroom, and the nursery'. Angered by her Welsh sisters' abandonment of 'picturesque national dress' and failure to teach their children 'the history, poetry, and legends of their own country', she conjures the 'Wives and daughters of Cymru', 'of the pure, native blood – as distinct from Norman houses and English settlers', to 'shake off the apathy of an inglorious past, and show the world of today . . . that the heroic virtue is not dead in you, has only been asleep'.

In the interests of furthering her mission to mobilise women to restore a lost 'Celtic' Wales, Mallt Williams seems to have sought out the company of like-minded single women. One such was Gwyneth

Vaughan, who in 1902 joined Williams in forming *Undeb y Ddraig Goch* (Union of the Red Dragon), an organisation based on the Gaelic League model, which pledged itself to protect and advance the cause of the Welsh language: '[I]f Wales is to retain its individuality,' the organisation's manifesto ran, 'it *must* preserve its language. The Undeb will devote its energies to the safe-guarding and propagation of the Cymraeg.'[55]

Mallt Williams's verbal portrait of her ally ('Madame Gwyneth Vaughan') appeared in volume VII of *Young Wales*.[56] Vaughan (see also chapters 2 and 4) is described as having worked as a physician in both England and Wales, served on the Caernarvon Board of Guardians and the District Council, and done much editorial work. An accomplished linguist (mistress of five languages), she had established 162 Branches of the British Women's Temperance Association and acted as Secretary to the Welsh Union of Women's Liberal Associations. 'But what Madame Vaughan esteems the greatest of all her successes,' Williams significantly emphasises, 'is the right to wear the white robe of a Druidess, and speak from the sacred Llog Maen – the only woman in modern times who has done so – and in her snowy satin robes, hand-painted with designs of the oakleaf, acorn, mistletoe, and leek, and coats-of-arms of her ancestors.' And it was those ancestors that particularly fascinated Williams, because, as Vaughan, a confirmed pan-Celtophile, informed *Celtia*, she was descended from no less a figure than Gruffydd ap Cynan, 'the last King of all Wales, who was brought up in Ireland, and who organised a Congress of Irish and Welsh bards in North Wales about AD 1100'.[57] Saluting *Celtia* from the 'Mountains of Eryri', Vaughan urged it to 'inspire with courage the old Celtic spirit that has slept so long with Arthur in the Isle of Avalon. And may you foster that love of the beautiful, the noble and the free that is inherent in every true-born Celt.'

* * *

Set Vaughan's fondness for donning 'Druidic' dress alongside Mallt Williams's penchant for dressing up as a 'Celtic' princess, and yet another facet of Celticism is revealed – its appeal not to the thoroughly domesticated wives and mothers addressed in 'Patriotism and the Women of Cymru', but rather to those women of the period who consciously or unconsciously felt strait-jacketed within the existing approved female roles, and yearned for opportunities to give fuller expression to their (frequently independent-minded and strong-willed) natures. Both Vaughan and Williams accordingly fantasised about the socially prominent and consequently powerful, role of women in ancient 'Celtic' society. Some manifestations of the movement might therefore benefit from being approached from the perspective of gender studies, and from being set in the context of 'the New Woman' and of experimentation during the 1890s with sexual preference and gender identity. One prominent figure attracted to the fashion for the Celtic, for instance, was Yeats's legendary muse, Maud Gonne, a singular personality, complex and formidable, whose passion for Irish independence was surpassed, if at all, only by her passion for her own.

While Gwyneth Vaughan's active support for progressive Liberalism and the rights of women mark her out as very much a vigorous modern reformer, her creative work exposes a vein of conservative Celticism broadly akin to what Mallt Williams had preached in her own fiction. As noted in chapter 4, this ideology found powerful expression in her two historical novels, *O Gorlannau y Defaid* and *Plant y Gorthrwm*, and in choosing two names from the Mabinogion – Rhianon and Olwen – for the two young daughters of Hafod Olau farm in the latter novel (the name itself signifies enlightened habitation), and in naming their young friend 'Dyddgu' after one of Dafydd ap Gwilym's most celebrated paramours, Vaughan was choosing to advertise the 'Celtic' credentials of her Welsh characters.

But her avowed pan-Celticism found its most overt expression in her allegorical fiction, 'The Old Song and the New'.[58] This is a lush druidic fantasy set 'in one of the years that are lost in the past when the world was young', and it opens with 'the strong sons and the fair daughters of the people that dwelt in the Isle of the Mighty' congregating to sing the fulsome praises of their land. They are blest by the visionary appearance of a group in white led by a venerable chief 'that had a circlet of gold round his brows, and a wreath of the sacred oak leaves was set upon the gold, which, when the sun cast its beams thereon, became so brilliant that the light therefrom gladdened the hearts of men'.

Their joyous celebrations are interrupted by a visit from a mysterious ship silently moving without sails and carrying a 'fair damsel' clad in a glittering rainbow-coloured dress. 'Sunder' is her name and her message is well suited to it, because she forecasts invasion and the scattering of the people by a powerful all-conquering enemy. This prompts the gathered assembly to volunteer five different courses of action, with three leaders opting to flee with Sunder to the safety of other locations, easily identified respectively as Ireland, Brittany and the Isle of Man, while another opts instead for the Highlands of Scotland, and a last declares an intention to stay put in what clearly is Wales. In reply, the 'damsel' murmurs a promise under her breath that their parting 'is not for all time, they will come back, and I may sunder them no more, for they shall be as one kindred again as heretofore'. The last part of the short narrative accordingly concerns the reunification, ages later, of the scattered Celtic peoples in response to the reawakening of Arthur, who gathers them together from Erin, the Isle of Man, Brittany, the Scottish Highlands and the 'Cymric mountains'.

In its cultural revivalist spirit, this fantasy resembles another published by Vaughan in the periodical *Cymru* under the title 'Breuddwyd Nos Nadolig' (A Dream on Christmas Eve).[59] This opens with the narrator sitting in front of a coal fire on a dark, snowy evening, entranced by faces from early youth forming in the glowing embers. This nostalgic scene dissolves into a dream vision. Standing aloft on a crag overlooking a Cardigan bay that had once been the familiar playground of youth, the dreamer hears a cry come from the darkness and makes out the indistinct form of a giant woman outstretched. Prone, helpless and suffering, she is passed first by a young aristocrat who disdains her, then a priest mockingly wishes her a speedy death, and finally a young blade, a mincing girl on his arm, vents his sarcasm at her expense.

At this point, the fantasy changes tone as the giant's slow recovery begins with angel voices hymning, as at Christ's nativity, but this time proclaiming 'Eu hiaith a gadwant' ('Their language shall they [the Welsh] retain'), a prophecy attributed by Iolo Morganwg to Taliesin. A soldier-poet next addresses to her a patriotic eulogy for the land of Wales, followed by a young poet who rejuvenates her with his love songs. Consequently transformed into a princess and clad in all the beauty of a second Eve, she receives elaborate ritual of homage from priests and is showered with treasures by an arch-druid. The apotheosis of her transfiguration is reached when a radiant figure wearing a glittering mitre places a crown of laurels on her head. The fiction ends with the firm assurance that the translation of the Bible by Bishop William Morgan in 1588 has ensured the survival for all time of the Welsh language.

This fantasy is confirmation that Vaughan's Celticism was rooted in her concerns for the future of the threatened Welsh language and its culture. It is also a clear example of the prominent tendency amongst many Welsh Celticists, like many other patriots, to sacralise their devotion to their land and its history. Raised as so many of them had been in a Nonconformist culture steeped in the Bible, it was natural for them to express their attachment to their nation in religious terms. Indeed, a significant minority of the young Welsh intelligentsia of this period went so far as to find in the religion of nation a comforting alternative to discredited religious belief.

Fables and allegories such as 'The Old Song and the New' and 'Breuddwyd Nos Nadolig' were very fashionable among the pan-Celticists, not least because in genre as much as in register they contrasted starkly with what was regarded as the sordid, dirty realism of so much of the new fiction of the day. Several contributors to *Celtia*, including the editor Fournier himself, published winsome little parables encapsulating the movement's aspirations. Such utopian forms of fiction allowed the devotees of Celticism to ignore the social, cultural and political realities separating the 'nations' whose union they were so determined to prophesy and celebrate.

* * *

There is a clear elegiac tone to Vaughan's Celtic writings, plangent records as they were of a fading language and the rural culture it had primarily supported. But while this sombre bourdon is also to be heard in the writings of many of the pan-Celticists from other countries of that time, it is not infrequently drowned out by its opposite – a triumphalist affirmation that it is the future, and not the past, that belongs to the Celtic peoples. There was, in particular, among many progressive Welsh Celticists a very active interest in developments in Ireland.[60] As Young Wales activists, they were naturally very conscious of Thomas Davis's Young Ireland movement (1842), modelled on the liberal Romantic vision of nationality advanced most influentially by Mazzini that had produced not only Young Italy but also Young Bohemia, Young Ukraine, Young Argentina, Young Tyrol, Young Austria and even Young America.

In choosing Young Ireland as the title of his movement, Davis had in mind not only all these other Europe-wide national movements, but to distinguish his initiative from the fading and sectional Old

Ireland movement of Daniel O'Connell, the great hero of Catholic Emancipation (1829). *The Nation*, the periodical that became the voice of Davis's new movement, was to prove an inspiration for those intellectuals of the Cymru Fydd/Young Wales movement who established a string of periodicals, in both English and Welsh, during the 1890s to advance their cause. Of those many different ideological factions of which Young Wales was in practice composed, it was those constituencies whose principal concern was the maintenance of unity of purpose that were most powerfully attracted to the particular, inclusive and ecumenical version of nationalism that had been formulated a half century earlier in Davies's *Nation*.

As J. Hugh Edwards, the editor of *Young Wales*, put it in 1896, 'we have preached the same gospel of Nationalism as did Thomas Davis and the other Young Irelanders in the pages of their periodical'.[61] But he regretted that he could not claim, in Davis's very words, to have broken 'that long habit of looking to foreign arms or English money for redress' and to have succeeded, as had the *Nation*, 'in impressing on the people that self-reliance is the only liberator'. A year later, in 1897, Edwards devotes another editorial to the same subject. He enviously recalls a letter a young villager sent in 1843 to Gavan Duffy, editor of *The Nation*, remarking that more copies of the periodical were sold in his locality than there were people to read it. And Edwards ruefully quotes another observer's recollection of seeing a crowd of young Irish 'peasants' listening to the *Nation* being read aloud, and 'swaying to and fro in the fever of a new faith for which they were impatient to labour and suffer'.[62]

The attraction of the Young Ireland gospel, of course, was also that it contrasted so decisively with the violent version of Irish nationalism that had succeeded it and that, along with ignorant superstitious Irish 'Papism', had so horrified a proudly educated, self-consciously sophisticated Welsh Nonconformist nation addicted to respectable quietism and correspondingly terrified of being seen by their powerful Anglo-Saxon neighbours as tarred with the same 'Celtic' brush as their barbarous, primitive, bog-ignorant cousins. A vitriolic commentary on Parnell in an 1891 issue of *Cymru Fydd* speaks contemptuously of 'Irish pertinacity and howling', sympathises deeply with the wronged and righteous Gladstone, and smugly announces that 'Wales is practically unanimous on Disestablishment; much more unanimous than Ireland is on Home Rule'. It ends: 'We hope that the moral revolt of the country against Mr Parnell will burn into the conscience of Young Wales everywhere that character is the principal thing, and that fear of God is the beginning of all wisdom.'[63]

In an essay for *Young Wales* on 'The National Unity of Wales', the charismatic T. E. Ellis, already a star of Gladstonian Liberalism and tipped as a future prime minister, attributed the nineteenth-century spread of nationalist ferment across Europe to the Irish example: 'Ireland has given a new significance to all schemes of local self-government by struggling and suffering for the principle of nationality . . . Nationality is now becoming a factor in English domestic politics. Catholic Ireland, Nonconformist Wales, and Presbyterian Scotland have emphasised their national existence in worship and in religious polity in face of pitiless persecution, and of the strenuous opposition of a large section of English opinion.'[64] But Ellis was, of course, not thinking of Parnellism, let alone Fenianism; he was recalling the example of Thomas Davis and his followers. This new, wary, highly selective late-nineteenth-century Welsh interest in things Irish was, therefore, firmly centred on such a generous vision of the national cause as had been voiced in Davis's *Nation* in the eloquent terms quoted by Edwards in a *Young Wales* editorial of 1897: 'a Nationality which will not only raise our people from their poverty, by securing to them the blessings of a Domestic Legislation, but inflame them with a lofty and heroic love of country – a Nationality of the spirit as well as the letter – a Nationality which will come to be stamped upon our manners, our literature, and our deeds – a Nationality which may embrace Protestant, Catholic and Dissenter – the native of a hundred generations and the stranger who is within our gates – a Nationality which would be recognized by the world, and sanctified by wisdom, virtue and prudence.'[65]

It's easy to see how such a vision of the nation appealed strongly to individuals like the fascinatingly maverick J. Arthur Price, a barrister and unorthodox Tory Anglican marching in the ranks of a Young Wales movement dominated by Liberal Nonconformists. In his two-part portrait of Davis for *Cymru Fydd*, he exulted in Davis's supposed Welsh ancestry, and claimed that his political ideas 'represent the ideal politics of a Celtic race'.[66] 'The prophet for all time of Celtic nationalism', Davis had favoured a four-nation federation as the cornerstone of a 'British' state. Price quotes a letter he'd written to Wellington: 'I ask you to give to Ireland a Senate of some sort elected by the people in part or in whole . . . This, were I an Englishman, I should ask for

England, beside the Imperial Parliament. So I would for Wales if I were a Welshman, and for Scotland were I a Scotchman.'

Although cautious talk of a Welsh-Irish alliance rarely got beyond rhetorical generalities, and was always bedevilled by rank Nonconformist anti-Catholic sentiment, there were occasional gestures towards practical cooperation.[67] In 1897, William O'Brien, that veteran of the Irish Land struggles, contributed an essay on the subject to *Young Wales*, urging Wales to remember the botched attempts by Gladstone and others to resolve the issue by Westminster legislation in order for Wales to avoid falling victim to the same experience. 'One of the permanent results of Mr Gladstone's Irish policy,' O'Brien hopefully argued, 'is that the Irish and Welsh nations, once so closely related in blood and history, have been drawing together again.'[68] The concept of Celtic kinship could thus still surface, if only as distant sentimental memory, even in the midst of the hard, difficult contemporary realities of radical social, religious and political differences. In 'Pat and His Four Ps', for instance, Arthur Mee (later of *Children's Encyclopaedia* fame) expressed the hope that by the end of the nineteenth century the old prejudices entertained by the Welsh against earlier immigrants from Ireland – 'the riff-raff of their country [who] loved to tipple and to squabble' – had now at last disappeared. Welcoming the rapprochement signified by the clasp of hands at the Eisteddfod between a Catholic priest (Father Hayde) and a 'Nonconformist pastor' (the Arch-druid Hwfa Môn), Mee urged the Welsh to identify and sympathise with the struggles of the 'winsome', good-natured and somewhat feckless Irish against their extortionate landlords.[69]

* * *

It was certainly only the vague rhetoric of a Celtic alliance that still survived, once the political hopes of Young Wales had been dashed by the notorious secession of the powerful South Wales Liberal Association from Lloyd George's cause of Home Rule in 1896 – although along with that went an interest in literary cooperation. Literature had always been central to the Mazzini version of nationalism espoused by both Young Ireland and Young Wales, as considered in chapter 4. Mazzini himself had begun life as a *littérateur*, and Thomas Davis was a poet. They both strongly believed in the power of literature and the other arts to shape national consciousness, to elevate the mind and to unify and mobilise an otherwise fatally divided and paralysed national community. Nineteenth-century history bore testimony to the efficacy of such a vision – Italian unity was in part born of Manzoni's novel *I promessi sposi*, and was achieved to the accompaniment of Verdi's great operas. There is a strong overlap between this Romantic concept of literature and the view of writing championed by modern discourse theory, which emphasises that writing (including literature) is not a product of culture, but an active producer of culture. It is, therefore, not a secondary but a primary cultural phenomenon, as powerful a determinant of cultural life as, say, is economics or politics. And there have been several important studies of nationalism as a discursive product.

By the 1880s, a talented group of young Irish writers of this kind of persuasion had attached themselves to the nationalist cause, and soon their vision of the national future took on a pan-Celtic character. In an important discussion of the subject, Daniel G. Williams has persuasively argued that the three-nations Home Rule favoured by the young W. B. Yeats and others has been conveniently airbrushed out of fashionable contemporary post-colonial Irish nationalist historiography.[70] But the Celtic Renaissance was in its day, as this chapter has already demonstrated, a movement of very considerable cultural reach and penetration in which Irish writers found ready partners for their nationalist enterprise, both in Wales and in Scotland. In keeping with nineteenth-century racial theory, the common denominator 'Celtic' was, of course, taken to be a scientifically proven racial category, and 'Celtic culture' assumed to bear the distinctive, supra-national imaginative character so potently described by Matthew Arnold.

A strain of pan-Celticism, compensating in part for the terminal breakdown in 1896 of an effective Liberal-led nationalist politics, becomes evident in the pages of *Young Wales* during the second half of the 1890s. Its chief spokesperson is probably Ernest Rhys, a figure who still earns a footnote in English cultural history as the visionary founder for Dent of the Everyman Library which he proceeded to edit with remarkable energy for the first forty years of the twentieth century. Everyman would, in fact, bear studying as a 'Young Wales Project'. Rhys's aim, from the outset, was to ensure Welsh materials sat alongside English materials in the series – one of the earliest volumes was a translation of the *Mabinogion*. At the same time, Rhys was discussing with his namesake, John Rhŷs, Oxford Professor of Celtic, the possibility of an edition of Malory's *Morte D'Arthur* with an introduction arguing for the Welshness of border country Malory. Arthur was, as the following chapter will show, a key figure in the Young Wales pantheon, and Rhys's approach to him was in a spirit that would nowadays be termed post-colonial – involving a reclamation for Wales of a figure appropriated by English culture. When he toured a lecture on 'the Revolt of the Celt', Rhys built to a climax that featured the retelling of the accidental reawakening of Arthur by a young boy who stumbled upon his cave and rang the great bell.

A man of letters whose working lifetime spanned from Browning to Dylan Thomas, and took in almost every writer of note during that period, Rhys (as noted earlier) thought of himself, by virtue of both his ancestry and his upbringing, as an Anglo-Welshman in the sense of part-Welsh, part-English. His 'unconventional' dual nationality and 'mixed' or 'mongrel' character alerts us to an under-estimated aspect of the pan-Celtic movement. It could usefully be set in the context of social reform movements that were such a dramatically prominent feature of the closing decades of the nineteenth century. There was clearly an overall impulse to review the constitution of established society in quite radical ways. And one evident consequence was the proliferation of innumerable models of alternative social structure, ranging from those based on the redressing of gender inequalities, through the reconfiguring of sexual identities, or the many different versions of proto-socialism, to the sometimes colourful spiritual and spiritualist experimentations of the period. Viewed against this background, pan-Celticism could be read as a critique of the way in which the 'Britishness' assiduously developed and promoted throughout what had been a triumphantly 'imperial' century was stiflingly monocultural in character. In addition, the effort implicit in pan-Celticism to construct a different, decentred and multi-cultural image of a federated Britishness was consistent with such attempts as are evident in the later nineteenth century to 'regionalise' England itself – attempts, in turn, frequently involving the serious recognition and appraisal of ways of life alien (and sometimes exotically intriguing) to dwellers in the great metropolis. Thomas Hardy was, of course, merely the most prominent and eminent example of the 'regional' novelists of the period.[71]

This kind of reading of pan-Celticism is particulary helpful when we consider the case of Ernest Rhys, because, as already suggested, it allows us to make sense of the continuities between his earliest work in the north-east of England where he had spent all his youthful years, and the work of his 'middle period' when the Welsh elements in his make-up were very much brought to the fore as he increasingly identified with the Cymru Fydd/Young Wales 'renaissance'. And, indeed, full acknowledgement of the several different 'regions' with which Rhys could legitimately claim intimate identification allows us further to recognise how, in pan-Celticism, he found a movement particularly suited to his own fractured case, as one of mixed Welsh-Geordie-Cockney-Irish inheritance. 'A Londoner born, as well as a Welshman in exile,' Rhys was to write towards the end of his life, 'I suffered from the mixed sympathies that are bound to affect a man of mixed race.'[72] It may be no coincidence that one of the ballads he originally contributed to the Rhymers' Club book and subsequently collected in *Welsh Ballads* features 'Howel of two passionate races', who is killed by his brother for being 'bastard bred' (i.e. of mixed race).

Rhys, then, felt most at home in the federated, multi-national pan-Celtic movement, becoming a fixed friend of Yeats in the later 1880s, joining him in establishing the famous 'Celt-fixated' Rhymers' Club in London in 1891, and going on to write a novel expressly intended for illustration by Yeats's artist brother, Jack B. Yeats. Balancing his interest in things Irish was his interest in things Scottish. He befriended the figure most closely corresponding to Yeats in the Scottish pan-Celtic movement, William Sharp. According to Rhys, Sharp actually concocted the name 'Fiona' – the only product of pan-Celticism still to enjoy a popular vogue today.

Rhys's first contribution to *Young Wales* was a piece about his vain search for Owain Glyndŵr's grave, during which he had been dismayed to discover how little memory of him remained in his native region.[73] The trope of lost cultural memory, signifying both source and symptom of loss of effective national identity, was a key trope of pan-Celticism. It was alternatively conceived in terms of a buried selfhood, imaged in turn by the figure of a mythic figure like Arthur or Glyndŵr, departed but not dead, and due to reappear one day; and the pan-Celticists proposed to assist in the process of restoration through their own creative work. Hence the interest of the young Yeats in Ancient Irish-language myth and legend and fairy lore, and hence, too, the parallel venture Rhys undertook in publishing *Welsh Ballads*, a collection that interleaved some of his own poems with translations from old Welsh poetry. In its very form, the collection was emblematic of the belief he shared with Yeats that his modern anglophone nation's ignorance of a past exclusively available to it in its declining indigenous language was accelerating the erosion of national identity. Equally important was the use of English to unlock 'the riches of [old Celtic] poetry and its romantic past to the outer world', as Rhys put it in a *Young Wales* interview.[74] Yeats, who had just praised in Lionel Johnson's poetry 'the Celt's futile revolt against the despotism of fact', warmed to Rhys's enterprise in a review he published of Rhys's *Welsh Ballads* (1898). He welcomed the work as representative of a new movement that

> has made painters and poets and musicians go to old legends for their subjects, for legends are the magical beryls in which we see life, not as it is, but as the heroic part of us, the part which desires always dreams and emotions greater than any in the world, and loves beauty and does not sorrow, hopes in secret that it may become. Because a great portion of the legends of Europe, and almost all the legends associated with the scenery of these islands, are Celtic, this movement has given the Celtic countries a sudden importance, and awakened some of them to a sudden activity.[75]

In Yeats's mind, Rhys and Sharp (Macleod) respectively represented Welsh and Scottish Celticism, and in another review (28 April 1897), this time of the *Spiritual Tales* (1897) of 'Fiona Macleod', he reaffirmed his belief in a multinational pan-Celtic movement that included such figures as the Belgian Maurice Maeterlinck. 'The truth is,' Yeats wrote of Macleod, 'that she, like all who have Celtic minds and have learnt to trust them, has in her hands the keys of those gates of the primeval world, which shut behind more successful races, when they plunged into material progress.' (*UP*, 40–1)

But this anglophone project championed by Yeats, Rhys and Sharp produced a fierce backlash on both sides of the Irish sea. In an article for *Young Wales*, Fournier argued that at the heart of the movement must lie the attempt at 'the revival of the Celtic languages'. He distinguished, with some heat, between the five movements dedicated to this cause, and the sixth movement 'variously referred to as "the Celtic Renaissance", "the Celtic Glamour", or "the Celtic Gift"', which was 'simply a special development of English literature, useful in opening up some of the treasures of Celtic lore to the monoglot English and to English-speaking Celts'.[76] With Fournier's vision in mind, the Cardiff National Eisteddfod of 1901, extensively covered by *Young Wales*, was specifically designated a 'Pan-Celtic Eisteddfod', and cries out for cultural analysis as such. And, as mentioned earlier, the same vision led to the convening in 1901 of 'the first Congress of the united Celtic peoples . . . in the beautiful capital of the Emerald Isle – the birthplace of the Celtic Association', as was reported in *Young Wales* that year by the sisters who wrote under the pseudonym 'Y Ddau Wynne'.

Rhys's contribution to pan-Celticism has received some attention from Welsh cultural critics; not so the contribution of his wife, Grace Rhys. She, however, is occasionally listed as a minor female writer in the bibliographies of Irish Edwardian fiction because she was born Grace Little, into a typically eccentric Anglo-Irish gentry family in County Roscommon. The Ireland-Scotland-Wales triangulation that was the matrix of pan-Celticism conveniently figures in the actual meeting between Rhys and his future wife. They first met at a garden party in Hampstead arranged by Yeats, and then got better acquainted at another party hosted by William Sharp's wife, Elizabeth, yet another ardent pan-Celticist. And the same triangulation seems to have been replicated in Grace Rhys's early writing career. While her first novel, *Mary Dominic* (1898), was based in Ireland, her second, *The Wooing of Sheila* (1901), was based in Wales. And before the publication of either, she seems – assuming that she did indeed adopt the pseudonym 'Gracie ap Rhys' – to have published in serialised form in *Young Wales* a novella that, although primarily Welsh in character, has a Scottish element. It is the Unionist Scots that are the villains of 'A College Tale', as they are the leaders of an anti-Welsh (i.e. anti-Young Wales) faction at one of Wales's new university colleges.[77]

Interestingly enough, in the same year as Rhys's 'A College Tale' appeared in its pages, *Young Wales* also printed an essay by J. Angus Wilson, Fordyce Lecturer at the University of Aberdeen, on 'Nationalism in Scotland'. It was, in effect, an argument against pan-Celticism on the solid grounds that the 'national sentiments' of the respective peoples involved were so widely divergent. Pointing to the congeries of feelings and aims involved in the Welsh case, Wilson argued that likewise in Scotland only a small fraction of its population could meaningfully be considered Celtic, and that otherwise, apart from a passionate attachment to their own separate legal system, Scots, while fiercely patriotic, were happily integrated into the British nation.[78] Nevertheless, a faint sense of common cause with their 'fellow Celts' in Scotland still lingered in the hearts of some Welsh Celticists. In 1901, *Young Wales* published a poem by W. Llewelyn Williams in the person of David Morgan, a Welsh Jacobite who, as he awaits execution, recalls the way he had waited in vain for Sir Watkin Williams-Wynn to lead a Welsh force in support of Bonnie Prince Charlie in 1745. 'Once more,' Morgan had hoped, 'the Cymro and the Gael/ would join in bravely fighting for country and for king.' But Morgan's trust in the Welsh gentry had been betrayed, to the eternal 'shame [of] our gallant country/ that never would be free'.[79]

However, it was the Wales-Ireland axis that was central to the pan-Celticism of both Grace and Ernest Rhys, and that found its prominent literary form in the *Celtic Anthology* on which they both collaborated.[80] It can be read as a revisionist version of *Lyra Celtica*, the anthology published by Elizabeth and William Sharp more than twenty years earlier.[81] It is revisionist because it includes an important section of translations from contemporary Welsh-language poetry by the leading poets of the twentieth-century Welsh Renaissance. Unlike the Sharps' anthology, it thus advertises the continuing vigour of Welsh as a modern Celtic language. And while the anthology is in some ways a very belated product of the 1890s pan-Celtic movement, it is also a bridge between it and the future, because one of its contributors was C. M. Grieve, alias Hugh MacDiarmid, who was to be a significant figure for the 'new wave' Anglo-Welsh generation of the 1930s and also for the young R. S. Thomas, who was himself so great a devotee of the work of 'Fiona Macleod' that he went searching for an authentic rural Gaelic society, first on Skye, and then, more satisfyingly, in the far west of Ireland, as the great Welsh-language poet, Gwenallt, had done before him.

* * *

Scholars of 'raciology' have recently become interested in the darker potentialities of Celticism noting, for instance, how many 'prominent linguist and race theorists in the German academy [were] figures important to the articulation of Germanicism' so that their identification 'with a Celtic struggle for national identity [can] be seen in parallel with the dramatic emergence of "Germany" in the nineteenth century'.[82] Their demonstration in the Irish context that the Celtic languages belonged to the Indo-European family and were thus Aryan had particularly unpleasant implications, because it was conveniently linked to 'linguists' attempt at an ethnography which tried to break any alignment of the Irish with an inferior indigenous race of "dark skinned" and "dark haired" natives.' In this connection, Heinrich Zimmer, for example, argued that this fact explained the emergence of a sophisticated civilisation on the remote Atlantic coast, the furthermost frontier of the West, with close affinities to that of the Aryan peoples; and such a contention allowed the dramatic reversal of the preferred English model of racial development, according to which the Celtic Irish were placed well below the Anglo-Saxons on the evolutionary ladder.

There are no visible signs, however, of such thinking impacting on the Celtophiles of Wales. When Ernest Rhys, for example, toyed with Aryanism in an essay for *Young Wales* on 'The Night of Welsh History', he did so in genially belletrist fashion:

> Meanwhile, we have a few landmarks in the Aryan night indicating the old highways we ['the West Brythons'] may have followed from east to west. And if it should prove, as Professor Rhŷs has seemed to suggest, that many of us Welsh who think ourselves Aryans, are only a kind of prehistoric Gypsies, who have stolen a Celtic coat or two from the backdoor of Europe, our interest in ourselves and our past need not be the less on that account.[83]

Welsh Celticism could, then, scarcely be accused of being dangerously racist in character. Instead, its history could be regarded as illustrating the unwritten law that any concept seminal to a given age becomes so because of its usefulness to that age. Moreover, it is certain to be flexible in meaning since to gain widespread traction it must be able to satisfy a variety of needs and to serve a multitude of different purposes (some of them even flatly contradictory). Far from merely reflecting and encapsulating important issues of the day, such concepts must generate new, creative means of addressing them. So, at least in historical terms, one could most fruitfully enquire not how intellectually coherent was any given key concept in its time, but rather how extensive was its range of applicability in its prime? What uses did it usefully serve in its period? What was its operational effectiveness within its social context? How many different interpretations did it prove capable of sustaining?

And when such questions are asked of Welsh Celticism and pan-Celticism, the multipurpose character of these terms immediately becomes clear. They could serve to unify a Nonconformist Wales riven by denominational rivalries and a would-be nation splintered into a plethora of tiny local communities. Forms of Celticism could be mobilised to reinforce a threatened linguistic identity, but they could also offer a means of transcending linguistic differences, since they enabled the construction of an emergent 'Welsh identity' not only in exclusively linguistic terms but also in the much less culturally restrictive terms of temperament – the latter proving particularly helpful at a time when English migration into Wales was threatening to undermine and destroy any identity exclusively premised on the Celticness of the Welsh language. And in this latter form of 'racial temperament', 'Celticism' facilitated the ready absorption of immigrants, whilst also allowing emigrants to continue to feel Welsh because they remained invincibly 'Celtic' in character. Further, in its variant forms Celticism provided Wales with the pedigree of antiquity crucial for the self-authentication of all the aspirational and emergent nations of nineteenth-century Europe. It also acted as a cultural vivifier, contributing to the emergence of a major twentieth-century cultural revival of Welsh-language literature. It facilitated easy slippage between the categories of 'nation' (still an unacceptable, politically destabilising and threatening expression for some) and 'people' (a category consistent with a progressive model of a British Empire composed of many different peoples). It allowed for the anodyne subordination of the political to the cultural – conveniently softening the threat of a separatist politics. Yet while it thus continued to accommodate the adoption of Arnold's reassuringly passive, quietist model of Celtic characteristics, it also allowed for its reversal, on appropriate occasion, into a politically active and potent form.

6

T. Gwynn Jones: The Once and Future Wales

An early symptom of the Arthurian craze that was to grip nineteenth-century England was *Le Morte D'Arthur*, a poem that the young Tennyson had written in 1833–4 and published in 1842. Reworked in 1869 as 'The Passing of the King', it movingly traced the final moments of the dying hero before duly dispatching Arthur to Avilion, 'to be king among the dead/ [But] after healing of his grievous wound/ He comes again'[1] – or so Sir Bedivere persists in hoping, although unable to suppress his lingering misgivings completely. And a coda reinforces the grieving knight's stubborn optimism:

[he saw]
Straining his eyes beneath an arch of hand,
Or thought he saw, the speck that bare the king,
Down that long water opening on the deep
Somewhere far off, pass on and on, and go
From less to less and vanish into light,
And the new sun rose bringing the new year. (*PT*, 1754)

Decades later, a young Welsh poet homed in on the same powerful story. His, though, was an altogether bleaker vision, his imagination gripped by the iron finality of Arthur's departure for Afallon (Avilion):

O drofâu'r llyn
Anial, lledodd niwl llwydwyn,
Yn araf cyniweiriodd,
Ac yno'r llong dano dôdd,

A'i chelu; fel drychiolaeth
Yn y niwl diflannu wnaeth.
Bedwyr yn drist a distaw
At y drin aeth eto draw.[2]

[From the windings of the desolate lake / crept a grey-white mist, / slowly gathering, / and there the ship melted into it / and was hidden; like a spectre / in the mist it disappeared. / Bedivere, sad and silent, / turned back again to the battle.]

With Arthur dead, the knight is left grimly alone to face a hostile world, bereft not only of his hitherto invincible leader but of the glittering, irresistible weapon of Excalibur. The age of heroism – and indeed of supernatural belief – over, Bedivere has to confront the question of 'what to make of a diminished thing?'[3]

So why was T. Gwynn Jones attracted to this particular episode in the Arthurian story? And why did he choose to provide his narrative with its darkling conclusion? A consideration of questions such as these should help bring out the complex and problematical character of a model of identity, predicated on a vision of cultural continuity, that was deeply attractive to leading figures among the turn-of-century Welsh-language intelligentsia.

* * *

T. Gwynn Jones's 'Ymadawiad Arthur' (The Departing of Arthur) turned out to be more than a poem: in short order it came to assume iconic status as, by brilliantly redeploying all the rich rhetorical resources of the great *barddas* tradition of the late Middle Ages, T. Gwynn Jones – a largely self-educated young journalist on a provincial paper – helped make possible a dazzling modern revival of Welsh-language literature. And its role as harbinger of cultural renaissance had, in turn, been made possible by a remarkable programme of cultural recuperation conducted over the two previous centuries.

It is the common fate of politically subordinated and marginalised peoples worldwide to see their culture remorselessly overwritten by the dominant culture to the point of total obliteration. Welsh history provides an advanced example of this process since, for centuries following the 1536 Act of Union, the country was steadily and successfully incorporated into the English state. Under such circumstances, the first significant signs of aboriginal reaction are always the efforts made by those whom Frantz Fanon termed 'native intellectuals' to recover and preserve such remnants of the original culture as have precariously survived. As Declan Kiberd has observed in the Irish context, this process takes on a peculiar urgency in the case of nations historically denied political expression:

> A writer in a free state works with the easy assurance that literature is but one of the social institutions to project the values which the nation admires, others being the law, the government, the army, and so on. A writer in a colony knows that these values can be fully embodied only in the written world; hence the daunting seriousness with which literature is taken by subject peoples.[4]

Beginning with the formidable Edward Lhuyd and Goronwy Owen, a wayward genius, a series of eighteenth-century scholars, antiquarians, philologists, lexicographers, grammarians and poets began to piece together the relics of the cultural history of the Welsh and, most importantly in due course for T. Gwynn Jones, to unearth such bardic and related manuscripts as fortuitously remained. It was a major effort at anamnesia – the restoration of a people's lost cultural memory. With the help of his mentor Lewis Morris, a man of substance and an accomplished antiquarian, the irascible Ieuan Brydydd Hir (Evan Evans) tramped the country in search of the mouldering manuscripts rapidly decaying in the dusty lofts of the anglicised gentry. Although eclipsed by the synthetic 'Celtic' effusions of Macpherson's *Ossian*, his authentic pioneering edition *Some Specimens of the Poetry of the Antient Bards* (1764) remains a landmark publication. Such efforts were fortified by the cognate activities of the two important Welsh societies established in London, the Honourable Society of Cymmrodorion and the Gwyneddigion. And the feats of recuperation accomplished against the odds by this first generation of 'Celtic Revivalists' were repeated in the succeeding generation by such astonishing individuals as Iolo Morganwg, who liberally laced authenticity with fabrication, as did his close acquaintance William Owen Pughe. A pair as well matched for eccentricity as for dubious originality, these two genuinely gifted scholars carried the work forward into the early decades of the nineteenth century by producing such notable compilations as the *Cambrian Register* and *The Myvyrian Archaiology of Wales.*[5]

Such labours were resumed, as the nineteenth century progressed, by 'a more educated and self-confident generation' (*GWLIV*, 185). And as the centre of production shifted from London to Wales, so too new alliances formed between native intellectuals and cultured incomers among the gentry – mostly the nouveaux riches of the new class of industrial magnates, no doubt motivated variously by an attraction to the exotic and a concern to acquire 'local' cultural credit. It is a development familiar to us today from nineteenth-century national revival movements in Ireland and on the continent. So Carnhuanawc (Revd Thomas Price), another myth-maker, inspired both Lady Llanover and Charlotte Guest with the cultural vision that resulted in such notable initiatives as the Abergavenny series of eisteddfodau, the ingenious concoction of a national dress – and, of course, Guest's historic translations of *The Mabinogion* (1849).[6] O. M. Edwards was, a half century later, to acknowledge the indebtedness of Cymru Fydd to this cultural nationalism in the pages of his influential periodical *Cymru*.[7] Edwards and others were concerned in part to ground Cymru Fydd on a new alliance between that earlier spirit of national awakening and the 'Nonconformist nation' that, between 1850 and the later 1880s, had deliberately suppressed and supplanted it.[8] But during those same decades the cool, dispassionate spirit of a new 'scientific' scholarship on the best Germanic model, shortly to be instigated by a cadre of academic professionals, was adumbrated in *The Literature of the Kymry*, an admirable work by a Unitarian chemist from the fiery industrial furnace of Merthyr. And as well as demolishing the cherished myth of Prince Madoc's medieval discovery of America, Thomas Stephens was unwittingly the first of several scholars to set about destroying the shibboleths of the eisteddfod; at that time, the embryonic national festival was in process of evolving from Old Iolo's dotty but brilliantly conceived druidic extravaganza at Carmarthen in 1819, starring the druidic Gorsedd of Bards of the Island of Britain, into a fervently patriotic celebration of popular culture.[9]

The most prominent and scathing of these new iconoclasts was John Morris-Jones, a severe young turk of a scholar trained at Oxford under Sir John Rhŷs, the first holder of the Chair of Celtic Studies established in the wake of Matthew Arnold's celebrated lectures on Celtic literature. Morris-Jones's formal university education had been significantly complemented by what he learnt as a prominent member of the Dafydd ap Gwilym Society, a seminal intellectual forum for Welsh students, where, along with his great friend O. M. Edwards, he had helped conceive and plan what became the Cymru Fydd/Young Wales movement.[10]

On his appointment as the first Professor of Welsh at the University College of North Wales, Bangor, John Morris-Jones embarked on the Herculean task of cleansing the Augean stables of Welsh culture. In a series of devastatingly rigorous scholarly articles, he demolished the claims of the Gorsedd of Bards to be of ancient British druidic descent. Afforded the prominent platform of the National Eisteddfod, where his immensely influential role as heavyweight adjudicator of one of the two major literary competitions (Chair and Crown) remained undisputed for two decades, he proceeded to launch a withering attack on that key national institution's debasement of standards to suit vulgar popular taste, its anglicised character and policy of systematic anglicisation, its tolerance of a bastardised Welsh, its rank amateurism, and its total ignorance of the demanding rules of strict-metre poetry. Simultaneously, in a series of magisterial volumes, he set about standardising Welsh orthography, producing an anatomy of Welsh grammar, and developing an intricate definitive taxonomy of *cynghanedd*. And, as a gifted poet of pronounced Europhile sentiments, whose translations of Heine reorientated Welsh-language literature, he was also able to produce a slight, but valuable, body of Parnassian lyric poetry intended, in part, to provide other aspirants with a model of best modern practice.

Nor was his self-appointed role as 'schoolmaster to the nation' (*JMJ*, 23) a mere pedagogical exercise. Behind his dazzling use of an arcane and somewhat archaic lexicon lay motives such as have been attributed to the great Italian Romantic poet, Giacomo Leopardi: 'he abhorred the present when it was stripped of its connections with its past . . . he saw in the modern age a catastrophic loss of poetic memory and an increasing impoverishment of this stereoscopic, or stratified, type of perception . . . poetry offered ongoing resistance against the tyranny of the real in its drive to abolish the recessive depths of time . . . diachronic time [was thus enabled to] overcome its isolation from the timeless.'[11]

Integral to Morris-Jones's vision of Cymru Fydd, the redeemed Wales of the future, was a cultural rapprochement and reunification of the nation with its pre-colonial past. In the modern parlance of postcolonial studies, such a hope could be anathematised as 'essentialist': in other words, it was regrettably predicated on a (typically nineteenth-century) supposition that there was a fixed, trans-historical national essence, most fully manifest at a single, arbitrarily chosen but highly prized period in what, post-colonialism would conversely (and surely correctly) insist, had in fact been a highly pluralised, fluid and indeed consistently conflicted Welsh past. But more recently, post-colonialism has come to recognise that a 'strategic essentialism' – a temporary, adventitious adoption of a selective, idealised reading of the pre-colonial past – has demonstrably proved to be an effective means of mobilising national consciousness during the initial stages of real historical anti-colonial struggles.[12] Viewed in this light, Morris-Jones's cultural ambitions become once more understandable and acceptable. Viewed against the background of the anglicised and politically progressive new industrial Wales of his time, whether they were advisable or indeed even viable is, as the following discussion will show, altogether more questionable.

It was John Morris-Jones who, confronted by 'Ymadawiad Arthur' in 1902, instantly recognised in this extraordinary classical 'awdl' that fusion of traditional *barddas* (the classic Welsh-language tradition of strict-metre poetry dating from the early Christian era) and modern practice of which he had long been dreaming and for which he had been diligently campaigning. In addition, T. Gwynn Jones's great poem was the grand apotheosis not only of two decades of recent radical 'scientific' scholarship but of two centuries of anti-colonial cultural endeavour. Moreover, the *awdl* was the very epitome of what, for John Morris-Jones, Cymru Fydd represented. Scornfully dismissing the sub-Tennysonian pastiches and the like which littered that year's Chair competition, Jones as adjudicator rejoiced in a poet who 'was at home in the Mabinogion and [the medieval Welsh Arthurian] Romances, in whose world he sings, and to whose characters and actions he makes reference in all his comparisons – to Olwen and Blodeuwedd and the birds of Rhiannon. His Welsh has borrowed its very beauty from theirs.' (*CB*, 1) In thus praising the 'native' qualities of T. Gwynn Jones's poem, however, John Morris-Jones overlooked one awkward question: how exactly did the figure of Arthur, as treated by the poet, fit into this ideal cultural schemata?

* * *

Arthur was, after all, English . . . or could he perhaps have been Welsh? To which nation did he 'really' belong? It is a complicated story . . . From Gildas's *De Excidio Britanniae* (*c*.540) onwards, the little that remains to us of Early and High Medieval Welsh literature contains several references to a figure called Arthur. But these are fleeting and fragmentary, and record history if at all only as already slippery with myth. Pondering these runes, modern scholarship has variously, tentatively, posited a heroic Brythonic leader of immediate post-Roman times, defender against Saxon incursions, and the existence of lost sagas of which 'Arthur' may have been the hero. But it is impossible to progress much beyond speculation. What is clear is that no fully developed heroic leader, complete with epic story, ever emerges from the tantalising early Welsh record. From such beginnings, the most recent scholarship has drawn (with the help of concepts such as that of Baudrillard's 'simulacrum', a copy with no original), the weary but surely accurate conclusion that 'there is no "original" Arthur and no originary or authentic Arthurian legend'.[13] Instead, modern attention has switched to an examination of the Arthurian cycle as 'a site of ideological struggle, a place where competing viewpoints engage in complex dialectics, interrogating contemporary concerns' (*CAL*, 1–2). In other words, stories have constantly emerged and evolved to serve the needs of different competing or succeeding social groups and interests.

Probably the single most influential version of the 'mature' Arthurian narrative remains the earliest and most elaborate available to us in written record. Geoffrey of Monmouth's *Historia Regum Britanniae* (1138) already contains the rich kernel of all modern Arthurian Romance.[14] And already, at this crucial early stage, Arthur is being 'remediated', as modern scholarship puts it, as a proto-*English* hero. While Geoffrey's vague mention of Brythonic source material leaves open the possibility of his working from some lost Welsh manuscripts, it is equally possible that his indebtedness, if any, was to Breton sources, since the Norman forces that first occupied Wales included many from Brittany in their ranks. Some scholars have even speculated that Geoffrey himself may have been of Breton descent. Once again, however, the issue of putative 'source' is less significant than is the ideology inscribed in Geoffrey's compelling narrative.

The thrust of his story-telling is that it is his own people, the Normans, the true descendants of Brutus, who have brought a new, sophisticated culture to Britain and therefore justly supplanted the original degenerate population. By the time that Geoffrey's tales had been modified, via Robert Wace's *Roman de Brut* (1155), for native consumption by the midlands writer Laȝamon at the beginning of the thirteenth century, they had taken on a much more committedly English complexion.[15] Meanwhile, a colourful chivalric Arthur had been fashioned by Chrétien de Troyes out of the *amour courtois* culture cultivated in eleventh-century Acquitaine, Provence, Champagne and Burgundy, and this new fashion strongly inflected both the post-Galfridian Arthurian Romances produced by the Welsh and the popular Arthurian stories widely circulating in England.[16]

Sensing the ideological potential of these potent and popular myths, the new Anglo-Norman rulers began to avail themselves of opportunities to give the stories pointed political expression by literally grounding them in native English soil. At the beginning of the twelfth century, Caradog of Llancarfan generated potentially lucrative publicity for the great monastery at Glastonbury by claiming, in his *Vita Gildae*, that Arthur had a close connection with that place. And when, later in that century, Henry II found himself discomfited by the political restlessness of the Welsh, he supplemented force with psychologically devastating symbolic action – he excavated the supposed remains of Arthur and Guinevere from their tomb at Glastonbury, thus vindicating his rule over the Welsh by demonstrating that he, and not they, was the true heir and custodian of the British past.[17] He also disposed of the myth that had been central to Welsh national survival – the myth (duly disinterred by T. Gwynn Jones) that Arthur, pending his return, rested in no known grave. From then on, James P. Carley has pithily written, 'the historical Arthur must be seen very much in the context of English imperial policy and the need of its rulers to impose themselves on their nearest neighbours.' (*AoE*, 50)

The major propaganda wars of the time continued to be waged in Arthurian terms. Following Edward I's defeat of Llywelyn the Great in 1277, the Welsh began to organise another rebellion under the banner of Arthur. In response, Edward returned to Glastonbury, disinterring Arthur's remains once again in order this time to bury them with due pomp, and reverence – and pointed finality. A few years later, the king organised a grand tournament in Nefyn to celebrate his decisive victory over the Welsh by disposing of their last Prince (1282). The 'golden crown' of Arthur was also formally presented to Westminster Abbey. And, over the succeeding decades, Arthurian tournaments were held all over England – the celebrated Round Table at Winchester Cathedral being a relic of all this prodigious pageantry.[18]

Arthur's Englishness was reaffirmed at the very dawn of the new revolutionary age of print. Malory's *Le Morte D'Arthur* (1485) had,

Caxton explained in his preface, been published at the express wish of gentlemen who had urged him to record the exploits of the 'worthy . . . Kyng Arthur, which ought moost to be remembed amonge us Englysshemen tofore al other Crysten kynges'.[19] The time had come to reclaim this quintessential English hero not only from the Italians, Spanish, French and Netherlanders whose possession he had become, but also from those pesky neighbours, the Welsh:

> Record remayne in wytnesse of hym in Wales, in the toune of Camelot, the grete stones and mervayllous werkys of yron lyeng under the grounde, and ryal vautes, which dyvers now lyvyng hath seen. Wherfor it is a mervayl why he is no more renomed in his own contreye. (*WM*, xvi–xvii)

The Englishness of the Arthurian story is underscored by Malory himself in the body of his work when he urges his countrymen, bloodily embroiled in civil strife, to draw the right moral from the fratricidal collapse of the fellowship of the Round Table: 'Lo, ye all Englysshemen, se ye nat what a myschyff here was? . . . Lo thus was the olde custom and usayges of thys londe, and men say that we of thys londe have nat yet loste that custom.' (*WM*, 861–2) Then, at the end of the fifteenth century, the Arthurian story moved back to the centre of the political stage for the last time as Henry Tudor claimed the English throne to be legitimately his by conveniently foregrounding his rather distant Welsh, and hence ur-British, ancestry. And, directly echoing Malory, the newly crowned Henry VII used the analogy of the Round Table both to bring the bloody civil strife between the rival royal Houses of Lancaster and York to an end, and (through his son) to effect the final assimilation of Wales by England.

The sceptical humanistic scholarship of the Renaissance proved, however, a powerful corrosive of the Arthurian myth. Once Polydor Vergil had exposed Geoffrey's fabrications to be fiction, serious English passion for Arthur and his suave knights rapidly evaporated, although the increasingly disempowered Welsh stubbornly clung on to this most potent myth of their nationhood. For the best part of three centuries, the stories circulated only in popular folk forms like the ballad, occasionally breaking surface, but in relatively apolitical and even decorative fashion, in high art – Spenser and Dryden (in partnership with Purcell) both produced notable work on Arthurian themes, while Milton dreamt of doing so, and, a century later, Thomas Wharton attempted to excavate historical memory of Camelot. But the grand cycle of stories had, it seemed, lost its social purchase and political potency just as Romance – the premier genre for such epic narratives – had fallen almost completely out of fashion. An additional disincentive to the enthusiastic development in England of these materials was that Malory was, for a period, supposed to be Welsh. But then, almost two decades into the nineteenth century, with Malory's Englishness gratifyingly reestablished, three editions of his *Le Morte D'Arthur* appeared in quick succession, and these proved to be both the auguries and the triggers of a spectacular change.

It may be no coincidence that Malory's classic narrative reappeared on the very cusp of the transition from the Regency to the Victorian period, from lasciviousness to prudishness. So flexible were the great stories of the Arthurian cycle that they could be reproduced in forms attractive to both cultures – it is in the multivalent character of myth that its astonishing power of survival after all inheres. And the history of the Arthurian craze in nineteenth-century England is testimony to this. In its new and multifarious manifestations, the cycle proved able to generate a vocabulary flexible enough to address a whole range of the century's most urgent concerns, including imperialism, industrialism, proletarianism, philistinism and socialism. They proved attractive alike to radical artists, intent on exploring the potentialities of alternative realities, and to the new consumer world of the affluent bourgoisie, enchanted by medieval kitsch. They made possible an unlikely fusion of the epic and the domestic. Their strong homosocial charge appealed subliminally to the closely interlinked and intensely male worlds of public schools, gentlemen's clubs and armed forces. But they also allowed cautious latitude to explore the torrid realms of heterosexual passion – in a reassuringly elevated and safely sublimated fashion. Always, though, when in English hands the cycle implicitly purported to provide the imperial warrior nation with the 'true' image of its cultivated, courteous, dignified self. And, most prominently in the hands of Tennyson, Arthur assumed the form of the quintessential English gentleman.

Since a strenuous rhetoric of Britishness was a prominent feature of nineteenth-century Arthurianism, it has taken scholars a very long time to appreciate the hard-core Englishness of that purportedly British vision. The situation has, however, changed of late. 'The past that they [the Arthurian stories] were used to construct,' Stephanie L. Barczewski has noted, 'was a narrowly *English* one which left out the other constituent parts of the British Isles.'[20] This was consistent with the nationalist spirit manifest in the *Encyclopaedia Britannica* identification of Malory's *Le Morte D'Arthur* as 'truly *the* epic of the English mind as the *Iliad* is the epic of the Greek mind'. Although, before completing *The Idylls of the King*, Tennyson, with typical diligence, went to considerable trouble to acquaint himself with such key Welsh texts as Guest's *Mabinogion*, William Owen Pughe's *The Heroic Elegies and other Pieces of Llywarch Hen*, and Carnhuanawc's *Hanes Cymru, a Chenedl y Cymry*, he did not allow these sources to compromise his pristine English vision. This crucial feature of his Arthurian cycle has been registered in recent scholarship:

> Neither is Arthur presented as a Celtic or, more particularly, as a Welsh figure. Tennyson thus appears very clearly separate from scholarly historians, topographers or participants in the Welsh Revival.[21]

In these respects, Tennyson typified the temper of his times, that saw the rise of an aggressively English, nationalist, version of Britishness[22] – his 'Anglocentric patriotism would not permit him to present Arthur as a Celt'. In 1861, Caroline Fox reported, on the strength of a conversation with the poet at dinner, 'The Welsh claim Arthur as their own, but Tennyson gives all his votes to us.' (*MNI*, 155)

It is not surprising, therefore, that contemporaries praised the impeccable and quintessential Englishness of Tennyson's Arthur. 'How happily characteristic of their English author, and their English theme,' wrote J. T. Knowles in a letter to the *Spectator*, 'seems to be the manner in which these *Idylls of the King* have become a complete poem.'[23] Tennyson even had Prince Albert in mind when fashioning his hero – 'who dares foreshadow for an only son/ A lovelier life, a more unstained, than his?/ Or how should England dreaming of *his* sons/ Hope more for these than some inheritance/ Of such a life, a heart, a mind as thine?' (*PT*, 1468) As Matthew Reynolds has recently observed, 'the *Idylls* present themselves as occupying "homogeneous, empty time", the time of "Englishness"'.[24] Tennyson shared the convictions of Garibaldi (whom he met) and other nationalist leaders of the time, that a nation could be stabilised only if it were completely unified (*RV*, 7 and 13). He was worried that this was not the case for the English nation at the time of writing the Arthurian cycle, since class differences and tensions were becoming very evident. Consequently, in a poem addressed to Queen Victoria, he expressed the concern that 'Britain' was on the point of becoming a 'sinking land,/ some third-rate isle half-lost among her seas' (*PT*, 1755). The final cataclysmic battle of Camlan therefore held an ominous appeal for him, 'The darkness of that battle in the West,/ Where all of high and holy dies away.' (*PT*, 1756) His account of the passing of Arthur gloomily emphasises that never 'yet had Arthur fought a fight/ Like this last, dim, weird, battle of the west' (*PT*, 1745). The western setting is significant. The Celtic fringe is viewed as 'A land of old upheaven from the abyss/ By fire, to sink into the abyss again;/ where fragments of forgotten peoples dwelt' (*PT*, 1745). Vaguely and portentously implicated in such a vision is a sense of the foreign, uncivilised otherness to England of the western lands of Cornwall and of Wales, and a fear of the threat accordingly carried by the aboriginal 'forgotten peoples' there. Far from recognising the Welsh dimensions of Arthur, therefore, Tennyson was instinctively inclined to view Wales as a potential source of internal social rupture and of consequent 'national' collapse.

* * *

As Ceridwen Lloyd-Morgan has pithily pointed out, 'The Arthur of the English was not the Arthur of the Welsh.'[25] But that Tennyson's Arthur was nevertheless attractive even to supporters of Cymru Fydd is evident, for instance, from the (rather fine) translation of a passage from 'The Passing of Arthur', by John Young Evans (Trevecca Academy), which in 1895 appeared in the pages of that flagship journal of the movement, O. M. Edward's *Cymru*. Appropriately, given the strong Nonconformist component of the Young Wales movement, it opens with Arthur's celebrated acknowledgement of the ways of Providence: 'Rhen drefn dan newid rydd i'r newydd le,/ A Duw amlyga'i hunan lawer modd' ('The old order changeth, giving way to new,/ And God fulfils himself in many ways').[26]

Evans's penchant for Tennyson was consistent with a long-standing readiness by the Welsh to conceive of Arthur as a 'British' rather than specifically Welsh hero. Thus, during his correspondence with Thomas Percy concerning the origins of Arthur, Ieuan Brydydd Hir (Evan Evans) could write, 'I am sure [the French] and all other nations must have borrowed [the tales] about King Arthur and his Knights originally from early British histories or Romances' (*MNI*, 109). But he was writing when, with Celtomania at its height, and the Scottish

Highlanders not just defeated but effectively exterminated at Culloden (1745), a new, relaxed concept of Britain, hospitably open to recognition of its historical (if not contemporary) heterogeneity, seemed to be developing. And with the Napoleonic wars came a new enthusiasm for a unitary 'Britishness', articulated by Welsh authors through the figure of Arthur. But the nineteenth century was to see a sharp, nationalistic reversion to the anglocentric model that treated Britain as virtually synonymous with England. And it was the very different climate of this time that prompted a sharp reaction in Wales, in the form of aggressive reclamation of Arthur. Both the Welsh-language and the English-language periodicals of Cymru Fydd therefore featured specifically Welsh versions of the Arthur story.[27] In 1895, for instance, Bryfdir's poem 'Pa le mae milwyr Arthur?' ('Where are Arthur's soldiers?) appeared in *Cymru*[28] and, in the same year, the Manchester Welsh Society was reported in *Cymru* as including a lecture by Mr H. E. Thomas on the 'Influence of Arthur on European Literature' in its programme of activities for the year.[29] This politico-cultural 'turn' taken during the last decades of the century was anticipated as early as 1818 by W. E. Meredith when, in his poem 'Llewelyn ap Iorwerth', he invoked Arthur as a hero of the Welsh against the invading Saxon English. Similar sentiments were expressed by Mrs Hemans in a poem collected by John Jenkins in his 1873 anthology *The Poetry of Wales*.

Her lyric 'The Grave of King Arthur' calls first on the sun to find 'with thy searching light,/ The island monarch's grave'; then 'the night's most lonely star' is asked 'where the slain of Gamlan lay', followed by the river and the winds who also are unable to oblige. Finally, the ocean waves bear the message that 'Long must the island monarch roam,/ The noble heart and the mighty hand;/ But we shall bear him proudly home/ To his father's mountain land.' What, exactly, Arthur was expected to do on his return was not, however, specified – telling evidence of the merely rhetorical power of this kind of hope. It was, predictably, this theme of Arthur as king-in-waiting that captivated Cymru Fydd followers. In a Welsh translation by 'Anthropos' of a poem by Lewis Morris – that establishment figure of the Victorian scene who cautiously allowed himself to be attached in his later years to the Young Wales movement – the king is traced to the cave in which he is sleeping, pending his recall in Wales's hour if not of need then of promise (felt in the stirrings of Cymru Fydd). The piece ends with a prayer to the hero to awake and arise, 'I godi'n hanwyl wlad' ('To raise our dear country'). This is a refrain repeatedly heard whenever the Arthur story resurfaces in the columns of these periodicals. And this defiantly Welsh Arthur was, in part, a response to a growing tendency in England throughout the later nineteenth century to represent the king not as Celtic but as Saxon, in keeping with the increasingly fashionable pseudo-scientific classifying of nations on a scale of 'evolution' that left the Celts languishing way behind the Saxons in the great race for life, as fit only for extinction.[30]

When the rising, versatile man of letters Ernest Rhys toured Wales in 1895 lecturing on the subject 'The Revolt of the Celt', the climax of his talk was the story of the little boy who, having stumbled on Arthur's cave, ventured to tip-toe in among the slumbering soldiers, only to brush accidentally against the great bell as he made his exit.[31] Rhys denied the rumour, spread by eager Cymru Fydd supporters, that his story was meant as an allegory of Lloyd George's 1894 'rebellion' against the Liberal party in the name of the Disestablishment of the Anglican Church in Wales. But he was pleased to see his tale being recognised as a nationalist comment on the contemporary political scene. And in his *Welsh Ballads* (1898), he included two Arthurian poems among the clutch of patriotic pieces centred on ancient Welsh history and literature that appeared in that collection.

In one of this brace of poems, a young lad is magically led to a lonely tombstone, 'Cast with Druid character'. It conceals steps leading down to the bowels of the earth, 'And within, a trembling twilight/ Surely shewed a thousand men,/ All asleep, in shining helmets./ Ah, to see them wake again.'[32] There lies Arthur, surrounded by his knights, among a hoard of treasure. The great bell sounds, the soldiers stir, but are commanded by the king to return to their sleep. The poem ends with Rhys dreaming of their eventual arousal and of the return of Arthur:

> Yet we wait the day of waking!
> But the grave its counsel keeps:
> Still within his Hall of waiting,
> With his warriors Arthur sleeps. (26)

This is an aspiration to which he returns in the second of the two poems, 'The Waking of King Arthur':

Little harp, at thy cry
He shall come in his time;
And thy sword-song on high,
High shall chime.

In cases such as this, Arthur seems to be functioning, in part, as a safe surrogate for Owain Glyndŵr, another deathless hero reputed to be awaiting recall by the nation.[33] Rhys unconsciously confirmed this when, in an article on 'The Grave of Glyndwr' in *Young Wales* (1895), he wrote as follows:

> All those elusive ideas that so peculiarly appeal to the Celtic races; all those lost causes that they have from time to time served with such devotion to the bitter end: were they not like the great Glyndwr, buried in an unknown grave? But no! all does not end there. Their spirit, like his, lives and is not forgotten . . . Other times, other weapons! The sword of Wales, if you will, lies buried in the grave of Glyndwr. But his tireless courage under disaster, his wit, his resource – these rise again for us, and refuse to be forgotten.[34]

Typically fuzzy in its political focus as Rhys's use of the narrative is, it contrasts with the incisively politicised Arthur referred to in a trenchant essay by J. Arthur Price.

To modern tastes, Price may well appear the most impressive, because the most unconventional and indeed original, of all the thinkers associated with Cymru Fydd. A convinced Conservative in an otherwise thoroughly Radical movement, he perceptively argued that, based as it was on a fundamental respect for the collective, Welsh nationalism was strictly incompatible with the Liberal cult of the unfettered individual. He further affirmed that in its deep reverence for tradition, Welsh nationalism was not, as Radicals contended, the offspring of the French Revolution but rather the exact opposite: it was a modern example of the national spirit of resistance aroused in Spain and England by the 'Revolutionary' armies of Napoleonic imperial France. Price's conclusion was that

> No doubt the Welsh are a democratic people, but their democratic ideas are not inconsistent with a respect for ancient blood. The nation that is still proud of the fact that, in its noble romance of a Welsh prince and his knights of the round table, it gave to Europe its medieval chivalry,

> cannot desire to assimilate its social or political life to that of the US of America, or to parody the vulgar democracy of modern Paris.[35]

In all such Welsh accounts, then, Arthur features not, as in Tennyson's poem, as a sepia emblem of national decline, but rather as an embodiment of hope, and as an omen (sometimes wistfully entertained) of cultural resuscitation and national revival. As such it epitomises the spirit of Cymru Fydd in its bullish heyday and, even after the political disaster of the 1896 Newport meeting, that spirit could still surface from time to time. Nowhere is this more apparent than in Ceinydd Morus's poem 'Behind the Veil', published in *Young Wales* in 1899, in which the earth itself is apostrophised because 'You ne'er forgot the gods who reigned of old/ Nor lost the mem'ries of your noble men':[36]

> In the red sunset sky I saw them – there
> On opal oceans Prydwen's bark did sail;
> Afallen Island shone eternal fair.

But that this red sunset presages a glorious dawn is made clear in the poem's concluding stanza:

> In the red sunset sky I saw him stand,
> The wounded king, beside the traitor slain.
> Arthur and Medrawd passing from Prydain Land,
> But Arthur, passing, swore to come again.
> Oh King, enthroned within thy shining isle
> Thy sword once more is flashing golden gleams,
> Out of the realm where thou dost dwell awhile
> To fill our darkness with immortal dreams.

In the intercultural dialogue between the Welsh and English Arthurian traditions, various subjects were at issue, such as the future shape of the British Empire. Whereas conservative English preference was for a strongly centralist model, very firmly directed from London, 'progressive' Welsh views such as prevailed in Cymru Fydd favoured (as chapter 4 has shown) the evolution of a Commonwealth structure, that would allow all the component peoples some degree of influence, according to their perceived status.[37] The resurgent Arthur was, therefore, a figure emblematic of hopes not only of a cultural revival but of a political change that would allow Wales at least a modest measure of (dutifully subordinate) control over its own affairs. As such, the treatment of the king by the Welsh contrasts with the uses made both of him and of Arthurian materials by English artists and intellectuals preoccupied with nineteenth-century imperial adventures. As Stephanie Barczewski has shown, the Indian Mutiny of 1857 triggered a dramatic shift in imperial interpretations of the legends. Previous to that uprising, supreme confidence in the project of Empire was reflected in heroic celebration of a band of impeccably gentlemanly knights intent on civilising the realm by reducing it to order. But subsequent to the Mutiny, growing anxiety about Empire meant featuring the lonely and uncertain attempt by isolated individuals to triumph over threats 'abroad', while behind them Camelot was collapsing into ruin (*MNI*, 201–30).

By contrast, the Welsh Arthur was not a by-product of concern with Empire, but a mirror image of the quintessentially English Arthur produced by the shift in England during the nineteenth century towards a firmly anglocentric and exclusionist model of Britishness. Recent scholars have pointed out that, far from being (as for so long fondly supposed) an exception to the European norm of constructing highly partisan versions of history to validate nationalist movements, nineteenth-century England conspicuously conformed to such practice in its warped versions of the 'British' past – hence the steady attempts, culminating in the 1890s, to co-opt the Arthurian stories to serve specifically English nationalist interests (*MNI*, *passim*). Hence, too, George Saintsbury's dismissal in 1897 of both Welsh and French claims on Arthur, while protesting that if 'the glory of the Legend be claimed for none of these, but for English or Anglo-Norman, it can be done in no spirit of national *pleonexia*, but on a sober consideration of all the facts of the case' (*MNI*, 112).

By the time of Jones's composition of 'Ymadawiad Arthur' five years later, only Welsh scholars like John Rhŷs (who connected the Arthurian materials with contemporary anthropologists' interest in solar myths)[38] and John Morris-Jones were still arguing for the Welsh antecedents of the Arthurian stories.[39] And theirs, too, was a conviction rooted as much in cultural need and political expediency as on 'sober consideration of all the facts'.

* * *

'The question which faced the decolonising world,' Declan Kiberd has written, 'the question to which it might become the answer, was: how to build a future on the past without returning to it?' And in this context, he recalls the striking remarks of Carlos Fuentes: '"the past is the only certifiable future we have," says Fuentes: "the past is the only proof that the future did, in effect, once exist." Hence his motto; "remember the future, imagine the past."'[40] As has already been repeatedly emphasised in this study, Cymru Fydd constantly wrestled with this paradox, recognising the recovery of a largely lost past to be central to securing the national future it was so eagerly attempting to imagine into being, and no one addressed himself to this challenge with more heroic, not to say manically self-destructive, energy than O. M. Edwards (as was demonstrated in chapter 3).[41] But, of course, as contemporary scholarship has emphasised, any appeal to history is fraught with innumerable tensions, complications and contradictions, because

> [c]ontests over the meaning of the past are also contests over the meaning of the present and over ways of taking the past forward . . . The forms of contestation . . . are very often not conflicting accounts of what actually happened in the past so much as the question of who or what is entitled to speak for that past in the present.[42]

This is everywhere evident in the writings of not only Edwards himself but those of the contributors to his periodicals and of a new, industrious generation of amateur and professional historians increasingly active during this period. Deep concern with the past was intensified by anxieties about Wales present and future. Conservative Nonconformists, for example, were inclined to lament a loss of piety, and the ungovernable dynamism of modern, industrial Wales generated even more widespread unease. A long poem about 'Ifor Wyn o'r Hafod Elwy', for instance, that appeared in 1895, urged the young to remember that the history of 'dear old Wales' remained an integral part of Cymru Fydd.[43] There were also serious misgivings that this new Wales, unlike its old pious predecessor, was far from immune to the blandishments of the corrupt popular culture of neighbouring England. As for Wales's relations with its many previous incarnations, one particular disagreement, both recurrent and pressing, concerned whether Cymru Fydd should align itself primarily with the Nonconformist or the pre-Nonconformist past, and related to this was a disagreement as to whether attention should primarily be given to Wales's recent or 'deep' history. Other issues involved the tension between extensive attempts to gather and record evidence of indigenous customs, dialects, memories and practices from the many widely diverse regions of Wales that correspondents anxiously emphasised were rapidly disappearing in the face of 'progress' and fears either that this would simply reinforce nostalgia and hamper advance, or that it would impede the attempt, vital to the success of Cymru Fydd, to replace the rival regional, sectional and denominational identities that had been the bane of traditional Wales with a new identification with the nation as a whole.

Acutely conscious as he was of the anti-Welsh bias of the new, 'enlightened' and 'progressive' system of primary, secondary and higher education loudly championed by Cymru Fydd, and of which late-nineteenth-century Wales was so inordinately proud, O. M. Edwards consciously intended to supplement the conspicuous deficiencies of the state system (as noted in chapter 3). As he sharply reminded one of his correspondents, the purpose of *Cymru* was not only to accumulate a treasury of information and knowledge, but specifically to educate its readership in the history of Wales, its language and its culture, while attempting to set it in its full European context.[44] The very format of the periodical was intended to advertise this multifaceted educational purpose. The contents of the ninth volume, for instance, were subdivided into more than a dozen subsections, including 'the History of Wales', 'the Literature of Wales', 'the Religion of Wales', 'the Regions of Wales', 'the Educational System in Wales', 'Welsh Life', and so on. As demonstrated in chapter 3, it is as if O. M. Edwards were formally devising an alternative syllabus of 'national' education. And it is no accident that 'the History of Wales' effectively heads the table of contents, closely followed by 'the Literature of Wales', and thirdly 'the Religion of Wales'. While respectfully acknowledging both the secular and the religious aspects of the Welsh past, Edwards implicitly favours the former: for him, history is the key to nationality: 'Wrth gofio am a fu,' he wrote, 'yr a cenedl ymlaen gyflymaf' (It is by remembering what has been that a nation most swiftly progresses).[45]

T. Gwynn Jones's 'Ymadawiad Arthur' can, then, usefully be viewed in the context of this widespread, deep, and vexed concern of how to relate modern and proudly progressive Wales to its past. In its own unique fashion, the *awdl* attempts to demonstrate how a loving familiarity with the legendary products of Wales's 'deep history' could offer the Welsh a valuable lens for bringing the Welsh present, and with it the Welsh future, into constructive focus. In Fuentes's powerfully suggestive terms, it is a remarkable creative attempt to remember the future, by imagining the past.

* * *

Given the radical, sweeping and often deeply problematic changes resulting from the explosive growth of industrial society with all its attendant developments during the nineteenth century, it is not surprising that a reassuring and stabilising relationship with a pre-industrial past should prove so appealing throughout this period. Of particular and urgent concern in England were ways of counteracting the new configurations of power and threatening tensions between social classes, while in Wales such issues were further complicated by the 'foreign' anglophone character of the rapidly emergent culture of the industrial south.

One 'native' response prominently favoured by the Young Wales movement was pithily encapsulated in 'Cymru Fu, Cymru Fydd', a catchphrase of the nationalist movement. Variously translatable (neutrally) as 'Wales past, Wales future', and (defiantly) as 'Wales has been and will continue to be', it was primarily attractive because the internal assonance ('fu' = 'vee', and 'fydd' = 'veethe') strongly implied that the present not only accommodated the past but comfortably incorporated it; that there was an internal, necessary, intimate and directly causal connection between Wales reassuringly 'ancient' and disconcertingly 'modern'. And no more powerful expression of this conviction could have been asked for than the *awdl* published by the young John Morris-Jones in 1891. Actually entitled 'Cymru Fu, Cymru Fydd', it anticipated T. Gwynn Jones's 'Ymadawiad Arthur' in trying to redeem the time by addressing contemporary concerns through the medium of the strict-metre tradition recovered by recent scholarship.

Fifteen pages in length and ornately crafted out of learned allusion, archaic lexis, and formal rhetoric in the high style, this *awdl* conforms to the classical requirements of its genre. And by displaying the poet's mastery of all the major forms and conventions of *barddas*, it functions as a verbal icon of its central message. Modern, anglicised Wales is a country in which Mammon has usurped the social power that was once the prerogative of those visionary custodians of culture, the poets. To ensure its survival, the nation urgently needs to reconnect itself with those ancient autochthonous sources of power, respectfully imbued by Morris-Jones, in true, religiose, late-Victorian manner, with solemn moral and spiritual authority. In a pivotal *englyn* at the centre of his *awdl*, Morris-Jones arrogates to himself the vaticinatory role of the strict-metre poets:

Ac fe ddaw it heirdd feirddion – i ganu
Gogoniant y cyfion;
Ac â newydd ganeuon,
A thanbaid enaid y dôn.

[And you (Wales) shall see handsome poets singing / the glory of the just; / with new poems / and fiery soul of song.][46]

When, therefore, Morris-Jones was faced with 'Ymadawiad Arthur' in 1902, it was natural for him to see in T. Gwynn Jones a 'mab darogan', the very son of his own youthful prophecy.

For Morris-Jones, the fate of the nation was inseparable from the fate of the Welsh language, which he saw as not only coming under increasing external pressure from the processes of anglicisation, but also (unsupported as it was by any educational institutions) as beginning to decay from within, thinning out in texture, limited in vocabulary and lacking the stiffener of grammatical correctness. For him, his poetry was part of a campaign to halt this decline. From the distinguished past, he quarried antique forms and archaic vocabulary, resources he felt were needed to enrich the language and ensure it became fit for all contemporary purposes. Such concerns were characteristic even of the dominant powers during this period, and so, following Arnold's argument that literature laid bare the very soul of a people, were attempts to create national literary traditions. England was no exception, as attention to the 'national' language and its culture began to replace study of the classics in the influential institutions for educating the new social elites. The English Association, The Oxford English Dictionary, The Cambridge History of English Literature, The Society of Pure English, the Early English Text Society, were all some of the renowned initiatives that resulted. And just as Morris-Jones was concerned that Welsh was becoming debased by the infiltration of English, so his contemporaries on the other side of the border worried about the effects on the language of both lower-class and colonial usage.[47] On its first, historic and prophetic appearance,

'Ymadawiad Arthur' therefore appeared to Morris-Jones to be not only a major poem but a culturally redemptive achievement.

* * *

What Morris-Jones shows no signs of considering in his influential adjudication of 1902, however, is the political dimension of T. Gwynn Jones's *awdl*, which is a little surprising considering that both he and the poet were ardent supporters of Cymru Fydd.[48] 'I have been a nationalist all my life,' T. Gwynn Jones wrote in a revealing article in *The Welsh Outlook*:

> I cannot well remember the time when I did not harbour a fiery desire to fight the ancient enemies of my race and see restored the independence of my country . . . I hated all the schools I ever attended because I felt they insulted me and everything I cared for, because the teachers never mentioned a word about Arthur or Gruffydd ap Cynan, Llewelyn ap Gruffudd or Owain Glyndŵr, and scores of other heroes of whom my father had told me.[49]

This makes it clear enough how, from earliest childhood, the figure of Arthur had been heavily politicised. As he further recalled in middle age, 'When a small boy I organized hundreds of imaginary armies, and won so many battles. Every cave seemed a resting-place for Arthur.' (*TGJ*, 35) There was therefore what might broadly be called a 'post-colonial' impulse in Jones's reclamation in 'Ymadawiad Arthur' of Arthur from Tennyson and the English, as Geraint Evans has most recently pointed out.[50] And it could also well be that, in valorising Arthur as a Welsh hero, he was drawing on very old oral materials and folklore still circulating in the popular culture of rural nineteenth-century Wales.[51]

For a decade or so previous to the composition of T. Gwynn Jones's poem, Cymru Fydd had experienced several crises that effectively robbed it of its political potency, causing it to turn again to the consolations of culture and precipitating its rapid decline. The year 1899 brought the early, untimely death of T. E. Ellis, the darling of the cultural wing of Cymru Fydd, a visionary politician whose original impassioned political advocacy of a cultural agenda for national self-fulfilment had already, before his death, begun to seem compromised by his acceptance of the key role of Liberal Chief Whip in the

Westminster parliament. Ellis had himself unconsciously encouraged the coupling of his name with Arthurian legend when, in a lecture on 'The Influence of the Celt in the Making of Britain', he had discoursed at scholarly length on the seminal importance of Arthur, following the appearance of Geoffrey of Monmouth's *Historia Regum Britanniae*, in the development both of English and of Continental literature. 'Arthur, in his struggle for the freedom, homes, and independence of the Cymry,' Ellis wrote, 'is the hero and inspiration of early English literature.'[52] And it may have been with comments such as this in mind that the poet Dyfnallt, in a lengthy elegy for Ellis completed in 1904 and considered in chapter 4, first depicted him in life as a knight who had awakened the sleeping Arthur of the Welsh nation with the resounding clangour of his bell-like call to action, and then likened him in death to the sleeping king, a continuing source of comfort and inspiration for his people: 'Daw fflam ei galon fel enw Arthur i losgi byth yn ysfa dy fryd' ('His heart's flame, like the name of Arthur, will come to burn forever in the yearnings of your nature').[53] Indeed, when the editor of *Young Wales*, J. Hugh Edwards, published a memorial tribute to Ellis immediately following his premature death, it was to the legend of Arthur that he instinctively turned for consolation:

> One thinks of Arthurian legend in which Arthur is represented as wounded and carried away to the Isle of Avallon. He has gone to heal his wound, the old Welsh said, and he will come again, healed and sword in hand, to save his people . . . The legend, with its deep note of pathos, finds its counterpart in the departure of Wales' true leader – Tom Ellis.[54]

By the turn of the century, Cymru Fydd had also implicitly lost its other charismatic leader. As has already been noted, Lloyd George effectively turned his back on the Home Rule movement within Cymru Fydd following the notoriously stormy meeting held at Newport in 1896. His defeat on that historic occasion was a direct consequence of the inter-lingual, inter-cultural and inter-regional rivalry between the rural, Welsh-speaking and largely Nonconformist north and the English-speaking industrial south, many of whose leading lights bitterly resented being bound to the triumphal wheels of Lloyd George's bandwagon. Piqued at his failure to win them over with his incomparable rhetoric or to outmanoeuvre them through his renowned political guile, the avidly ambitious Lloyd George abruptly turned his back on the Welsh national vision and swaggeringly committed himself instead to cutting a swathe through establishment, centralist British politics.[55] In 1900, just two years before 'Ymadawiad Arthur', T. Gwynn Jones lambasted all such Cymru Fydd turncoats in a bitter English squib, 'My Conversion'. In it, a backslider explains that 'I used to be a Radical of yore,/ I claimed the widest form of devolution,/ Told Mr Bull to mind his own, and swore/ Nought but Home Rule could bring the true solution . . . But now, I bow unto my betters.' (*TGJ*, 117)

Since he was writing very much with these raw recent losses in mind, it is not surprising that Jones's imagination was haunted not by legends of Arthur's return but by the powerful narrative of his final departure, central to which, of course, was the account of the sacrifice of that omnipotent instrument of power, Excalibur. And Bedwyr's reluctance to consign the sword to the dark, deep waters of the lake is specifically voiced in terms of a nightmare vision of a nation suddenly rendered utterly defenceless and vulnerable to annihilation. 'Ai rhaid yw arnaf,' the surviving knight brokenly asks, 'ddinistrio'r deyrnas?' ('Have I no choice but to destroy the kingdom?'):

Ar fod ynghadw'r hen arf dynghedus
Y saif rhyddid ein teyrnas fawreddus;
Cwympem, pe'i collid, rhag llidus – alon
A rhuthr ach estron, dan orthrech astrus. (*CB*, 47)

[The liberty of our great kingdom is dependent/ on this ancient, fateful weapon;/ we would fall, should it be lost, under terrible oppression,/ prey to inflamed enemies and the onslaught of a foreign people.]

Thus does Jones fashion a great tragic allegory of the national condition, as he saw it, out of the story of Arthur's passing, finding a modicum of comfort only by mobilising the age-old hope of a defeated and politically neutered people that culture may yet defiantly prove to be the final irreducible refuge of national being. This, of course, had been one of the great implicit hopes of the poets of the *uchelwyr* (the minor Welsh gentry), writing as they were during the golden age of Welsh *barddas* that directly followed the killing in 1282 of the last prince of Wales. By brilliantly exhuming the strict-metre poetry tradition Jones was therefore knowingly fashioning a deeply traditional icon of elegiacally inflected cultural resistance. Accordingly, when Bedwyr speaks of Afallon, he conjures up a recessive image of cultural memories:

Yno, fro ddedwydd, mae hen freuddwydion,
A fu'n esmwytho ofn oesau meithion;
Byw yno byth mae pob hen obeithion,
Yno mae cynnydd uchel amcanion. (*CB*, 52)

[In that happy vale dwell old dreams/ that have soothed the fears of innumerable ages;/ eternally living there are all the old aspirations,/ and high ambitions thrive and flourish.]

The tone of the rhetoric is subtly pitched between wistful elegiac nostalgia and enabling, invigorating conviction. Similarly, the summation of this vision is hauntingly ambiguous:

Yno y mae tân pob awen a gano,
Grym, hyder, awch pob gwladgarwr a 'mdrecho,
Ynni a ddwg i'r neb fyn ddiwygio,
Sylfaen yw byth i'r sawl fyn obeithio;
Ni heneiddiwn tra'n noddo – mae gwiwfoes
Ac anadl einioes y genedl yno! (*CB*, 52)

[There may be found the flame of all talent and song,/ the power, hope, appetite of every patriot who struggles,/ it brings energy to any who begin to droop,/ and offers firm foundation to all who persist in hope;/ we shall not age while it nurtures us – the very quick/ and breath of the nation's existence dwell there.]

Jones specifically identifies himself as an inhabitant of this Afallon, and therefore as an implicit exile from post-1896 Wales, when he signs off with the pseudonym 'Tir na n-Og', the fabled Celtic land of eternal youth he has just made virtually synonymous with Avilion.

* * *

The foregoing narrative highlights for us, however, only one facet of what, regarded culturally, is a poem in whose Janus face even present-day Wales may descry the very image of its own troubled cultural doubleness. In this connection, it is worth reminding ourselves again how deeply and intransigently English a figure was the Malorian and Tennysonian Arthur who remains, despite all Welsh cultural finessing, the central hero of T. Gwynn Jones's poem. And not only did Jones openly acknowledge his indebtedness to Malory, he also admitted that, as a boy, he first succumbed to the allure of poetry when introduced to Scott's 'The Lady of the Lake' at school. Nor did his dalliance with English end in childhood. As a young poet, he debated whether Welsh or English should be his medium, and even after committing himself primarily to the former, he continued from time to time to produce English compositions, motivated by a wish to educate both English incomers and his monoglot English compatriots in the history and culture of the country.

It is, then, Jones's conflicted feelings about his ambiguous cultural positioning that are inscribed in 'Ymadawiad Arthur', a poem whose central ambivalence is perfectly emblematised in the cross-currents between its vatic epigraph and its elegiac conclusion. While the *awdl* ends with a bereft but sadly resolute Bedwyr, on a darkling shore, faced by an ominously hostile and implacable future, its epigraph – taken from lines in the ancient *Englynion y Beddau* (Poems of the Graves) rejoicing that Arthur's grave remains undiscovered – provides a chink of vaticinatory hope for the redemptive hero's eventual return.[56] Jones was similarly divided between pessimistic fears for the future of Welsh and hope that the language could reach some effective accommodation with its aggressive invader. In a letter he wrote following his success with 'Ymadawiad Arthur', he specifically noted that Wales was rapidly becoming a bilingual country, but hoped the language might yet survive if properly taught by the state education system. However, noting how unsatisfactory hitherto had been the modes of teaching in this connection, he was inclined to place his faith instead in the exciting new literature, worthy of a small European nation, that young writers might yet produce. The fate of the language, he concluded, was the only battle worth the fighting, and there could be no laying down of arms in such a struggle – a figure of speech that, of course, directly echoes the concluding lines of 'Ymadawiad Arthur' describing Bedwyr's downhearted but determined return to the fray (*TGJ*, 129).

Deeply disturbed as they were by the fluidities and indeterminacies of the new dynamic and cosmopolitan culture of the industrial south, it is not surprising that members of Wales's new intellectual elite, like Morris-Jones and T. Gwynn Jones, should have been seduced by the fallacy of origins: the supposition that the present and its future could most safely be anchored to a single point in a pristine, aboriginal past such as seemed to them to be supremely represented by the golden age of the strict-metre tradition. However, contrary to Jones's own most cherished suppositions, it may well have been by unconsciously incorporating the radical doubleness of his own times into the very body of his *awdl* that he was most faithful to the actual practice of classical *barddas*, in its Late Medieval prime.

Recovery of *barddas* had always been integral to the vision of the Welsh-language 'wing' of the Cymru Fydd movement: 'Prif nodwedd y deffroad Cymreig,' its flagship periodical announced in 1890, 'ydyw'r dyddordeb gymerir yn hen feirdd Cymru.' ('The main feature of the Welsh awakening is the interest taken in the the old Welsh poets.')[57] The assumption, of course, was that this tradition constituted the backbone of authentic, aboriginal Welsh culture. But the recent 'post-colonial turn' in Welsh Medieval Studies has resulted in scholarly concentration on the (frequently tense) multi-cultural character of the post-Conquest Wales that saw the golden age of *barddas*. 'The ironies and ambivalences that characterised the position of the *uchelwyr* are of particular interest as so many of the renowned strict-metre poets of the period either belonged to that class or were dependent on it for patronage.'[58] But the *uchelwyr* were increasingly reliant for their social status on the 'occupying powers' of the Anglo-Norman political ascendancy, to whose service they assiduously attached themselves. And inevitably, for all the periodic rhetoric of cultural resistance favoured by the *uchelwyr* and their poets, mentioned above, the ambiguities of their compromised inter-cultural position found repeated expression both crude and subtle in their poetry. Morgan T. Davies has shown, for instance, how Dafydd ap Gwilym's celebrated poem of dialogue with his shadow can be read as a symbolic reenactment of the drama of inner psychological division.

In these ways, then, classical *barddas* was already culturally hybrid at source. What 'Ymadawiad Arthur' therefore demonstrated, however unintentionally, was not only how impossible would be any dream of a modern Welsh monoglot identity but how groundless, too, were ambitions to underpin, validate and empower it by appeal to some 'purely Welsh' past. Any concept, however heroic, of cultural resistance in the form of 'continuity' modelled on such an assumption was likewise doomed to founder. Instead, what 'Ymadawiad Arthur' could offer was a different model of continuity involving (from the Welsh-language perspective) risky accommodation and conceiving of place as what post-colonial studies has called 'a cultural palimpsest built up over centuries and retaining the traces of previous engagements and inscriptions' (*PCS*, 175). The modern Guayanese writer Wilson Harris has likened it to a fossil bed, taken as a 'sign of the continuation of the forms of the past in the living present. No single feature of past or present can be singled out as an origin, since all are related to an endless and multiple set of processes, an "infinite rehearsal" that never ends and in which "history" is located as a transient structure.' (*PCS*, 175)[59]

However compelling, and indeed hauntingly tragic, was the narrative rendering by 'Ymadawiad Arthur' of the Welsh language's threatened condition in modern industrial Wales, the only future available to it by 1902, in hard truth, was in permanently uncertain and constantly changing relationship with English. As has been seen, this truth was already inscribed in the very body of the poem, informing both its core substance (the culturally ambiguous figure of Arthur) and its signature form (a classical strict-metre poetry whose quintessential Welshness was, from its late medieval heyday, already a cultural alloy produced by intimate trafficking with another culture). This was a difficult truth more easily accepted by the anglophone Young Wales wing of the national movement than by the Cymru Fydd wing. In fairness to the latter, however, it should be noted that in the Welsh context the model of linguistic resistance was not so much incompatible with the model of linguistic accommodation as a necessary precondition of it. Unless Welsh could exert a very significant counter-cultural force, its 'accommodation' with English could result only in its capitulation and eventual obliteration. And the internal tension in 'Ymadawiad Arthur' between epigraph and conclusion, between the respective appeals of the residual Welsh Arthur and the dominant and dynamic English Arthur, can be regarded as the poet's unconscious recognition of this cultural 'given'.

With its strong tragic overtones, T. Gwynn Jones's 'Ymadawiad Arthur' is the great textual encapsulation of the central dilemma facing the cultural elite that formed the core of the Welsh-language 'wing' of the Cymru Fydd/Young Wales movement: could the 'ancient' Wales with which they strongly identified be perpetuated through any meaningful connection with the new, still amorphous, and culturally unaligned society of industrial south-east Wales, a society largely given over to an imperial language so powerfully invasive that it already inhabited the consciousness even of traditional Welsh-language Wales? Could there really, beyond the convenient accident of assonance, be any substantive connection between 'Cymru Fu' and 'Cymru Fydd'? Could the Arthur of the Welsh, after all, prove himself to be not only the once but the future king? These were the fateful questions that haunted those of Jones's persuasion between 1890 and 1914, who were stricken by the vision of the possible demise of the Welsh language and its rich culture.

7

Evan Roberts: the Ghost Dance of Welsh Nonconformity

Many decades after Wales had been convulsed by the great religious revival of 1904–6 with which his name remains indelibly associated, Evan Roberts (1878–1951) happened to bump into an old acquaintance. 'Don't you pine for a return of those wonderful days,' his friend passionately enquired, 'when the Holy Ghost graced us so liberally with its presence?' 'Yes indeed,' replied Evan Roberts sadly, 'if it *was* the Holy Spirit.'[1]

By then, Roberts had retreated back into those shadows of history from which, for a brief, meteoric period, he had so blazingly emerged. When he eventually passed away in 1951, in an old people's home in Cardiff, it is said that very few if any of the people there had any knowledge of his astonishing past. He died incognito; the enigma he had always been, even at the very height of his charismatic fame. As Gwyn Thomas put it, 'Few writers exposed to the more powerful myths of south Wales life can fail to be attracted by the name and mystery of Evan Roberts, the evangelist . . . He was the wind that came, and like the wind he went. He chose a dangerous and impossible task but he made it brief, and in that fact alone . . . our endless curiosity is rooted.'[2]

Striking antecedents for the conflict of our present-day estimates of him can readily be found in the contrasting 'readings' of 'his' revival that were already circulating in his own day. Evangelically-inclined Christians viewed him straightforwardly as the instrument of the Holy Spirit, while more mainstream believers voiced sceptical reservations about the inflamed passions and vulgar mass hysteria so brazenly displayed in his tastelessly intemperate meetings. Professional psychoanalysts concentrated both on the animal energies that seemed to be precariously sublimated into ecstatic spiritual experiences and on the social tensions underlying the whole remarkable, culturally belated, phenomenon. Even many close acquaintances of his, from his Newcastle Emlyn days onwards, had periods of suspecting that he suffered from mental derangement. His success was attributed in some quarters to the most fashionable and 'progressive' pseudo-sciences of his day, 'mesmerism, occultism, hypnotism and magnetism'.[3]

Conservative ministers astutely remarked on the role played by the *Western Mail* and the London press of the day in creating the myth of Evan Roberts and in feeding the frenzy. As the eminent Revd John Williams (subsequently of Brynsiencyn) astutely noted, 'the Press is a mighty power in every direction, and it did its part in bringing the Revival and the Revivalist to the notice of the world' (*ER*, 421). Even the famous W. T. Stead, father of the 'new journalism', was involved in shrewd promotion of what he dubbed, with an eye on widening interest in its sensational aspects well beyond Wales, 'The Rising Revival in the West' (*ER*, 299). Other level-headed commentators objected to the personality cult of Roberts himself. Not only, they argued, had many, including Joseph Jenkins (New Quay) and Seth Joshua (originally Cardiff), been labouring for years before him to prepare the ground for the Revival, but when eventually it arrived, it had been blessed with many talented spiritual leaders, of whom Evan Roberts was only one. Influential ministers, anxious to establish that Roberts was no 'meteorite', as Gwyn Thomas was to put it, but rather an evangelist heavily indebted to decades of groundwork by the chapels, referred back to the Great Welsh Revivals of 1859, 1876 and 1879 and viewed 1904–6 as the latest in the series.

As to what follows, it will predominantly view the Evan Roberts Revival as the Ghost Dance of Welsh Nonconformity. In 1890, it will be remembered, the Sioux peoples, faced with cultural extinction, were persuaded by their shamans that all the millions of buffalo that had roamed their plains before the murderous arrival of the white man with his killing guns could be miraculously recalled from under the ground by spirit-robed dancers who gyrated themselves into visionary trance and ultimate exhaustion. The golden hunting age of the Plains Indians would thus be restored. The sad outcome of it all, of course, was the death of Sitting Bull at the hands of the Sioux nation's own Indian police, and the massacre at Wounded Knee.[4]

As adopted and practised by the Sioux, this dance, which had been first devised by the Paiute shaman Wovoka, seemed to some white observers to exhibit a marked millenarian character and to resemble some of the rituals of Seventh-Day Adventists. In other words, the Ghost Dance was a hybrid phenomenon, part reversion to traditional Native American spiritual beliefs, and part the result of exposure to Christian eschatology: Wovoka himself also went under the name of Jack Wilson, having been adopted by a white family when a boy. The same hybridity could be said to have characterised the Evan Roberts Revival. A part of its leader's appeal lay in his embodiment of previous Welsh Revivalists – he 'reminded one of the portraits to be seen in many Welsh homesteads of men who were leaders in the two previous religious revivals in Wales' (*ER*, 252) – but piquancy also lay in the unexpected, unconventional features of the services over which he presided and, as will shortly be seen, this twentieth-century Revival differed very significantly in tone from its predecessors. It is precisely the hybrid character of both the Sioux and the Welsh phenomena that is for anthropologists the sure sign of their being 'revitalisation movements', such as are triggered by the extreme psycho-social stress experienced by a social group struggling to adapt to radically changing circumstances. The natural social response to such a crisis is an urgent review, reorientation and re-energising of the group's hallowed socio-cultural practices, which normally culminates in the establishment of a significantly modified socio-cultural order.[5]

* * *

The 'Evan Roberts Revival' conforms neatly to the paradigm of a 'revitalisation movement' that failed, just like that of the Sioux. By 1904, Welsh chapel culture – which was, at core, a Welsh-language phenomenon – was under threat from many directions, as was the language which had sustained it. It was becoming increasingly marginal to the new, dynamic anglophone culture of the industrialised south-east. And it was being swamped by the burgeoning sport and entertainment sectors of mass industrial society – a letter to the young Evan at Newcastle Emlyn from his brother Dan at home in Loughor sounds the note of alarm:

> The football worshippers are numerous at Bwlchymynydd, taking the minds of the young and middle-aged people. There was a match between

> them and those at Llanelly last Saturday . . . There was much drinking and a great deal of row among them. I should like to see the Holy Spirit coming powerfully to drive these games out of the country. (*ER*, 40)

Thanks to his brother, the Holy Spirit was soon to oblige.

The price paid for the social influence and prestige of a new generation of well-trained ministers was loss of electrifyingly direct connection with the psycho-social needs of their flocks; chapel communities had become socially stratified in a way that mirrored the divisions within industrial society at large; services had become less enthusiastic and more temperate and rational in tone, as educated men steadily replaced the self-educated in the pulpits – Evan Roberts himself, writing to a close friend about his intention fairly late in life to train for the ministry, observed that he had first entertained the idea much earlier, but 'when I understood that the influence of the "schools" destroyed the spirit of the ministerial students, I had no heart within me any more to venture there' (*ER*, 94). Part of the secret of Roberts's eventual success was that he appeared untutored, spontaneous, sincere, authentic. Indeed, at the very outset he felt he'd been prompted to consider the pulpit not only because it was 'a passionate desire of my soul', but because he could hear 'the voice of the people' in its call (*ER*, 94). His popular appeal rested in part on the perceived ordinariness of his character and intellectual gifts. This meant he was embraced as a representative figure, intensifying popular conviction that his astonishing charisma was a spiritual gift potentially within the grasp of all.

So strong indeed was Robert's instinctive, even visceral reaction against the programme of formal education which aspirants to the Presbyterian (Welsh Calvinistic Methodist) ministry were required to follow in his day, that even after overcoming his own deep misgivings and enrolling as a mature student in Newcastle Emlyn Grammar School with a view eventually to proceeding to Trefecca College, he found himself physically incapable of studying anything but the Bible itself.

> Only opening the Book of books would he obtain peace. On one occasion he was learning a lesson in Welsh Grammar, and after committing to memory about twelve lines, he suffered most terribly in body and mind, and was obliged to throw the book from his hands, and take up the Bible. (*ER*, 102)

It is a profoundly emblematic episode, in which can be found the secret of at least part of his astonishing appeal to a working population, the large majority of which found itself excluded on the basis of insufficient academic talent from the newly established state grammar schools system. It was his very lack of such an education that was to set Evan Roberts apart from the aristocrats of the pulpit in late Nonconformist Wales, and to enable him to sound like 'the voice of the People'.

At the beginning of the twentieth century, strife was not confined to industrial relations. It had long been endemic to the many denominations (principally the Welsh Presbyterians – Welsh Calvinistic Methodists – Congregationalists [or Independents], Baptists and Wesleyan Methodists) that constituted the very loose and informal alliance that came to be designated 'Nonconformist Wales'. For decades, they had been rivals for spiritual ascendancy, social influence, educational clout and political power. Not the least significant aspect of Evan Roberts's appeal was his emphatic public dissociation of himself from every denomination, raised though he had himself been in Moriah, the Welsh Presbyterian chapel in Loughor. 'Some people had said he was a Methodist,' Roberts remarked of hmself in Trecynon in the autumn of 1904, but 'he did not know what he was. Sectarianism melted in the fire of the Holy Spirit, and all men who believed became one happy family.' (*ER*, 253) It was a core conviction of his, evidenced by his repeating not just the same sentiments but much the same words at a November (1904) meeting in Cilfynydd, where 'his great point was the duty of sinking all sectarian differences, and for all to meet as one family' (*ER*, 273).

'Nonconformist Wales' was, then, under increasing stress in 1904, and that at a time when coalfield society in south-east Wales was for the first time heading towards class conflict. Just four years earlier, in 1900, Keir Hardie's election as one of the two MPs for Merthyr had signalled the advent of the new politics from which would emerge the dominant twentieth-century image of Wales as the 'Socialist Nation'. Hardie's election had also silently announced the terminal decay of 'Mabonism', the conciliatory, consensual, classless form of unionism named for its great representative, Mabon (William Abraham), darling of the Welsh chapels. A mere six years before Evan Roberts's birth in Island House, in the very shadow of the large tinplate works on the far bank of the Loughor river, Mabon had begun his career as miners' leader in that very same region, when he was elected agent for the

Loughor district of the Amalgamated Association of Miners (AAM). A mere six years after the 1904 Revival, Mabon switched his allegiance from the labour wing of the Liberal party to the newly-established Labour Party proper. He thereby underlined how radically and irreversibly class relations within industrial society had changed. His switching of allegiance was an implicit acknowledgement of the displacement of the old Nonconformist nation by a new, emergent Socialist nation. The Gospel was being replaced by the Social Gospel; working people were turning for guidance and leadership more to the officials of the 'New Unionism' than to ministers of religion. In at least one of its aspects, then, the 1904–6 Revival was the chapels' fightback, a fightback that now, in the rear-view mirror of our today, may perhaps be viewed again as the rearguard action of the doomed Nonconformist nation.

Crisis mentality was not, however, confined to the populous, incipiently cosmopolitan industrial districts of the south. The Great Strike at the Penrhyn Quarry – one of the most epic in the annals of British labour – had at last been brought to resentful conclusion after three years of bitter stalemate, only a matter of months before Revival fever began, and the slate-quarrying communities of the north-east of Wales were to prove notably receptive to Evan Roberts's message. The rural regions of Wales, that had been the turbulent site of the people's Tithe Wars during the 1880s, had been in steady decline throughout the second half of the nineteenth century, as a substantial percentage of its population migrated to the boom-time industrial areas not only of south-east Wales but also of the USA. And, by the end of the nineteenth century, Liverpool – which was to welcome Roberts with open arms – was just one of many of England's rapidly growing cities that had become home to a strong and influential deraciné community of Welsh exiles.

Although writing more than half a century after the event, Gwyn Thomas, the greatest mythographer of south Wales coalfield society, intuitively understood the socio-historical role Evan Roberts had performed in the psycho-social drama of his period. 'The atmosphere of the times must have been charged with a sense of cataclysm', Thomas wrote of his native Rhondda at the turn of the twentieth century (*HH*, 47). 'Not a seam was to be left unripped. Mines could be gutted by flame, villages decimated by death. To live with an angry roughness took some pain from part of the outrage. The valley brimmed with hopes and dreads, longing for a focus.' 'The great agitators of the colliers' union,' Thomas concluded, 'provided [that focus] in part,' but for many, 'the Messenger, in the Mohammedan sense of the term, would need a wider field of reference than coal or politics.'

What Evans Roberts offered anxious, tense communities was, as experienced observers noted at the time, subtly but arrestingly different not only from what the chapels were offering but also from what had been offered by celebrated revivalists from the Welsh past. Evan Roberts was offering release, joy, even rapture:

> The doctrines burn hearts like red-hot fire, and scorch the spirit of the unforgivers, the doubtful, the disobedient, the sceptical, and the gloomy. The sound of reconciliation of forgiveness, of confession and self-denial, and the joy of salvation fill the place . . . When the scholars drew out plans for the future revival, they asserted that that revival would be very different from all its forerunners . . . 'Here is love, vast as the ocean' [an English translation of the great Revival hymn, 'Dyma gariad fel y moroedd'] is the rallying point of the new world . . . Evan Roberts has been a glorious instrument to elevate the Christian Church in Wales to the assurance of faith, the assurance of hope, and the assurance of love, into a high spiritual atmosphere, into the fellowship with the eternal, into possession of the joy of salvation, and the joy of the Holy Spirit. The tone of religion altered, and under God's blessing, a direction was given to the revival in Wales. (*ER*, 285)

'The tone of religion altered': Roberts didn't in any way downplay the traditional Calvinist emphasis on full – indeed public – confession of sin, and search for forgiveness, but he certainly did, in practice if not in intention, fast-track sinners' progress towards a blissful state of grace, and removed the terrible, debilitating, Calvinist uncertainty over the personal spiritual privilege of election. The tone of his religion was, so the scale and extent of his Revival was to prove, thus perfectly suited to soothe what Gwyn Thomas called 'the atmosphere' of his deeply troubled times.

When indeed then this 'Messenger', as Thomas was to style him, eventually arrived, he duly manifested all the credentials necessary for the effective performance of his redemptive role, and it is Gwyn Thomas again who puts his finger on one key feature of Evan Roberts's biographical profile in this regard that few subsequent commentators have noticed. 'He came roaring out of the West, his own conscience on fire, and left a multitude of minds charred and astonished.' (*HH*, 47)

Thomas is in fact mistaken – Roberts was born and raised not in rural west Wales but in a western corner of the coalfield itself, part of the substantial Swansea industrial hinterland, and he'd spent more than a dozen years working underground, having started as an eleven-year-old door-boy. But this factual error serves only to underline how in such cases fact may be far less pertinent and potent than myth: the necessary myth concerning Evan Roberts being the supposition of many of his industrial listeners that he had 'come . . . out of the West'.[6]

That mythical 'truth' was so potent because to workers and their families in the mining, steel and tinplate heartlands of the south Wales coalfield, as in the seminal quarrying districts of the north-east, Roberts seemed to offer an escape from the conditions that oppressed and bewildered them, in the form of a steadying, vivifying reconnection with their own 'roots' in the rural world of the pre-industrial west. And, indeed, Robert had himself undertaken after a fashion precisely such a mythic return journey to primal rural western source. Having been born and raised in industrial Loughor, and having worked as a young man in several of the mines both in that area and as far afield as Mountain Ash in the Cynon Valley area, he had then travelled west to Newcastle Emlyn in the very heart of the lovely Cardiganshire countryside, to prepare himself for admission to Trefecca training college by first attending the private preparatory school grandiosely entitled Newcastle Emlyn Grammar School. Very shortly after his arrival in the town, he attended a service at nearby Blaenannerch, and it was there that he experienced his extraordinary spiritual 'awakening'.

* * *

One vital aspect of the Revival that seems to have received no attention was its thoroughly bilingual character, which is highlighted at one point in a key account of 1904–6. At Pentre (Rhondda Fawr), 2–4 December 1904, it is reported, 'young converts took a prominent part, in Welsh and English . . . That was a pleasant surprise [to Roberts], because from that he could infer that the Revival had laid hold of the English section of the populous valleys.' (*ER*, 286)

As D. M. Phillips, an intimate of the evangelist and one of the earliest and most thorough chroniclers of the Revival, makes clear, Evan Roberts, raised in a Welsh-speaking home and local environment, a working-class boy who had had to abandon schooling when he was only eleven, made painstaking efforts at night after work not only to master the grammar of the English language but to make himself thoroughly literate in it. In time, his library, as Phillips interestingly records, was to be evenly divided between heavyweight improving texts in Welsh and in English, with D. Silvan Evans's celebrated Welsh–English Dictionary serving as a kind of bridge between the two (*ER*, 55). He thereby equipped himself to lead a Revival that was thoroughly, and fascinatingly, bilingual and bicultural in character. This proved to be a crucial factor, enabling him to campaign as effectively in the great new anglicised industrial areas as in the traditional rural areas of the Welsh-speaking heartlands. As the great hymn-writer Elfed noted in his memoir of the Revival, *With Christ among the Miners*, 'If we have spent most of our time among the miners – using the term in its broadest sense – it is simply because they form the majority of the nation, and affect the whole directly.'[7] Roberts was thus effectively able to span the very socio-cultural divide that was such a threat to the future of Nonconformist Wales. His Revival could profitably be studied in the context of the 'English Cause' of the nineteenth century – an organised attempt by Welsh Nonconformity to make common cause with English-speaking Wales by establishing English-language chapels under the auspices of Welsh denominations. In one way, Evan Roberts's Revival represented one further, and final, step in this doomed Welsh Nonconformist attempt to reach out to anglophone Wales, in an effort to survive the slow and seemingly terminal decline of the Welsh language.

The 'international' language of music served a very useful purpose in this connection, although far too much has been made by writers, artists and popular historians alike of this famous dimension of the Revival experience. Roberts himself was always at least as suspicious as he was appreciative of the enormous emotional power of hymn-singing: 'Do not sing too much in the meeting,' he advised trainee ministers, 'and that without any spirit in it. In such a meeting I am compelled to sit, although that is very hard, and see the meeting go down . . . Do not sing until we are full of the spirit of prayer. The spirit of prayer must possess us before we can sing prayerfully.' (*ER*, 441) And he had similar misgivings about the emotions that a Revival meeting could arouse. 'Too much importance should not be given to feeling,' he emphasised (*ER*, 436); '[i]t is not feeling we want but belief.'

Roberts's origins in Loughor seemed emblematic of his inter-cultural role. The township was situated towards the far edge of the south Wales coalfield, forming a kind of hinge between the Welsh-speaking

West (including the renowned tinplate town of Llanelli) and the increasingly English-speaking East (represented locally by the major metallurgical centre of Swansea). At the time of his birth, the upstart town of Gorseinon – which would eventually expand to more or less incorporate the ancient Norman borough of Loughor – began to develop apace into an industrial centre that anglicised rapidly as it grew. And Roberts's bilingualism served one other vital function. It allowed him to mediate the *hwyl* or religious enthusiasm that had traditionally characterised the Welsh-language chapels to the new anglophone regions of the industrial south. This missionary effort was, however, to prove Welsh Nonconformity's last hurrah.

The traditional hold of the chapels over the communities of Loughor and its environs was probably prolonged by the distinctive socio-political character of this particular corner of the south Wales coalfield. Overlooked by historians, this important feature of Evan Roberts's background was identified early with unconscious accuracy by D. M. Phillips, a minister at Tylorstown, in the heavily congested Rhondda Fach. Visiting Loughor, he was accordingly struck by the relative spaciousness of an area largely devoid of the terraced miners' houses that clogged up the steep slopes of the narrow south Wales valleys.

> The town [of lower Loughor] has no form after the manner of [the cramped, crowded] towns of later years. We find here a number of old houses, but not more than from two to six of them are joined together. So it may be said of houses built in later years – two here and two there, three in one place and four in another. You would not find a street of twenty houses in the town . . . It seems that every one chose his own spot to build a house. (*ER*, 9)

What a contrast with the congested terraces of company housing in the Rhondda. Island House itself – where Evan Roberts was born and raised – was a not insubstantial building, standing in solitary isolation and able to boast a large garden that on one famous occasion the boy single-handedly dug with dogged determination, to ensure his family would have enough home-grown produce to sustain it. It was a semi-rural, semi-industrial environment a world away from the Rhondda, and it produced an independent, self-sufficient, individualist streak in its inhabitants that made them imperfect collectivists and lukewarm unionists compared to the industrial proletariat of the south-eastern valleys of the coalfield. Consequently, the union militancy, which by the early 1900s was attracting some chapel faithful away in those regions and attaching them to the new charismatic leaders of the Labour cause, was never as readily attractive to this western part of the coalfield where chapel ministers could still hold considerable sway.

Roberts himself typified the relatively un-militant, socially and politically conservative character of his particular locality, and was thus able to function during the Revival as a kind of reassuring reminder of an earlier era of owner-worker relations, less fraught and riven by class hostility than that dawning in 1904. Indeed, his earliest biographer, who knew him extremely well, chose to highlight this feature of his personality. 'Distinction of class does not bias his mind,' claimed D. M. Phillips; although, he hurriedly added, 'were he to incline towards one class more than the other, the benefit would be given to the poorer.' (*ER*, 184) That last term, 'poorer', smacks far more, of course, of the Bible than of the socialist vocabulary that marked the emergence of a proletarian consciousness. 'He is at home with all classes of society,' added Phillips, '[h]e has no desire to stay with people of high rank when on his mission, because he thinks he can do more good amongst the middle and lower classes, and can, thereby, glorify God better.' (*ER*, 185) The comment is all the more pointed in that, by 1904, the ministers of Welsh Nonconformity were themselves comfortable, even at times self-satisfied, members of the middle classes of Wales.

There is evidence that the attention of the middle classes across Britain was attracted to the Revival partly because it seemed to promise an antidote to working class militancy. When W. T. Stead, the most prominent and innovative London journalist of the day, attended a Revival meeting in Maerdy, at the very top of the Rhondda Fach (soon to become known as 'little Moscow'), he first cunningly reported that it prompted 'the thought that Welsh religious enthusiasm may be destined to impart as compelling an impulse to the Churches of the world as Welsh coal supplies to its navies' (*ER*, 299). Then, having thus represented the Revival as a working-class phenomenon, he assured his readers that the meeting had been 'as orderly, and at least as reverent, as any congregation I ever saw beneath the dome of St Paul's', even though the place 'was aflame with a passionate religious enthusiasm' totally unlike any experienced in that grand monument to Wren. 'There was absolutely nothing wild, violent, hysterical, unless it be hysterical for the labouring breast to heave with sobbing that cannot be repressed and the throat to choke with emotion as a sense of the awful horror and shame of a wasted life suddenly bursts upon the soul.' (*ER*, 301)

Stead then embarked on a paean of praise for the civilising effect of the Revival on an industrial working class that, in consequence, had not only given up drink, gambling, swearing – and sport – but (crucially) had become less 'idle' and more productive: 'Waste is less, men go to their daily toil with a new spirit of gladness in their labour.' (*ER*, 300) Stead also made much of the unstructured character of a Revival that in some ways seemed refreshingly leaderless. The spontaneous cooperation evident in meetings – several reporters wonderingly mentioned their 'go-as-you please' air, more Quaker than Nonconformist in character – was very reassuringly different from the organised collectivism of the threatening new unionism with its leadership cult, and seemed to Stead to augur the alternative development of what he called an 'industrial democracy'. He also shrewdly noted how the sermon that had traditionally formed the centrepiece of chapel worship had been displaced in Revival meetings by both solo and congregational hymn singing. 'It is to other revivals what the Italian opera is to the ordinary theatre', he suggestively remarked, anticipating Gwyn Thomas. The Revival, we should remember, was in one of its aspects both the grand climax of the Cymanfa Ganu (hymn-singing festival) cult that had become such a feature of late Nonconformist culture and a subversion of it. In yet another of its aspects (deeply mistrusted, as we have seen, by Roberts himself), it was, thanks to the theatricality of the singing, the chapel culture's riposte to the new cult of the music hall and its various offshoots in the popular culture of the day.

Reporting of the Revival from the 'sophisticated' metropolitan perspective of London always found eventual reassurance in its Welsh primitive emotionalism, even while careful to couch such in the hallowed terms of the Bible. Thus, for W. B. Hodgson of the *Daily News*, the key feature of Evan Roberts was that he had 'the heart of a child' (*ER*, 313). Hodgson proceeded to dilate at length on this admirable quality, and his condescension extended to other members of the Welsh working class to which Evan Roberts seemed, to this 'sophisticated' metropolitan outsider, transparently to belong: 'this afternoon as a great collier was pleading with the sharp tones of deadly anguish of soul, with fists upraised and clenched as though the knuckles must come through the skin, there came a soft undercurrent of exquisitely undulated harmony.' (*ER*, 314) The emasculation – indeed, the soft feminisation – of the threatening Welsh 'collier' was a sight in which London might well rejoice, particularly given how otherwise threatening the burly figure of the miner could be when associated with the increasingly violent labour disputes of the day.[8]

Given, then, the unorthodox character of the Revival meetings, shrewdly noted by an outsider like Stead, it is not surprising that Roberts was reputed by the militant proletariat in the thickly-sown industrial valleys of south Wales to himself be an outsider, to have 'come from the West'. It qualified him in their eyes to help the industrial working class deal with the psycho-social crisis occasioned by strange, disorientating new conditions, as he was the mythically authorised bearer of a reassuringly familiar explanatory language of spiritual struggle – an augur, so to speak (to revert to the analogy of the Ghost Dance) of the buffalos' return. Time after time, Roberts refused to act the traditional revivalist's part of inspired guru and saviour. Time after time he turned his individual listeners back on themselves, referring a working people radically disempowered by circumstances to their own extraordinary supra-personal inner resources. They should attend, he insisted, not to him but to the quiet and totally unpredictable promptings of the Spirit within. And it wasn't by his words so much that they were moved as by the electrifying example he set himself, as he sat before them in agonised silence for an hour or more at a time.

Gwyn Thomas thus intuited Evan Roberts's mythic stature and healing mission accurately enough, but went factually awry again when he characterised the evangelist as 'a bilingual, simple-minded meteorite'. Bilingual Roberts certainly was, but he was also an intensely intelligent, highly sensitive, naturally introspective and extremely complex human being. Having dropped out of school before he was eleven to help his father who had been injured in a pit accident, he nevertheless continued to feed his brooding, enquiring mind voraciously on religious books. As a young man, he had briefly entertained the idea of migrating to the US, with the intention of making sufficient money by his labours there to retire back to Wales at an early age and spend the rest of his life absorbed in study. Somewhat nearer the mark was Thomas's other comment that, 'like all dynamic South Wales talents' (no doubt Thomas was thinking partly of himself), the naturally introverted Evan Roberts was 'a fugitive from pit-labour and neurosis' (*HH*, 48). But it was probably this very 'neurosis' that so perfectly attuned him to the mass neurosis of his Wales. Consequently, for a brief period – a period he seems retrospectively to have viewed as both terrifying and tragic – he was to find himself acting as the lightning conductor not only for the Holy Spirit ('if indeed it *was* the Holy Spirit') but for his people and his age.

* * *

No more dramatic manifestation could have been imagined of the terrible strain Evan Roberts was under after two years of evangelising than his shockingly abrupt abandonment of his mission in 1906. At what seemed to be the very height of his controversial fame, he suddenly bolted, headed for psycho-spiritual refuge in distant, placid suburban Leicestershire, at the home of one of his most ardent supporters, Mrs Jessie Penn-Lewis, and never again risked prolonged public exposure. It was as if some latter-day King Arthur, grievously sick not from physical but from psychic wounds, had retired in sympathetic female company to distant Afallon to be cured of his ills, leaving a stricken, bewildered people dreaming of his redemptive return.

Evan Roberts, most would agree today, had suffered 'burn out' – the term is hospitably vague. A qualified psychiatrist has recently hazarded a more precise and fashionable diagnosis: 'post-traumatic stress disorder'.[9] There has been no shortage of opinions, both lay and professional, as to the exact nature of Roberts's spectacular meltdown, with explanations centrally divided between those who give serious credence to the spiritual character of both his mission and his collapse, and those who believe both can be wholly accounted for in the secular terms of modern psychological and psychoanalytical analysis.

What is certain is that Evan Roberts had been very deeply troubled mentally for some considerable time before his final precipitate sequestration. His letters testify copiously to that, as can be seen from the following disturbing passage dated 13 September 1915:

> The ladies are seen to wear their pearly chains day after day. But I believe that the white, crystal, and priceless pearls of the fiery seer excel them ten thousand times, and yet ten thousand more. But there, I must call back my imagination lest I speed over the steep descent, and then, and there, only destruction for myself and those under my care will be found. And so, now we shall slacken the pace in time lest the wheels take fire from the furious speed. The car has now come to a standstill. Down we go. Now for a word before we part. (*ER*, 447)

Here Roberts demonstrates admirable self-awareness: conscious of how excitable his imagination is, he polices it very carefully. One feature of his sensibility that has largely escaped critical notice is that he was a poet – of sorts, at least. In truth, his religious effusions in both Welsh and English are embarrassingly trite, but he certainly did have a sensitivity to language that found most effective written expression in his prose. He could, for instance, rejoice in 'the blue beauty of life', (*ER*, 449) and could remark that 'in the past, I believed that the line from my eyes to the horizon was the radius of life's circle. Ah, me! I know now that life has no horizon, nor sleep – turning circle after circle – it opens – extends – deepens – and what else? I know not. I feel sin to be hell without a drop of blood to cool it.' (*ER*, 451)

This vividness of imagination and gift for striking expression was a mixed blessing. It undoubtedly contributed significantly to the magnetism that made him such a compelling visionary witness to Gospel truth, as he experienced it; but, as he himself shrewdly understood (his impressive natural intelligence should never be underestimated), his creative sensibility was also a constant threat to his mental stability ('but there, I must call back my imagination lest I speed over the steep descent . . .'). Reports of his conduct, both private and public, repeatedly give the impression of a mind suspended precariously over dangerous chasms. He may very well have inherited this volatile temperament; an early associate who knew both Roberts and his family well, observed of his father Henry that 'his face tells us that he is a man who belongs to the nervous temperament class. It is from this class most often men of great talents arise . . . This temperament is an excellent one, if kept under control, and if accompanied by a high degree of intellect . . . Henry Roberts may be grateful that he possesses a lively and electric nature.' (*ER*, 14) 'Electric': an adjective to which we will shortly return when considering the temperament of Henry's famous son.

Anyone seeking an explanation for the way Evan Roberts suddenly and irrevocably absented himself from the theatre of his great psycho-spiritual triumphs in 1906 need perhaps look no further than such a passage as this from a letter he wrote late in 1905:

> The people cannot understand why I do not move: and I fail to understand why I am staying! But this I know, that I am moving swifter than ever – so swift, indeed, that I cannot perceive myself moving. What a commotion there is in the tents! My soul is a kind of tabernacle, and

> self dwelling in innumerable tents around it, and what takes place is the slaughtering of the troublesome, howling, thankless, rebellious inhabitants, and so on. Oh! Some ceaseless moving continues! The old man and the pure heart enraging, and getting furious for victory. I see today that 'self' has its houses, palaces, and dens. But how cunning this can be in this den! But away after him! Behold he fleeth into his cave! Here cometh the Divine searchlight on its strong wings. Satanic. Ha! Ha!! Ha!!! Lo! He is made a corpse by the pointed arrow. Is that the end now? No, no! The beginning of the end, and the end of the beginning. Is it so? Is it indeed? What shall I do next? Return to my strong castle, or seek for another enemy? Beware! What then? On thy knees in an instant, and in gratitude let thy lips move. Moving the knee and lip? Is it not, Doctor? Then, moving into peace. (*ER*, 448)

Rhetorical, yes; theatrical even, one might almost say; but also unmistakeably anguished, tortured. Though the tropes are at bottom conventionally Biblical, the language of spiritual self-scrutiny far from unconventional – it may readily be sourced to the self-examination of intense believers from St Augustine through George Fox and John Bunyan (*Pilgrim's Progress* was one of Roberts's personal favourites; *ER*, 66) to the present – there is no mistaking the desperate vehemence here of a self-baffled soul.

The letter pivots around a distinction between movement and stasis, and there is ample evidence that, from 1904 to 1906, Roberts's own life alternated with dramatic unpredictability between the one and the other. There are examples galore of his almost pathological inner restlessness, as of his bewilderingly sudden shifts during the course of his Revival meetings from ecstatic dancing on the tips of his toes to an almost catatonic stillness and silence. Indeed, he became dubbed 'the silent Evangelist' during his Liverpool expedition and, accordingly, compared to the Quakers. 'The thing specially notable,' wrote one newspaper correspondent, 'the distinctively new trait in evangelism – is the silence, which much overbalances the speech. The trait which has been least mentioned as to Evan Roberts, but which has been most new, has been the entire absence of personal push.'[10]

This is not to assert that Roberts was a manic-depressive. It was during the Liverpool period that he was specifically referred to several eminent psychiatrists who, following a thorough examination, pronounced their patient to be completely sane, a sensibly cautious diagnosis confirmed by a clinical psychiatrist of our own time. But that is not to rule out the surely tempting possibility that – to use another clinical term of our day – Roberts was a 'borderline personality'. This is not to deny that he had a strong, authentic mystic streak. 'There is a great deal of mysticism in him,' noted the celebrated minister John Williams ('Brynsiencyn') (*ER*, 421), and it found expression in experiences such as the following which he reported in November 1904 to his close friend Sydney Evans:

> I had a vision last Thursday morning. Here it is. Near me I could see a candle burning, and casting its light around. Far away in the distance, I could see a man rising. And, Oh! what a sight it was. Not a winter nor an autumn sun, nor the sun of spring, but the sun of a summer's morn. Well, there was something divine in it. Its beams were like long arms, extending across the heavens. And the candle continued to burn. There were three or four inches of the candle unburnt. Now, Syd, what is the meaning of this? Turn to interpret. It is quite simple. Day is at hand. This is the beginning of a Revival. But, Oh! the great sun of the Revival is near at hand. (*ER*, 225)

But he was also subject to episodes of religious mania and even of psychotic delusion. Witness his erratic emotional behaviour, his extreme and unpredictable alternations of mood, his self-admitted tendency to mental hyper-stimulation, his polarisation of his mesmerised congregation into the scions of Satan and the beloved of Christ. There seems little doubt that on any spectrum of the sane, Roberts would be placed on occasions fairly far out towards the perilous limits.

What's more, it was perhaps precisely by thus so palpably living on what Browning termed 'the dangerous edge of things' that Roberts was able to generate the frisson, the electricity, that so galvanised his extraordinary meetings. His listeners never knew what to expect, and could never predict which Evan Roberts would turn up – if, that is, one turned up at all, since he was notoriously given to breaking his engagements at the very last minute. But then he was equally liable to materialise suddenly, half way through a meeting. He might then simply sit in silent immobility for long hours, sunk in prayer (he never indulged in public displays of his genius for praying), and not registering an awareness of anyone else's presence. Or he might abandon himself to inspired impassioned prophecy. By ominously blaming unnamed individuals in his appalled congregation for preventing the Spirit from speaking through him, he might turn every man against his neighbour, every woman against her companion. He was as liable to break down in floods of tears as to break out in ecstatic Hosannahs. At his meetings, no one ever knew what would happen next.[11]

* * *

Interestingly enough, Evan Roberts had visited a phrenologist in Swansea before devoting himself to the ministry. This 'Professor Williams' had stated that Roberts 'would (a) succeed, and (b) excel in electricity' (*ER*, 94), and had urged him to consider the pulpit. 'Electric' was a designation utilised by the fashionable pseudo-science of phrenology to characterise an individual of highly nervous temperament and unstable mind, and history continues to furnish many examples of the extraordinary fascination such edgy characters seem to exert, possibly because they mediate raw, barely controllable primal forces. Electricity is, of course, a highly dangerous source of energy which needs extremely careful handling, and Roberts was intelligent enough to be very mindful of the highly volatile character of the extraordinary power with which he had been ambivalently blessed.

His great public meetings were occasions when he was exposed to the greatest psychic risk, precisely because they were such highly charged occasions. On the one hand they afforded him an indispensable safe opportunity for discharging all the latent electricity of his peculiar nature, but on the other, instinct as they were with mass hysteria, they provided opportunities for mental over-stimulation and over-excitation of his highly susceptible imagination. Something of their extraordinary character is well captured in the cool reports of Roberts's Revival meetings in Liverpool that the local correspondent Gwilym Hughes contributed to the *South Wales Daily News*.

The strangest of these meetings, without a doubt, were those held in 1905 on Tuesday 11 April, and Friday 14 April. In the first of these, the Revivalist 'was convulsed with heartrending sobs', reported Hughes, before he was able to break free from his psycho-spiritual constraints and testify that God had authorised him to proclaim that the Free Welsh Church in Liverpool was not firmly anchored to the Rock of Ages. 'The sensation caused by this declaration is painful', wrote Hughes, as several faithful members of the Free Welsh Church were present in the meeting. A minister accordingly rose to voice a protest on their behalf, upon which Evan Roberts's whole demeanour changed dramatically in an instant:

> What a change! The revivalist is now all smiles. He laughs merrily, joyously, and his laugh is contagious. But suddenly he becomes serious. 'Don't think so low of me,' he pleads, 'as to believe that I am taught by man. I never repeat from the pulpit what man says, but what God bids me speak.' (*ERR*, 75)

Predictably, the proceedings of that evening raised a huge storm that raged around Roberts's head for the rest of the week, so that the Friday meeting was avidly awaited. For the first and last time in the history of the Revival, women were denied admission because trouble was expected. As for the site of the meeting, it happened to be the very chapel in Chatham Street where one of the most prominent of the Free Church ministers had been pastor for many years. As anticipated, the result was mayhem. One minister leapt to his feet to claim that Evan Roberts was prevented by his guilty conscience from opening his mouth. Other ministers reached for their coats in protest and made ready to leave. An aged minister laboured to his feet only for his words to be drowned out by the enthusiastic congregational hymn-singing. Another minister sank back into his seat protesting that '"This is not the work of the Holy Ghost; it is the work of the genius of man. All that has taken place here tonight is mockery."' (*ERR*, 84)[12] He then attempted to climb on top of his seat to address the congregation, but was silenced by hostile shouts, as yet another hymn was struck. In the end, the meeting was brought to an extremely hurried conclusion, and Evan Roberts was bundled out secretly by a back-door exit. The following day he was examined by four of the most prominent medical men in Liverpool, who declared, '"We find him mentally and physically quite sound. He is suffering from the effects of overwork, and we consider it advisable that he should have a period of rest."' (*ERR*, 89)

What happened in Liverpool seems to have been rare in the history of the Roberts Revival. It was not his practice to single out individuals or groups by name. Rather, his preferred strategy was to demonise unnamed and therefore unidentifiable members of the congregation, thereby unnerving all the rest and rendering them highly suggestible. This externalisation of his wrestlings with his own demons proved a highly successful means of mass manipulation, but such sinister unfocused scapegoating remains disquieting to read about even a century later. He would compellingly announce, for example, that the spiritual recalcitrance of one of his listeners who was refusing to yield to Christ's piteous importunings was freezing his tongue, or was reducing him to uncontrollable tears. Gwilym Hughes memorably recorded one such occasion in Westminster Road, Kirkdale, 10 April 1905:

> His mood is distinctly black; his features betray indications of recent tears. He opens the Bible, finds the verse he needs, and is on the point of reading it when his face is convulsed. He bends his head in silent prayer. Three or four times is this repeated. At last he speaks gaspingly: 'Well, I am not allowed to read this verse. There is someone here who knows why.' (*ERR*, 67)

By such means, he could work up his listeners to a fever pitch of hysterical anxiety, but at the price of spreading mutual suspicion abroad. On occasions, he further intensified the effect by locating his targets more precisely:

> We witness that wild, rapid glance of his surveying the congregation up and down. Again he closes his eyes, his face is twitching, and his hand is firmly pressed against the back of his head. 'Over there,' he cries, gesticulating wildy, and pointing to the gallery at the far end of the building. 'Over there in the gallery.' (*ERR*, 64)

Under the pressure of such unremitting emotional blackmail, more often than not some poor soul would buckle, capitulate, confess his or her 'sins', and beg for mercy and forgiveness.

When Evan Roberts was questioned as to the state of his health at the conclusion of his Liverpool visit, he replied that '[h]e felt strong . . . but his nerves were a bit unstrung' (*ERR*, 94). His response neatly encapsulates the ambivalent character of his experience as a Revivalist. Psychically reinforcing though they were in one respect, they were dangerously destabilising in another. He insisted on pushing on with his work, but a few months later he finally cracked under the cumulative strain of two and more years of soul-wrenching, mind-bending campaigning.

* * *

Roberts found sanctuary in the comfortable bourgeois home of Jessie Penn-Lewis (1861–1927) and her husband William, in Leicester. Having spent the best part of two years trying, however unintentionally and unconsciously, to satisfy his people's craving for spiritual solace, it must have been a huge psychological relief for him to place a significant physical distance between himself and their insatiable demands and psychic pressures. Not that this was his first attempt at self-protective withdrawal. Indeed, his career as evangelist had been punctuated by brief but dramatic periods when he suddenly became unreachable and incommunicable. He had once spent a whole week in Briton Ferry holed up in one small room, refusing to speak to anyone save Florrie Evans, one of his most trusted followers. Indeed, a striking feature of Evan Roberts was his almost certainly innocent fondness for female company and his public reliance on female helpers and even performers. His readiness to allow women their voice has probably been what has most endeared his Revival to social historians in recent years. His own deeply empathetic (stereotypically 'feminine') temperament may well have inclined him to favour the company of women at a time when gendered male and female characteristics were much more rigid and pronounced than they are today. The girls had, after all, outnumbered the boys in his own family by five to three, and he had been particularly close to the youngest of his sisters, Mary, whom he had helped raise when his mother was greatly weakened after her birth.

Whatever the reason, Evan Roberts obviously felt comfortable in the company of women, and afforded them starring roles in his Revival meetings. In that way, he radically modified traditional Nonconformist practice according to which, consistent with Victorian convention, women's voices were deferentially silent in chapel and could be raised only within the domestic confines of home and family. And moreover, unintentionally but providentially, Roberts for the first time allowed the New Woman (considered in chapter 2), who had been such a startling product of the 1890s, a loud public voice in respectable religious circles. It was at long last possible for a young woman both to remain safely within the chapel fold and also to satisfy whatever secret longings had been timidly stirred in her by the colourful and controversial figures of the Women's Movement.

It was probably no coincidence, therefore, that it was to a woman – herself a New Woman of sorts – that Roberts turned for help when his great psycho-spiritual collapse eventually occurred. Jessie Penn-Lewis was a married woman of middle age, who had been raised on a comfortably bourgeois, religiously devout hearth in Neath, a dozen miles from Loughor.[13] The grand-daughter of a leading Welsh Calvinistic Methodist divine, she nevertheless had no knowledge of Welsh and exhibited instead all the personal and social confidence of the upwardly mobile and proudly anglicised Welsh middle-class into which she had been born. Iron-willed and an indefatigable religious busybody, she could, one imagines, be something of a tyrant at times, but then her father had been a hard-headed mining engineer and her mother a doughty campaigner for the Temperance League. Plagued by ill health as a child, she had not only been denied prolonged formal education but also forbidden to tax her brain or indulge in physical exercise. At the same time, she was greatly indulged as the apple of her father's eye, and was allowed to mix freely with her brothers. 'My play-fellows,' she later recalled, 'were boys. In the garden we played cricket and climbed trees, and had our own little "reading nests" in various ivy corners.' (*TT*, 3) On the one hand, therefore, she had been granted liberties unusual for a Victorian girl; but, on the other, these liberties had served only to highlight her irksome confinements and to render them unbearable to one of her strong-willed and highly spirited nature. Early rage at such unreasonable constraints left an indelible mark on her mature character. Yet even as late as the date of her marriage, she was deemed so delicate that her young husband William, a promising borough accountant, was warned that he was taking on an 'invalid for life'. Their partnership proved to be a highly durable and successful one, but had first to survive an early period when she was prostrated by a lethargy that seems pretty clearly to have been a physical expression of her resentment at being so crampingly confined to the role of an obedient wife. Release for her mercifully came in the form of a momentous experience of religious conversion.

With the entry of the Holy Spirit into Penn-Lewis's life came liberation. What male could possibly deny a woman the right to dedicate her entire life to the Spirit's dictates? As time passed, she discovered she was commanded by it to spend much of her life away from home, on missionary expeditions that grew ever more intrepid. The remarkable book jointly authored by Penn-Lewis and Evan Roberts during his Leicester period records the view, presumably shared by both, that women faced the difficulty of having to operate within a male-dominated social structure. The point is made via an ingenious reinterpretation of the passage in the book of Genesis where Adam is reputed to have been first tempted by Eve. After reiterating the familiar theological argument that it was also by woman that salvation came to mankind, the authors then proceed an original step further. The Devil, they argue, was so incensed by the birth of the Messiah that,

> Henceforth it is also war by Satan upon the womanhood of the world, in malignant revenge for the verdict of the garden. War by trampling down of women in all lands where the deceiver reigns. War upon women in Christian lands, by the continuance of his Eden method of misinterpreting the Word of God, insinuating into men's minds throughout all succeeding ages, that God pronounced a 'curse' upon the woman, when in truth she was pardoned and blessed; and instigating men of the fallen race to carry out the supposed curse, which was in truth a curse upon the deceiver, and not the deceived one. (Genesis 3:14)[14]

This throws a fascinatingly bizarre light in retrospect on the prominent role afforded to women in the Evan Roberts revival. It also lays bare, it seems to me, the mainspring of Jessie Penn-Lewis's life of evangelising.

So it is little wonder that she became besotted with the Holy Spirit. A divine, liberating, incomparable, irresistible – and tacitly 'male' – force, it authorised and enabled her to overcome any obstacle set in her way by established male-dominated society wherever in the world it was to be met. Indeed, ecstatic illumination (*TT*, 27) had first come to her in 1892 from Africa, through a book entitled *The Spirit of Christ* (*TT*, 14; *MPL*, 14), written by the missionary Andrew Murray, and thereafter hers was to remain a global vision of the struggle between light and dark. It was in this setting she was to persuade Evan Roberts to view the 1904–6 Welsh Revival.

* * *

Jessie Penn-Lewis herself became something of a world traveller as she evangelised, organised, campaigned and innovated with inexhaustible energy. Initiatives to improve the condition of women remained ever close to her heart. While mixing mostly with the affluent, influential middle-class, she was particularly concerned with the welfare of working-class women such as domestic servants and factory workers. Her own early experiences no doubt had made her sensitive and sympathetic to the plight of young women who were denied social expression of their gifts and energies. 'I think that if a person goes to the theatre,' she wrote (and the concern already noted in Evan Roberts's case with the potentially irresistible attractions of the new popular forms of mass entertainment is again evident),

> there is within a craving for something they lack, but it is mis-directed. It is natural to want *life*, and all these things point to unsatisfied souls crying out for 'life' . . . I am intensely sympathetic with young folk when they see the old folk jog-trotting to prayer meeting! Have you no sympathy? Would *you* have gone? That is what draws me into the work among young girls – I had such sympathy with them. They want life, and if we do not give them the right kind of 'life', they will get the wrong kind. (*MPL*, 61–2)

One of her first initiatives was to establish a home for girls, and she worked closely with the YWCA. Institutions into which she poured her energy quickly expanded – the number of women attending classes at Richmond Institute, for instance, doubled to 13,000 a year – so that she eventually gained prominence sufficient for her to rub shoulders with such legendary evangelisers as Dwight Moody at the Keswick Evangelical Convention in 1892. Inspired by the success of Richmond, she established a like Institute in her native Neath, which proved so successful that another was soon established in neighbouring Swansea.

Young women trained in her Bible classes and prayer groups began to venture into evangelising themselves, while Penn-Lewis became a notable public figure and capable platform speaker, and author of copious religious and improving books. A growing interest in the missionary cause in China opened a new door for her onto the evangelical movement worldwide. In 1896 she ventured to Sweden, and then to Russia the following year, meeting with the aristocratic elite and intrepidly attempting to win women away from the Russian Orthodox Church. She returned via Sweden, and then resumed her hectic schedule of visits to towns and cities the length and breadth of the United Kingdom. The following years saw her visit Russia, Sweden, Denmark, Canada, the USA, Germany, Egypt and India.

Always eager to serve her own native land – although Wales seems to have been merely a 'Principality' for her – she joined forces in 1902 with Dean Howell of St Davids Cathedral and two prominent Nonconformist ministers (J. Rhys Davies and D. Wynne Evans) to establish a branch of the celebrated and highly successful annual Keswick Evangelical Convention in Llandrindod Wells. It was with some justice, therefore, that she was later to claim in her book, *The Awakening in*

Wales, that she had been one of those who had prepared the way for the Revival. That book also serves as a useful introduction to the worldview to which Penn-Lewis was to convert her house-guest Evan Roberts, following his precipitate withdrawal from the Revival. She was living anew, or so she believed, in the Pentecostal Days of the first Apostles, when the Holy Spirit had been so dynamically present in the lives of the followers and disciples of the newly resurrected Christ. The Spirit's presence was for her conclusive proof that she was living in the Last Days, and that Christ's triumphal return could therefore be confidently and imminently expected. And, in accordance with the prophecies, it also meant that the Devil had been loosed from his chains and was once more destructively abroad in the world along with his evil accomplices, whose very particular targets were naturally the 'saints', the elect company of those saved by grace. The signs of these terrible times were everywhere to be read, from the great turmoil in Australia and China right across to India, on through Continental Europe and the British Isles, and finally convulsing the USA.

In 1903, the grand Evangelical Convention at Keswick had begged the Holy Spirit for assistance to counter Satan's spiritual depredations, and response to urgent prayer had indeed been promptly forthcoming, manifest first in India and then, most gloriously in 1904, in 'the little Principality of Wales' of all unlikely places, where such evangelical initiatives as the Forward Movement had been for some time busily preparing the ground. 'Partnership with the Holy Ghost in service', enthused Penn-Lewis with ardour, 'is more romantic than any earthly romance' – and in *The Awakening in Wales*, she herself attempted to write a kind of spiritual romance.[15] Evidence may indeed there be found of her gift for narrative and other salient features of story, and this may help us understand her otherwise rather baffling appeal to the wounded soul of Evan Roberts. Penn-Lewis's account of the Revival is an interesting example of her passionate desire to construct a highly original explanatory system, aspiring to be rigorously intellectual in character and comprehensive in conspectus. It was only once he was safely held in the authoritative embrace of that system that Evan Roberts was slowly able to recover a degree of mental stability.

* * *

Jessie Penn-Lewis's global contextualisation of Evan Roberts's Revival may well have struck a chord with him because it involved a reading of Nonconformist Wales that accorded perfectly with that which it held of itself. A cardinal belief of Welsh Nonconformity by the end of the nineteenth century was that Wales had become one of the most devout nations in the world and, as such, could serve as an example to other nations worldwide, not least those supposedly proud members of the Great British Empire. Welsh missionary expeditions abroad could boast a number of spectacular achievements, such as Swansea-born Griffith John's sixty years of Christian labour in China. John's mastery of many Chinese dialects as well as of Mandarin Chinese equipped him to undertake the pioneering translation of both the New and the Old Testaments into those languages, and he became a renowned preacher to the Chinese in the language that they spoke.

John's first wife was the daughter of David Griffiths (1796–1841), celebrated missionary to Madagascar, who, along with his fellow Welshman David Jones (1796–1841), had been the first translator of the Bible into Malagasy, after the former had devised an orthography for that language. Evan Roberts was undoubtedly persuaded by Penn-Lewis to view the Revival in this international context. In due course, his younger sister Mary, to whom he was particularly close, served for a period as a missionary in Africa before marrying Roberts's closest friend, Sydney Evans. For more than half a century after the Revival, Evans dedicated his life to evangelising in north-east India, and served a long term as principal of the theological college in Cherrapunji, in the Khasi Hills. The people of that mountainous region had first been introduced to Christianity by Thomas Jones (1810–49), the controversial Welsh missionary described on his gravestone as 'the founding father of the Khasi alphabet and literature'. Thanks, then, to the export-version of the Revival patented by the likes of Sydney Evans, Roberts's brother Dan and his sister Mary, Welsh Nonconformity was to enjoy a curious, ghostly afterlife in foreign fields long after it had lost its vigour in Wales itself.[16]

As for the openly millenarian aspect of Jessie Penn-Lewis's unorthodox theology, it not only brought the latent millenarianism of the 1904–6 Revival into clear focus, but also exposed another of the ways in which (by-passing Nonconformity in its ultra-respectable, socially powerful, late nineteenth-century guise) it reconnected modern Wales with its disreputable 'pristine source' in the sometimes chaotic puritan, Dissenting sects of the English Civil War and Commonwealth.[17] In retrospect, this turn back to its roots in seventeenth-century Dissent could be seen as a symptom of a late nineteenth-century Welsh Nonconformity under pressure and in crisis. Several of the great Welsh founding fathers of that earlier day – William Erbery, Morgan Llwyd (however briefly) and Vavasour Powell – had, for instance, been associated with the Fifth Monarchist Movement of the early 1650s, whose members eagerly expected the imminent arrival of King Christ. And on the assumption that they were indeed living in the Last Days (as predicted not only by the Book of Revelation but in the strange, heterodox writings of the Father of Modern Millenarianism, Joachim of Fiore), they declared themselves to be obedient to no moral, social, political or spiritual authority save that of the Holy Spirit that had returned to earth for the first time since the period of the original Apostles.[18] 'Accompanying this dynamic principle of pressing on, through and beyond all outward and imprisoning forms, to attain the full liberty of the Holy Spirit, was a powerful eschatological consciousness.' (*HS*, 108). 'I am persuaded,' wrote Morgan Llwyd in the heady days of 1652, 'that you may probably live to see more blessedness then ever our fathers thought any of their posterity should be made to understand.'[19]

Evan Roberts was likewise to place himself publicly, in each of his Revival meetings, at the unpredictable disposal of that Spirit, much to the understandable discomfort of the chapel faithful and the delight of his ecstatic followers. In that sense, his Revival was a radical movement of renewal through reconnection with primal source – again rather like the Ghost Dance of the Sioux – referring the staid, moribund late-nineteenth-century Nonconformist denominations to their origins either in the radical sectaries, 'experimental' enthusiasms, spiritual anarchy and wild disorder of the Civil War and inter-regnum periods, or in the St Vitus Dance of early eighteenth-century Methodist 'enthusiasts'. In thus having its roots firmly within the radical, ecstatic, evangelical wing of the Welsh tradition of religious Dissent itself, the Revival remained very much *sui generis*, even while it shared obvious similarities with the many other eschatological charismatic movements worldwide of its age that included the Pentecostal Movement – to which some of Roberts's followers were eventually to gravitate – which is usually dated back to Charles Fox Parkham's Bethel Bible School at Topeka, Kansas, 1900, and the Azusa Street Revival in Los Angeles, 1906, led by Parkham's student William J. Seymour. Women played as prominent a part in such movements as they did in the Welsh Revival.

Very broadly speaking, Christian Millenarians down the centuries have been divided into two groups: the Social Revolutionaries and the Spiritual Revolutionaries. The former has tended to expect the coming of a radical new social and political order based on universal fairness and justice; the latter, completely internalising its chiliastic beliefs, has expected only a transfiguration of the soul-scape of the saved. In belonging essentially to the latter kind, Evan Roberts was of the company of the great seventeenth-century Puritan mystic Morgan Llwyd and, like him, Roberts found important confirmation of his beliefs in the work of a singular German (*ER*, 68). In Llwyd's case, that German had been the remarkable Lutheran visionary cobbler Jacob Böhme, some of whose work he translated into Welsh. In Roberts's case, the German in question was George Müller (1805–98) who, though a native of Prussia, had made his home in Bristol. There, he proceeded to make his name by establishing an orphanage funded entirely by contributions elicited through prayer. This was perfectly in keeping with his unorthodox theology, which uncompromisingly insisted on the need to open oneself up to the Holy Spirit in ceaseless Prayer and to rely exclusively on its power to deliver even the basic material needs of the day, a faith grounded in Müller's strict Calvinist belief in the miraculous efficacy of special election. Evan Roberts's Revival meetings had always been, despite all the celebrated hymn-singing (about which he himself had considerable misgivings), in essence prayer meetings. And once he had begun to recover a degree of stability in the home of the Penn-Lewises, Roberts was reliably reported to spend up to eighteen hours a day in prayer.

* * *

Insufficient attention has been paid to the many respects in which the 1904–6 Revival typified the eschatological character of its age. This was, after all, the age of Utopian Socialism and of pseudo-scientific movements such as Mesmerism, Theosophy and Spiritualism, and millenarians of every conceivable kind abounded. The eminently rational and sceptical George Bernard Shaw, for instance, confidently expected the evolutionary progress of human intelligence shortly to usher in a New Age. W. T. Stead, the famous London newspaper man who had reported on that meeting in Maerdy in the early days of the

Revival, treated it as heartening evidence that a new era was dawning. It was, he reported, 'the precursor of progress, the herald of advance' (*ER*, 298). In accordance with the zeitgeist, Stead was an enthusiastic Spiritualist, and in 1893 established a Spiritualist paper appropriately entitled *Borderland.*

Seth Joshua, whose evangelical work in New Quay had famously prepared the way for the Revival, actually complained to Jessie Penn-Lewis in a letter of April 1905 that everywhere there were false prophets (as predicted, of course, in the Book of Revelation) and that these threatened to swamp believers in the true Apocalypse:

> A very hard fight is going on with the forces of darkness. Nearly every error under the sun finds roots in this place [Joshua was writing from Merthyr, at the dark centre of modern, turbulent, industrial Wales]. The Spiritualist Society, the Ethical Society, the Agnostic Group, the Christadelphians, the Seventh Day Adventists. The last inspiration would be the 'Pentecostal Dancers' who are drawing a strong following at Dowlais . . . It is dangerous these days to speak too freely. Never was Satan so on the attack. (*TT*, 122)

Those 'Pentecostal Dancers' surely evoke echoes of the Ghost Dancers. Penn-Lewis, in her turn, reverted to the same theme in the year when Revival fervour began to subside:

> If we look back at the history of the past decade, up to the time of the awakening in Wales, we can see how the Prince of Darkness was working insidiously among the people, undermining their faith in the Scriptures as the Word of God, silencing the preaching of the Cross to the utmost of his power, and drawing off great numbers into Theosophy . . . Christian Science . . . and Spiritism. (*MPL,* 229, quoting from *The Warfare with Satan and the Way of Victory*)

Pentecostalism was, likewise, soon to be condemned by her.

Some of the more showy aspects of the Revival may then be seen as products of its attempt to see off this 'competition'. There is no doubt that Seth Joshua, Evan Roberts and Jessie Penn-Lewis were very aware of the challenge that came from these other 'cults', but equally it is now possible for us to see how from a different perspective their own movement could itself be regarded as another expression of the excited spirit of eschatological expectation that was abroad at the time. For Jessie Penn-Lewis, though, all these other movements were evidence that in accordance with the prophecy of Revelation the Devil had indeed been loosed in the latter days, to wreak such havoc as he could in the souls of men. *War on the Saints*, the remarkable book Penn-Lewis co-authored with Roberts, goes so far as to tabulate some of these instances of Satan's work:

> **IN THE CHRISTIANISED WORLD**, some doctrines of demons, *tested by these two primary principles* [namely, complete obedience to the full message of Scripture, and acceptance of the theology of Sin and the Cross] may be mentioned as:
>
> Christian Science: no *sin*, no Saviour, no Cross.
> Theosophy: no *sin*, no Saviour, no Cross.
> New Theology: no *sin*, no Saviour, no Cross. (*WS*, 23)

Judged by these same two cardinal principles, the Revival, of course, scored highly on both the counts specified. 'Plyg ni, Arglwydd, Plyg ni' (Bend us, O Lord, Bend Us) became Evan Roberts's celebrated mantra, the anguished signature tune of Revival theology. It stressed the difficult need to begin, always, by first admitting the terrible sinfulness of the human Self, preliminary to complete abandonment of one's proud, stubborn will to the Spirit that could alone be the mediator of grace and forgiveness and redemption. 'The great difficulty was to bend,' he admitted of his 'grop[ing] in the darkness' in Newcastle Emlyn, 'but I had to bend. By bending our will is not restrained but melt it does, and act in harmony with the great will of God.' (*ER*, 414) In this respect, again, Roberts was actually attempting to reconnect with the Calvinistic theology that had traditionally lain at the very core of Dissent and Nonconformity but that had gradually faded from the sight of believers in the later nineteenth century as the chapels became 'infected' and 'softened' by the liberal humanism and new theology of the age. Once more, then, a Nonconformity in crisis was trying, through the Revival, to access its lost sources of energy.

Homeopathy, Vegetarianism, even Feminism, all were in some respects expressions of the heady days of millennial expectations, while some particularly venturesome individuals such as Havelock Ellis and Edward Carpenter went so far as to question established gender roles and sexual practices. Background to many of these new philosophies was the confident supposition that continuing dramatic advances in science and technology would result in revolutionary social change. Very much in keeping with this intoxicating spirit of her age, Jessie Penn-Lewis became completely convinced that an age of new understanding would shortly dawn as the Holy Spirit began to enlighten human consciousnesses and enable the development of a Higher Knowledge. Women, she believed, would play a crucial central role in this process, and in this regard again she was very much a creature of her period:

> Throughout the nineteenth century, women put religion to many and various uses. Primitive Methodism defended women's preaching, utopian socialists called for a 'Female Messiah', and women in the spiritualist movement used their role as trance mediums both to subvert and confirm separate-spheres ideology.[20]

There are even broad parallels to be drawn between Penn-Lewis as a kind of unorthodox Christian guru and exotic figures of the period such as Madame Blavatsky and Annie Besant (with the Penn-Lewis/Roberts relationship bearing a fascinating resemblance to that between Besant and Jiddu-Krishnamurti), and one may safely interpret the close collaboration between her and Roberts on the writing of *War on the Saints* as in part an expression of her passionate belief in the equality of intellectual capacity between male and female. In fact, Penn-Lewis appears to have been a much more securely grounded personality than Roberts himself, despite her history of occasional physical and mental prostration. It was in his weakness and psycho-spiritual confusion that he turned to her for help in 1906, and *War on the Saints* bears the very heavy imprint of her influence on his subsequent thinking.

* * *

As Brynmor Pierce Jones, Jessie Penn-Lewis's most recent biographer, has established, Evan Roberts was not the first wounded soul for her to nurse psychically. Indeed, she had something of a disturbing history of unhealthy interest in such cases. There was, for example, the tempestuous case of 'Nursie Laura', a reputedly 'schizoid' girl (*TT*, 81), who had found sanctuary in Penn-Lewis's home for an extended period. And there is also substantial evidence in Pierce Jones's biography of the numerous mentally disturbed individuals from Wales and across the world who wrote Penn-Lewis beseeching letters. No doubt her own troubled background rendered her particularly responsive to hysterical conditions, a predisposition strongly reinforced by her obsessive interest (which may also have been a result of her own early psychic battles) in the fateful struggle between the Trinity and the Devil within every human soul, as will become apparent in what follows. In consequence, she was avid for evidence of this apocalyptic struggle wherever in the world it might be found.

Throughout the period when the mass enthusiasm of the 1904–6 Revival was at its height, Penn-Lewis actually kept disturbingly close tabs on some of Evan Roberts's wilder pronouncements about the spirit world. Indeed, she actually kept a tally of such statements in her diary; very occasionally, she even intervened. After receiving an exasperated letter from one minister, for instance ('What shall we do with this boy?' he despairingly enquired), she pursued Roberts with letters urging him to join her in Leicester before he was utterly defeated by the Devil (*TT*, 121). He seems to have ignored these missives – until, that is, his final breakdown.

Pierce Jones makes it clear that the reason why Penn-Lewis targeted Roberts so remorselessly in these ways was because she was convinced she had been destined by the Holy Spirit itself to prepare the evangelist to lead a Revival worldwide by introducing him to her own privileged worldview. The biographer also shrewdly notes how, not long after his arrival at her Leicester home, Roberts began to adopt Penn-Lewis's somewhat arcane terminology and her peculiar theological tenets. Nevertheless, Pierce Jones very strongly disputes the view that Roberts became Penn-Lewis's tool and that he ended up in effect both her physical and her psychological prisoner. There is certainly compelling evidence in the meantime that she offered him extensive physical therapy and spiritual support throughout a stay that eventually extended over several decades, and was terminated only by the death of her husband.

Given therefore that the exact nature of the intense and complex relationship between Roberts and Penn-Lewis is unlikely ever to be fully fathomed, and that it is likely to have been highly ambivalent in character and multifarious in outcome, it may be useful to bear in mind the psychologist D. W. Winnicott's suggestive concept of a 'holding environment'.[21] Winnicott, who specialised in child psychology, had noticed how children could lose themselves in play – an activity he credibly regarded as crucial to healthy mental development – only when they felt wholly comfortable in their surroundings and could relax. In other words, it was only when they felt psychologically secure in their external surroundings that they could venture to explore, through play, their own, private, inner worlds of imagination and experience.

The same could be said to have been true of Evan Roberts. Psychically tortured, anguished and confused as he clearly was when he arrived in Leicester, he could begin to risk exploration of his potentially destructive inner chaos of mind and turmoil of soul only in an environment in whose independent, objective, resilient, supportive strength he felt he could implicitly trust. That unshakeably secure environment functioned in effect as the guarantor of the eventual survival of the essence of his personality, however changed it might be by his risky inner journey. According to Winnicott, this is precisely the kind of 'enabling environment' that every good-enough parent unconsciously provides for a child, and it is notable how Penn-Lewis acted in a kind of maternal capacity in relation to an Evan Roberts who had, in a way, been infantilised by the breakdown of his mature adult personality. Indeed, during his crucial period in her home he significantly took to referring gratefully to her as his 'spiritual mother'. (This unfortunately also involved a separation from his loving biological mother – a break such as is sadly to be seen occasionally to occur today in the case of individuals who choose to enter certain extreme cultic groups.)

But Roberts found more than just a 'holding environment' in Leicester; he found a grammar and vocabulary of belief there that enabled him to ease his psychic pain by giving it satisfactory expression, thus providing it with intelligible shape and making it accessible to rational explanation. This new elaborate structure of belief was, of course, supplied by Penn-Lewis, but Roberts could never have been profoundly persuaded of its truth had it not very significantly dovetailed with deep-seated convictions of his own that had undoubtedly been magnified by his Revival experiences. They were agreed on a view of the contemporary world as a millenarian battleground between the Devil and the Holy Spirit. But Penn-Lewis had evolved a far more elaborate, almost parodically rational, explanatory system for this belief than ever Roberts had entertained. What's more, she had already identified a crucial role for Roberts himself to play in her world-redemptive system. Gradually, as his inner psychic state was brought into full, eagerly willing correspondence with Penn-Lewis's system, Roberts began to regain a degree of mental composure.

* * *

War on the Saints was some eight years a-making, and the fruit of Evan Roberts's strict adherence to a regime of prayer, reading and writing – overseen, of course, by Jessie Penn-Lewis. It is in many ways a bizarre volume, bearing, at least to this reader, the unmistakeable imprint of minds in the grip of religious mania, while also curiously reminiscent of so many religious tracts of the Civil War period. But it is a document fascinatingly revealing of the feverish mental climate of the Revival era, and the closest we have to the spiritual autobiography of Evan Roberts, that Revival's most charismatic figure.

Perhaps the most prominent feature of the book is its obsessive detailing of the almost innumerable, fiendishly different, ways in which the ever resourceful Devil is able to deceive and infiltrate the minds of believers. Such has often been the consequence down the Christian centuries of a total reliance on indwelling divine presence that leaves the confused, bewildered believer uncertain how to distinguish between the voice of the Spirit and the voice of the fancy – or even of Satan. The desperate thoroughness of paranoid itemisation in *War on the Saints* appears to have been powered by a kind of manic intellectual ingenuity. The whole exercise seems to be the symptom of a disordered mind suffering from a compulsive-repetitive disorder. Included in the volume are elaborate 'flow-charts' designed to assist the reader in tracking the twists and turns of the Devil's psychological wiles. Bold print is used from time to time, in newspaper fashion, to alert us to the urgent relevance of the message.

The book was under production during a period when it was believed modern and reliably 'scientific' methods had been devised for definitively surveying the world of psychic 'realities'. The 'Society for Psychic Research' had recently been founded for this very purpose, and it was also the period that saw the publication of the earliest of Sigmund Freud's works on the 'science of mind'. It therefore seems likely that Evan Roberts found substantial mental consolation in the supposition that the rather wild eschatological speculations in which he and Penn-Lewis were indulging were the product of the kind of authoritative rational enquiry that modern 'science' endorsed. But to most modern readers, *War on the Saints* is likely to resemble a mad chess handbook straight out of *Alice in Wonderland*. The repeated attempts made to outwit Satan and to outflank him by anticipating, and thus in a sense countering, his every move, seem the record of a precarious intelligence fearful of subversion and anxiously seeking to defend itself.

But from the therapeutic point of view, it may be that the most salient feature of *War on the Saints* is the narrative form to which it approximates, in its peculiar fashion. Reference has already been made to Penn-Lewis's basic story-telling powers, and the book may perhaps profitably be read as an interesting instance of what is nowadays classified as 'psychonarratology', a form of therapy based on the recognised power of story to assist a mental sufferer regain a degree of control over his or her inner life. *War on the Saints*, then, may well have afforded Roberts the opportunity of profiting from 'narrative therapy':

> In striving to make sense of life, persons face the task of arranging their experience of events in sequences across time in such a way as to arrive at a coherent account of themselves and the world around them. Specific experiences of events of the past and present, and those that are predicted to occur in the future, must be connected to a literal sequence to develop this account. This account can be referred to as a story or self-narrative. The success of this storying of experience provides persons with a sense of continuity and meaning in their lives, and this is relied upon for the ordering of daily lives and for the interpretation of further experiences.[22]

Only story has the power to drive out story. When a person – in the present case, Evan Roberts – has fallen prisoner to a particularly powerful story of self and world (which had steadily gathered psychic strength through endless repetition during the Revival) – then he can be helped to find release only through the medium of another story he comes to regard as even more compelling: 'the interpretation of . . . current living circumstances [shifts] radically with the generation of [a] new story that [proposes] an alternative history and future' (*NM*, 11).

As Frank Kermode has long since shown in what has become a classic study, universal fascination with an Apocalypse is the natural outcome of our permanent primitive craving for a story that conclusively provides Time itself with humanly intelligible shape – that is, a beginning and an end. The micro-narrative structures of novel, play and lyric, the patterns of visual image, the harmonies of musical composition, are all minor instances of this major compulsion. And as Kermode further demonstrated, the *fin de siècle* period preceding a new millennium regularly sees an intensification of human anxiety about Time, bringing in its wake a search for major new narratives of reassuring order. The 1890s were no exception to this rule:

> Certainly there was a great deal of apocalyptic feeling at that time, not least in the revival of imperial mythologies both in England and in Germany, in the 'decadence' which became a literary category . . . in the utopian renovationism of some political sects and the anarchism of others . . . the whole concurrence of *fin de siècle* phenomena amply illustrates Foucillon's thesis, that we project our existential anxieties on to history.[23]

By way of example, Kermode cites the cases of prominent writers such as Yeats, Eliot, Pound, Wyndham Lewis and D. H. Lawrence along with a number of other figures across the art forms. And this Apocalyptic tendency was, as Kermode implied, even more evident in the hectic religious life of the day, witness the Revival and *War on the Saints*.

* * *

In *War on the Saints*, history is divided into three different periods very much along the lines of the influential thinking of Joachim of Fiori, the father of modern Christian millenarianism.[24] That remarkable medieval monk had distinguished between three successive 'dispensations', providentially arranged, each respectively governed by one of the three Persons of the Holy Trinity. Thus, the first had belonged to the Father, the second belonged to the Son, and the third would belong to the Holy Ghost, with each period corresponding in turn to those of the Old Testament, the New Testament and the eventual pre-millenarian age. Tending ultimately very much towards the same divisions, *War on the Saints* begins its story in the Garden of Eden with the temptation of Adam and Eve that resulted in humankind's inability to recognise its own spiritual condition. This state was somewhat relieved during the Old Testament stage of the Father, and very much further improved during the second stage following Christ's rending of the veil. But only with the third stage, and the coming of the Holy Spirit preparatory to the triumphal return of Christ to earth, was the Holy Spirit, according to Roberts and Penn-Lewis, now empowered to embark on the task of finally fully illuminating the minds of the elect, of whom they, of course, were two of the most privileged.

Roberts had made occasional references to the millennium during the Revival itself.[25] These references had, though, been few and far between, but the situation changed dramatically after he had settled in Leicester.[26] There, a vision of the Apocalypse began to dominate his entire mind. Very simply put, sensing the Revival was somehow going astray, Roberts had increasingly blamed himself towards the end for what he had eventually in consequence come to regard as its 'failure' – or rather, and far worse, its change from an instrument for good to an instrument for evil. But by supplying a fully developed account of the Apocalyptic context – that is, by placing his Revival in the minutely detailed context of a global struggle between the Devil and the Holy Spirit and confirming that this struggle was a cataclysmic manifestation of the Last Days – Penn-Lewis relieved Roberts of the terrible personal responsibility he had guiltily felt for what had happened in what now, in this world-wide perspective, seemed no more than a preliminary marginal skirmish in the Great Spiritual Battle of the End of Days:

> mixed 'manifestations' . . . have come upon the Church of God, since the Revival in Wales; for, almost without exception, in every land where revival has broken forth, within a very brief period of time, the counterfeit stream has mingled with the true; and, almost without exception, *true and false had been accepted together*, because of the workers being ignorant of the possibility of concurrent streams. (*WS*, 77)

What happened in the Revival, therefore, had subsequently happened in countless other places around the world. What enormous reassurance Evan Roberts must have gained from such a doctrine. And while Penn-Lewis had obviously originally intended to prepare Roberts to reemerge and lead a worldwide Revival, she gradually came to resign herself to his stubborn (and psychologically shrewd) belief that he could best contribute to such an initiative through intense and prolonged prayer, without ever leaving the psychic sanctuary of her Leicestershire home.

Her mind-cure seems even to have relieved Roberts of the periodic bouts of depression from which he had clearly suffered throughout the Revival years. (Penn-Lewis herself may well have experienced the same during her early years of psychic frustration.) It is difficult to read the chapter in *War on the Saints* entitled 'Passivity The Chief Basis of Possession' without deeply sympathising with what at one time they both had probably suffered. 'The physical feelings,' we are there informed, 'become deadened, or atrophied, and the affections seem petrified, and stoical. This is the time when deceiving spirits suggest that he [the sufferer] has grieved God beyond repair, and a man goes through agonies of seeking the Presence he thinks he has grieved away.' (*WS*, 63) This does not mean, it continues,

> that 'passivity' in its full extent means no 'activity'; for once the man becomes passive in volition and mind, he is held by deceiving spirits without power to act, or is driven into Satanic activity; that is, uncontrollable activity of thought, restlessness of body, and wild, unbalanced action of all degrees. The actions are spasmodic and intermittent, the person sometimes dashing ahead, and at other times sluggish and slow; like a machine in a factory, with the wheels whirring aimlessly, because the switch of the centre control is out of the hand of the master. (*WS*, 69)

A few years later, a T. S. Eliot who had sought help in a psychiatric hospital in Lausanne for a very similar condition, was to use the French word 'aboulie' to define it, and to admit that his struggle with it had effectively given rise to 'The Waste Land'.

One recalls the spasmodic alternation between furious activity and catatonic stillness that had been the hallmark of Roberts's compelling conduct throughout the Revival years. In particular, one may recall that remarkable episode of abrupt, complete withdrawal in Briton Ferry previously referred to, one of the most dramatic instances of his refusal to move or speak until commanded by the Spirit. *War on the Saints* includes one passage that ends with what seems to be a reference to exactly such a state of paralysis that renders the sufferer vulnerable to Satan:

> On the believer's side, we may say, however, that there is a waiting for God, whilst the Holy Spirit deals with, and prepares, the one who has put in his claim, until he is in the right attitude for the influx of the Holy Spirit into his spirit, but this is different from 'waiting for Him to come', which has opened the door so frequently to Satanic manifestations from the unseen world. (*WS*, 49)

The volume's explanation of this latter, demonic, state is that it is the fault of the expectant believer, because that believer has relinquished his or her will without first ensuring the saving, supporting presence of the crucified Christ.

Jessie Penn-Lewis, then, came to exert a very considerable influence over Evan Roberts's mind, and class difference may also have played its part in her ascendancy. Roberts was, after all, a typical product of the lowly Welsh-speaking working class, whereas Penn-Lewis had not only been born into the socially superior, anglicised middle class in Wales, but had also further enhanced her social status through her marriage to one who became a very successful borough accountant. The unmistakeable tones of the ruling class of an imperial power are to be heard from time to time in Penn-Lewis's writing and pronouncements, as when she refers condescendingly to her visits to 'primitive' Russia, where she met 'spiritually child-like Russian ladies' (*MPL*, 124), and her interpretations of the 1904–6 Revival are steeped in similarly condescending assumptions about the simple emotionalism of the Welsh. The longer Roberts spent in her company, the more he seems to have unconsciously adopted something of her attitude along with something of her accent. A great-niece of his who visited Roberts from time to time in his later life was to recall that

> To us girls he seemed like a distinguished English businessman, although he still talked to my mother in good Welsh. The twenty-year exile in Leicester had taken Uncle Evan out of Welsh life and culture too completely.[27]

There was, no doubt, a pressing psychological as well as social reason for Roberts's distancing himself from his former, Welsh, self. Distancing himself from Wales, from Welsh, and from even the closest of his Welsh family members, had probably been a necessary step towards being able to place the terrible mental turmoil and spiritual agony attendant upon the Revival years in a savingly distant perspective.

Co-authoring *War on the Saints* was, of course, another vitally important step in the very same direction, and consistent with the advice he had received from the physicians that he had consulted shortly after his arrival in Leicester. They had warned him in no uncertain terms that he should abandon public evangelising immediately for the sake of his mental health, an instruction he was careful to obey to the letter until the very end of his life. Consequently, he avoided any recurrence of his total psychic collapse in 1906, although continuing to be tormented from time to time by periods of depression. Instead of conducting a public campaign of evangelising, he devoted himself to the work of being what Penn-Lewis ingeniously described as a 'prayer warrior', giving himself entirely to prayer for hour after long hour. And having established such a rigid routine in Leicester, he was to adhere to it religiously (in more senses than one) throughout his subsequent period of retirement in Cardiff. Although not unwilling occasionally to socialise with kindred spirits, and always very willing to correspond with a multitude of followers all over the world, he seems to have mainly kept his own company. It is as if one part, at least, of that touching adolescent dream of his – of making sufficient money in the US to allow him to retire early to Wales and to devote himself to study and religious meditation – had, indeed, been realised.

From time to time, snippets regarding Roberts's current state of mind appeared in the press. The 'London Correspondent' of the *Western Mail* reported, on Thursday, 16 April 1925, that he had met the evangelist in London and could confirm that 'he seems still to be suffering from nerves'. 'While listening patiently to his old friends,' he added, 'he seems unable to stand the strain of enforced attention in a crowded room, and at first opportunity slips quietly away.' Seven years later (Friday, 23 September 1932) the same paper scotched rumours that Roberts was planning a come-back in Anglesey. Commenting on the rumours, he emphasised that he devoted all his time to 'what the Scriptures call "Labouring in Prayer"'. It was, he added, extremely hard work, engaging thus with 'problems national and international' and 'seeking solutions for them. All these problems have to deal with life – the life of mankind as it was, is, and what it is to be.'

Two months earlier (on 13 July 1932), the *Western Mail* had carried an extended report by a Bristol vicar of his meeting with Evan Roberts in Cardiff. It included an intriguing discussion of the evangelist's reputed gift of second sight. While modestly preferring to call it 'guidance', Roberts confirmed he had, indeed, been able to foretell the future and cited an example. Before addressing a meeting in Pyle, he had handed a sealed envelope to an attendant who, opening it only at the end of the service, had discovered it contained a piece of paper on which Roberts had accurately predicted how many souls would be saved by him that evening. But in conversation with his English vicar friend, he placed emphasis not on the past but on the present, arguing a Christian duty to alleviate the sufferings of the poor during the Depression and prophesying the coming of a New Age 'under the government of God'. The most persistent thing about Roberts, the vicar stated, 'is his cosmic view' – clear evidence of the continuing influence of Jessie Penn-Lewis's millenarian visions on his thinking: 'The whole world is his parish. He revels in the great changes taking place in the world . . . He even had a good word to say about Russia.'[28]

Underlying such normality as he was able to achieve, then, was always a highly nervous sensibility, as had become evident at the time of the First World War:

> The first sign of tension [between him and Jessie Penn-Lewis] was over the results of Evan Roberts' unexpected revelation in November, 1913, that he had been given an exclusive 'Burden Message' for the whole world. God's time for the translation [we would nowadays say *rapture*] of all the saints into Heaven was absolutely imminent, he announced. The news spread like a bush fire into the United States, Europe, and Asia. But when nothing happened and when hell on earth spread over the battlefields of Europe instead, the question naturally arose as to the true status of this Welsh prophet. (*TT*, 246)

A similar episode occurred slightly later, when

> Evan started to persuade the group that he had the secret of casting off the old nature and obeying new spiritual laws. He was misunderstood and rebuked sternly for preaching *sinlessness*. While Jessie was away for the weekend, the others tried to cope with Evan who was bubbling over with joy and shouting about his wonderful new body that had become strong by faith. 'Nine years are over!' he shouted. 'Glory to God!' Yet, twenty four hours later he was knocked out completely with strain and was going against the rest of the group and even criticizing one of the lady members, who wrote, 'Then his voice changed and he said he was all right, but I sobbed and sobbed. He put a cloak on and went out and I followed around roadways – cursing the evil spirit. I met Evan Roberts and we walked awhile and I asked him gently, 'Why?' In the drawing room he broke down and wept and was very weak at supper, but I talked with others and got through.' (*TT*, 248)

It is a poignant portrait of a man totally baffled by the dark labyrinth of his own unpredictable nature.

This radically disturbed sensibility should be constantly kept in mind as one reads *War on the Saints*, and Roberts himself was often at pains to emphasise how important the experience of writing the book had been for him. In an open letter he published in Penn-Lewis's paper *The Overcomer* in December 1913, explaining why he'd fled to Leicester, he underlines the significance of their collaboration:

> Those who proclaim unbelief in my work only the louder proclaim their own blindness. Have they seen my messages in 'The Overcomer'? Then why could they not see the signs of God in them? Have they read *War on the Saints* – my unnamed biography? Do they not hear the depths of experiences in this book calling great mysteries by their right name? Are these truths in it an unveiling of 'the deep things' of Satan? And who could reveal them without knowing them?
>
> My co-work with Mrs Penn-Lewis in *War on the Saints* was of God. For spiritually I was too burdened to write it myself, and apart from me, neither could she write it, and it would have been useless to search elsewhere for a pen to do so. I know of no one equal to her in understanding of spiritual things; she is a veteran in heavenly things. (*IR*, 68)

* * *

'*War on the Saints* – my unnamed biography.' Or rather, as Roberts goes on to imply, 'my unnamed autobiography'. The book was, after a fashion, the last will and testament of Evan Roberts the Revivalist; and as such it was also a last will and testament of the Welsh Nonconformity of which he had been such a spectacular belated product. At the distance of a century, a pathos seems to me to attach itself to Roberts's story and to become associated, too, with the twentieth-century history of the chapel culture out of which he had come. Within a decade of the end of the 1904–6 Revival, the chapels were to start their long decline. Their social and spiritual power steadily waned even though they retained their austere physical presence in the Welsh landscape.

There is one striking coincidence that highlights the fateful transitional character of the Evan Roberts phenomenon. One of those who testified most ardently, eloquently and perceptively to the success of his late Liverpool mission was the Revd John Williams, minister of the Welsh Calvinistic Methodist chapel in Princes Road at the time, but soon to win popular renown as 'Brynsiencyn', Anglesey. He noted the 'exceptional celebrity' Roberts had attained in such a startlingly short time (*ER*, 420), registered that 'some mystery attached to him which defies all explanation' (*ER*, 421), admired his 'strong and brilliant mind', and compellingly concluded that 'I have never seen anyone so godly; I have never seen anyone so sensitive to the shadow of untruth' (*ER*, 423).

That was in late 1905. A decade later, 'Brynsiencyn' was to achieve a national prominence that would soon change to notoriety, as Lloyd George's 'recruiting sergeant' of a minister, charged with the task of assembling a 'Welsh Army'. Dressed in full military uniform, and proudly sporting the insignia of a Colonel, 'Brynsiencyn' set about his task with such vigour that 100,000 Welshmen had joined the forces by the end of 1915, and by 1918 this number had increased to over 250,000. Of these, 35,000 did not return – one of the highest per capita losses of any of the participating nations.

The (unintentional) contribution made by 'Brynsiencyn' to this mass carnage has been deemed by historians to be part cause and memorable symbol of the Welsh Nonconformist establishment's disastrous support for a conflict that was to destroy the long-standing respect of the Welsh people for the chapels. 'Brynsiencyn', then, it was who effectively presided over the demise of 'Nonconformist Wales'.

The Evan Roberts Revival certainly revivified at least some chapels for a while, and it also stimulated the creation of an 'alternative' network of worship represented by the Gospel Halls and Pentecostal churches that mushroomed across Wales. But as the grand, central power of the Welsh Nonconformist denominations steadily diminished after the Great War, so too did Evan Roberts begin his slow inexorable fade from public memory until he died, in 1951, in that Cardiff old people's home – a virtual unknown, unrecognised, and little mourned except by the elderly 'veterans' of his remarkable Revival.

8

Arthur Machen: Border Disputes

As his current global reputation as a master of 'horror' literature seems happily to testify, Arthur Machen is a rum and riddling writer. His ponderously portentous occult fictions continue to enjoy cult appeal worldwide. Literary scholars, too, have shown an increasing interest in tracing the many intersections between his work and the culture of decadence of the 1890s and the years leading up to the Great War. As a popular professional writer, not only was Machen avowedly indebted to a number of prominent authors and movements of the period, he also ingeniously devised his own distinctive vocabulary of form, plot and symbol for articulating some of its deepest concerns and fears:

> Not the least enduring interest of his work is the way it provided the cultural aspirations and anxieties of his age with feverishly heightened narrative shape and symbolic expression. Into the nightmare forms of his demonic femmes fatales were crammed the sexual fears aroused at the *fin de siècle* by the dangerously liberated figure of the New Woman . . . As for Machen's arrogantly meddling scientists, those Nineties descendants of Frankenstein whose experiments exposed the human brain to the invasion of evil, they eerily anticipated the era of Psycho-analysis and of Neurosurgery. And the sinister powers of many of his characters are attributed to their mixed, and therefore indeterminate, racial origins at the very time that Empire was giving rise to fears that the white race might be running the risk of taint by miscegenation. There is plenty of insolently casual racial prejudice in Machen.[1]

In a letter to his publisher, Machen himself drew an implicit parallel between his breakthrough novella *The Great God Pan* (1894) and Robert

Louis Stevenson's study of *The Strange Case of Dr Jekyll and Mr Hyde* (1886).[2] Yet, whereas that classic has long been read as coded expression of a central psycho-social feature of Scottishness – what Gregory Smith so influentially termed 'the Caledonian Antisyzygy'[3] – only recently have critics ventured to explore the equally peculiar, yet strangely exemplary, form that Machen's Welshness takes in his key writings. Yet, viewed in the context of the present volume's concerns, his life and work do actually assume an unexpectedly representative character. The momentous social, economic and cultural developments of the later nineteenth century had left Wales riven by disturbing dualities, the site of bewildering juxtapositions, and the locus of unpredictably eruptive forces. The gothic – that genre born of unease, and Machen's chosen medium – could therefore be said to have readily made itself at home in this new Wales, so tumultuously at odds with itself.[4] As the present study has attempted to show, the whole radically unsettled country had come to exhibit something of a marchland condition of fluid plurality and indeterminacy, a condition empowering at some times, but overpowering at others, and a phenomenon which for Machen was (paradoxically) grounded, with immensely suggestive imaginative power, in his own beloved native locality of Gwent. His border positioning licensed him to assume multiple identities, to live the life of a professional shape-shifter, to perform several different roles. 'The Transmutations', the sub-title Machen adopted for his novel *The Three Imposters*, could well stand as a summary both of his life and of his career as an author.

In Machen's best-loved fiction, the ultimate source of the horror remains unspoken not so much because it is morally unspeakable but because, being inherently inchoate, it actually defies rational articulation and clear-cut representation. It therefore violates the categories of normal, ordinary understanding in a way closely approximating to that which happens in what anthropologists term liminal states and boundary situations. The following passage, from *The Great God Pan*, is typical of Machen's writing:

> Clarke tried to conceive the thing again, as he sat by the fire, and again his mind shuddered and shrank back, appalled before the sight of such awful, unspeakable elements enthroned, as it were, and triumphant in human flesh.[5]

The point has been made even more clearly earlier on, when Clarke is brought 'face to face . . . with a presence, that was neither man nor beast, neither living nor dead, but all things mingled, the form of all things but devoid of all form' (*P*, 11). The structural counterpart of this indefiniteness is the 'nested' character of the actual narrative, to which Machen specifically draws the reader's attention when Villiers reflects that 'a case like this is like a nest of Chinese boxes: you open one after another and find a quainter workmanship in every box' (*P*, 28). Machen thus deliberately foregrounds the strategy of endless deferral that he, as master narrator, has painstakingly constructed.

The signifier of this chronic undecidability is Pan, an elusive figure that, as used by Machen, is culturally ambiguous and plural, and thus possesses its own interestingly mysterious indeterminacies.[6]

> It was indeed an exquisite symbol beneath which men long ago veiled their knowledge of the most awful, most secret forces which lie at the heart of all things; forces before which the souls of men must wither and die and blacken, as their bodies blacken under the electric current. Such forces cannot be named, cannot be spoken, cannot be imagined except under a veil and a symbol, a symbol to the most of us appearing a quaint, poetic fancy, to some a foolish tale. (*P*, 65)

While Machen specifically associates Pan with the Roman legionaries at Caerleon, the goat-footed satyr was in origin a figure not of Roman but of Greek mythology, and moreover seems in the novella to have become the malign resident spirit of the sometime Romano-British landscape of the Monmouthshire of Machen's day. As scholars have noted, from the moment of his emergence in Ancient Greece, Pan had been a creature of border regions:

> Vase painters of the fifth and fourth centuries frequently link Pan with Dionysos. The goat-god, master of territorial liminality and the metamorphic borderline between man and animal, is a natural companion of satyrs and silenes; these in turn are the companions of that popular god whose crucial role in the sacred calendar includes within the institutional center elements of otherness and imbalance.[7]

These psycho-cultural instabilities actually inscribed in the very history of the Pan myth seem, in Machen's fiction, to infect those who are possessed by the satyr and thus become a running motif of the novella. The most salient feature of the successive incarnations of Pan is their mixed 'racial' character (what we would describe as cultural differences, being readily interpreted in the nineteenth century as racial differences). On her first appearance in the tale, the young girl 'Helen V' is ominously described as an orphan 'of a very different type from the inhabitants of the village; her skin was a pale, clear olive, and her features were strongly marked, and of a somewhat foreign character' (*P*, 16). Upon her subsequent sinister appearance as the wife of Herbert, we further learn that 'she was . . . the child of an English father and an Italian mother' (*P*, 27). Machen seems to have opted to conceive of himself (son of a Welsh vicar proud of his Welsh pedigree and of a Scottish mother who had a half-Welsh grandfather) as being of mixed race, which for him was the ethnic equivalent of a border character. This fitted well with his passion for multiple identities – at various times, as occasion suited, he would identify as English, as Welsh, as Western English, as Celtic English, as Welsh Celtic and as 'Silurian'. Conveniently, even the surname Machen, by which he became well known, was not only his mother's maiden name, legally adopted as that of the family by his father in order to benefit from an advantageous will, it was also the name of a Monmouthshire town very near Caerleon. Master of the uncanny though Machen is supposed by his fans to be, his interest in the context of the present study is as a canny exploiter of the multiple identities afforded him by his border origins and by the cultural perceptions of his day.

* * *

Whichever of these identities Machen at any given time opportunistically and strategically chose as his own always existed in unstated dialectical relationship with one or more of the others and, from the point of view of his writing, it is the dialectical relationship between his self-perceived 'Celticness' and his 'Englishness' that matters most deeply. Here, again, it is helpful to remember the culturally ambiguous character of Pan. Not only was the satyr a Grecian import, not native to Rome (whose equivalent figure was Faunus), he would also have been from the point of view of the ruling Roman Imperial classes an unwelcome foreigner, a figure of licence and licentiousness that threatened to undermine the good order and discipline upon which the Empire depended. His popularity among the legionaries, such as the soldiers of the Second Augustan that was based at Caerleon, would have seemed another instance of the way in which military 'culture' had become progressively debased as Rome had begun to recruit its soldiers from the many 'inferior' peoples and races it had conquered and (incompletely) 'civilised'. It was in this 'decadent' context of the later Empire that Eastern mystery religions such as the Mithraic cult began to thrive, and Machen not only published a long poem (*Eleusinia*, 1881) on the Greek Mysteries as a young man but, in later life as we shall see, associated the emergence of his own preferred version of Christianity with this unstable background.[8]

Just as Pan, then, had functioned in classical Roman history rather as Dionysus (or so Nietzsche had just claimed in Machen's own day [1886])[9] had functioned in ancient Greece – as the dark anarchic counterpart of rational established order – so Machen used his novella *The Great God Pan* to undermine the arrogantly self-satisfied 'civilisation' of an imperial England that believed in its God-given duty to bring civilisation to the whole world. From the age of eleven the young Machen had, as biographers have repeatedly if rather uncomprehendingly noted, spent five years away from his beloved Gwent at the celebrated cathedral school in Hereford. The primary function of such English public schools at this period was, of course, to train up the future rulers, managers and administrators of the British Empire, and indeed several of Machen's contemporaries at Hereford duly proceeded to significant service in the 'colonial' field. 'John Walmsley (1867–1922), four years Machen's junior, became Bishop of Sierra Leone, while his almost exact contemporary, Alfred York Browne (1861–1906), was military chaplain at Bombay and Aden.' (*AM*, 12) Fundamental to the training the boys received at Hereford, as at every other English public school, was intensive civilising instruction in 'Classics', in the study of which Machen is known to have excelled (*AM*, 12).

Perhaps the most truthful glimpse of Machen's period at Hereford is supplied in the form of Lucian Taylor's fictive recollections of public school in the opening pages of *The Hill of Dreams* (1907). Lucian is represented as an odd-ball in that setting, highly proficient at his studies but also a loner and misfit, tolerated kindly enough by his contemporaries but distinctly unorthodox in his recondite tastes. 'His school-fellows thought him quite mad, and tolerated him, and indeed were very kind to him in their barbarous manner.'[10]

> He liked history, but he loved to meditate on a land laid waste, Britain deserted by the legions, the rare pavements riven by frost, Celtic magic still brooding on the wild hills and in the black depths of the forest, the

> rosy marbles stained with rain, and the walls growing grey. The masters did not encourage these researches; a pure enthusiasm, they felt, should be for cricket and football, the *dilettanti* might even play fives and read Shakespeare without blame, but healthy English boys should have nothing to do with decadent periods. (*HD*, 6–7)

In his later novel *The Secret Glory* (1922), Machen launched a frontal attack on the English public school system. A young Welshman, Ambrose Meyrick, is desperately unhappy at his Midlands school, subject to the bullying of Canon Horbury, his uncle, who dreams of becoming headmaster one day and of turning the school into a model of its kind.[11] Horbury clearly sees the institution as making a huge contribution to the maintenance of Empire and looks forward to the time when the barbaric school game of 'rocker' has become an established 'part of the great Anglo-Saxon inheritance', played 'wherever the English flag floated: east and west, north and south; from Hong Kong to British Columbia; in Canada and New Zealand' (*SG*, 43).

The programmes of study at all such public schools were intended to elevate the minds of the young sons of Empire and to discipline their natures, and so they necessarily entailed an exposure to classical authors that was as restricting as it was restrictive. There could be no room for Pan, a Greek figure from the ancient underworld, on the Classics syllabus at Hereford. Machen's sly adoption of the notorious goat-god as the central figure in his novella can, therefore, be seen as the subversive gesture of a 'Celt' who, while not unhappy at school, never ceased to regard his stay there as anything other than 'an interlude among strangers'.

Read in this incipiently postcolonial light, aspects of Machen's fiction hitherto overlooked by critics begin to loom significantly into view. That the relationship at the beginning between 'Raymond' and 'Clarke' (as, later, between 'Herbert' and 'Villiers') dates back to public school days is implied by their use of each other's surnames, in the approved fashion of those stiff and stuffy institutions of the English middle class as of their counterparts, the Oxbridge colleges. The first person to invoke the name of the Great God Pan is Raymond, and it is he, too, whose callously experimental brain surgery (his cool acceptance of his poor victim's ensuing 'idiocy' reeks both of class and of racial arrogance) enables the satyr to manifest himself, even though Clarke had had premonitions of his appearance when a boy some fifteen years previously. And the location for the experiment is not

Gwent, but somewhere distant and in a deliberately unspecified setting distinctly English in its middle-class character. Likewise, the origins of 'Helen V' are emphasised to have been at a remove from 'the borders of Wales' where she is eventually settled by an adoptive father, keen to bury her in a remote region by buying the cooperation of a local 'yeoman' farmer. In other words, far from being native to Monmouthshire, as commentators have carelessly assumed, the human creatures of Pan in the novella are specifically identified as having come from elsewhere – that elsewhere being strongly implied to be some part of England. This is consistent with the suggestion made above that, for Machen, the figure of Pan was not some kind of 'natural' expression of the Gwent countryside but rather a character born of the ascription to Gwent, as to Wales, by the ruling English middle-class establishment of the day, of a troubling, primitive 'otherness'. Thus, the modern English practice of exporting Pan to the borders of Wales paralleled the original action of the legions in importing him from Greece, via Rome. As we shall see, Machen saw the 'othering' that was manifest in this English practice as the external expression of that internal repression, by the English, of their own 'inner Celt' – the fearful denial by them of what was for Machen (following Arnold) the valuable latent Celtic strain in the English nature.

Such an association of Pan with the Celtic West was easily made at the time. After all, a few short years after Machen's novella about the goat-god, the cavalierly philandering Lloyd George came routinely to be dubbed the 'Welsh Goat' by both the English press and the English public. But what Machen does in his novella is not to passively accept that foreign attribution, but rather to turn it back on its originators by embracing it, refashioning it, and redirecting it to his own, culturally subversive and retributive, purposes – thus facilitating what might, taking Freud's lead, be termed a graphic instance of the return of the repressed. In Machen's novella, the sojourn of Pan's creatures in Gwent is brief. They soon leave the border country to haunt the streets of the imperial capital, London, which, as Conrad's narrator Marlow was so famously to observe in *Heart of Darkness* just five years after the publication of *The Great God Pan*, proves to be 'one of the dark places of the earth'.

These two novellas by Machen and by Conrad surely cry out for close comparative attention. Both are open to the charge – so eloquently brought against *Heart of Darkness* by Chinua Achebe in a classic essay – of being colonial texts.[12] But both are also susceptible of being conversely defended as incipiently post-colonial in character, because they share the same central structure of a journey expected to be into a distant outpost of empire, a supposedly remote primitive region of moral and spiritual darkness, but that proves, instead, to be a journey back to the dark centre of the supposedly 'civilised' imperial world instead. Both novellas are therefore radical subversive exercises in irony.

* * *

Machen well understood the mechanism of psycho-social 'projection' that produced monsters such as Pan. He actually anatomised it at length in *The Hill of Dreams*, pithily noting how for the brooding adolescent Lucian 'the wild domed hills and darkling woods seemed symbols of some terrible secret in the inner life of that stranger – himself' (*HD*, 33). The young man Lucian's feverishly tumescent imagination briefly flirts with the idea of writing a defence of Swift's Yahoos in *Gulliver's Travels* – and Machen would certainly have known that Swift intended the Yahoos to represent the bestial view of the colonised Irish espoused by the 'Houyhnhnms', those desiccated representatives of the 'rational' English enlightenment (*HD*, 44). The Yahoos, Lucian reflects, 'were in many respects a simple and unsophisticated race, whose faults were the result of their enslaved position, while such virtues as they had were all their own'. His home town of Caermaen itself becomes implicated in Lucian's disgust. As he views its mean, sordid streets from an eminence overlooking the town, the voices of its inhabitants 'came up to him on the hill, as if it was an outland race inhabited the ruined city and talked in a strange language of strange and terrible things' (*HD*, 47). In this mood, it seems to Lucian as if 'the Celt assailed him, becoming from the weird wood he called the world, and his far-off ancestors, the "little people", crept out of their caves, muttering charms and incantations in hissing inhuman speech; he was beleagured by desires that had slept in his race for ages' (*HD*, 52). Within a few pages, however, a Lucian brought to his senses by happier experiences recognises these images of Caermaen and the Celtic to have been nothing but the sick fantasies of a disordered adolescent mind.

Sadly, however, Machen's resourceful awareness of the socio-psychological mechanism, by which he as a 'Celt' had been 'othered', and rendered strange by ruling English ideology, did not prevent him from visiting the same fate on other similarly marginalised groups and peoples. Indeed, his hostility to 'foreigners', whether represented by the industrial working class or by incomers from overseas, may well have actually resulted from the negative aspects of his periodic identification of himself as a 'Celtic' outsider. As was noted in chapter 3 in consideration of O. M. Edwards's response to the Jews, it is not uncommon for individuals who feel vulnerable to being 'monstered' as threateningly foreign to respond by exaggeratedly stressing their own 'normality' at the expense of monstering others. This depressing syndrome seems not infrequently to have been at work whenever Machen chose to present himself simply and unproblematically as English, and nowhere is this more evident than in his racially disturbing short story 'The Shining Pyramid'.

From the very beginning, the Caerleon area in which 'The Shining Pyramid' is set is described as situated in the 'West of England'. This allows the tale that follows to deal with the threat to Englishness from an invasion of foreign sailors via the booming industrial port of Castletown (Newport, Monmouthshire):

> Castletown is a large seaport, you know, and some of the worst of the foreign sailors occasionally desert their ships and go on the tramp up and down the country. Not many years ago a Spanish sailor named Garcia murdered a whole family for the sake of plunder that was not worth the sixpence. They are hardly human, some of these fellows, and I am dreadfully afraid the poor girl must have come to an awful end. (*P*, 82)[13]

This unpleasant racist theme is reinforced throughout the tale, as when the shape of the human eye that engrosses Dyson's attention as an element in the sinister cipher he is attempting to decode is likened to a 'Mongolian eye' owing something, perhaps, to that of 'a gilt Chinaman on a tea canister in the grocer's shop' (*P*, 91). Machen brings both his tale and his xenophobia to a climax by invoking the legend of the 'dark little people', whom anthropologists of his day were routinely identifying with the Iberian people that had supposedly occupied Wales long 'before the Celt set foot in Britain'. This enemy within is identified as being a far greater threat than that from without, such as 'a blackguard sailor on the tramp' (*P*, 105). At this point, Machen actually pinpoints the deepest root of his paranoia in the very act of seemingly denying it, as Dyson speculates as to the nature of the malign assembly he had witnessed congregating in the Caerleon amphitheatre at dead of night:

> In Ireland or China or the West of America the question would have been easily answered; a muster of the disaffected, the meeting of a secret society, vigilantes summoned to report; the thing would be simplicity itself, but in this quiet corner of England [*sic*], inhabited by quiet folk, no such suppositions were possible for a moment. (*P*, 109)

Here, Machen throws interesting new light on his 'border' positioning. He reveals himself to be a beleaguered native of the rural Monmouthshire that lay to the east of the teemingly cosmopolitan industrial port of Newport and its hinterland, who was desperately anxious to place a safe distance between himself and the south Wales whose nineteenth-century reputation in England for social unrest and violence dated back to the Merthyr Rising of 1831, the Rebecca Riots of 1839, and the Chartist attack on Newport in the same year. If that was what it meant to be Welsh, then Arthur Machen, or so he set out implicitly to inform his readers in 'The Shining Pyramid', was very anxious indeed to be accounted English.

It was a point he reinforced in an essay, some thirty years after the appearance of his short story, on the subject of 'Superstition – or Instinct'. He concluded his discussion by deploring contemporary tendencies to contrast '"backward and undeveloped peoples"' unfavourably with 'industrial and commercial peoples'.[14] Recalling his own childhood in 'a little valley in the West of England' he nostalgically remembered it as an idyllically small rural community of 'some four or five homesteads: two farms, let us say, and three cottages'. But now, he mused, 'if I revisited that valley, I might very likely find the clear brook transmuted into a black scum-sewer, great chimneys vomiting poisonous smoke into the air, the goodly old houses and their orchards and gardens replaced by rows of mean, jerry-built houses, by emporiums of margarine, and vile cagmag, and bad drink, and every kind of abomination' (*S*, 140). Monstrous Newport, that outlier of the sprawling industrial society of south Wales, had, he thus implicitly imagined, at last comprehensively devoured Caerleon. The sinister Welsh proletariat was on the move.

* * *

Intriguing and revealing instances of Machen's canny deployment of the multiple identities attendant upon his indeterminate cultural positioning as a borderer can be found in *The House of Souls* (1906), an anthology of some of his supernatural pieces, including *The Great God Pan*. The work is prefaced by an extraordinary lengthy introduction in which Machen proffers a parodic image of himself as a bona fide 'English' novelist that is based on a satiric account of prosperous, practical, late nineteenth-century bourgeois England's smug preferred image of itself. 'In England,' Machen mockingly asserts, 'we lay stress on usefulness and serious aims, and Imagination itself is expected to improve the occasion, to reform while it entertains, and to instruct under the guise of story-telling.'[15] Such robust common sense, he continues, is the legacy 'of our sturdy Puritan ancestors, those architects of England's true greatness, fathers of huge banking accounts, of flourishing industrial communities, of Gower Street, of Manchester and its environs'. In matters literary, the result is 'that the English Novel' is only deemed great 'when it is a sermon, or tract, or a pamphlet in disguise. The hard-headed men of business, whose judgement is, very properly, supreme in all questions of art and letters, have never disguised their intolerance of imagination qua imagination, since they have rightly felt that in the imaginative world, pure and simple, they have no part.' It is true that exceptions such as Dickens may occasionally be indulged, but even his 'strange fantasies' are 'forgiven' only 'for the sake of his zeal for reform in Church and State' (*HS*, viii). Superstitious medieval love of sacrament, and rite, and mystery have so long been gloriously banished from the English scene that 'we can hardly realize the bondage, the Egyptian darkness, from which we have been delivered' (*HS*, xi).

Machen brings his mock eulogy to an end by claiming that,

> it is entirely from the Puritan standpoint that I wish to rest my plea for these tales of mine. In the first place, I may say that only a very thoughtless reader will fail to note the moral which underlies each story. How plain, for instance, is the warning in the tale of 'The White People', where we see the necessity of the careful supervision of young females; while in 'The Great God Pan' the dangers of unauthorized research are clearly and terribly indicated. (*HS*, xii)

Machen is, he thus sarcastically protests, a dutiful 'English' novelist, ever conscientiously mindful of his duty to bend the knee to the holy trinity of Puritan (and, he implies Philistine) England: reason, morality and common sense. In a late twist, he pretends guiltily to confess to nevertheless having written tales concerned with a spiritual reality that 'transcends the experience of Bethel and the Bank'. But then, finally, he humbly defends his apparent transgression by claiming the authority of Science itself for them, since even that august 'guide of Life . . . has admitted many transcendental conceptions into her scheme of things'. As conclusive witness to the seriousness and sincerity of his intentions he cites the approbation of the Theosophists (whom Machen had, by this time, come to despise as charlatans) for his work. Numbered in their ranks, he facetiously adds, are 'atheists, men about town, journalists, hard-headed men of affairs, in fine . . . the thinking classes' (*HS*, xiii). He can, therefore, legitimately claim to be a 'sober portrayer of a certain side of life', and to have written solely for the attention of 'serious and practical people, who have no time to waste on idle reverie or flimsy fancies'.

There were several reasons for Machen's blistering attack on contemporary English taste. By 1906, he was struggling to maintain a hold on the affections of the Edwardian reading public. There had been a 'reaction against the outré' following the Wilde trials (*AM*, 82). Furthermore, a new generation of writers was emerging, some of whose appeal to the mass popular market rested on novels of social realism, contemptuously compared by Machen in his preface to the trivial gossipy letters of a country aunt 'giving the last news of six parishes, with births, marriages, deaths, dances, and engagements, to say nothing of the hunting' (*HS*, ix). So discomfited was he that he devoted several transparently autobiographical pages of his novel *The Hill of Dreams* (1907) to a jaundiced attack on the torrent of bland novels that currently appealed to the English reading public. 'Harmless amusement', he imagined one reviewer noting approvingly,

> a gentle flow of domestic interest, a faithful reproduction of the open and manly life of the hunting field, pictures of innocent and healthy English girlhood such as Miss Sanders here affords us; these are the topics that will always find a welcome in our homes, which remain bolted and barred against the abandoned artist and the scrofulous stylist. (*HD*, 37)

His typical reply was to publish a belated masterpiece of decadent fiction, *The Hill of Dreams*, which is nothing but a graphically lurid study of the steadily more feverish life of an 'abandoned artist' and 'scrofulous stylist'. It was a bold thing to do, given that his own stock as a professional best-selling author had at that time fallen so low that he'd been forced to take to the stage as an actor for a period.

His parodic assumption in the preface to the *House of Souls* of the role of an English author was, then, prelude to an attack on contemporary literary fashion. But it was also paradoxically an inverted assertion of the 'Celticness' he so deliberately affected on other occasions, and which was a crucial dimension of some of the tales in his anthology. In addition to 'The Great God Pan' and other tales, the anthology included 'The Novel of the Black Seal'. This was a self-contained 'episode' from an earlier, singular, composite work entitled *The Three Imposters* (1895), a collection of four very loosely linked tales of the supernatural. Commentators have been baffled by Machen's own variant on the venerable genre of the 'explained supernatural' and have been indignantly nonplussed by his insouciant advertising of the outrageousness of the 'falsehoods' represented by these tales. But from the point of view of the present study, this archness is very much to the point. It is an instance of Machen's periodic mocking of his English readers with a demonstration of how susceptible was their vaunted reason and common-sense to the most extravagant products of the 'Celtic' imagination, even when explicitly accompanied by a sober authorial warning of their unreliability. An encounter with Machen in this mode should warn us not to dismiss lightly the time he spent treading the boards as a mere unfortunate hiatus in his career as a writer. There is a theatricality verging on the camp to many of his horror tales, and recognition of this should in turn alert us to his great admiration for Poe, another arch manipulator, titillator and hoaxer who likewise practised so deftly on the gullibility of his readers.

Transferred from its original position in *The Three Imposters* to the *House of Souls*, 'The Novel of the Black Seal' has its original function of subverting rational English complacency augmented by its dialectical relationship with the work's preface, considered above. The story, as narrated by the sinister unreliable narrator Miss Lacy, is located once more in the mesmerically magical region of the Gwent countryside specifically characterised as a border country, and thus mysteriously duplicitous: 'in the distance I saw the white streak of a road that climbed and vanished into some unimagined country. But the boundary of all was a great wall of mountain, vast in the west, and ending like a fortress with a steep ascent and a domed tumulus clear against the sky.' (*HS*, 355) There, Miss Lacy meets the eminently reasonable Professor Gregg, who reminds her of a mysterious secret that he had previously mentioned – 'nothing definite, I mean, nothing that can be set down in hard black and white, as dull and sure and irreproachable as any blue-book' (*HS*, 355).

An incidental detail, wholly innocuous and negligible to an English reader, that reference to a 'blue book' would have rung alarm bells in the ears of any Welsh reader of the period. The enquiry commissioned by Westminster into the state of education in Wales had, in 1847, resulted in an official multi-volume report – popularly known from the colour of their covers as The Blue Books – whose scathing attack on the ignorance, poverty, licentiousness, superstition and depravity of the ordinary Welsh population had not only outraged public opinion but had permanently scarred the Welsh mind (see chapter 3). 'The Treachery of the Blue Books', as the episode universally came to be known (with historic reference to the notorious Treachery of the Long Knives that had supposedly first allowed the Saxons under Hengist and Horsa to gain ascendancy over the Celtic Welsh), had effectively determined the whole subsequent tenor of Welsh social, cultural and political life right down to Machen's time.[16]

Machen's strong Welsh Anglican connections would most certainly have alerted him to the whole traumatic affair, since the powerful vocal Nonconformist majority in Wales placed responsibility for the fiasco firmly at the door of the Church of England, whose representatives the commissioners (who interviewed monoglot Welsh speakers, despite their own complete ignorance of the language) were plausibly accused of being. Machen had no truck with Welsh Nonconformity – 'Dissent' in whatever form was absolute anathema to him, the very image of the puritanism he so deplored – but neither had he any sympathy for the Church of England in its established form, as we shall see. He could well, therefore, have regarded the Treachery of the Blue Books as an instance of how the ordinary people of Wales, whom he fondly believed still retained living connections with their ancient, pre-puritan roots, had been travestied and betrayed both by the Anglican commissioners and by their would-be defenders, the Welsh chapels.

There is, therefore, an interesting sense in which 'The Novel of the Black Seal' can be read as a 'Celtic' response to the Treachery of the Blue Books, a demonstration that even the most supposedly level- headed of readers, and the most 'scientific' of Englishmen such as Professor Gregg preens himself on being, are after all as prone to 'ignorant' superstition as allegedly had been the Welsh 'peasantry'. And as for Professor Gregg's assumption that the Blue Books – those 'dull and sure and irreproachable' instruments of Westminster political bureaucracy – represent a gold standard for factual accuracy, Machen had after all proof positive from recent Welsh history that Blue Books could be productions as 'imaginative' as any work of fiction.

One seems to be positively invited to attempt this kind of post-colonial reading of 'The Novel of the Black Seal' by the traces of colonial outlook embedded in the narrative itself. Confronted by the wild country and the 'barren and savage hills' of Gwent, for instance, Miss Lacy views it with trepidation as 'a territory all strange and unvisited, more unknown to Englishmen than the very heart of Africa' (*HS*, 357). It is in this mood that she finds herself reading an ancient book by a geographer of Imperial Rome about the strange sub-human peoples of Libya, on the very fringes of the Empire, who 'dwell in remote and secret places, and celebrat[e] foul mysteries on savage hills' (*HS*, 359). Soon, Miss Lacy discovers that traces of the 'stone Hexecontalithos' mentioned as sacred to the Libyans have recently been discovered in the Gwent countryside, and that the malign hissing that characterised the Libyans' incomprehensible speech had been heard emanating from the mouth of a local lad, Cradock, reputed to be a bit 'queer', and 'a little "simple"' (*HS*, 364). 'I heard him answering the gardener in a queer, harsh voice that caught my attention; it gave me the impression of some one speaking deep below under the earth, and there was a strange sibilance, like the hissing of the phonograph as the pointer travels over the cylinder.' (*HS*, 364)

On a later occasion, the 'babble of sounds' that come 'bursting and rattling and hissing from [Cradock's] lips . . . seemed to pour forth an infamous jargon, with words, or what seemed words, that might have belonged to a tongue dead since untold ages, and buried deep beneath Nilotic mud, or in the inmost recesses of the Mexican forest' (*HS*, 367). Tellingly from the postcolonial point of view, the lad's gibberish is at first suspected by Professor Gregg to be some form of Welsh (the Greek word 'barbarian' derives, as we know, from the contemptuous supposition that the speech of all non-Greeks was nothing but mangled sounds), but in the process of assuring him that the lad is not speaking Welsh, the local parson Mr Meyrick whimsically suggests that if Cradock's speech 'belongs to any language, I should say it must be that of the fairies – the Tylwydd [*sic*] Teg, as we call them' (*HS*, 370). Thus forewarned, we duly discover, at the conclusion of the tale, that 'Professor William Gregg, F.R.S. etc.' has indeed been persuaded of there periodically occurring locally a kind of horrible 'witches Sabbath' celebrated by the Little People, or fairy folk, whom he chooses to describe in pseudo-scientific terms as the products of reverse evolution; 'horrible' examples of human reversion to pre-human, bestial nature.

'The Novel of the Black Seal' has, however, been narrated by Miss Lacy, whose unreliability has been established at the very outset. Thus – and this is what readers apparently can still find inexplicable, baffling and disconcerting – the whole tale seems to become an outrageous fabrication and its conclusion a bewildering anticlimax. But taken in conjunction both with the post-colonial reading offered above, and with the mocking preface already examined very much in mind, the whole affair makes a different kind of possible sense. The tale could be in part a demonstration to the supposedly sophisticated and rational English reader of how easy it is for a self-styled 'Celt' such as Machen to practise on his or her credulous naivety, not least because the English had long been susceptible to the colonialist view so vigorously promulgated by Matthew Arnold and his many politico-cultural disciples that the Celts were peculiarly gifted with a natural magic, and so were readily persuaded to suspend their disbelief.

In 'The Novel of the Black Seal', therefore, Machen in his persona as a 'superstitious Celt' (counterbalancing the equally exaggerated presentation of himself in the preface as a commonsensical English Saxon) could be said to be holding up a distorting mirror to the supposedly rational and level-headed English, which renders their inherent deep superstitiousness mockingly apparent. As we shall see, he viewed the credulousness of the contemporary English ruling class that prided itself on its rational scientific outlook as a perversion of the spiritual sensitivity the 'Saxon' English had lost by suppressing (and monstrously projecting onto the Welsh) the inherent inherited 'Celtic' dimension of the English temperament.

The tone of the tale has, after all, been set from the outset in the presentation of one of the characters, Charles Phillips, as an individual who, 'flattering himself with the title of materialist . . . was in truth one of the most credulous of men' (332). And he it is who is snared by a tall tale told by Miss Lacy, the decidedly unreliable narrator with a 'twinkling as of mirth about her eyes' (340). When English figures like Professor Gregg, a central actor in the story, tentatively venture as far as the borders of Wales, they are liable to find what they expected to find; and when English readers likewise read a tale by a Celtic author, they too are liable to find in it exactly what they expected and wanted to find, however extravagantly unlikely the whole narrative may actually advertise itself as being. Nowhere is the absurdity of the story more apparent than in its approach to its conclusion, when the 'scientific' professor observes with apparent disciplined dispassion the transmutation of the body of a boy, Jervaes, into a distended bladder from which emerges a sight

> horrible, almost beyond the power of human conception and the most fearful fantasy. Something pushed out from the body there on the floor, and stretched forth, a slimy, wavering tentacle, across the room, grasped the bust upon the cupboard, and laid it down on my desk. (*HS*, 393)

In the *House of Souls*, therefore, Machen sets up a fascinating dialectic between the conspicuously exaggerated 'English' persona he affects in his outrageous introduction and the correspondingly exaggerated 'Celtic' persona he implicitly affects in his transparently outrageous tale of the Black Seal. These personae are interdependent, and their interaction in this particular case constitutes perhaps the most complex of Machen's own public reflections on his multiple, or compound, or hyphenated, identity – as that curious hybrid creature of border country, a 'Celtic Englishman'.

* * *

A very similar dialectical dynamic is generated by the relationship between Machen's tale, 'The Bowmen of Mons' and the introduction he was subsequently persuaded to furnish for that celebrated text in an attempt to disabuse his contemporary English readers of the truth of his fantasy. During the last week of August 1914, the small British Expeditionary Force of experienced professional soldiers that had been sent to France became involved in its first major action on the Western Front at Mons, on the border between Belgium and France, in an attempt to prevent a direct German advance on Paris. In the face of attacks from an enemy roughly three times its size, the force found itself having to stage a heroic fighting retreat for some 250 miles, before it was able to regroup and counter-attack in company with the French at the Battle of the Marne. Hearing the news, Arthur Machen envisaged 'a furnace of torment and death and agony and terror seven times heated, and in the midst of the burning was the British Army'.[17] He had already begun to supply London papers with factual articles about the war but, moved by this nightmare vision of Mons, he turned again to fiction, producing several stories the least satisfactory of which, in his estimation, was 'The Bowmen of Mons', a tale that many of his readers immediately mistook for fact.

Shorn of the customary ornate stylistic embellishments on which Machen so prided himself, the story has about it a spare, bare, quality that helps explain the extraordinary impact it immediately made, in its stark clarity, on a traumatised public and the status it has subsequently enjoyed as a classic myth of modern warfare.[18] Demonstrating a pitch-perfect ear for the kind of wry black humour that the British of the day loved to associate with the incorrigible 'Tommy', Machen contrives a low-key opening to his story that seems to vouch for the veracity of what purports to be a report from the front. The transition to a different key is effected with disarming casualness, as in the heat of battle an insignificant British soldier is moved to repeat aloud a motto he's seen on a restaurant plate adorned with the blue figure of St George: '*Aduit Anglis Sanctus Georgius* – May St George be a present help to the English' (*BM*, 33). No sooner has he spoken the words than they seem to be taken up and augmented into a battle cry by innumerable spirit voices echoing in the surrounding air, 'and as the soldier heard these voices he saw before him, beyond the trench, a long line of shapes, with a shining about them. They were like men who drew the bow, and with another shout, their cloud of arrows flew singing and tingling through the air towards the German hosts.' (*BM*, 35)

Machen was astounded and nonplussed when learned clergymen and scholars, as well as the general reading public, positively insisted on treating his fantasy as gospel fact, some of them asserting even in correspondence with the flabbergasted author himself that there was hard evidence (never of course actually adduced) for the truth of the story. Keen to set the record straight, he was readily prevailed upon to reprint 'The Bowmen' in 1915 in company with other similar wartime stories of the supernatural, and to provide a preface that clearly laid out the circumstances that had given rise to the fiction. In that preface, Machen repeatedly identifies himself as English and refers to the British Expeditionary Force as an English army. Such an identification allows him the insider's privilege, and authority, to launch an attack on England as 'a nation [so] plunged in materialism of the grossest kind' that, having become insensible to authentic spiritual experience, it falls prey to crass superstitions it views as rationally enlightened or 'scientific' in character such as spiritualism and theosophy: 'It took hard, practical men of affairs, business men, advanced thinkers, Freethinkers, to believe in Madame Blavatsky and Mahatmas.' (*BM*, 26) But it's at this point that the advantage of Machen's other, twin, identity as a Celt becomes apparent. As a western Englishman, a borderer, a native of Gwent, he is also a Celt, a fact that is underlined in an interesting way in his preface when Machen records his response to a Londoner who criticised him for allowing the English archers in his story to utter their battle-cries in French.

> I reminded him that, as a matter of cold historical fact, most of the archers of Agincourt were mercenaries from Gwent, my native country, who would appeal to Mihangel and to saints not known to the Saxons – Teilo, Iltyd [*sic*], Dewi, Cadwaladyr Vendigeid [*sic*]. (*BM*, 13)

The battle of Agincourt had not, then, been won by the 'Saxon' English, as they liked to claim, but rather by the 'Celtic English' from whom Machen believed himself to be descended. And in his devout opinion it was likewise the 'Celtic English' who, as we shall see, had kept faith with those spiritual beliefs that the modern materialistic Saxon English had so arrogantly and fatally abandoned. Core to these beliefs was the vital understanding, so Machen roundly stated at the end of his introduction, that 'Christianity . . . is a great Mystery Religion; it is THE Mystery Religion. Its priests are called to an awful and tremendous hierurgy; its pontiffs are to be the pathfinders, the bridge-makers between the world of sense and the world of spirit.' (*BM*, 27) This was the great truth that the church of England, the church of materialistic Saxons corrupted by the rational dogmas of Puritanism, had so disastrously denied.

* * *

As has been demonstrated in chapter 5, 'Celticism' was, by the turn of the century, a conveniently fluid, passionately contested, fashionable term. Machen's variant of it may have been most immediately inherited from Yeats and his 1890s acolytes, but it was Matthew Arnold who was undeniably the great originator and promoter of the concept.[19] There are several features of the scholarly account of Celticism offered by Arnold in his immensely influential work, *On the Study of Celtic*

Literature (1867), that have a direct bearing on Machen's particular case. Arnold first addresses the difficult matter of living Celts, the Welsh and Irish who (despite his protestation that he feels for them the sympathy a good modern Liberal must always feel for any unfortunate minority doomed to be one of history's losers) Arnold can view only as the pathetic, hopeless remnants of a once great, Europe-wide culture. In sentences that were to acquire a notoriety in the twentieth century, he bluntly asserts that 'the sooner the Welsh language disappears as an instrument of the practical, political, social life of Wales, the better; the better for England, the better for Wales itself. Traders and tourists do excellent service by pushing the English wedge farther and farther into the heart of the principality; Ministers of Education, by hammering it harder and harder into the elementary schools.'[20] And the reason for this? 'The fusion of all the inhabitants of these islands into one homogeneous, English-speaking whole, the breaking down of barriers between us, the swallowing up of separate provincial nationalities, is a consummation to which the natural course of things irresistibly tends; it is a necessity of what is called modern civilization.' (*SCL*, 197)

Machen's response to such nakedly colonialist sentiments are nowhere on record. But what is evident is that he shows very little sympathetic interest (except of the kind shortly to be considered below) in the *Pura Wallia* beyond his border country of Monmouthshire as it actually existed at the turn of the century. One reason for this was that 'Gwalia beyond Gwent' had, by the end of the nineteenth century, become the impregnable stronghold of the very form of Protestant culture most abhorrent to Machen. 'Celtic' Wales had turned into that abomination; a Nonconformist nation. His loathing found expression in a late story 'The Gift of Tongues', set in the region of Treowen, 'one of a chain of horrible mining villages that wind in and out of the Monmouthshire and Glamorganshire valleys'. This town, 'as dismal and detestable as the eye can see', is home to no fewer than 'three chapels of the Methodists and Baptists and Congregationalists; architectural monstrosities all three of them'.[21] However, set apart from these on the bare uplands above the town, there stands 'Bryn Seion', an 'old meeting house . . . a simple, square building, devoid of crazy ornament'. It is there that the Revd Thomas Beynon, one Christmas Day morning, suddenly astonishes his congregation by beginning to speak in a strange tongue, and to mime the celebration of an invisible Mass. Then, as he raises his hands as if he were involuntarily elevating a Chalice, 'there came the final tinkle of a bell from the sheep grazing high up on the mountainside'. It is as if, Machen concludes by suggesting, this Nonconformist minister, perhaps unconsciously recalling some Mass he'd inadvertently attended at nearby Newport or Cardiff, had unawares reverted to the order of service of the ancient Church of his distant Celtic forebears.

Given his loathing, then, for Nonconformist Wales, it is unlikely that Machen would have sympathised with the politico-cultural aims of an uncomfortably dynamic Cymru Fydd movement that was essentially rooted in chapel culture. Instead, he would probably have shared Arnold's dim view of 'the political and social Celtisation of which certain enthusiasts dream' (*SCL*, 303). For Machen, as for Arnold, Celtic culture in its vigorous political, social and cultural aspects was a phenomenon of the remote past, to be viewed with nostalgia. Arnold had ominously prefaced his study with an epigraph from Ossian that for him summed up the history of the Celts: 'They went forth to the war, but they always fell.' Arnold's preferred Celts were no-hopers when it came to effective practical action, and so were Machen's. 'The Celts,' he wrote in his essay on 'Celtic magic' (echoing Arnold's celebrated phrase about 'natural magic'), 'have been ineffective': 'it is the sense of a great loss which lies at the root of all the Celtic magic, the Celtic mysticism, the Celtic wonder.' (*S*, 143) Again like Arnold, he insisted that the only contribution the Celts could make to the modern world was through providing 'a little leaven in the somewhat solid, somewhat mundane Anglo-Norman lump'. Having summarily disconnected the notion of 'the Celtic' from specific inconveniently modern Celtic languages such as Welsh and Gaelic, Arnold and Machen were able to convert the term into a marker of vague ethnic, racial features that allowed them to argue that, as the Saxon tongue and culture had overlaid the aboriginal Celtic culture of early England without destroying it, and as Saxon had freely mated with Celt, there still lurked within the modern-day English a potential for 'Celticism' that remained untapped. It was with this assumption and its resultant possibilities very much in mind, then, that Machen strategically chose on occasion to insist he was a native of 'the west of England', and to present himself in so much of his fiction as a Celtic Englishman. A borderer he may have repeatedly emphasised he was, but more often than not he chose to treat his rural part of Gwent as if it lay on the English, rather than the Welsh, side of the border.

Moreover, he wrote several stories specifically intended to illustrate how a long-latent strain of 'Celticism' could suddenly manifest itself in the life and character of even the most seemingly solid and four-square of English men. One such story was 'A Fragment of Life', a tale centring on Edward Darnell who, though a clerk condemned to the drudgery of counting coupons in the city, had about him 'the curious hint of a wild grace, as if he had been born a creature of the antique wood, and had seen the fountain rising from the green moss and the grey rocks'. It takes more than fifty rather tortuous pages before Darnell begins to intuit even in London's dreary streets the pulse of some ancient alternative life, and it is many pages more before he finally acquires psychological impetus and the material means to trace these mysterious revivifying energies to their source – discovering in the process that his wife, too, has had similar hallucinations of a light glowing from behind the grey walls of London's grimy commercial buildings, and has formed the impression that 'the mystic fragrance of incense was blown to her nostrils from across the verge of that world which is not so much impenetrable as ineffable, and to her ears came the dream of a chant that spoke of hidden choirs about her ways' (*HS*, 95). Together, they establish that Darnell's ancestors bore a Welsh surname and that the family went back 'far into the dim past, beyond the Normans, beyond the Saxons, far into the Roman days' (*HS*, 96). The story's protracted conclusion has the Darnells fall completely under the spell of a richly mysterious form of litany, ritual and ceremonial worship known to Edward's saintly ancestors:

> In such things Darnell found a wonderful mystery language, which spoke at once more secretly and more directly than the formal creeds; and he saw that, in a sense, the whole world is but a great ceremony or sacrament, which teaches under visible forms a hidden and transcendent doctrine. It was thus that he found in the ritual of the church a perfect image of the world; an image purged, exalted, and illuminate, a holy house built up of shining and translucent stones . . . So day by day the house of his life became more magical. (*HS*, 100–1)

Significantly, this successful quest for illumination has been precipitated by an episode in which Mrs Darnell's aunt is discovered to be insane, and the cause of that psychological breakdown is ominously identified as a Nonconformist minister, a 'little Welsh skunk named Richards. He's been running some sort of chapel over at New Barnet for the last few years, and [the demented aunt] . . . had been going to his damned schism shop for the last twelve-month.' (*HS*, 89) The tale thus adumbrates a struggle between Welsh writer and Welsh preacher, between pen and pulpit, for mastery of imagination through control of the word, a struggle that was to become a central, defining feature of early twentieth-century 'Anglo-Welsh' literature. And the story also highlights yet another facet of Machen's strategic adoption of a border identity. If, as we have seen, it enabled him to claim a power, as Celtic Englishman, to activate the Celtic spirit latent within the English, it also enabled him to claim a power to reconnect the Welsh with that precious identifying strain of Celticness that had been grotesquely repressed in them by contemporary Welsh Nonconformity. In being free to be truly Celtic, Machen the borderer felt himself to be, in effect, free to be more Welsh than the Welsh of modern Wales itself; he was the remembrancer of its Celtic past and the visionary prophet of a once and (so Machen implies) future *Pura Wallia.*

Both Machen and Arnold, then, valued Wales not for anything (such as a 'democratic' religious community, a radically progressive Liberal politics, and a world-leading industrial civilisation) it had actually to offer in their own day, but rather for that rich past to which it provided entry. In Arnold's case, this primarily meant the body of poetry produced by the Celts from the early Christian centuries down to the late Middle Ages, a unique repository of 'natural magic'. As for Machen, his nostalgia was for a magic of a rather different kind, and this, too, he attributed to the remote Welsh past. By the time of the First World War, his dream of a spiritually exalted Celtic antiquity had begun to take the form and substance of a historical myth, strongly hinted at in 'The Bowmen of Mons', that was to become articulated with a kind of obsessive repetition in his later fiction. Nor, as we shall see, did that myth originate entirely with him, and it is this which makes his adoption and radical modification of it so culturally suggestive.

* * *

The Great Return, first published in 1915 as another of Machen's wartime books, features his adoption, for the first time, of another of his multiple identities. Here he chooses to represent himself as being 'Welsh Celtic', by which he means a borderer of Gwent now keen to advertise his close connections with Wales on his father's side of the family. Interestingly, this realignment is explicitly addressed early in the novella, through an encounter between the narrator (with whom Machen consciously identifies) and Mr Evans, the rector of Llantrisant, the mysterious village in the far south west of Wales where the action is set. Displaying what for the fictional 'Machen'[22] is a disconcertingly detailed acquaintance with his ancestry, the old man accuses him of having betrayed his Welsh family's history by becoming a 'bitter railer', the notorious scourge of an Anglican Church supposedly rotten with 'Protestantism', despite the fact that his great-grand-uncle Hezekiah, 'ffeiriad coch y [*sic*] Castletown – the Red Priest of Castletown – was a great man with the Methodists when he administered the Sacrament'.[23] In the rector's judgement, this debunking spirit means that 'Machen' is 'not worthy of this mystery that has been done here' – the very mystery that, it turns out, *The Great Return* is destined to reveal.

Mr Evans's extraordinarily detailed knowledge of this family background prompts the narrator to reflect that 'it is curiously true that the Welsh are still one people, one family almost, in a manner that the English cannot understand' (*GR*, 237). While aware that 'I only know modern Wales on the surface', 'Machen' nevertheless claims to be sufficiently inward with Welsh tradition, thanks to family roots, to be alive 'to the possible survival', in contemporary Wales, 'of old tradition in a kind of dormant, or torpid, semi-conscious state' (*GR*, 244). The novella is littered with Welsh phrases (usually slightly incorrect), because Machen the author, like his fictional counterpart, is convinced that the language retains traces of ancient legend and lore, and thus acts as a carrier of the remnants of secret knowledge. 'So [the Welsh] come trailing, let us say, fragments of the cloud of glory in their common speech; and so, on this Saturday, they began to display, uneasily enough in many cases, their consciousness of things that were of their ancient rite and former custom.' (*GR*, 220)

'The things that were reported' relate to the matter that 'Machen' has come to Llantrisant to investigate, namely rumours of the villagers' strange visionary encounters with some supernatural phenomenon that has left them spiritually transfigured, morally transformed, illuminated from within by a glorious, exalting light. The first clue as to the cause of 'the enigmas of Llantrisant' (*GR*, 211) comes when the narrator notices the strange interior design of the parish church. Where the rood screen would normally be found, there stands a solid wall with a narrow opening under a rounded arch leading to the sanctuary and altar beyond. 'Machen' realises this is 'a typical example of a Welsh parish church, before the evil and horrible period of "restoration"', which means that it retains 'that primitive division between nave and chancel which only very foolish people decline to recognise as equivalent to the Oriental iconostatis' (*GR*, 229). This discovery chimes with news of the occasion when the handful of parishioners seated in the holy of holies beyond the division streamed out to the main body of the church, having witnessed an exalting revelation of divine mysteries. The miracle also connects with fishermen's stories of seeing a strange red light gleaming over the sea and seeming, on occasion, to come to rest in the old church of St Teilo, situated in a remote limestone cleft on Chapel Hill.

Piecing together such pieces of evidence, 'Machen' realises that the inhabitants of Llantrisant have been made privy to a vision of the mystic Mass of the Sangraal, a privilege granted them because theirs is a fishing village in a land whose patron saint is Dewi (David), known as 'Dewi Ddyfrwr' (David the Waterman), the original 'King Fisherman' (or 'Fisher King') of Grail tradition (*GR*, 236). With the mystery thus explained, the novella ends with a detailed description of 'The Mass of the Sangraal', opening with a ritualistic call to worship by an 'old Calvinistic Methodist deacon' (*GR*, 288), and proceeding to a liturgy in a mixture of Welsh and Church Latin. Central to the rite are the ringing of a bell that gives voice even to the birds of the air, the displaying of a 'lost altar that they once called *Sapphirus*', 'which was like the changing of the sea and of the sky, and like the immixture of gold and silver', and the elevation 'high over the altar [of] a cup that was red with burning and the blood of the offering'.

This version of the Grail legend, which came to obsess Machen during the final decades of his life, giving rise both to a number of fictions and to a series of essays on the subject, is an idiosyncratic mishmash of Celtic tradition, popular lore and the (sometimes rather wild) 'scholarship' of his own period. Recently reintroduced to the public through such exalted works as Tennyson's *Idylls of the King* and Wagner's opera *Parsifal*, the tangled nexus of Grail legends had not only re-entered popular consciousness but attracted the attention of occultists, anthropologists, psychologists, and an assortment of scholars ranging from the colourfully dubious to those sobered by genuine learning. Machen enthusiastically contributed his own soaring flights of theoretical fancy to the general mix, connecting the Grail stories to the Bran story of the Talking Head from the Mabinogion, and arguing in the process that 'there were doubtless [Celtic] legends, as bare and unadorned as this, from which the Anglo-Normans and the Germans constructed the *Quest of the Sangraal*, the *Parsifal*, the whole Arthurian mythos' (*S*, 144). The Arthurian corpus was particularly dear to Machen's heart, because ever since a boy he had believed that Caerleon had been the original site of Camelot, no less.

In an essay on 'The Holy Grail', Machen strongly recommended *The Hidden Church of the Holy Graal: Its Legends and Symbolism*, a book by his friend A. E. Waite, an authority on the history of the occult as a spiritual movement. In particular, he heaped praise on its learned analysis of the range of key primary sources, in prose and verse, 'written in Old French, Dutch, and German . . . roughly speaking between the years 1170 and 1230' (*S*, 146), regarding Waite's discussion as a valuable corrective to the casual English assumption that the Arthurian Grail Romances needed to be traced only to their supposed source in Malory's *Le Morte D'Arthur*. Machen tracks the core Grail legend back to the story of Joseph of Arimathea's vision of the Grail on the eve of his voyage to bring the Christian faith to Britain, and this prompts him to highlight his dissent from Waite's theories in one crucial respect. Whereas Waite was of the opinion (in keeping with several weighty subsequent scholars) that the origins of the Grail legends were to be found in the history of Medieval Christian theology, Machen continued to side with older scholars (including Sir John Rhŷs and Jessie Weston) in arguing that they were a radical Christian redaction of materials drawn from ancient pre-Christian Celtic legend and lore.

At this point, however, Machen proceeds to elaborate his own highly idiosyncratic version of the stories of the Grail. The Knights, he argues, were originally 'Welsh saints in armour', the Grail cup itself deriving from a magical portable altar of Saint David that took on the attributes of the famed 'Cauldron of Rebirth' of pagan Celtic tradition. As Celtic Britain was reduced to a waste land by the depredations of the Saxons following the departure of the Roman legions, so the sacred relic was spirited away rarely to be glimpsed, giving rise to the history of the elusive Holy Chalice. These were the materials that came to the attention of the Normans, following the 'discovery' of St Joseph's tomb at Glastonbury, and were duly expanded by their gifted authors into the elaborate tales that enchanted the whole of Medieval Europe.

* * *

Machen's growing post-war preoccupation with the Celtic Church of Dewi Sant/Saint David and his correspondingly more frequent identification of himself as a 'Celtic Welshman', find their most expansive and ambitious expression in the novel *The Secret Glory* (1923). Disgusted with the corrupt, cramping, environment of his English public school, the young Welshman Ambrose Meyrick becomes subject to a series of visions, beginning with one of a majestic medieval cathedral, ornamented with delicate and wonderful stonework radiantly alive with images of the birds, beasts, flora and fauna of the natural creation (*SG*, 23–4). Within the walls of the great church, he hears 'the modulations of a final and exultant ecstasy, the chant of liberation, a magistral [*sic*] *In Exitu*' (*SG*, 53), culminating in 'bells ringing for a feast, organ rolling, ministrants in white, endless litanies, great torches of wax, golden and vermilion ornaments, tapers, silver censers tossing a pale cloud into the air' (*SG*, 54).

Reading such a passage, heady with Machen's enthusiasm for the hieratic, it is easy to believe A. H. Palmer's observation that his friend was an '*anima naturaliter catholica* who had never made the move from Canterbury to Rome largely on account of his attachment to the old Celtic Church of Dewi Sant. He remained an Anglican but never ceased to vent an intense and seditious disapproval of the Protestant origins of Anglicanism.' [24] And as Meyrick, leaving the great church behind, ventures ever farther into the forest of his vision, it is indeed at the sea-girt land of the Celtic saints that he finally arrives, pausing before a 'very ancient little chapel' (*SG*, 55), its bell 'ringing clearly and so sweetly that it was as it were the singing of the angels'. Entering, he scents the odours of Paradise, while a spectral choir sings more enchantingly even than ever did the Birds of Rhiannon in the Mabinogion. A door opens in the screen and an old man in shining white emerges. On his head there sits a golden crown, and he is gravely proceeded by a young bell-ringer, accompanied by torch-bearers. In his hands, the old man '[bears] the *Mystery of Mysteries* wrapped about in veils of gold and of all colours', and radiating the 'light of heaven'. Having paraded ceremonially, he then exits by a door on the other side where 'the Holy Things [are] hidden' and, from within, an awful voice is heard declaring 'Woe and great sorrow are on him, for he hath looked unworthily into the Tremendous Mysteries, and on the Secret Glory which is hidden from the holy Angels.' (*SG*, 57)

Rapturously exalted by this vision, Meyrick is moved to recall what he had learnt from his Welsh father before ever he was sent to the detested English public school:

> He remembered his father's oft-repeated exclamation, 'cythrawl [*sic*] Sais!' He understood that the phrase damned not Englishmen *qua* Englishmen, but Anglo-Saxonism – the power of the creed that builds Manchester, that 'does business', that invents popular dissent, representative government, adulteration, suburbs, and the Public School system. It was, according to his father, the creed of 'the Prince of this world', the creed that made for comfort, success, a good balance at the bank, the praise of men, the sensible and tangible victory and achievement; and he bade his little boy, who heard everything and understood next to nothing, fly from it, hate it and fight against it as he would fight against the devil – 'and', he would add, 'it *is* the only devil you are ever likely to come across'. (*SG*, 69)

That last observation should give one pause, if we recall that the early Machen was much given to invoking a whole legion of devils in his 'terror' fiction. The comment here reinforces the argument presented earlier, that those devils were sometimes the figments of the imaginations of the Saxon English who had become worshippers of material success. Moreover, the whole thrust of this passage – and it is surely difficult not to believe it had some foundation in an actual exchange between the Machens, father and son – seems to reinforce the suggestion already made that there are incipiently postcolonial dimensions to some of Machen's work. Implicit even in his adoption of the identity of a 'Celtic Englishman' was the idea that thereby he could encourage the Celtic strain to prevail over the Saxon strain in the English temperament. And implicit in that aspiration, in turn, was the old vaticinatory dream of the modern Welsh (so cunningly exploited by the Tudors) that one day they would regain control over the whole island of Britain that had once been theirs to rule in its entirety.

A neat example of Machen's flirtation with such a tradition occurs at the point in *The Secret Glory* where young Ambrose Meyrick, fortified by the extraordinary glimpse he's shared with his father of St Teilo's Holy Cup (a dazzlingly bright bowl, 'its surface was a marvel of the most delicate intertwining lines in gold and silver, in copper and in bronze, in all manner of metals and alloys'; *SG*, 80), is provoked into revealing the secret when one of his fellow-pupils at his hated English public school boasts of having recently viewed the Crown Jewels (*SG*, 85). It is as if Machen were symbolically expressing his 'Welsh Celtic' dream of seeing the English monarchy replaced by such true heirs of the ancient spiritual culture of Wales as Mr Cradock, 'an old [Welsh-speaking] farmer with a small freehold up here on the mountain side [whose] English is no better than that of any other farmer in this country. And, compared with Cradock, the Duke of Norfolk is a man of yesterday. He is of the tribe of Teilo the Saint.' (*SG*, 84)

* * *

Ambrose's father reads out to his son 'all the histories of Teilo, Dewi, and Iltyd [*sic*]' (*SG*, 159), and then shows him the mysterious traces of the 'venerable saints' still evident to initiates in the sacred landscape of Gwent. The boy is taught to sing that landscape into being by chanting ancient verses such as the following:

> 'The cell of Dewi is in the City of the Legions,
> Nine altars owe obedience to it,
> Sovereign is the choir that sings about it.
>
> The cell of Cybi is the treasure of Gwent,
> Nine hills are its perpetual guardians,
> Nine songs befit the memory of the saint.' (*SG*, 72)

Machen was clearly familiar with the claim made in Rhigyfarch's eleventh-century Life of Saint David that although Dewi had become Bishop of St Davids his ecclesiastical seat was at Caerleon.

Ambrose's father recalls with passion the early centuries when the old Mass of the Britons was celebrated in Gwent. 'And then,' the old man continues,

> [c]ame the Yellow Hag of Pestilence, that destroyed the bodies of the Cymri [*sic*]; then the Red Hag of Rome, that caused their souls to stray; last is come the Black Hag of Geneva, that sends body and soul quick to hell. No honour have the saints any more. (*SG*, 73)

But while Machen himself took much the same view of fifteen hundred years of Welsh ecclesiastical history, he modified it in one important respect, as is apparent in this key passage from *The Great Return*:

> The question is as to the continuance of tradition; more especially as to the continuance of tradition among the Welsh Celts of today. On the

> one hand, such waves and storms have gone over them. The wave of the heathen Saxons went over them, then the wave of Latin medievalism, then the waters of Anglicanism; last of all the flood of their queer Calvinistic Methodism, half Puritan, half pagan. (*GR*, 237)

Unlike Mr Meyrick Senior, Machen believed that, throughout those long centuries of spiritual aberration, the Welsh had never entirely lost their ancient memory of the 'true Faith' of the early Celtic saints and their 'church'.

And, indeed, Machen would certainly have been aware of the solid (if inverted) evidence for this to be found in those versions of their own past that had been adopted first by the Anglican Church in Wales and subsequently by the Dissenting/Nonconformist sects. Shortly after the first emergence of Tudor Anglicanism, Bishop Richard Davies prefaced his great inaugural translation in 1567 of the New Testament and the Book of Common Prayer into Welsh with an 'Epistol at y Cembru', an epistle addressed to his obstinately Catholic countrymen. In it, he argued that the apparently new and foreign Anglican Church, whose representative he was, had in fact restored to the Welsh that pure, primitive form of religion they had known back in the time of the early Celtic saints. This 'new' Church of England was therefore actually the old Church of Wales restored.[25] A century later, the pioneering missionaries of puritan Dissent were to claim exactly the same distinction for their own forms of worship. Machen, dismissive both of Welsh Anglicanism and of Welsh Nonconformity, accepted neither line of argument, but he did recognise in them enduring racial memories of the primacy and spiritual authenticity of the early Christian church in Wales.[26] And it is on this premise that the central action of his novel *The Great Return* is actually based.

* * *

As one reads Machen's fictions, then, awareness steadily grows that his fantasies are constructed from a very interesting assortment of the cultural materials available to him at the time, and that in them his beloved border land of Gwent/Monmouthshire takes on several very different aspects, varying from the unsettled and unsettling haunted landscape of Pan and his peers to ground permanently and palpably sanctified by the ancient presence of the Celtic saints. But, as has been suggested, far from being the products of two incompatible modes of perception, these contrasting features can be regarded as two faces of a single belief – Machen's belief in the ambiguous consequences of Monmouthshire's border condition, its Celticness (which he variously inflected as Welsh Celtic/Celtic English) mediating the complex relation between Wales and England. And Machen's constant transmutations of identity – variously identifying as Welsh, Welsh Celtic, Celtic English, Western English, Silurian, and sometimes even deceptively as 'plain' English – were calculated to serve exactly the same purpose. Moreover, when it came to dealing with Wales itself, Machen was able to work a similar alchemy. By transmuting them into the peculiar forms congenial to his own fantastical imagination, Machen was able to synthesise in his fictions several of the competing, even conflicting, variants of Welsh identity with which this study has been concerned, proving, in the process, to be a figure most unexpectedly representative, in his own weird way, of the unstable condition of a dynamically changing Wales at the juncture of the nineteenth and twentieth centuries. The researches by bona fide scholars into the myth and legend of Wales's early, Celtic, past versus the resolutely anti-'pagan' prejudices of the primly devout chapels; the competing claims of the Church of England and Nonconformity on the Welsh soul; the division between traditional rural Wales and the new, raw, industrial societies of the south Wales coalfield; the tug of war between the intellectual and political leaders of a would-be self-governing *Pura Wallia* and an England-orientated industrial elite; these and other divisive but distinctive features of the Wales of his day are given expression in various fantastical guises and strange combinations in fictions, in which Machen the writer claims for himself the shape-shifting freedom proper to a product of border country, an inveterately proud native of Gwent.

Notes

1 Emblematising the nation

1 *City Hall, Cardiff: Visitor Information Guide* (2nd edn: City and County of Cardiff, May, 2006).

2 As John Davies has arrestingly written, 'A quarter of the population of Wales lives within the boundaries of what were the lordships of the Bute estate.' John Davies, *Cardiff and the Marquesses of Bute* (Cardiff: University of Wales Press, 1981), vi.

3 As John Ellis has explained, 'The appointment of the Marquess of Bute as Mayor of Cardiff in 1890 reconciled him not only to the city, but to the nation as well. With his political power destroyed, the Marquess was transformed into a symbolic figure-head, Cardiff's foremost citizen associated with the city's and, by extension, the nation's cultural and social aspirations.' John S. Ellis, *Investiture: Royal Ceremony and National Identity in Wales, 1911–1969* (Cardiff: University of Wales Press, 2008), 79, hereafter *I.*

4 Gwyn A. Williams, *When Was Wales?* (London: Penguin Books, 1991), 224.

5 Gareth Elwyn Jones and Trevor Herbert (eds), *Wales 1890–1914* (Cardiff: University of Wales Press, 1988), hereafter *W.*

6 K. O. Morgan, *Rebirth of a Nation: Wales 1880–1980* (Cardiff: University of Wales Press, 1981); *Wales in British Politics, 1866–1922* (Cardiff: University of Wales Press, 1963); *Revolution to Devolution: Reflections on Welsh Democracy* (Cardiff: University of Wales Press, 2014).

7 Hereafter the terms 'Cymru Fydd' and 'Young Wales' will be treated as interchangeable.

8 Denis Mack Smith, *Mazzini* (New Haven: Yale University Press, 1994).

9 Dewi Hughes, *Cymru Fydd* (Cardiff: University of Wales Press, 2006), hereafter *CF.*

10 K. O. Morgan, *David Lloyd George, 1863–1945* (Cardiff: University of Wales Press, 1981); John Grigg, *Lloyd George and Wales* (Aberystwyth: The National

Library of Wales, 1988); John Grigg, *The Young Lloyd George* (London; Methuen, 1973).

11 *Cymru Fydd* 1 (1888), editorial.

12 *Young Wales* 1 (1895), 235.

13 Neville Masterman, *The Forerunner: the Dilemmas of Tom Ellis, 1859–1899* (Llandybie: Christopher Davies, 1972).

14 W. Llywelyn Williams, 'Through Welsh Spectacles,' *Young Wales* 2 (1896), 30–3.

15 William George, 'Our Sunday Notebook,' *Young Wales* 2 (1896), 17.

16 *Young Wales* 1 (1895), 21.

17 *Young Wales* 1 (1895), editorial.

18 *Young Wales* 2 (1896), editorial.

19 W. Llewelyn Williams went on to publish a fictional account of 'Wales: Fifty Years Hence'. *Young Wales* 9 (1903), 43, 49, 56, 93, 97.

20 *Young Wales* 9 (1903), 261. See also J. Arthur Price, 'Has Welsh Nationalism Failed?', an impressive analysis, from the viewpoint of a conservative Anglican supporter of Cymru Fydd, of the decline of Welsh nationalist feeling (*Young Wales* 10 [1904], 77).

21 *Young Wales* 2 (1896), 121.

22 Reported by O. M. Edwards, *Cymru* 9 (1895).

23 Beau Riffenburgh, *Shackleton's Forgotten Expedition: The Voyage of the Nimrod* (London: Bloomsbury, 2004), 16.

24 Private correspondence, reproduced with consent.

25 Peter Lord, *The Visual Culture of Wales: Imaging the Nation* (Cardiff: University of Wales Press, 2000), hereafter *IN*.

26 D. R. Jones, *Illustrated Catalogue of the Welsh Historical Sculptures presented to the City of Cardiff by the Rt Hon. Lord Rhondda of Llanwern* (1916).

27 John Gwynfor Jones, 'Y Ddelwedd Gymreig Ddinesg yng Nghaerdydd *c.*1885–1939,' in Hywel Teifi Edwards (ed.), *Merthyr a Thaf* (Cardiff: University of Wales Press, 2001), 325–63.

28 See for example Ursula Masson, *'For Women, for Wales, and for Liberalism': Women in Liberal Politics in Wales, 1890–1914* (Cardiff: University of Wales Press, 2010).

29 'The Grave of Glyndwr,' *Young Wales* 1 (1895), 3–4.

30 Wyn James, *Glyndŵr a Gobaith y Genedl: Agweddau ar y portread o Owain Glyndŵr yn llenyddiaeth y cyfnod modern* (Aberystwyth: Cymdeithas Lyfrau Ceredigion, 2007), 40, hereafter *GGG*; Elissa P. Heinken, *National Redeemer: Owain Glyndŵr in Welsh Tradition* (Cardiff: University of Wales Press, 1996); R. R. Davies, *The Revolt of Glyndŵr* (Oxford: Oxford University Press, 1997); 'Beriah Gwynfe Evans: A Pioneer Playwright Producer,' in Hywel Teifi Edwards, ed., *A Guide to Welsh Literature, c.1800–1900* (Cardiff: University of Wales Press, 2000).

31 'Y Frenhines yn y Bala,' *Cymru Fydd* 3 (1890), 62. See Hywel Teifi Edwards and E. G. Millward, *Jiwbilî: Y Fam Wen Fawr* (Llandysul: Gwasg Gomer, 2002), 5.

32 *Ceremonial to be observed at the Investiture of His Royal Highness The Prince of Wales, KG., Carnarvon Castle, 13th July, 1911.*

33 *The Book of the Investiture*, Swansea Local Education Authority Souvenir Booklet.

34 *Wales and her Prince: The Investiture and All About It* (*The Daily News*: London and Manchester).

35 Hywel Teifi Edwards, *Cofféu Llywelyn, 1856–1956* (Llandysul: Gwasg Gomer, 1983); and, *Jiwbilî: Y Fam Wen Fawr, Victoria.*

36 Gwaenfab, 'Cofgolofn Llywelyn,' *Cymru* 8 (1895), 211.

37 Huw Pryce, *J. E. Lloyd and the Creation of Welsh History: Renewing a Nation's Past* (Cardiff: University of Wales Press, 2011), hereafter *JEL*.

38 'Wales and the First World War,' in *Revolution to Devolution*, 145–73.

39 Historians have argued that the opportunity to fashion a modern, bilingual Wales had been lost several decades earlier, between 1850 and 1880. This, they've added, was due not to industrialization per se, nor, at that juncture, to substantial in-migration, but rather to such factors as the lack of a sophisticated, university-trained intellectual leadership, and the preoccupation of the leaders of Welsh Nonconformity both with religious and sectarian issues and with the individualistic and utilitarian values they'd acquired from English Liberalism. See, for example, John Davies, *A History of Wales* (Harmondsworth: Penguin, 1993), 403. Other historians would undoubtedly want to emphasise the demoralising effect of the Blue Books Report of 1847 that instilled in the Welsh a cultural cringe that lasted well beyond even the end of the nineteenth century. See Prys Morgan, ed., *Brad y Llyfrau Gleision* (Llandysul: Gwasg Gomer, 1991); Gwyneth Tyson Roberts, *The language of the blue books: the perfect instrument of empire* (Cardiff: University of Wales Press, 1998). For the divisions in Welsh society that also contributed to this situation see Prys Morgan, 'Early Victorian Wales and its Crisis of Identity,' in Laurence Brockliss and David Eastwood, eds, *A Union of Multiple Identity: the British Isles, c.1750–c.1850* (Manchester: Manchester University Press, 1997), 93–109.

40 Richard G. Fox, ed., *Nationalist Ideologies and the Production of National Cultures* (American Anthropological Association, 1990), 3, hereafter *NI*.

41 Cairns Craig, *The Modern Scottish Novel: Narrative and the National Imagination* (Edinburgh: Edinburgh University Press, 1999), 30, hereafter *MSN*.

42 See Paul James, *Nation Formation: Towards a Theory of Abstract Communities* (London: Sage, 1996), 14–15.

2 Performing political identity

1 The following discussion of the Pageant is totally dependent on the brilliant study by Hywel Teifi Edwards, *The National Pageant of Wales* (Cardiff: University of Wales Press, 2009), hereafter *NPW*.

2 Judith Butler, *Gender Trouble: Feminism and the Subversion of Identity* (New York and London: Routledge, 1999), hereafter *GT*.

[3] John Gwilym Jones, 'Dramâu Beriah Gwynfe Evans', *Swyddogaeth Beirniadaeth* (Dinbych: Gwasg Gee, 1977), 303–15.

[4] For Evans's career see E. G. Millward, 'Beriah Gwynfe Evans: A Pioneer Playwright-Producer', in Hywel Teifi Edwards (ed.), *A Guide to Welsh Literature, c.1800–1900* (Cardiff: University of Wales Press, 2000), 166–85; E. Wyn James, *Glyndŵr a Gobaith y Genedl* (Aberystwyth: Cymdeithas Lyfrau Ceredigion, 2007), 43–67.

[5] Sian Rhiannon Williams, *Oes y Byd i'r Iaith Gymraeg: y Gymraeg yn Ardal Ddiwydiannol Sir Fynwy yn y Bedwaredd Ganrif ar Bymtheg* (Caerdydd: Gwasg Prifysgol Cymru, 1992).

[6] E. Morgan Humphreys, 'Beriah Gwynfe Evans', in *Gwŷr Enwog Cynt (Yr Ail Gyfres)* (Aberystwyth, Gwasg Aberystwyth, 1953), 120–31.

[7] See Aled Gruffydd Jones, *Press, Politics and Society: A History of Journalism in Wales* (Cardiff: University of Wales Press, 1993).

[8] Beriah Gwynfe Evans, *Dafydd Dafis: sef Hunangofiant Ymgeisydd Seneddol* (Wrexham: Hughes and Son, 1898), hereafter *DD*.

[9] Benedict Anderson, *Imagined Communities: reflections on the origins and spread of nationalism* (London: Verso, 1983), 123–4.

[10] Beriah Gwynfe Evans, *Y Cyngor Plwyf. Pa Fodd i'w Ethol a'i Weithio, sef Llawlyfr Deddf Llywodraeth Leol 1894*.

[11] Beriah Gwynfe Evans, 'The Parish Councils Act: its message to Wales', *Young Wales* 1 (1895), 10–11.

[12] See K. O. Morgan, *Wales in British Politics, 1868–1922* (Oxford: Clarendon Press, 1981).

[13] Interestingly, Evans chose to translate the title as *The Confessions of a Parliamentary Candidate*, when listing his publications.

[14] As K. O. Morgan has pointed out, Welsh Liberalism had been all-ways over Irish Home Rule at the time of the great schism of 1886: 'There were prominent defectors from Gladstonian ranks, mainly on grounds of sympathy for Protestant Ulster, and detestation of Irish Catholicism. Some leading Welsh Liberals veered towards Liberal Unionism; seven Welsh Liberal MPs voted against the second reading of Gladstone's Irish Home Rule Bill in June 1886. The celebrated publicist, Thomas Gee, editor and publisher of *Baner ac Amserau Cymru*, the eminent Methodist theologian, the Revd J. Cynddylan Jones; the barrister-critic, T. Marchant Williams; even the young Caernarvonshire solicitor David Lloyd George – all flirted with Liberal Unionism.' K. O. Morgan, *Rebirth of a Nation* (Oxford: Clarendon Press and Cardiff: University of Wales Press, 1981), 43, hereafter *RN*.

[15] Beriah Gwynfe Evans, *The Life Romance of Lloyd George* (London: 'Everyman', n.d. but 1915/1916), 10, hereafter *LRLG*.

[16] Thomas E. Ellis, *Speeches and Addresses* (Wrexham: Hughes and Son, 1912), especially 3–84; Peter Lord, *The Visual Culture of Wales* (Cardiff: University of Wales Press, 2000), 325–6.

[17] J. Hugh Edwards, 'Leading Young Welshmen VII: Thomas Ellis MP', *Young Wales* 2 (1896), 94.

18 Anwen Jones, *National Theatre in Context: France, Germany, England, Wales* (Cardiff: University of Wales Press, 2007).

19 Ursula Masson, *'For Women, for Wales and for Liberalism': Women in Liberal Politics in Wales, 1880–1914* (Cardiff: University of Wales Press, 2010), hereafter *UM*. Also, Kay Cook and Neil Evans, '"The Petty Antics of the Bell-Ringing Boisterous Band": The Women's Suffrage Movement in Wales, 1890–1918', in Angela V. John (ed.), *Our Mothers' Land: Chapters in Welsh Women's History 1830–1939* (Cardiff: University of Wales Press,1991), 159–88.

20 Leonora Philipps (née Gerstenberg), Lady St Davids, 'was a considerable figure in her own right, both as a strong supporter of women's rights and as an able platform speaker. In Wales, she took an interest in folklore, performed recitations, had a leading part in the Welsh National Pageant of 1909, and, supported the National Eisteddfod, being the lady president at a concert during the Abergavenny Eisteddfod in 1913.' (*Dictionary of Welsh Biography*) She was married to Wynford Philipps, Lord St Davids, a member of an old Pembrokeshire family who, having amassed a fortune through cavalier investments in Argentinian railways and other enterprises, became intent, from 1895 onwards, on a career in Liberal politics and developed into a key financial backer of Lloyd George. Ursula Masson discusses Philipps's seminal contribution to women's rights in Wales and beyond in *'For Women, for Wales, and for Liberalism'*, *passim*, particularly 52–5. The fact that Philipps was the English-born daughter of European Jewish parents (*UM*, 63) may possibly have predisposed her to sympathise with marginalised peoples like the Welsh.

21 See, for example, Gwyneth Vaughan, 'Women and their questions', *Young Wales* 3 (1897), 19–20. Vaughan, whose real name was Annie Harriet Hughes, became in due course secretary of WUWLA.

22 Mrs Wynford Philipps, 'Notes on the Work of Welsh Liberal Women', *Young Wales* 1 (1895), 17–19, 19. Masson has pointed out that Philipps was a leading advocate in Wales of Josephine Butler's 'separate spheres' approach to gender issues (*UM*, 16).

23 Mrs Wynford Philipps, 'Notes on the Work of Welsh Liberal Women', 37–41. The Welsh Liberal MPs Philipps had in mind included Bryn Roberts – ironically, given the way he's depicted in *Dafydd Dafis* – D. A. Thomas, Alfred Thomas and Mabon, and she adds that 'Mr Lloyd-George [*sic*] has recently spoken in sympathy with [women's] political aspirations'.

24 A confirmed bachelor who enjoyed a distinguished career as lawyer and judge, J. Bryn Roberts was Liberal MP for South Caernarvonshire from 1885 to1906. In being a fierce, unclubbable individualist, he was a Liberal of the old school who had no interest either in socialism or Cymru Fydd nationalism, and was never a reliable ally of Lloyd George. See *Dictionary of Welsh Biography*.

25 *Young Wales* 3 (1897), 232–3.

26 Sir William Harcourt served as Home Secretary under Gladstone from 1880 to 1885 and as Chancellor of the Exchequer first in 1886 and then from 1892 to 1895 (the year in which he became Liberal MP for West Monmouthshire).

27 Susannah Gee was the daughter of the renowned campaigning editor of *Baner ac Amserau Cymru*. As Masson points out, when Gee became a member of the WUWLA executive she 'provided the link between it and the Welsh Disestablishment Campaign Committee' (*UM*, 28).

28 For gendered representations of national identity, see Kirsti Bohata, *Postcolonialism Revisited* (Cardiff: University of Wales Press, 2004) and Masson, *For Women, for Wales, for Liberalism*, particularly Introduction (18), along with chapters 3 and 6.

29 John J. MacAloon, *Rite, Drama, Festival, Spectacle: Rehearsals Toward a Theory of Cultural Performance* (Institute for the Study of Human Issues, 1984), 1.

30 Millward, 'Beriah Gwynfe Evans', 171.

3 Keeping track of the gwerin

1 O. M. Edwards, *Cartrefi Cymru* (Wrexham: Hughes and Son, 1896), hereafter *CC*. Edwards (1858–1920), who was knighted in 1916 for his services to the literature of Wales, was a giant on the cultural scene and greatly beloved by the rural Welsh-speaking Wales of his day. The son of a tenant farmer from Llanuwchllyn, on the outskirts of Bala, he acquired English only at the village school before going on to a stellar academic career, first at the new University College of Wales in Aberystwyth, then at Glasgow University and finally at Balliol College, Oxford, where, as a student of modern history, he scooped most of the glittering prizes. In 1889 he was appointed Fellow and tutor in history at Lincoln College, Oxford, and remained in that post until appointed Chief Inspector of Schools of the Welsh Board of Education in 1907. Driven by his desire to educate Welsh-speaking Wales in its own history, his output of publications for popular consumption was astonishing. His two dozen books ranged from historical studies through travelogues to anthologies and an autobiography; he was the founding editor of seven periodicals; and the editor of seven series of Welsh popular classics. Succinct introductions to his life and work include the entry in Meic Stephens (ed.), *The New Companion to the Literature of Wales* (Cardiff: University of Wales Press, 1998); and Hazel Walford Davies, *O. M. Edwards* (Cardiff: University of Wales Press, 1988), hereafter *OME*.

2 For a full treatment of the seminal concept of *y werin* ('the gwerin'), see Prys Morgan, 'The Gwerin of Wales – Myth and Reality', in J. Hume and W. T. R. Pryce (eds), *The Welsh and their Country* (Swansea: Christopher Davies, 1986), 134–52.

3 For discussion of the Nonconformist nation, particularly in relation to Wales's anglophone literature, see M. Wynn Thomas, *In the Shadow of the Pulpit: Literature and Nonconformist Wales* (Cardiff: University of Wales Press, 2010). A defence of O. M. Edwards's strategic deployment of the *gwerin* concept may be found in Lowri Angharad Hughes, 'O. M. Edwards: Ei Waith a'i Weledigaeth', *Ysgrifau Beirniadol* XXIX (Denbigh: Gwasg Gee, 2010), 51–77.

4 The distorted picture of Welsh rural life implicated in the *gwerin* myth has been repeatedly criticised by recent scholars. See, for instance, Alun Llywelyn-Williams, 'Owen M. Edwards: Hanesydd a Llenor', *Y Traethodydd* 114 (1959), 1–16; Hywel Teifi Edwards, *O'r Pentre Gwyn i Gwmderi: Delwedd y Pentref yn Llenyddiaeth y Cymry* (Llandysul: Gwasg Gomer, 2004); T. Robin Chapman, *Meibion Afradlon a Chymeriadau Eraill: Golwg ar y Dymer Delynegol, 1891–1940* (Cardiff: University of Wales Press, 2004). A more favourable account of the myth is offered by J. E. Caerwyn Williams in 'Gweledigaeth O. M. Edwards', in *Taliesin* 4, 5–29. For an authoritative historian's view of Welsh rural life during the period in question, see Russell Davies, *Secret Sins: Sex, Violence and Society in Carmarthenshire, 1870–1920* (Cardiff: University of Wales Press, 1996).

5 'The Literary Revival,' in Dafydd Johnston (ed.), *A Guide to Welsh Literature, 1900–1996* (Cardiff: University of Wales Press, 1998), 1–21 (2–3).

6 At the prompting of William Williams, Welsh MP for Coventry, the Government appointed three young English lawyers to conduct an inquiry into the state of education in nineteenth-century Wales, with particular reference to the means provided for 'acquiring a knowledge of the English tongue'. The inexperienced lawyers, who knew no Welsh, were three Anglicans charged with taking the educational measure of Nonconformist Wales. When published in 1847, their three-volume report (the Blue Books) prompted a storm of outrage across Wales because, while it usefully highlighted egregious weaknesses in the meagre existing educational provision, it also branded the Welsh-speaking 'peasantry' as ignorant and licentious. Nonconformist Wales likened the 'treachery' of the Blue Books to that of the Night of the Long Knives, when the Saxons had taken advantage of a parley to seize the larger part of Britain by violence from the original Britons (the Welsh). Traumatised by the report, Victorian Wales became obsessed for the remainder of the nineteenth century with rebuilding its reputation by conspicuously advertising its cultural respectability, its religious piety and its humble, peaceful devotion to the British crown. For discussion of the whole issue, see Prys Morgan (ed.), *Brad y Llyfrau Gleision* (Llandysul: Gwasg Gomer, 1991); Gwyneth Tyson Roberts, *The Language of the Blue Books: the Perfect Instrument of Empire* (Cardiff: University of Wales Press, 1998).

7 Declan Kiberd, *Inventing Ireland* (London: Cape, 1995).

8 St Davids had become a site sacred in the eyes of Cymru Fydd adherents. See, for instant, the article on the cathedral city by 'Y Ddau Wynne' in *Young Wales* 5 (1899), 'dear to every Cymric heart is this quiet mother Church'.

9 Gerald De Barri (Giraldus Cambrensis, 1146–1223), Gerald of Wales, responded to repeated refusals by the King and the Archbishop of Canterbury to appoint him Bishop of St Davids by spending years gathering evidence, which he three times presented to the Pope in Rome, in support of his claim that St Davids used to be an archiepiscopal church. He attributed the failure of all his campaigning to English hostility to the sympathy he felt for the Welsh, natural to one whose grandmother was Nest, daughter of the last king of Deheubarth and a renowned beauty.

10 For more information on the claims of Welsh Catholics, Anglicans and Nonconformists alike to be the true heirs of the original Celtic church of Saint David, see Glanmor Williams, 'Some Protestant Views of Early British Church History', in *Welsh Reformation Essays* (Cardiff: University of Wales Press, 1967), 207–19.

11 *Cymru* 10 (1896), 116.

12 Frantz Fanon, *The Wretched of the Earth* (Harmondsworth: Penguin, 1967).

13 Gareth Elwyn Jones and Gordon Wynne Roderick (eds), *A History of Education in Wales* (Cardiff: University of Wales Press, 2003), 71, hereafter *HEW*.

14 The discussion that follows draws upon the following texts: Don Mitchell, *Cultural Geography: an Introduction* (Oxford: Blackwell, 2002); Denis Cosgrove and Stephen Daniels (eds), *The Iconography of Landscape* (Cambridge: Cambridge University Press, 1988); Peter Jackson, *Maps of Meaning: An Introduction to Cultural Geography* (London and New York: Routledge, 1989).

15 Benedict Anderson, *Imagined Communities* (London: Verso, 1991).

16 See Dorian Llywelyn, *Sacred Place, Chosen People: Land and National Identity in Welsh Spirituality* (Cardiff: University of Wales Press, 1999).

17 There is a need for a comprehensive study of Wales's relations with Europe. In the absence of such, a beginning may be made by consulting the following: 'Wales and Europe: From Revolutionary Convention to Welsh Assembly, 1789–2014', in Kenneth O. Morgan, *Revolution to Devolution* (Cardiff: University of Wales Press, 2014), 271–86; M. Wynn Thomas, 'Ewtopia: Cyfandir Dychymyg y Cymry', in Geraint H. Jenkins (ed.), *Cymru a'r Cymry 2000: Wales and the Welsh 2000* (Aberystwyth: University of Wales Centre for Advanced Welsh and Celtic Studies), 99–118.

18 An anthology of his periodical writings was edited, in three volumes, by D. Myrddin Lloyd: *Erthyglau Emrys ap Iwan I* (Dinbych: Gwasg Gee, 1937); *Erthyglau Emrys ap Iwan II* (Dinbych: Gwasg Gee, 1939); and *Erthyglau Emrys ap Iwan III* (Dinbych: Gwasg Gee, 1940), hereafter *EI1, EI2, EI3*. For a summary of his life and work, see D. Myrddin Lloyd, *Emrys ap Iwan* (Cardiff: University of Wales Press, 1979); and T. Gwynn Jones, *Emrys ap Iwan: Dysgawdwr, Llenor, Cenedlgarwr* (Caernarvon; Cwmni'r Cyhoeddwyr Cymreig, 1912).

19 Knighted in 1907, Rhŷs was a renowned philologist and Celtic scholar, educated at Oxford and at the Universities of Paris, Heidelberg, Leipzig and Göttingen. In 1877 he was appointed to the new Chair of Celtic at Oxford, and in 1895 became Principal of Jesus College.

20 O. M. Edwards, *O'r Bala i Geneva* (Bala: Davies ac Evans, 1889; all references to second edition, 1908), hereafter *OBG*.

21 Quoted from the entry in the *New Companion to the Literature of Wales*.

22 In all, O. M. Edwards was to publish three books of continental travel – ones on Italy and Brittany following hot on the heels of *O'r Bala i Geneva* – and one each on his journeys through north and south Wales.

23 For a definitive study of relations between the Welsh and the Jews, see Jasmine Donahaye, *Whose People? Wales, Israel, Palestine* (Cardiff: University of Wales Press, 2012).

24 This fascination with the feminine, in particular as specifically associated with the carnal, may help explain an otherwise puzzling (and indeed astonishing) passage in *Cartrefi Cymru*, where Edwards, normally ever the prim, puritanical Victorian, suddenly goes out of his way to commend the work of Gwerful Mechain (fl.*c*.1462–1500), a poet notorious for an arresting poem celebrating the female genitalia in the very frankest of terms. He rates her alongside Ann Griffiths, the religious visionary, as 'dwy brydeddes oreu Cymru' (Wales's two leading female poets), and while recognising that Gwerful Mechain (whom he mistakenly conflates with Gwerful Fychan) devoted her genius to the weaving of 'caneuon aflendid' (impure songs), ends by daringly suggesting that 'y mae bron â medru gwneud yr aflan yn brydferth' (she almost succeeds in making the impure itself beautiful) (*CC*, 85). For the work and life of Gwerful Mechain, see Nerys Ann Howells (ed.), *Gwaith Gwerful Mechain ac Eraill* (Aberystwyth: University of Wales Centre for Advanced Welsh and Celtic Studies, 2001); Dafydd Johnston (ed. and trans.), *Canu Maswedd yr Oesoedd Canol/Medieval Welsh Erotic Poetry* (Cardiff: Tafol, 1991), which includes 'The Female Genitals', an English translation of Gwerful Mechain's 'Cywydd y Cedor'. A feminist approach to Gwerful Mechain is offered by Ceridwen Lloyd Morgan, '"Gwerful, Ferch Ragorol Fain": Golwg Newydd ar Gwerful Mechain', *Y Traethodydd* 16 (1990), 84–96; and Marged Haycock, 'Merched Drwg a Merched Da: Ieuan Dyfi v Gwerful Mechain', *idem*, 97–110.

25 For Liberal Romantic Nationalism, see, for instance, Anthony D. Smith, *Theories of Nationalism* (London: Duckworth, 1971).

26 'Amcan y llyfr hwn yw cysegru daear Cymru i'w phlant, a rhoddi rhai o gymhwynaswyr pennaf ein cenedl yn gynllun ac yn esiampl i fywyd ein pobl ieuainc. Ceisir gyrru'r bachgen neu'r eneth ar bererindod adeg gwyliau i un o gartrefi prydferth sanctaidd, yn lle ymdyrfu tua'r mannau y dylifa gwagedd a phechod iddynt.' (*Cymru* 10 [1896], 116)

27 'On Bilingual Education in Schools', in Sir Alfred T. Davies (ed.), *O.M. (Sir Owen M. Edwards): A Memoir* (Cardiff and Wrexham: Hughes a'i Fab, 1946), 88, hereafter *M*.

4 Literature and the political nation

1 *Young Wales* 1 (1895), 2.

2 Dyfnallt, 'Tom Ellis: pryddest eil-oreu y Goron yn Eisteddfod Genedlaethol y Rhyl, 1904' (Ystalyfera: E. Rees a'i Feibion, 1905), hereafter *TE*.

3 *The Late T. E. Ellis' Statue Unveiling: Souvenir Programme* (Bala: Brython a'r Eryr Office, 1903).

4 Peter Lord, *Imaging the Nation* (Cardiff: Unversity of Wales Press, 2000), 350–2.

5 This was pointed out in the appeal that had been launched by the periodical *Cymru* in 1902 for contributions to a fund to erect a memorial to Ellis in Bala. *Cymru* 22–3 (1902), 199, editor's footnote to Huws elegy (see below).

6 'The Memory of the Kymric Dead', in T. E. Ellis, *Speeches and Addresses* (Wrexham: Hughes and Sons, 1912), 3–28, hereafter *SA*.

7 See, for instance, those by W. Llewelyn Williams, Alfred Thomas, Isambard Owen, Albert Spicer, Dr Edward Jones, Richard Jones, Artemus Jones, J. Hugh Edwards, *Young Wales* 5 (1899), 75–87.

8 W. W. Williams, 'A Tribute of the Muse to T. E. Ellis', *Young Wales* 5 (1899), 108.

9 Sir Lewis Morris, 'In Memoriam, Thomas Ellis MP', *Young Wales* 5 (1899), 73–4.

10 *Cymru* 28 (1905), 217–19

11 *Young Wales* 5 (1899), 86.

12 *Cymru* 22–3 (1902), 199.

13 J. Hugh Edwards, 'Leading Young Welshmen VII: Thomas Ellis MP', *Young Wales* 2 (1896), 94.

14 J. Hugh Edwards began his portrait of Ellis (see above) with an arresting account of how his father had been threatened with eviction simply because one of his dogs had coursed (but not caught) a hare on his landlord's estate. Ellis had included a reference to this incident in his testimony to the Land Commission.

15 Eifion Wyn, 'O'r Deffroad', *Cymru* 14 (1899), 245.

16 The issue of unity became an important one for every nineteenth-century nationalist who claimed descent from Mazzini. See Denis Mack Smith, *Mazzini* (New Haven: Yale University Press, 1994).

17 *Cymru* 10 (1896), 244.

18 *Cymru* 9 (1895), 233.

19 Rosanne Reeves, *Dwy Gymraes, Dwy Gymru – Hanes Bywyd a Gwaith Gwyneth Vaughan a Sara Maria Saunders* (Cardiff: University of Wales Press, 2014).

20 Gwyneth Vaughan, *O Gorlannau y Defaid* (Carmarthen: Spurrell; London: David Nutt, n.d.); *Plant y Gorthrwm* (Cardiff: Educational Publishing Company, n.d.).

21 D[aisy] Hugh Pryce, *The Ethics of Evan Wynne* (London: Everett and Co., 1913), 76, hereafter *EW*.

22 The thorough mendaciousness with which the unappealing Stanley reported his early Welsh circumstances in his influential *Autobiography* has been devastatingly revealed in Emyr Wyn Jones, *Sir Henry M. Stanley: The Enigma* (Denbigh: Gee and Son, 1989), hereafter *E*; see also Lucy M. Jones and Ivor Wynne Jones, *H. M. Stanley and Wales* (St Asaph; Published by the H. M. Stanley Exhibition Committee, 1972). A much more charitable view of Stanley is, however, offered in Tim Jeal's revisionist biography, *Stanley: The Impossible Life of Africa's Greatest Explorer* (London: Faber and Faber, 2007).

23 An interesting comparison of Stanley with Conrad as instances of outsiders (Welshman and Pole) desperately anxious for full acceptance by the Imperial Establishment is made by Stephen Hendon in 'Civilizing the Natives: Henry M. Stanley's and Joseph Conrad's Narratives of Identity', Katie Gramich, ed., *Almanac: Yearbook of Welsh Writing in English* (Cardigan: Parthian, 2010), 1–35.

24 For Welsh reactions to the Jubilee, see Hywel Teifi Edwards and E. G. Millward, *Jiwbilî y Fam Wen Fawr* (Llandysul: Gwasg Gomer, 2002).

25 For Wales's earlier engagements with the British Empire, see Neil Evans, 'Writing Wales into the Empire: Rhetoric, Fragments . . . and Beyond?', in H. V. Bowen (ed.), *Wales and the Overseas Empire: Interactions and Influences, 1650–1830* (Manchester: Manchester University Press, 2011), 15–39.

26 *Cymru* 9 (1895), 288.

27 *Young Wales* 2 (1896), 126.

28 J. Young Evans, 'Wales and the Empire,' *Young Wales* 2 (1896), 150–2.

29 *Young Wales* 2 (1896), 18.

30 Revd Richard Hughes, 'Conditions of National Progress,' *Young Wales* 2 (1896), 25–8.

31 David Boucher and Andrew Vincent, *A Radical Hegelian: The Political and Social Philosophy of Henry Jones* (Cardiff: University of Wales Press, 1993), 134–40. I am grateful to David Boucher for bringing this volume to my attention.

32 *Westminster Review* 133/1 (1890), 403–4.

33 Edward Jones, *Cymru Fydd* 2 (1889), 681.

34 Quoted in Ronald Hyam, *Britain's Imperial Century, 1815–1914: A Study of Empire and Expansion* (London: Macmillan, 1993), 250. See also Max Beloff, *Britain's Liberal Empire, 1897–1921* (London: Macmillan, 1987).

35 Hyam, 235.

36 J. Arthur Price, 'The Union of Wales and England,' *Cymru Fydd* 3 (1890), 182–9. For a succinct account of Price's refreshingly unorthodox views on a range of issues see Frances Knight, 'Welsh Nationalism and Anglo-Catholicism: The Politics and Religion of J. Arthur Price (1861–1942),' in Robert Pope (ed.), *Religion and Nationality: Wales and Scotland 1700–2000* (Cardiff: University of Wales Press, 2001), 103–22.

37 K. O. Morgan, *Rebirth of a Nation: Wales 1880–1980* (Oxford: Clarendon Press, 1981), 113. When E. T. John became Liberal MP for East Denbighshire in 1910, he conceived, along with Beriah Gwynfe Evans, 'schemes for Welsh self-government as part of a wider framework of imperial devolution. A single-chamber Welsh legislature would be established, to deal with domestic issues, including power over local taxation.' (Ibid., 139) As Neville Masterman has pointed out, when Ellis was convalescing in Egypt a year earlier (1889) he developed a sympathy for the 'colonised' state of the Egyptian people, drawing broad parallels between them and the Welsh. 'It may be argued,' Masterman adds, 'that Ellis's radical Welsh nationalism prevented him from having what might be called the stock imperialist emotion after his visit to Egypt.' Neville Masterman, *The Forerunner: the Dilemmas of Tom Ellis, 1859–1899* (Llandybie: Christopher Davies, 1972), 125 and 133.

38 Revd W. G. Edwards-Rees, 'The Welsh: A Neglected Imperial Asset', *Young Wales* 8 (1902), 73–9.

39 Speech at Caernarvon, 29 May 1891, quoted in K. O. Morgan, *David Lloyd George, 1863–1945* (Cardiff: University of Wales Press, 1981), 113.

40 While *Lady Gwen* was published anonymously, Neville Masterman has confidently claimed (but without corroborating evidence) that the author was J. Arthur Price (*Forerunner*, 155).

41 *Lady Gwen*, *Cymru Fydd* 3 (1890), 335. See the extensive discussion of the novel in Kirsti Bohata, *Postcolonialism Revisited* (Cardiff: University of Wales Press, 2004), 62–72.

42 For a full account of Rhoscomyl's extraordinary life, see John S. Ellis, 'Making Owen Rhoscomyl (1863–1919): Biography, Welsh Identity and the British World', *The Welsh History Review/ Cylchgawn Hanes Cymru* 26 (June, 2013), 482–511.

43 Owen Rhoscomyl, 'As To Some Conventions', *Young Wales* 5 (1899), 49–58.

44 For a period after publishing his first two novels, Rhoscomyl cultivated a studied anonymity, following Scott's example with the publication of *Waverley.* In an interesting sketch in *Young Wales*, the Merthyr journalist John Jones sought at this time to promote the mysterious Rhoscomyl's aims of being the 'Great Wizard' of Wales, as Scott had been for Scotland. 'Scott,' Jones wrote, 'by making them students of the past, made his countrymen sturdy and earnest patriots . . . What Scott did for Scotland, Rhoscomyl seeks to do for Wales.' *Young Wales* 2 (1896), 233.

45 Owen Rhoscomyl, *Old Fireproof: Being the Chaplain's Story* (London: Duckworth & Co., 1906), hereafter *OF*. John Ellis has found in Rhoscomyl's personal story evidence that at this time 'Welshness was in many senses a global project concurrently undertaken across Wales, Britain, the colonies and the world beyond,' and claims that 'rather than a solvent reducing peoples to a homogenous Britishness, there is an increasing recognition that the imperial experience actually developed and enhanced the various cultural and national identities of the empire.' ('Making Owen Rhoscomyl', 482, 483–4.)

46 Owen Rhoscomyl, *Flame Bearers of Welsh History* (Merthyr Tydfil: The Welsh Educational Publishing Company, 1905), hereafter *FBWH*.

47 Rhoscomyl was much preoccupied with establishing the true origins of the 'Cymry', being convinced that English historians were intent on denying to the early Welsh the respect they paid the Saxons of treating them as a properly organised social polity. See Arthur Owen Vaughan (another of Rhoscomyl's aliases), *'The Matter of Wales', Preliminary Volume: 'Cymru as the native name for Wales'* (Cardiff: The Education Publishing Company Ltd, 1913).

48 Marie Trevelyan, *Britain's Greatness Foretold: The Story of Boadicea, The British Warrior-Queen* (London: John Hogg, 1900), hereafter *BGT*.

49 Born Emma Thomas, daughter of a Llantwit Major stonemason, Marie Trevelyan (her nom de plume) turned to writing after it became apparent that the marriage to a Frenchman that made her Madame Puclieu was bigamous, and that she would have to fend for herself as well as provide for her child.

50 Gerry Smith, *The Novel and the Nation: Studies in the New Irish Fiction* (London: Pluto Press, 1997), 76.

51 Stefan Berger, Linas Eriksonas and Andrew Mycock (eds), *Narrating the Nation: Representations in History, Media and the Arts* (Oxford: Bergahn Books, 2008).

5 The Celtic Option

1 E. Weber, 'Who sang the Marseillaise?', in J. Beauroy, M. Bertrand and E. T. Gargan (eds), *The Wolf and the Lamb: Popular Culture in France from the Old Regime to the Twentieth Century* (Saratoga, 1976); also Douglas Johnson, 'The Making of the French Nation', in Mikulas, Teich and Porter (eds), *The National Question in Europe in Historical Context* (Cambridge: Cambridge University Press, 1993), 35–62.

2 See Anthony D. Smith, 'The Nation: Invented, Imagined, Reconstructed', in M. Ringrose and A. J. Lerner (eds), *Reimagining the Nation* (Buckingham: Open University Press, 1993), 9–28.

3 'On The Study of Celtic Literature', in R. H. Soper (ed.), *The Complete Prose Works of Matthew Arnold*, Vol. III: Lectures and Essays in Criticism (Ann Arbor: University of Michigan Press, 1962), 291–386, 197; Rachel Bromwich, *Matthew Arnold and Celtic Literature* (Oxford: Clarendon Press, 1965); John V. Keller, 'Matthew Arnold and the Celtic Revival', in Harry Levin (ed.), *Perspectives of Critism* (Cambridge, Mass.: Harvard University Press, 1950), 197–221.

4 See Prys Morgan, *The Eighteenth-Century Renaissance* (Cardiff: University of Wales Press, 1981); Katie Trumpener, *Bardic Nationalism: The Romantic Novel and the British Empire* (Princeton: Princeton University Press, 1997).

5 Ossian's poetry was respectfully disinterred by leading Scottish Celticists of the late nineteenth century. In his introduction to the 1896 *Centenary Edition of the Poems of Ossian*, published in Edinburgh by Patrick Geddes's press, William Sharp gushingly proclaimed that 'of this there can be no question: that the ancient poetry, the antique spirit, breathes through this eighteenth-century restoration and gives it enduring life, charm, and all the spell of cosmic imagination' (xxiv).

6 Prys Morgan, 'Lady Llanover (1802–1896), "Gwenynen Gwent"', *Transactions of the Honorable Society of Cymmrodorion* 13 (2007), 94–106.

7 Rhŷs was not averse to popularising his Celtic scholarship on occasion. See, for example, his *Celtic Britain* (1882 and 1908).

8 See Miranda J. Green (ed.), *The Celtic World* (London: Routledge, 1995).

9 Ceinydd Morus (Kenneth Venmor Morris), 'Progress', *Young Wales* 4 (1898), 113–14; 114.

10 The end-matter of *The Fiddler of Carney* (Edinburgh: Patrick Geddes, 1896) lists a dozen or so similar press notices of the works of 'Fiona Macleod', who was variously hailed as 'the most remarkable figure in the Scottish Celtic Renascence' (*Irish Independent*) and 'the central figure in the Scots-Celtic Renascence' (*Daily News*).

11 Beriah Gwynfe Evans, *The Life Romance of Lloyd George* (London: 'Everyman', n.d., but 1915/1916), 213, hereafter *LRLG*.

12 René le Roux, trans. F. Vallier (Breton) and Rhys Phillip (Welsh), *Notennon Diwar-Benn ar Gelted-Koz/Nodiadau am yr Hen Geltiaid.* Completed in 1917, it claimed to be the first ever instance of translation from Breton into Welsh.

13 Quoted in Marjorie Howes, *Yeats's Nations: Gender, Class and Irishness* (Cambridge: Cambridge University Press, 1996), 5.

14 *Yeats's Nations*, chapter 1 *passim*.

15 Owen Rhoscomyl, 'As to Some Conventions', *Young Wales* 4 (1899), 49–58, hereafter *ASC*.

16 R. S. Hughes, 'Scientific and Technical Education in Wales', *Young Wales* 4 (1896), 97–102; 97–8.

17 *The Poetry of the Celtic Races, and Other Essays* (London: The Walter Scott Publishing Co., 1896).

18 Ivor Bowen, 'Welsh Radicalism and German Socialism', *Cymru Fydd* 2 (1889), 57–62, 60.

19 R. Foulkes-Griffiths, 'The Responsibility of Young Wales in Relation to Historical Research', *Cymru Fydd* 2 (1889), 74–84, 79.

20 *Young Wales* 7 (1901), 44.

21 Robert Bryan, 'Welsh Literary Jottings', *Young Wales* 7 (1901), 45. Bryan (1858–1920) is a character of interest not least for his connections with Egypt through his three brothers who, by the 1930s, had established stores in Cairo, Alexandria, Port Said and Khartoum that were well known throughout the Middle East. See Siân Wyn Jones, *O Gamddwr i Gairo: Hanes y Brodyr Davies Bryan (1851–1935)* (Wrecsam: Llyfrau'r Bont, 2004).

22 *Young Wales* 7 (1901), 197–8.

23 Thomas E. Ellis, 'Dyled Prydain i'r Celt', in *Gwlad Fy Nhadau; Rhodd Cymru i'w Byddin* (London: Hodder and Stoughton, n.d., but 1915), 120–1; 121. Produced by The National Fund for Welsh Troops 'to provide additional comforts for Welsh Regiments at home and abroad', the anthology was actually edited by John Morris-Jones.

24 Yeats's most considered statement on the subject of Celticism can be found in 'The Celtic Element in Literature', *Essays and Introductions* (London: Macmillan, 1961), 173–88.

25 See chapter 9, 'What a Welshman you would have been', in M. Wynn Thomas, *Transatlantic Connections: Whitman US / Whitman UK* (Iowa City: Iowa University Press, 2005), 228–38.

26 Flavia Alaya, *William Sharp – 'Fiona Macleod,' 1855–1905* (Cambridge, Mass.: Harvard University Press, 1970), hereafter *FM*.

27 For the important association of Patrick Geddes with the Celtic Renaissance in Scotland see Megan C. Ferguson, *Patrick Geddes and the Celtic Renascence of the 1890s* (PhD, University of Dundee, January 2011). *The Celtic Library* published by Geddes's press included most of the important works of the movement in Scotland.

28 Fiona Macleod, *The Sin-Eater and Other Tales* (Edinburgh: Patrick Geddes and colleagues, n.d. but copyright 1895), 5, hereafter *SE*.

29 For a detailed study of Irish Celticism, see Jeanne Sheehy, *The Rediscovery of Ireland's Past: the Celtic Revival 1830–1930* (London: Thames and Hudson, 1980).

30 *http://www.irishhistorylinks.net/Historic_Documents/The_Gaelic_Revival.html.*

31 John F. Frayne and Colton Johnson (eds), *Uncollected Prose by W. B. Yeats* (London: Macmillan, 1975), 187.

32 John Rhŷs and Brynmor Jones, *The Welsh People* (London: Fisher Unwin, 1900), xxiv.

33 Peter Lord, *Imaging the Nation* (Cardiff: University of Wales Press, 2000), 318, hereafter *IN*.

34 For the Caernarvon Congress see Marion Löffler, *'A Book of Mad Celts': John Wickens and the Celtic Congress of Caernarfon 1904 / John Wickens a Chyngres Geltaidd Caernarfon 1904* (Llandysul: Gomer, 2000). See also Löffler, 'Pan-Celticism around 1900', in *Celtes et Gaulois dans l'histoire, l'historiographie et l'idéologie moderne. Actes de la table ronde des 16 et 17 juin 2005 à Leipzig (D.)*, ed. Sabine Rieckhoff (Glux-en-Glenne, 2006), 143–51.

35 *Young Wales* 5 (1899), 180–7.

36 *Cymru* 11 (1896), 214. See also Seamus Deane, *Celtic Revivals: Essays in Modern Irish Literature, 1880–1980* (North Carolina: Wake Forest University Press, 1987); Ann Saddlemyer, 'Pan-Celticism in the Nineties', in *The World of W. B. Yeats: Essays in Perspective* (Dublin: Dolmen, 1965).

37 Murray Pittock, *Celtic Identity and the British Image* (Manchester: Mancheser University Press, 1999); Ann Saddlemeyer, 'The Cult of the Celt: Pan-Celticism in the Nineties', in Robin Skelton and Ann Saddlemeyer (eds), *The World of W. B. Yeats: Essays in Perspective* (Dublin: the Dolmen Press, 1965), 19–21; George Boyce, *Nationalism in Ireland* (London: Croom Helm and Dublin: Gill and Macmillan, 1982); Andrew Lang, 'The Celtic Renaissance', *Blackwood's Magazine* 975 (February 1877).

38 In an essay in *Young Wales*, Henry Jones insisted that Cornwall 'is Celtic to the core', while attacking the fashionable stereotype of the melancholy Celts, and heatedly enquiring 'where is the justification for these familiar impertinences?' *Young Wales* 5 (1899), 88, 89. For the Celtic Revival as it related to Cornwall, see Philip Payton and Paul Thornton, 'The Great Western Railway and the Cornish-Celtic Revival', *Cornish Studies*, Three (1995), ed. Philip Payton (Exeter: Institute of Cornish Studies, University of Exeter Press), 83–103; Ronald Perry, 'Celtic Revival and Economic Development in Edwardian Cornwall', *Cornish Studies*, Five (1997), ed. Philip Payton (Exeter: Institute of Cornish Studies, University of Exeter Press), 112–24; Ronald Perry, 'The Changing Face of Celtic Tourism in Cornwall 1875–1975', *Cornish Studies*, Seven (1999), ed. Philip Payton (Exeter: Institute of Cornish Studies, University of Exeter Press), 94–106; Alan M. Kent, '"Lyonesse" Meets "A Cornish School"?: English Literary Margins and Celtic Revivalism, 1890–1940', in *The Literature of Cornwall: Continuity, Identity, Difference 1000–2000* (Bristol: Redcliffe, 2000), 147–94; Philip Payton, 'Paralysis and Revival: The Re-construction of Celtic-Catholic Cornwall 1890–1945', in *Cornwall: The Cultural Construction of Place*, ed. Ella Westland (Penzance: Pattern Press, 1997), 25–39. I am extremely grateful to Dr Katherine Stansfield for drawing this body of work to my attention.

39 Roy Foster, *W. B. Yeats, A Life* 1 (Oxford: Oxford University Press, 1998), 130. Heareafter *WBY*.

40 *Young Wales* 7 (1901), 231–5.
41 *Young Wales* 7 (1901) carried a mention of the launch of this magazine.
42 *Celtia* 2 (February, 1901).
43 *Young Wales* 7 (1901), 45.
44 'The Pan-Celtic Idea', *Young Wales* 5 (1899), 1–5.
45 'Parable,' *Young Wales* 6 (1900), 46.
46 Dr J. Llewelyn Treharne, 'Impressions of the Breton Eisteddfod at Vannes', *Young Wales* 5 (1899), 211–16.
47 *Celtia* 2 (Feb. 1901), 17.
48 *Celtia* 3 (March, 1901), 35.
49 *Dictionary of Welsh Biography* entry on Mallt Williams's brother Walter Retlaw Williams; Jane Aaron, *Nineteenth-Century Women's Writing in Wales* (Cardiff: University of Wales Press, 2007), 176
50 While the story in the form serialised in *Young Wales* ends with this marriage, it concludes differently in its novel form, which sees Tangwystl trampled to death by ponies on the eve of her wedding: *A Maid of Cymru: A Patriotic Romance* (London and Carmarthen: Simpkin, Marshal & Co., and Spurrell & Son, n.d. [1901]).
51 'Y Ddau Wynne', 'Things Celtic: Some Suggestions', *Young Wales* 5 (1899), 98.
52 *Young Wales* 6 (1900), 279.
53 'The Passing of Mamgu Pali', *Young Wales* 6 (1900), 18.
54 'Un o'r Ddau Wynne', *Young Wales* 4 (1898), 115. She is here identified as 'author of *One of the Royal Celts*, *What the Celts are Doing* and *A Plea for Our Celtic Place Names*', which would seem to dispose of the otherwise plausible theory recently advanced by Marion Löffler, in an important article, that Mallt Williams was not the author of the first of these publications. Marion Löffler, 'A Romantic Nationalist', *Planet* 121 (1997), 58–66. In the frontispiece photograph to *Young Wales* 6 (1901), 'Miss Alice M. Williams' (i.e. Mallt Williams) is included alongside Ernest Rhys.
55 *Young Wales* 8 (1902), 4.
56 *Young Wales* 7 (1901), 188.
57 *Celtia* (February 1901), 20.
58 'The Old Song and the New', in Jane Aaron (ed.), *A View Across the Valley: short stories by women from Wales c.1850–1950* (Dinas Powys: Honno, 1999), 37–44.
59 'Breuddwyd Nos Nadolig', *Cymru* 29 (December, 1905), 245–8.
60 For a full, balanced view of relations between Wales and Ireland in this period see John Davies, 'Wales and Ireland', *Planet* 95, 7–16; Paul O'Leary, *Irish Migrants in Modern Wales* (Liverpool: Liverpool University Press, 2004).
61 *Young Wales* 2 (1896), 299.
62 *Young Wales* 3 (1897), iii.
63 *Cymru Fydd* (1891), 45.
64 *Young Wales* 2 (1896), 153–6.
65 *Young Wales* 3 (1897), iii.

66 'A Celtic Statesman', *Cymru Fydd* 3 (1890), 625–37; 723–32.
67 Even during the course of another warm and friendly sketch of the Irish he had met while travelling the country, O. M. Edwards cannot refrain from regretting the dirtiness of the Catholic natives. *Cymru* 8/9 (1895).
68 'Cymru and Gael', *Young Wales* 3 (1897), 75–6.
69 Arthur Mee, 'Pat and his four Ps', *Young Wales* 5 (1899), 199–201.
70 Daniel G. Williams, *Ethnicity and Cultural Authority: From Matthew Arnold to W.E.B. Du Bois* (Edinburgh: Edinburgh University Press, 2006).
71 See K. D. Snell (ed.), *The Regional Novel in Britain and Ireland, 1800–1900* (Cambridge: Cambridge University Press, 1998).
72 Quoted in J. Kimberley Roberts, *Ernest Rhys* (Cardiff: University of Wales Press, 1983).
73 'The Grave of Glyndwr', *Young Wales* 1 (1895), 3–4.
74 *Young Wales* 1 (1895), 132–5.
75 W. B. Yeats, 'Mr Rhys' Welsh Ballads', in *Uncollected Prose*, 91–4; 92, hereafter *UP.*
76 *Young Wales* 5 (1899), 1–5.
77 Grace ap Rhys, 'A College Tale', *Young Wales* 2 (1896), 245–51; *Young Wales* 3 (1897), 21–2; 45–7; 92–4; 210–12; 238–9.
78 J. Angus Wilson, 'Nationalism in Scotland', *Young Wales* 2 (1896), 51–3.
79 W. Llewelyn Williams, 'Waiting for Sir Watkin', *Young Wales* 7 (1901), 187.
80 Grace and Ernest Rhys (eds), *Celtic Anthology* (London: Harrap, 1927).
81 E. A. Sharp and J. Matthay (eds), *Lyra Celtica: an Anthology of Representative Celtic Poetry* (Edinburgh: Oliver and Boyd, 1896): introduction by William Sharp.
82 Len Platt (ed.), *Modernism and Race* (Cambridge: Cambridge University Press, 2011), 29.
83 Ernest Rhys, 'The Night of Welsh History, I,' *Young Wales* 5 (1899), 87.

6 The once and future Wales

1 All references to Tennyson's poems are to Christopher Ricks (ed.), *The Poems of Tennyson* (London: Longmans, 1969), hereafter *PT*.
2 *Cyfansoddiadau a Beirniadaethau Eisteddfod Genedlaethol Bangor, 1902*, 52, hereafter *CB.* Before reprinting the poem in 1925, the author made significant changes to the text.
3 'The Oven Bird', Robert Frost, *Selected Poems* (Harmondsworth: Penguin, 1963), 81.
4 Declan Kiberd, *Inventing Ireland* (London: Cape, 1995), 118.
5 Branwen Jarvis (ed.), *A Guide to Welsh Literature, c.1700–1800, vol. IV* (Cardiff: University of Wales Press, 2000), hereafter *GWLIV.*
6 Prys Morgan, 'Lady Llanover (1802–1896), "Gwenynen Gwent"', *Transactions of the Honourable Society of Cymmrodorion* 13 (2007), 94–106.

7 O. M. Edwards, 'Fel y gwelais Arglwyddes Llanofer', *Cymru* 10 (1896), 144.

8 Prys Morgan, 'Early Victorian Wales and its crisis of identity', in Laurence Brockliss and David Eastwood (eds), *A Union of Multiple Identities: the British Isles, c.1750–1850* (Manchester: Manchester University Press, 1997), 93–109.

9 Hywel Teifi Edwards (ed.), *A Guide to Welsh Literature, c.1800–1900, vol. V* (Cardiff: University of Wales Press, 2000).

10 Allan James, *John Morris-Jones* (Cardiff: University of Wales Press, 1987), hereafter *JMJ*.

11 Robert Pogue Harrison, 'The Magic of Leopardi', *New York Review of Books* (10 February 2011), 34–7.

12 See the entry on 'essentialism' in Bill Ashcroft, Gareth Griffiths and Helen Tiffin (eds), *Post-Colonial Studies: The Key Concepts* (London: Routledge, 2000), hereafter *PCS*.

13 Helen Fulton (ed.), *A Companion to Arthurian Literature* (Chichester: Wiley-Blackwell, 2009), 1, hereafter *CAL*. Alan Lane, 'The End of Roman Britain and the Coming of the Saxons', in *CAL*, 15–29.

14 A. O. H. Jarman, *Geoffrey of Monmouth* (Cardiff: University of Wales Press, 1966); Helen Fulton, 'History and Myth: Geoffrey of Monmouth's *Historia Regum Britanniae*', in *CAL*, 44–57.

15 James P. Carley, 'Arthur in English Literature', in W. J. R. Barron (ed.), *The Arthur of the English: The Arthurian Legend in Medieval English Life and Literature* (Cardiff: University of Wales Press, 1999), 47–58, hereafter *AoE*.

16 Robera L. Krueger, 'Chrétien de Troyes and the Invention of Arthurian Courtly Fiction', *CAL*, 160–74.

17 For Wales's relation to England during this period, see R. R. Davies, *The First English Empire: Power and Identities in the British Isles, 1093–1343* (Oxford: Oxford University Press, 2000).

18 Juliet Vale, 'Arthur in English Society', *Arthur of the English*, 185–96; Karen Jankulak and Jonathan M. Wooding, 'The Historical Context: Wales and England 800–1200', in *CAL*, 73–83.

19 Eugene Vinaver (ed.), *The Works of Malory* (London: Oxford University Press, 1966), hereafter *WM*. Raluca L. Radulescu, 'Malory and the Quest for the Holy Grail', in *CAL*, 326–39.

20 Stephanie L. Barczewski, *Myth and National Identity in Nineteenth-Century Britain: The Legends of King Arthur and Robin Hood* (Oxford: Oxford University Press, 2000), hereafter *MNI*. W. J. Barron, Francoise Le Saux and Lesley Johnson, 'Dynastic Chronicles', in *AoE*, 11–46; Felicity Rudd, 'Reading for England: Arthurian Literature and National Consciousness', *Bibliographical Bulletin of the International Arthurian Society* 43 (1990), 314–32.

21 Roger Simpson, *The Arthurian Revival and Tennyson, 1800–1848* (London: D. S. Brewer, 1990), 223; Tom Peete Cross, 'Alfred as a Celticist', *Modern Philology* 18:9 (January1921), 485–92; Geoffrey and Kathleen Tillotson, 'Tennyson's Serial Poem', *Mid-Victorian Studies* (London: Athlone Press, 1965), 80–109; Inga Bryden, 'Arthur in Victorian Poetry', in *CAL*, 368–80.

22 Declan Kiberd has interestingly related crucial developments in late nineteenth-century Irish nationalism to England's concern with (re)inventing itself as a nation from 1880 onwards. (*The Invention of Ireland*, 150ff.)

23 J. T. Knowles, letter to *Spectator* (1 January 1870), in J. C. Jump (ed.), *Tennyson: The Critical Heritage* (London: Routledge and Kegan Paul, 1967), 316.

24 Matthew Reynolds, *The Realms of Verse, 1830–1870* (Oxford: Oxford University Press, 2001), 18, hereafter *RV*.

25 Ceridwen Lloyd Morgan, 'The Celtic Tradition', in *AoE*, 1. For the Welsh Arthur see Rachel Bromwich, A. O. H. Jarman and Brynley F. Roberts (eds), *The Arthur of the Welsh: The Arthurian Legend in Medieval Welsh Literature* (Cardiff: University of Wales Press, 1991); Helen Fulton, 'Arthur and Merlin in Early Welsh Literature: Fantasy and Magic Naturalism', in *CAL*, 84–101.

26 'Ymadawiad Arthur', *Cymru* 8–9 (1895), 105.

27 Amateur scholars of the period, however, continued cheerfully to reinforce the sparse authentically Welsh Arthurian materials with others drawn from the English and French Arthurian traditions, while claiming they all related to the 'Welsh' Arthur. See, for example, E.H., 'The Welsh Romance', *Young Wales* 3 (1897), 75–7.

28 'Pa le mae milwyr Arthur?' *Cymru* 9 (1895), 151.

29 *Cymru* 9 (1895), 162.

30 The foregoing discussion of the nineteenth-century English Arthur, including quotation from Felicia Hemans, is heavily dependent on Barczewski, *Myth and National Identity*, 144–61.

31 J. Hugh Edwards, 'An interview with Mr Rhys', *Young Wales* (1895), 132.

32 Ernest Rhys, *Welsh Ballads* (Carmarthen: Spurrell; Bangor: Jarvis & Foster; London: David Nutt, 1898), 23.

33 See Wyn James, *Glyndŵr a Gobaith y Genedl* (Aberystwyth: Cymdeithas Lyfrau Ceredigion, 2007).

34 *Young Wales* 1 (1895), 4.

35 J. Arthur Price, 'Welsh Nationalism and Revolutionary Politics', *Cymru Fydd* 2 (Awst, 1889), 424–37, 434–5.

36 Ceinydd Morus, 'Behind the Veil', *Young Wales* 5 (1899), 196.

37 See, for example, Edward Jones, 'Nationalism', *Cymru Fydd* 2 (December, 1889), 680–91.

38 John Rhŷs, *Studies in the Arthurian Legend* (Oxford: Oxford University Press, 1891). The book was based on the Hibbert lectures on 'Celtic Heathendom' delivered in 1886. See also an essay by J. Gwenogfryn Evans, one of Rhŷs's young acolytes, 'Welsh Colleges and Professors of Welsh', *Cymru Fydd* 3 (Rhagfyr, 1890): 'The influence of Bledri, of the Mabinogion, of the Brut of the "Kelt of Monmouth" is easily traceable from the twelfth century down to *King Lear*, *Idylls of the King* and *Locrine*. But how few Welshmen know anything of the originals . . .', 749.

39 For an authoritative recent discussion of 'the Arthur of the Welsh', see O. J. Padel, *Arthur in Medieval Welsh Literature* (Cardiff: University of Wales Press, 2000).

[40] Kiberd, *Inventing Ireland*, 292.

[41] In his editorial for *Cymru* 9 (1895), 116, he launched a blistering attack on the Senate of the newly established University of Wales for deciding, in its wisdom, to omit the study of Welsh literature and history from its syllabus.

[42] Katherine Hodgkin and Susannah Redstone (eds), *Memory, History, Nation: Contested Pasts* (New Brunswick, NJ: Transaction Publications, 2001), 1.

[43] 'A chofiwch hyn bob dydd/ Fod hanes annwyl Cymru Fu/ Yn rhan o Gymru Fydd' ('Remember this daily/ that the history of dear Old Wales/ remains a part of Cymru Fydd'). *Cymru* 9 (1895), 233.

[44] *Cymru* 10 (1896).

[45] *Cymru* 10 (1896), 244.

[46] John Morris-Jones, *Caniadau* (Rhydychen: Fox, Jones and Co., 1907), 66.

[47] *Myth and National Identity*, chapter 4; Brian Doyle, 'The Invention of English', in Robert Collis and Philip Dodd (eds), *Englishness; Politics and Culture, 1880–1920* (Kent: Croom Helm, 1986), 89–135.

[48] Saunders Lewis, in a typically incisive short article, highlighted the political dimension of the poem in 1971, seeing in it a continuing affirmative expression of Cymru Fydd's hopes for the Welsh future: 'Ni allai awdl T. Gwynn Jones ar destun "Ymadawiad Arthur" fod yn ddim llai na symbol o holl obaith a holl gynnwrf cenedlaetholdeb Cymru o'r pryd yr aeth Tom Ellis i senedd Westminster yn 1886 . . . O'r cychwyn felly epiuion deffroad cenedlaethol Cymru yw "Ymadawiad Arthur" Gwynn Jones. Hynny sy'n rhoi i'r gerdd ymchwydd arwrol.' (T. Gwynn Jones's *awdl* could be no less than a symbol of all the hope and national excitement of Welsh nationalism from the time Tom Ellis entered Westminster in 1886 . . . From the beginning, therefore, "Ymadawiad Arthur" was a product of the national awakening of Wales.') Gwynn ap Gwilym (ed.), *Saunders Lewis, Meistri a'u Crefft* (Caerdydd: Gwasg Prifysgol Cymru, 1981), 203–8.

[49] David Jenkins, *Thomas Gwynn Jones* (Dinbych; Gwasg Gee, 1973), 35, hereafter *TGJ*.

[50] 'Modernist Arthur: the Welsh Revival', *CAL*, 434–48.

[51] Elissa R. Hanken, *National Redeemer: Owain Glyndŵr in Welsh Tradition* (Cardiff: University of Wales Press, 1996), particularly the discussion of the sleeping warrior/ saviour motif in Welsh folklore featured in stories about Arthur, Owain Lawgoch and Owain Glyndŵr (84).

[52] 'The Influence of the Celt in the Making of Britain', Thomas E. Ellis, *Speeches and Addresses* (Wrexham; Hughes and Son, 1912), 97. He later (107) quotes from Tennyson's 'The Passing of Arthur' ('The old order changeth, yielding place to new . . .'), in connection with the argument that 'the leaders and the rank and file in the movement for land reform, which really means social reform, are Celts.' (108)

[53] Dyfnallt (J. Dyfnallt Owen), *Tom Ellis: Pryddest* (Ystalyfera: E. Rees a'i Feibion, 1905), 34–6, 36.

[54] J. Hugh Edwards, *Young Wales* 5 (1899), 86.

[55] Dewi Rowland Hughes, *Cymru Fydd* (Caerdydd: Gwasg Prifysgol Cymru, 2006).

56 'Bedd i Farch, bedd i Wythur,/ Bedd i Wrgawn gleddyfrudd,/ Anoeth bid bedd i Arthur.' ('A grave for a horse, a grave for Gwythur/ A grave for Gwrgawn of bloody sword,/ But a grave for Arthur is a mystery.')

57 *Cymru Fydd* 3 (1890), 65.

58 Morgan T. Davies, 'Dafydd ap Gwilym and the shadow of colonialism', in Helen Fulton (ed.), *Medieval Celtic Literature and Society* (Dublin: Four Courts, 2005), 248–74, 253.

59 Harris is prone to take a rather utopian view of the benefits of cultural hybridity, dreaming of future 'rainbow arcs or bridges between cultures', asserting that a ceaseless restless intermixing of cultures is true to 'a harlequin cosmos at the heart of existence'. His ultimate hope of bringing 'into play certain disregarded yet exciting pathways into the reality of traditions that bear upon cross-cultural capacities for genuine change in communities beset by complex dangers and whose antecedents are diverse' is an attractive one. Wilson Harris, *The Womb of Space: the Cross-Cultural Imagination* (Connecticut: Greenwood Press, 1983), 31, 92, xv.

7 The ghost dance of Welsh Nonconformity

1 I am deeply grateful to the late Professor R. Geraint Gruffydd for sharing this anecdote with me.

2 Gwyn Thomas, *High on Hope* (Cowbridge: D. Brown and Sons, 1987), 47, hereafter *HH*.

3 D. M. Phillips, *Evan Roberts: The Great Welsh Revivalist and his Work* (London: Marshall Brothers, 8th edn, 1923), 189, hereafter *ER*.

4 See Dee Brown, *Bury My Heart at Wounded Knee* (London: Pan Books, 1975); Jerome A. Greene, *American Carnage: Wounded Knee, 1890* (Norman: University of Oklahama, 2014).

5 See James Mooney and Anthony F. C. Wallace, *The Ghost Dance Religion and the Sioux Outbreak* (Chicago: Chicago University Press, 1965); Anthony F. C. Wallace, 'Revitalization Movements', *American Anthropologist* 58 (1956), 264–81.

6 A brief personal note may be in order here. When I was a boy, living in the post-war Rhondda, neighbours used to refer to my family's regular visits to the Gorseinon-Loughor area (my mother's home district) as a journey 'down West', exactly as if we were headed not to another corner of the same coalfield but to the country.

7 Quoted in Hywel Teifi Edwards, *Arwr Glew Erwau'r Glo* (Llandysul: Gwasg Gomer, 1994), xvi.

8 For a penetrating discussion of influential images of the Welsh collier, see Hywel Teifi Edwards. 'The Welsh Collier as Hero, 1850–1950', *Welsh Writing in English: a Yearbook of Critical Essays* 2 (1996), 22–48.

9 Gaius Davies, 'Evan Roberts: wedi ei ddifa gan y tân?', in Noel Gibbard (ed.), *Nefol Dân: Agweddau ar Ddiwygiad 1904–05* (Bryntirion, Bridgend: Gwasg Bryntirion, 2004), 160.

10 Sir Edward Russell (Editor of the *Liverpool Daily Post and Mercury*), 'Mr Evan Roberts and the Mission', in Gwilym Hughes, *Evan Roberts, Revivalist* (Dolgelley: E. W. Evans, 'Goleuad' Office, 1905), 11, hereafter *ERR*.

11 Reports of the Revivalist meetings held by Roberts across south Wales are collected in *The Religious Revival in Wales, 1904, by Awstin and other Special Correspondents of the Western Mail* (no publication details).

12 It should be noted, however, that the minister publicly recanted and admitted he had misjudged Evan Roberts. See the discussion of the matter at the end of *ERR*.

13 Brynmor Pierce Jones, *The Trials and Tribulations of Mrs Jessie Penn-Lewis* (North Brunswick, New Jersey: Bridge-Logos, 1997), hereafter *TT*. Also Mary N. Garrard, *Mrs Penn-Lewis: A Memoir* (Bournemouth: Excelsior Press, n.d., but foreword dated June, 1930), hereafter *MPL*.

14 Mrs Jessie Penn-Lewis in collaboration with Evan Roberts, *War on the Saints: A Text Book on the Work of Deceiving* (Burgess Hill: Diggory Press, 2005. Originally published, 1912), 11, hereafter *WS*.

15 Jessie Penn-Lewis, *The Awakening in Wales and some of the Hidden Springs* (London: Marshall Brothers, n.d. but preface dated April, 1905), 34.

16 Nigel Jenkins, *Gwalia in Khasia* (Llandysul: Gomer, 1995); Andrew J. May, *Welsh Missionaries and British Imperialism: The Empire of Clouds in North-West India* (Manchester: Manchester University Press, 2012); D. Ben Rees (ed.), *Vehicles of Grace and Hope: Welsh Missionaries in India, 1800–1970* (William Carey Library, 2002); Aled Jones and Bill Jones, 'The Welsh World and the British Empire, *c*.1851–1939; an exploration', in *Journal of Imperial and Commonwealth History* 31/2 (2003), 57–81.

17 See Geoffrey Nuttall, *The Holy Spirit in Puritan Faith and Experience* (London: Basil Blackwell, 1946), hereafter *HS*.

18 See Norman Cohn, *The Pursuit of the Millennium: Revolutionary Millenarians and Mystical Anarchists of the Middle Ages* (London: Secker and Warburg, 1957).

19 John H. Davies (ed.), *Gweithiau Morgan Llwyd o Wynedd* 2 (Bangor: Jarvis and Foster, 1908), 250.

20 Joy Dixon, *Divine Feminine: Theosophy and Feminism in England* (Baltimore and London; Johns Hopkins University Press, 2001), 7.

21 D. W. Winnicott, *Playing and Reality* (London: Routledge, 1971).

22 Michael White and David Epston, *Narrative Means to Therapeutic Ends* (New York: Newton, 1911), 11, hereafter *NM*. Also Peter Dixon and Marisa Bortolussi, *Psychonarratology* (Cambridge: Cambridge University Press, 2003); and the relevant entries in David Herman, Manfred John and Marie-Laure Ryan (eds), *The Routledge Encyclopaedia of Narrative Theory* (London: Routledge, 2005).

23 Frank Kermode, *The Sense of an Ending: Studies in the Theory of Fiction* (New York; Oxford University Press, 1967), 97.

24 For a summary of Fiore's thinking, see *Pursuit of the Millennium*, 108–10.

25 See, for example, his poem 'Descriptions of the Religious Condition of Wales in the Winter of 1905': 'King Jesus riding/ In majesty;/ And multitudes shouting –/ We're free! We're free.' (*ER*, 534).

[26] See Dewi Arwel Hughes, 'Yr Ail Ddyfodiad a'r Diwygiad', in *Nefol Dân*, 135–45.

[27] Brynmor Pierce Jones, *An Instrument of Revival: The Complete Life of Evan Roberts, 1878–1951* (South Plainfield, NJ: Bridge Publishing, 1995), 247, hereafter *IR*.

[28] I am very grateful to Dr Alyce von Rothkirch for bringing all these press reports to my attention.

8 Border disputes

[1] Quoted from an essay of mine for Helen Fulton and Geraint Evans (eds), *The Cambridge Companion to the Literature of Wales* (Cambridge: Cambridge University Press, forthcoming).

[2] Mark Valentine, *Arthur Machen* (Bridgend: Seren, 1995), 26, hereafter *AM*.

[3] Gregory Smith, *Scottish Literature: Character and Influence* (London: Macmillan, 1919).

[4] Jane Aaron, *Welsh Gothic* (Cardiff: University of Wales Press, 2013).

[5] Arthur Machen, *The Great God Pan* (Cardigan: Parthian, The Library of Wales, 1895), 22, hereafter *P*.

[6] For a succinct learned survey of the treatment of Pan in ancient and modern art, see John Boardman, *The Great God Pan: The Survival of an Image* (London: Thames and Hudson, 1997).

[7] Philippe Borgeaud, *The Cult of Pan in Ancient Greece*, trans. Kathleen Atlass and James Redfield (Chicago and London: University of Chicago Press, 1988), 178.

[8] For the kinds of circumstances that provided a fertile breeding ground for the spread of new cults, see Tom Holland, *Rubicon: The Triumph and Tragedy of the Roman Republic* (London: Little Brown, 2005), 171–2: '[in the first century BC] across the Mediterranean, wherever men from different cultures had been thrown together, whether in slave barracks or on pirate ships, [there] was a desperate yearning for the very apocalypse so feared by Posidonius. Rootlessness and suffering served to wither the worship of traditional gods, but it provided a fertile breeding ground for mystery cults. Like the Sibyl's prophecies, these tended to be a fusion of many different influences: Greek, Persian and Jewish beliefs. By their nature, they were underground and fluid, invisible to those who wrote history – but one of them, at least [the Mithraic cult], was to leave a permanent mark.'

[9] Friedrich Nietzsche, *Die Geburt der Tragödie aus dem Geiste der Musik* (London: Verlag E. W. Fritsch, 1872).

[10] Arthur Machen, *The Hill of Dreams* (Cardigan: Parthian, Library of Wales, 2010), 7, hereafter *HD*.

[11] Arthur Machen, *The Secret Glory* (London: Secker, 1923), 33 ff, hereafter *SG*.

[12] Chinua Achebe, 'An Image of Africa: Racism in Conrad's *Heart of Darkness*', *Massachusetts Review*, 18 (1977). Reprinted in Robert Kimbrough (ed.), *Heart*

of Darkness, An Authoritative Text, Background and Sources Criticism (London: W. W. Norton and Co., 1988), 251–61.

13 The Garcia story is repeated at greater length in *The Secret Glory*.

14 Arthur Machen, *The Secret of the Sangraal* (London: Tartarus Press, 1995), hereafter *S*.

15 Arthur Machen, *The House of Souls* (London: Grant Richards, 1906), vi.

16 Gwyneth Tyson Roberts, *The Language of the Blue Books* (Cardiff: University of Wales Press, 1998).

17 Arthur Machen, *The Angels of Mons* (London: Simpkin Marshall, 1915), hereafter *BM*.

18 See, for instance, the discussion in Paul Fussell, *The Great War and Modern Memory* (Oxford: Oxford University Press, 1975; 2000 edn), 116.

19 See Daniel G. Williams, *Ethnicity and Cultural Authority: From Arnold to Du Bois* (Edinburgh; Edinburgh University Press, 2006).

20 'On The Study of Celtic Literature', in R. H. Soper (ed.), *The Complete Prose Works of Matthew Arnold*, vol. 3: Lectures and Essays in Criticism (Ann Arbor: University of Michigan Press, 1962), 291–386, 197, hereafter *SCL*.

21 Arthur Machen, 'The Gift of Tongues', in Dai Smith (ed.), *Story: The Library of Wales Short Story Anthology* (Cardigan: Parthian, 2014), 3–9, 5, hereafter *SSA*.

22 The name is placed within inverted commas in order to distinguish Machen the author from the narrator with whom he clearly shared many important features.

23 Arthur Machen, *The Great Return*, in *The Caerleon Edition of the Works of Arthur Machen*, vol. 7 (London: Martin Secker, 1923), 189–245, 202, hereafter *GR*.

24 Christopher Palmer (ed.), *The Collected Arthur Machen* (London: Duckworth, 1988), 10.

25 See Glanmor Williams, *Welsh Reformation Essays* (Cardiff: University of Wales Press, 1967), 183–4.

26 The term 'Celtic Church' is, in fact, a misnomer. See Oliver Davies, *Celtic Christianity in Early Medieval Wales* (Cardiff: University of Wales Press, 1996).

Index